THE WORKS MGs

MGs

SECOND EDITION

More books from Veloce ...

www.veloce.co.uk

First published in 2000 by Haynes Publishing, second edition published June 2011. Reprinted in October 2018 by Veloce Publishing Limited, Veloce House, Parkway Farm Business Park, Middle Farm Way, Poundbury, Dorchester DT1 3AR, England. Tel +44 (0)1305 260068 / Fax 01305 250479 / e-mail info@veloce.co.uk / web www.veloce.co.uk or www.velocebooks.com.
ISBN: 978-1-787113-65-7 UPC: 6-36847-01365-3.

THE WORKS MGs

SECOND EDITION

THEIR STORY IN PRE-WAR AND POST-WAR RACES, RALLIES, TRIALS AND RECORD BREAKING

MIKE ALLISON & PETER BROWNING

VELOCE PUBLISHING
THE PUBLISHER OF FINE AUTOMOTIVE BOOKS

CONTENTS

ACKNOWLEDGEMENTS AND BIBLIOGRAPHY

Introduction to this classic reprint

This book started as a production by Peter Browning, who asked if I would be prepared to cooperate with him and write the pre-war section, while he wrote the post-war history. Having known Peter for many years, I readily agreed. The two previous editions of this book were a record of the competition activities of the MG Car Company at Oxford and Abingdon before the collapse, under government control, of the British Leyland Motor Corporation in the 1980s. The workforce was always small; in 1967, when we were building some 12-1300 cars a week, the total payroll was 1250 people. A large proportion of the output was exported and so the fame of the cars spread worldwide. Since the product was classed as a sports car, these were entered in events of all types, and it was natural that clubs for enthusiasts would evolve. Promoting various motorsport activities, the first, the MG Car Club, was founded in 1930.

This book, then, was a review of motorsport with MG cars since 1924, when the first six cars were produced, through the 1930s, when MG cars were pre-eminent in their classes. After the Second World War, MG helped Great Britain back to economic wealth by selling its cars in many foreign markets, as well as returning to the competition world, with many successes both national and international. The authors have tried to cover all these using reminiscences of those who took part as both competitors and technicians, alongside personal records.

Even the accepted meaning of the term 'sport' when applied to the motor car has changed, and it is now in 2018 seen attached to all sorts of unlikely vehicles. However historical fact cannot change, and the words in this edition remain much as the last with a few minor corrections, but with a new publisher, who considered the work sufficiently important to continue production.

These vehicles are now made in a country far from rural England, and it is difficult to see them as sporting vehicles. However, what is interesting is that it was the MG marque which was favoured over the others the current owners acquired when they bought the assets of MG-Rover. Motorsport has changed, and there is little in which an enthusiast can now participate without specialising their vehicle, but the clubs continue to cater for their needs, and those of older models which are still participating in suitable events.

To Rod Grainger and his staff at Veloce go our thanks for their enthusiasm in re-publishing the work which we hope will enthuse a new generation of MG car owners, keeping the name alive in the current climate of those who cannot believe that some cars were built for the fun and pleasure of driving.

We dedicate the book to those who created the MG cars of the story, and the many who have used them over the years, as indeed it is still possible, at the time of writing, to see the cars in action, maintained and driven by their enthusiastic owners at suitable club events.

Photographs were taken, in the main, from personal files purchased by and donated to me over a period of 40 years or more interest in the exploits of the marque MG. The National Motor Museum at Beaulieu was especially helpful, and I cannot fault the assistance of the staff of the archive, who must get bored with people like me looking for photographs which have not previously been published.

Much help was received from the files of the MG Car Club Triple-M Register, of which, at the time of writing, I am the Honorary President. Gratefully I acknowledge considerable help given by Malcolm and Andrea Green, Stephen Dear, and John Kidder, and to many of the members and committee of the Triple-M Register, who have helped along the way although they might not have been aware of this at the time.

Lastly, and by no means least, I thank my wife and family for helping, and generally 'putting up' with my octagonal obsession, but of which, at least, they have known no different form of life, since it pre-dates them all. However, without their continuing support and help, none of this would have been possible. My son, David, kindly read the whole manuscript and offered several suggestions which have been incorporated.

The initial writing was done on my personal computer, using the Microsoft Word program, Version 7, which I hope one day to fully understand and to be able to use in full! In this day when 'computer errors' are so common, I would like to declare that: computer errors are created by the operator, but this applies not only to this book! Any errors in Part One are mine alone, but, as I have made every effort to avoid these, I would be pleased to hear of any detected so that they can be corrected in the future.

All photographs are from the authors' collections unless stated otherwise.

Bibliography

Purposely I did not use John Thornley's wonderful book *Maintaining the Breed* as a reference source, simply because I knew that this book might then have ended up being a rewrite of that magnificent work, and such a thing is simply not possible. However, I here acknowledge that had it not been for reading his book for the first time around 1953, I might never have formed the interest in MG cars which has lasted to this day. If many of the stories are found in both books then this must be because they are true – the source was the same. The following books have been used for reference purposes:

Combat, Barré Lyndon, Foulis, c1932

Luck of the Game, Barré Lyndon, MG publicity booklet, c1932

Circuit Dust, Barré Lyndon, Foulis, c1934

Mille Miglia, Humfrey Symons, MG publicity booklet, c1934

Luck of the Game Again, Barré Lyndon, MG publicity booklet, c1935

Grand Prix, Barré Lyndon, Foulis, c1936

Magic M.P.H., Lt Col A. T. Goldie Gardner, OBE, MC, Motor Racing Publications, 1951

Grand Prix Facts and Figures, Roland King-Farlow, Foulis, 1964 edition

MG by McComb, F. Wilson McComb, Osprey, 1978 edition

The Racing Fifteen-hundreds, by David Venables, Transport Bookman Publications, 1984

The Magic of the Marque, Mike Allison, Dalton Watson, 1989

The following contemporary periodicals were used throughout to check on facts:

A file of press cuttings, once the property of Cecil Kimber, relating to the 1933 Mille Miglia race, and given to me by Grace Lewis, who had been John Thornley's secretary for many years.

MG Magazine, 1933 to 1934, the original bi-monthly MGCC magazine

Sports Car, 1935 to 1939, the monthly replacement for *MG Magazine*

The Motor, 1924 to 1939

The Autocar, 1924 to 1939

The Light Car, 1924 to 1939

A file of letters and memos, once the property of George King, relating to the preparation of cars for competition purposes. George allowed me to copy this for my personal files.

A report of a lecture given by H. N. Charles in February 1935, entitled Small Racing Cars. Proceedings of the Institute of Automobile Engineers, Volume 29, pp500–538.

The engine power curves were given to me by Reg Jackson, when he retired, along with many of his other personal records and handbooks, and which have been used freely throughout.

Personal notes and files made and recorded by personal interview with those mentioned in the text, during the period 1963 to 1977, when I worked for the British Motor Corporation and its successors. When I first went to work at Abingdon, the factory was still officially the MG Car Company Ltd, but this was a wholly owned subsidiary company of the British Motor Corporation Ltd.

Mike Allison

PART ONE

THE
PRE-WAR
CARS

INTRODUCTION TO PART 1

Another MG history? So far as the pre-war part of the story goes it is on one hand difficult to see what additional information can be put down, while on the other it is a fantastic tribute to the men who built the cars that, so many years after it all happened, there are still people who want to know the story.

Of course, everyone thinks they have a new angle, and the whole problem is that the actual story of MG and its participation in motorsport has been told by so many people that the true story has got more than a little clouded. Over the years I have been involved with running MG cars I have been more than a little horrified to find new exploits being invented to explain various fables, which some would like to believe.

The approach from Peter Browning to tell the pre-war part of the MG competition history was an opportunity I welcomed, and then two years later realised that what I had taken on had become something of an iceberg. However, after a couple of 'editorial' meetings we decided to tell the story as it was told to us when we worked at Abingdon, as it was first-hand from those who had actually been there.

I was fortunate to have worked with Reg Jackson for some three years, and had known him for a number of years prior to that. To have also worked with Cecil Cousins, Alec Hounslow, Syd Enever, Bert Wirdnam, Sam Nash, Henry Stone, Frank Stevens, Harry Herring and many others helped me to realise how fortunate I was to have known all these genial, though modest, and clever men.

As far as possible, this story is theirs. Where necessary I have tried to check facts in contemporary literature and reports. If there are any conflicts with previously published stories, then I can only repeat the previous two sentences, and those guys are the people who made the stories, and I have recorded these as faithfully as I can.

The book title, *The Works MGs*, is something of an anomaly, because MG as a company seldom raced officially. In general, the cars were sold to customers, who raced them as privateers, but with works backing, so in this respect I have chosen to tell the story of all these people. Works backing came in the shape of notification of the latest parts and tuning hints. If a customer was racing, then he was quite likely to be assisted by Reg Jackson, or one of his men, and once he was established as a driver, this help came more readily . . . if not for free! There was no system of bonus payments, but often parts were supplied at discounted prices, and labour bills were often reduced to a bare cost level for those who were successful.

This policy was in marked contrast to some manufacturers, preparing cars at their factories, and racing them against customer cars. They said nothing about their latest 'demon tweaks', or even sold on last year's models immediately before bringing out a new version, which was then raced against the hapless purchaser of the older car!

Neither Peter Browning nor I have tried to trace the histories of actual cars through to the present day, since this is a minefield in which we have chosen not to tread. As time passes, parts are replaced, and the car which won a race in its heyday is almost certainly not really the same car which we see now. Wilson McComb once wrote that of the 33 K3s actually built there are at least 90 survivors, and that was in 1959! Wilson and I spent some considerable time between 1963 and 1966 trying to trace all the surviving MG racing cars and were able to positively identify around 40 of the 140 or so which were built. This was done by tracing all the known MG cars, and checking back their provenance to pre-war days. We also researched all the known road registration numbers of cars, and positively shut the door on several cars lost to sight. Then there were at least two cars which had been 'cloned' by the works . . . the story goes on. Some of the cars we wrote off in those days have apparently resurfaced subsequently.

It would indeed be nice to believe that every Tigress, 12/12 M-type, C, J4, Q, R and K3 was still extant, but in the nature of things this is not possible. I personally agree with the current FIA ruling that once a car is broken up it ceases to exist, but unfortunately even 'they' are not consistent in that they have accepted reconstituted cars of all types: surely the worship of Mammon, rather than of reality? If you intend to buy a piece of history, do research the claimed stories carefully, and remember that the files of the Triple-M Register of the MG Car Club are able to identify all the MG racing cars with a fair degree of positiveness, even if you or the seller do not want to agree with the findings!

Then there are the stories of the cars which never were: for instance, I have said a little about the S-type racing car which was never much more than a pipe dream, and what I have recorded is the truth as told to me by various people. I trust that this finally dispels the rumours that one is hiding in a shed in Oxford, or wherever!

I trust that the whole story again comes to life, especially for those to whom 'MG' cars are built by a German-owned company. For consistency we have used 'MG' throughout although the old way of writing the Company name was M.G., which was the way Kimber wrote it down, "...as a tribute to Lord Nuffield". If it was Kimber who made MG it should never be forgotten that it was William Morris that provided the initial inspiration with his Morris cars, and if these had not had such a wide appeal it is doubtful whether MG would have been the success it was.

There is a little about Wolseley Motors within, and what I have discovered has created a further interest for my researches, for I have rediscovered many long forgotten facts about the cars of the old Birmingham company, with help from my friend Stephen Dear and others. However much one applauds the foresight of Morris or Kimber, or the designs of Wolseley which started it all, it must never be forgotten that it was the men of Abingdon who actually created the cars and made them the success they were.

Throughout the story I have written in the first person, attributing first-hand stories as necessary: I trust that the reader approves of this more friendly approach.

Lastly I would like to record my thanks to all those who have told me their stories, many of whom are no longer with us, and to others who have helped during the compilation, mostly fellow members of the MG Car Club, but also the staff of the National Motor Museum at Beaulieu. However much all these people have helped, nothing would have been finished without the full backing and continual encouragement of my wife Anne.

Mike Allison

CHAPTER 1

ESTABLISHING THE BREED 1924–30

THE 14HP AND 18HP CARS, WOLSELEY MOTORS AND THE DEVELOPMENT OF THE MIDGET

'Old Number One'. Acknowledged by Kimber as the first MG sports car; built at the Longwall Street workshops by Frank Stevens and Cecil Cousins, and used by Kimber to achieve a Gold Medal in the 1925 Lands End Trial.

In 1921 the term 'sports car' probably meant much the same as it now does: *a special car with higher than normal performance based on an ordinary production model*. The term does not seem to have come into common usage until after the turn of the century. Until the advent of the first grand prix in 1902, the term 'racing car' had not emerged either. The idea that these two types of vehicle might be one and the same did not come about until after the Great War. In general, the original sports cars were fitted with four-seat bodies and large capacity engines, while racing cars had these bodies stripped off, and a lightweight two-seater *carrosserie* fitted. From 1908 there was a growing interest in *voiturette* racing, using engine displacements of 1.5 litres or less, and with this came an interest in the possibilities of cars with smaller engines. The notion of a two-seater sports car did not come into prominence until after the First World War. Large engine capacity four-seat sports cars persisted until the outbreak of the Second World War, but their popularity waned considerably after 1930. Truth to tell, they were never 'popular', in the grammatical sense of the word, because they were expensive to buy and, while new, could naturally only appeal to the few who were wealthy enough to purchase them.

It was an economic fact that 'popular' cars could only be truly popular if they were made to be affordable to a wider group of buyers, something that Henry Ford came to realise before the First World War, when he produced his Model T. William Morris was one of the first Europeans to follow this example and Morris

The original Morris Cowley Sports: much had to be learned about sports cars!

Motors had started to produce small, and relatively inexpensive cars just before the war. To supplement this a two-seater Sports Cowley was produced in 1921 to supplement their production range of cars, but found little market at £321. Almost certainly the lack of commercial success was due to a total absence of aesthetic appeal: the car rode high off the ground, it was unbalanced and was, frankly, plain ugly. The small number sold may well have coloured Morris's view that sports cars were not worth producing.

Contemporary with the original Morris Cowley cars, other manufacturers had sought to appeal to the small-budget would-be motorist with a range of so-called 'cycle-cars', but these had limited appeal, and although the GN Company was relatively successful, this market was killed off when Herbert Austin went another route, and in 1922 announced his 'Seven', which was cheap enough for almost anyone to buy.

The Oxford distributor for Morris Motors was Morris Garages Ltd and was actually owned by William Morris, but as a venture separate from the car manufacturing wing. Formed from Morris's original bicycle company Morris Garages Ltd they not only supplied the standard range of Morris cars, but also a wide range of supplementary equipment, and by 1924 also offered a selection of special bodies to be fitted to chassis frames. By this time the company was managed by an enthusiastic Cecil Kimber who had stepped into the job following the sudden death of his predecessor by his own hand. Kimber had been head-hunted by William Morris from one of his supplier companies during 1921, and was appointed to be Sales Manager. He became General Manager during 1923.

Morris Garages supplied a wide range of special

Jack Gardiner's Special 14/28 built by Morris Garages, using coachwork by Hughes of Birmingham.

equipment for fitting to new Morris cars, ranging from special instruments, ashtrays and travel rugs, to special trunks and travelling cases. They also provided a series of bespoke bodies for Morris Oxford and Cowley cars, but these were in the form of well-equipped saloons and tourers, sold at prices considerably above those of the standard cars. The cars appealed to those who could not afford the more exotic machines to which they aspired, but appreciated the more luxurious appointments added to a much respected, if comparatively cheap, car.

One of the popular services provided by Morris Garages was the tuning of cars and motorcycles for extra performance and the workshop foreman, Cecil Cousins, was expert at getting the best from the side-valve engines which powered the majority of production vehicles. He later told me that he also offered carburettor conversions for Morris Cowley cars using an SU Sloper in place of the Smith Five Jet unit used on the standard car. The SU Company was at the time not part of the Morris group of companies, but their instruments were used on the very exclusive Bentley sporting car, so the sporting pretensions of the carburettor were obvious.

Kimber did not share the official Morris Motors view that the Cowley Sports did not merit building, but believed that it merely lacked aesthetic appeal. He therefore re-thought the idea and sketched a close-coupled open body and this he had drafted properly and constructed by Raworth of Oxford, a well respected coach-building firm. This model was called a Chummy and was mounted on a Cowley chassis. The result was the sort of thing we nowadays call a 2 + 2.

Even though the passengers were high off the ground, the Chummy was readily distinguished from its parent by having the suspension lowered and by being trimmed in leather. It was also painted in lighter colours than the standard car. The Chummy sold in small, but profitable, numbers through 1923. Two of this model, at least, managed to pick up Gold Medals in the Lands End Trial of the Motor Cycling Club, one driven by Kimber himself and the other by Russell Chiesman. Thus started the relentless progress towards the production of a sporting car by Cecil Kimber.

Morris offered their own Chummy model for the following year, at a much lower price, and so it was that early in 1924 Kimber ordered half a dozen special two-seat bodies from Raworth for mounting on the Cowley chassis and these were marketed as the MG Super Sports Morris. At £350, nearly double the price of the standard Cowley, it was hardly a cheap car, nor was it particularly good looking. It took a long time to sell the six from stock which in the event did not matter because two remarkable things happened which really started Morris Garages moving into the sporting car market.

The first was that an order, in the latter part of 1924, for a special body on a car was placed by one of the Morris Garages employees, Jack Gardiner. Gardiner stayed with the MG company until he retired in the late

1960s, and told me that he had his own ideas about what a car should look like. He was fortunate in that he had been bequeathed sufficient money to indulge his fantasy, and took some sketches to Kimber. They then went to the sidecar building firm of Hughes of Birmingham, who interpreted the drawings and built the body, which was mounted on a suitably modified Oxford chassis.

This turned out to be spectacularly attractive, and resulted in orders for further cars to be built in a similar vein, which established a line of cars that proved the linear antecedents of the MG marque. They were referred to in all the early sales literature, hurriedly produced as typescript with actual photographs for illustrations, as the 14/28 MG Super Sports Morris Oxford. One of these cars, driven by Billy Cooper, took the first MG track award at a Motor Cycling Club (MCC) High Speed Trial in 1924, and was frequently seen at Brooklands where Cooper was a regular track official. However clumsy the name was this car represented the first real production car of the MG Car Company.

To add to the revised thinking of the Morris Garages special bodies, the second happening which pushed the company towards true sporting cars was the building, starting also in the latter part of 1924, of a very special car which although based on Morris components was nothing like one of the standard Morris cars at all: the chassis frame showed original thought, even featuring a special overhead valve engine. This car was, of course, the car we now refer to as Old Number One and regarded by many, including Kimber himself, as the first true MG sports car, although it did not see the light of day until April 1925, well after the first 14/28 cars had been delivered.

Now the production cars could not really be described as sports cars, even in two-seater form, for they were little more than rebodied and mildly tuned Morris Oxfords, so it is my view too that FC 7900, while perhaps not the first MG, was the first MG sports car . . . far be it for me to argue with the company's founder!

The whole car, even though it was built largely from Morris parts, displayed a line of original thinking which was foreign to that coming from Cowley Design Office at the time. The chassis frame was derived directly from the Morris Oxford model but was specially constructed for this car. Like the Oxford and Cowley models, simple channel side members were held apart by channel cross members, with a large space at the front into which the engine and gearbox fitted. The frame was riveted together. Unlike the Morris Oxford the rear of the chassis was carried back to the rear spring shackles, over the rear axle, and suspension was by semi-elliptic leaf springs. The revised rear chassis side members

were made by Frank Stevens starting with steel plate in the Longwall Street forge, and then welded to the front part of an Oxford chassis frame.

The radiator was a standard Morris Cowley unit, but with a special badge attached. The engine was a Hotchkiss unit originally destined for the long-forgotten firm of Gilchrist Cars. An overhead valve four-cylinder unit of 68mm bore and 102mm stroke gave it a capacity of 1,482cc. It was a strong and willing unit, if a little lacking in the oil supply department, and proved capable of giving the Special a lively performance by the standards of the day. The performance was matched by an excellent steering lock. A three-speed gearbox and torque tube transmission lifted from a scrapped, accident-damaged Cowley was used, and brakes were to all four wheels: the foot brake working the four shoes at the rear, while the handbrake operated those at the front. The bodywork was constructed from sheet aluminium by Cousins and Stevens and was based on photographs they had seen in a magazine of the Bugatti racing cars which were just emerging as successful racing cars in Continental events, about which, of course, Cousins was reading everything he could in press reports.

That this car won a gold medal in the Lands End Trial for Kimber on its debut is a well known story. In the best traditions of motorsport this achievement was not easily obtained, for the evening before setting off for the start, Cousins found that the chassis frame was badly cracked, ahead of the place where the modified rear section had been welded in place. Most of the night and the following day was spent plating the chassis in the weak area to ready the car for the event, which started that same evening! It could be said with some justification that the MG personnel learned something about the importance of normalising welded areas, but similar problems never again happened at MG.

This result was, however, the first positive result obtained by an MG works car, and in the same event gold medals were taken by both Russell Chiesman and R.V. Saltmarsh in their 14/28 MG Super Sports cars. The Special was sold on but was eventually bought back by Kimber early in 1931, saving it from the ignominy of being scrapped. The car is now kept at BMI Trust, Gaydon, but many years ago when working at the MG factory I was fortunate to be able to drive it for a considerable distance on the road, and found it to be a wonderful car of the period, displaying performance and handling of a level well above that of the standard Cowley-built car.

The MG 14/28

The chassis frame of the production cars was pure Morris Oxford, the springs were flattened, but the rest of the hardware was from Morris Motors parts bins. Engine and gearbox were likewise readily identified with the parent, as were axles and brake gear. The engines were very carefully tuned, by dismantling them and polishing the ports and combustion chambers and matching manifolds to ports. The cars were spirited performers for their day and the ability to cruise at high speed was assisted by raising the rear axle ratio over that of the standard Oxford, this being possible since the MG version was significantly lighter in weight than its parent. This was probably no bad thing since the engine connecting rods were known to seek daylight if the engine speed was raised too far above the standard 3,500rpm!

The steering box was bolted to the chassis, whereas on the Morris it was attached to the engine, and this modification probably did more for the feeling of confidence when driving the car than anything else. The rake of the column was lowered, and the gear lever and handbrake were cranked back, which allowed for a lower scuttle line, and therefore for very rakish body styling.

Body styles were very attractive, having curved side panels, at a time when most of its competitors in the price range were slab-sided and square when

A production 14/28 of 1927 with Mrs Kimber at the wheel, taken at the Bainton Road Factory, just before the move to Edmund Road.

viewed from almost any angle. These were set off by imaginative colour schemes, which from 1925 included two-tone colours, with different shades used above and below the waistline on closed models, probably the first instance of this being used on a production car of any make. Open cars had polished aluminium sides, and painted wings and top panels.

The success of the car was helped more than a little by the fact that Kimber had befriended Hubert Charles of the Morris Motors design staff, and got quite a bit of free advice and actual design help in the engineering modifications made to the cars. This advice was passed down to Cousins who had the benefit of actual drawings to work from, while he himself learned how to make engineering drawings.

Quite a few journalists, aided by the infinite wisdom of hindsight, have sought over the years to show that the early side-valve MG was some form of confidence trick, not really being a different car from its parent Morris at all. The cars may have looked similar and been more expensive than the standard product, but to a large measure this was justified by a better build quality, better trim, and a better performance all round, with much nicer road handling qualities. That it was a nicer car to look at was a bonus. However, in all honesty, these early MG cars were not sports cars, but neither were they the boring touring cars of the type seen every day; they would now probably be described as 'sporty' cars. The manufacturer today might even append the, then unknown, letters 'G.T.' to the nameplate!

The model ran for five years, during which time over 1,200 were built, and a few were run in rallies and trials with some success. As time went on the car was improved in the braking department. In 1927 Morris introduced the upright square radiator in place of the attractive Bullnose type, and this helped MG to begin to form its own identity, being the starting point for the traditional MG radiator, carrying the MG octagon boldly for all to see.

In 1927, following removal to a new purpose-built factory unit at Edmund Road, Cowley, the MG Car Company (Proprietor: W. R. M. Morris) had been officially formed, and from this date Kimber worked to establish MG as a separate marque. However the close connections with the somewhat humdrum parent car were very difficult to shake off, no matter how much better the product was or was claimed to be. During the year came the first report of a race win for MG, when two Frenchmen succeeded in running away from all opposition in Buenos Aires, of all places.

By 1928 the car was being advertised as having sporting links with more than a little justification, and having above average performance. The cars were scoring successes in rallies and trials, but the works were not involved with this activity at all. The following year it became the 14/40 Mark IV, because it was the fourth year of production I believe, and the year after

that the company moved to Abingdon, and production was being centred on the new Midget with the side-valve car finally being removed from the catalogue. The fact is that the side-valve MG was merely a step in the progression towards a true sports car, capable of both road and competition use.

The MG Six

Prior to 1928 Kimber was obsessed with the idea of a Le Mans type of sports car, able to carry up to four people at high and effortless speed. His philosophy was that the car should produce this performance with ease, and yet the complete car should be relatively inexpensive to buy. The 14hp cars did not quite fit the bill for this notion, for although they were not expensive, the engine was a little too small at 1.8 litres and had side valves, and therefore had a limited range for tuning. He knew that it was not going to be possible for MG to buy an engine from outside the Morris empire, but he needed a unit with around 2.5 litres displacement to put the car on level terms with rival makes in the medium price category.

Morris Motors were themselves looking for a family of engines to replace the old Hotchkiss-designed unit which had its origins in 1912. In view of Morris's own reservations about any form of valve operation apart from side-by-side layout, quite how the engine arose is not known, but Frank Woolard of Morris Engines was designing a 2.5-litre ohc unit for a range of larger cars to be built at Cowley. This engine must have taken shape late in 1925 or early 1926, probably as a result of the lack of success of the side-valve six of that period. Woolard and Kimber were friends from

'Ol' Speckley 'en', the car which caught the imagination of the Abingdon brewers Morlands in 1979 when they released their new brew, Old Speckled Hen, to celebrate 50 years of MG at Abingdon.

The 18/80 Six chassis as displayed at the 1929 London Motor Show.

their days at E. G. Wrigley, prior to their employment with Morris, and had no doubt got together to discuss likely overhead camshaft arrangements for a mid-sized engine, and might have started in 1924 or '25, but this is pure conjecture. The fact is that the new engine was available by late 1926.

Around the same time Morris bought the bankrupt Wolseley Company, and although there came with the assets of that company a whole range of new engines, it seems likely that the new Morris engine was too far down the design track to be aborted in favour of the newly acquired Adderley Park units. However, these engines would feature in high relief for the next eight years, as we will see.

The new car, using the Morris engine, was announced during 1927. The Chassis Design Department at Cowley was not forward-looking and the car they produced was not a particularly good one, with narrow track, flexible chassis and a three-speed gearbox, all inherited from the Oxford. The prototype Morris Light Six excited very little interest, and it was left largely to Kimber to produce a car

based on these components. Morris Motors did try once more to use the engine, producing a car which subsequently became the Isis, which was a limited commercial success and ran until 1934. Kimber's car was however altogether a better proposition. The engine carried on in marine configuration for some time after that, known as the Commodore.

MG had the early prototype Light Six, and constructed a body for it which was easier on the eye than the original Cowley design one had been. Kimber had Gordon Crosby redesign the 14/40 radiator shell. Using sketches made by Cecil Cousins, he came up with a really stunning new shell, which was to feature on MG cars for the next 20 years and more. The car, named the MG Six, was announced at the 1928 Motor Show, and the prototype two-door saloon was on show, with open four-seat tourers being offered, together with a range of bodywork in the style of Morris Garages. The birth pangs of the new car caused considerable problems and it was finally in production early the following year, but even then not in the numbers that Kimber had anticipated, causing it to be relaunched as the MG 18/80 Six. It was hoped that cars could be sold with a guaranteed top speed of 80mph to justify this name-tag, but this was not to be achieved until 1930

The 18/80 Mark II show chassis for the 1930 London Motor Show, displaying the stronger chassis, four-speed remote change gearbox and the larger brake drums. Unfortunately all this added to the overall weight of the car.

when the true sports version of the car, known as a Speed Model, was introduced, and by this time a Mark II version of the 18/80 had been announced, running alongside the original design, now called the Mark I.

The Mark II featured a much more robust chassis and running gear, including wider track axles, which would allow the construction of wider and more comfortable bodies. Neither the axles nor the chassis frame were used on a Morris car, but they endowed the new MG with better handling characteristics than the earlier cars. A four-speed gearbox was designed for the car and built by the ENV company. The redesigned, wider-track rear axle was connected by a propeller shaft enclosed in a torque tube in the time-honoured Morris tradition.

The new model, therefore, taking a leaf direct from the book of W. O. Bentley, was seeking to provide a good basis for a luxury car. There is no doubt that the Mark II was a superior car in almost every way to its predecessor, but it was considerably heavier and therefore suffered with a resultant loss in performance as the output of the engine had not been enhanced.

The cruel fact was that the car, whether Mark I or Mark II, as designed was about three years too late: for the day of the large sports car was over. Kimber had ignored the lessons of economic depression and the fact that the whole motor industry was in decline. Even the highly respected firms of Bentley and Lagonda were struggling, with only the technically advanced Talbot and respected Alvis companies

succeeding in producing cars which were selling in this price category: to break into this market was to prove a very difficult prospect for MG. Both the 18/80 models offered a specification which should have attracted buyers in droves, for the cars offered spectacular value for money. The Mark I was offered at around £400 and the Mark II at a hundred pounds more, much the same sort of money as being asked for the somewhat staid Wolseley cars. The MGs were described as sports cars, and indeed looked the part, but unfortunately there was no sporting heritage, apart from a few relatively minor achievements in trials and rallies. Furthermore the potential buyers were licking their financial wounds following the stock market crises of the time, and £400–£500 was a considerable sum in the days when the average pay was barely £100 a year.

In 1929, Captain Francis Samuelson entered his 18/80 Mk I saloon for the Monte Carlo Rally, and asked Kimber what support he could have. Kimber seconded an enthusiastic R. C. Jackson to the job of co-driver and mechanic, but Reg's story told to me years later when I was working for him, was illuminating as an essay in the relative places of master and man in those days. It certainly coloured his views on participation in rallies and he never went again! In the event after many excitements, Samuelson finished and recorded the fastest time in the Mont des Mules hill-climb event which was part of the rally, and was the first significant result for the MG marque in a Continental event.

The special-bodied 18/80 Mark II built for Mrs Gough, which was used in British-based rallies, and won the coachwork class in the 1931 RAC Rally.

There was little doubt in Kimber's mind that to sell a sports car that car had to be tested against its peers on the race track. He would not have found a sympathetic ear with William Morris, who was strongly opposed to racing, but Kimber reasoned that if he could find buyers for the car, then there was not much wrong in the Factory lending support to owners who wished to race their own vehicles. Morris could see the logic of this argument but would not agree to direct involvement of the Factory. In fact Kimber himself wrote that he disagreed with works involvement in racing, which led to reduced entries due to the private owners being blown away by professional teams. The trick, therefore, was to produce a car which could be sold 'ready-to-race' at a sensible price offering a performance to attract the wealthy amateur racing driver . . . and in 1929 there were very few professionals.

The Tigress

Thus was born the notion of the first MG racing car, the Tigress. Based on the Mark II, the Tigress featured a race-prepared specification and, it was hoped, a guarantee of 100mph. The Tigress went forward, with an entry being made for the prestigious Double Twelve Race at Brooklands in 1930, and plans were laid for entries to the Le Mans 24-hour Race later the same year. Kimber made provision for a production run of 25 of these cars, for which special engines, gearboxes and bodies were ordered. The rest of the

parts were expected to be drawn from the production stores. In the event quite a few special parts were fabricated at Abingdon, for large fuel tanks were required and the engine oil system was by dry sump. However an initial batch of five cars was laid down, at a price of £895 ready-to-race. Parts were ordered for a further four such batches, presumably to keep parts prices as low as possible.

One car was completed in time for the race, and was entered by L. G. Callingham with H. D. Parker as co-driver. These two were personal friends of Kimber, with Parker being able to offer help from the Shell Company. In practise it ran reliably but not fast enough. Its lap speed was around 88mph, well down on the targeted 100mph, and not fast enough to keep pace with the Talbot 90 cars of similar engine size but simpler design. In the race, after two hours' running, the MG engine failed due to a small screw from a carburettor throttle plate becoming detached, causing the throttle to jam wide open and resulting in the engine over-revving.

This event proved to be the only official competition appearance for the Tigress, because its importance was overtaken by the smaller Midget, which had coincidentally been introduced at the same Motor Show as the original MG Six.

Some work continued with the development of the

*The first MG racing car: the 18/100 MG Six Mark III, later known as the Tigress,
although not officially. Note the attention to detail and the inherent strength which was
considered necessary for long-distance racing. This is the car which raced in the 1930
Double-Twelve Race at Brooklands, but the engine failed after two hours' running.*

engine, a Mark II Saloon, registration JO 29, previously used by Lord Nuffield, which was loaned to the Shell Company, through Parker, and fitted with a Tigress engine for this purpose. Shell, of course, were keen to prove that it was not their oil which had caused the engine's demise at Brooklands, while Kimber had hoped that they might find the horsepower necessary to give the car the 100mph performance which he sought. In this he was to be disappointed, for reasons easy to understand now, but this car was used as a factory hack through 1931 and 1932 and the chassis has survived to this day to form the basis for a Tigress look-alike. However two Tigress cars still exist from the five built, and are acknowledged by all as beautiful examples of the final stages of the history of the vintage sports car.

At this stage the story moves back to 1928, and before continuing we need to take a look at one of the other companies owned by William Morris.

Wolseley Motors

Wolseley Motors was one of the oldest car manufacturing companies in Britain, with surviving examples of the marque dating back to the 19th century. Prior to making cars the parent company had been involved in the manufacture of agricultural machinery, and one of their machinery designers, Herbert Austin, had brought them into car production.

One of the two surviving Tigress cars, originally owned by Lord Rothschild, but never raced or rallied.

After the First World War Wolseley had gone into the single overhead camshaft engine in a big way, producing engines of all capacities from around one litre to about three, all using valve gear based on that of the Hispano-Suiza aero engine. Originally designed by Marc Birkigt, these had been built during the war at Adderley Park under licence. The car engines were fitted to a bewildering array of Wolseley and Stellite cars using four, six and eight-cylinder designs. Although the cars were well made, they were not particularly inspiring from the technical point of view, except for their engines. Also it has to be said that they were not marketed in an imaginative way, overlapping as they did earlier side-valve engined designs, nor were they especially cheap. The model range for 1926 was positively perplexing, one suspects because they had unsold older designs in the Factory which no-one wanted to buy. Unable to find a market for their cars, Wolseley Motors laboured their way towards bankruptcy, and during 1926 the company was put up for sale by the receivers.

However, the strong suit of company policy was not car manufacture but in design and production of engines and transmissions. If the gearboxes had poor ratios, they at least had four speeds and were

practically unbreakable. This was something that Morris needed for his own range of cars, and therefore he bought the company's assets at much the same time as he also bought the SU Carburettor Company, and so forming the basis for what would become the Nuffield Group, some ten years later. The Wolseley Company was re-launched as Wolseley Motors (1927) Ltd, with Sir William Morris as proprietor, in the way he owned MG.

For the 1928 season, there was an array of overhead camshaft power units already in production. These were two four-cylinder units of around 1,250cc, a six of 2,025cc, a six of 2,677cc and an eight of 2,682cc. The two fours were an 11hp (called the 'Ten'!) with two main bearings, and a 12hp with five, and these were sold in a variety of identical cars. None of the cars were sporting in pretension, indeed it may be said they were touring cars of the type then favoured, but they were expensive when compared with the Morris production cars. Obviously these were overlapping each other and must have caused mayhem in the factory, while the sales people must have been somewhat mystified by the general overlapping of models. At one stage it seems that there were actually two models being marketed concurrently, both called the 21/60, one with six cylinders and the other with eight!

In addition to those engines, there were three brand new designs ready, a four-cylinder unit of 847cc capacity, a six of 1,271cc and a six of 2,025cc. The last of these units was a development of an existing design but it shared similarities of layout with the smaller engines, and showed a development of a family line which needs mention at this stage of the story. Wolseley had started the design of a new car, the 16/45 model,

A Wolseley 16/45 of 1927, which was a competitor of the Morris Isis cars which led to the 18/80 design. The engine of this car featured the vertical shaft drive to the overhead camshaft, and also had a four-speed gearbox, but styling and chassis design were behind the Oxford cars.

but at this stage there were no production plans for the smaller engines.

Under the Morris regime, in 1928, the two existing four-cylinder engines were dropped, but the Wolseley 16/45 appeared on an up-dated Oxford chassis, using the two-litre engine. This model was later called the Viper.

At the 1928 London Motor Show the Morris Minor was introduced, featuring the new little four-cylinder engine. Then in 1929, a Wolseley Hornet model using the smaller six in a lengthened Minor chassis appeared, offering the sophistication of a six-cylinder engine in a small up-market car, perhaps a forerunner of the 'hot-hatch' concept, popular some 50 years later.

For the purposes of this story it is the smaller engines which concern us. They all had a rigid crankcase-cum-cylinder block which was provided with plenty of water cooling for the cylinders. The four-cylinder had two main bearings, the small six had four, while the two-litre unit had seven. In the case of the smaller two engines, the front bearing was a ball race, with thrust being taken at the front end of the ball race housing. The rear main was a cylindrical bush, while the intermediate main bearings fitted to the six-cylinder engines were cast into bronze backing shells located in split cast aluminium housings which were assembled onto the crankshaft before the crankshaft was fitted into the crankcase.

The 16hp engine was basically very similar, although the intermediate mains were carried in split housings, and the front bearing was a white-metalled bronze bush, like the rear one. The result in all cases was an immensely stiff crankcase, something of a novelty for the period, and if the crankshafts of the smaller engines was not correspondingly strong, this matter was put to rights with a few years of development.

Connecting rods were of duralumin alloy, with pinch-bolt small ends to clamp the piston gudgeon pins, and bronze shells lined with white metal forming the big end bearings. The engines were distinguished from contemporary units by being very strong and ran smoothly and, as we shall see, were capable of considerable development.

The camshaft was carried in the detachable cylinder head on cast iron bearing housings lined with split white metal bushes, and driven by a vertical shaft by spiral bevel gears. In the two smaller units the dynamo sat vertically on end and the armature formed part of this shaft, above which was an exposed spring coupling before the shaft disappeared into a casting under the cylinder head. This layout was translated to the larger engine when the car became the Viper in 1931. Slightly inclined valves were actuated by finger rockers, which

The Morris Minor car led to the MG Midget. Here, two early models are in convoy in the late 1940s.

featured eccentric bronze bushes at their pivot point, which led to a great deal of misconception in the retail trade, and consequent poor running of the engines.

The Morris Minor presented a real competitor to the Austin Seven, offering as it did a far more modern car with superior appointments at much the same price and must have caused quite a bit of consternation at Longbridge, and perhaps even more in the Singer and Triumph factories of Coventry. William Morris was hoping to get the price of the Minor down to £100, but he did not achieve this goal until 1932, by which time Cowley was back to side valves again!

The Hornet when introduced in 1929 was well received by the press, being amongst the first production cars to offer the Lockheed hydraulic brakes as standard, as well as a high degree of interior appointments not previously featured on such comparatively low-priced cars. Wolseley Motors (1927) Ltd as being set up as the quality end of the Morris car production range.

If good handling was not amongst these new cars' attributes, then this was a characteristic shared with most vehicles built at the time. The idea that all cars should handle like a sports car had not yet become a requirement for designers, or even car users. Car ownership was still not widely available, and users at that time tended to pigeon-hole activities. Cars were, it seemed, built for different purposes. Touring cars

were for touring, generally at relatively low speeds, and it was not expected that such a car would be used for sporting purposes. Sports cars were seen as large, expensive cars and were used by people with sporting aspirations, who probably were actively participating in trials or even racing. So far as the Morris Group of companies was concerned sports cars were the province of the MG Car Company. What they succeeded in doing, using the parts of the Wolseley and Morris cars, was to redefine the meaning of the term 'sports car' and created a whole new outlook on this term which was probably to have the effect of helping to create the car as it is now known, for which there are no such readily perceived barriers of use.

Let us now return to our story as it affected MG at Edmund Road and to the chronology at 1928.

The MG Midget

Sometime late in the summer of that year, R. C. Jackson was sent to Morris Motors on an errand connected with the production of the 18/80 model, and there saw the Morris Minor chassis, and the prototype cars. Reg Jackson was a man with his feet on the ground, and although at that time he used a motorcycle himself, he aspired to, but could not afford, car ownership. He realised that there were many more like himself, unable to afford other than the humblest and cheapest of vehicles. Furthermore he was a keen follower of motorsport and had been inspired by the activities of Austin Seven cars and to a lesser extent those of small

Triumph and Singer cars, so he was quick to realise the potential of the Morris Minor. He was so excited about what he saw at Cowley that he reported back to Cousins. Equally enthusiastic, Cousins reported to Kimber that here was the basis for a new MG model: a small engined car which could meet the Austin Seven and Triumph Seven cars head on, and what was more would have the benefit of an overhead camshaft engine, all this at a potentially attractive low price, within the abilities of far more people to afford than the 14 and 18hp cars.

Kimber went to see for himself, not completely convinced about the commercial value of a small sports car, but realised that the publicity which the sporting achievements of the Austin Seven had received was of great value. Ever open to opportunity, he arranged for a rolling chassis to be shipped to Edmund Road, where Jackson, under the eagle eye of Hubert Charles, built up a prototype body, featuring a boat tail in the fashion of the day, from wood and fitted it. Nothing was done to the engine, but a radiator grille similar in style to that of the 18/80 was made up, and the engine space covered with a folding bonnet. The embryonic vehicle was whisked off to Carbodies of Coventry, who made two production prototypes panelled in plywood and covered with Rexene, and returned it to Abingdon. At this stage there was only the one powered chassis, but this was quickly built up into a running car, while the

The nearside of the engine bay of an early Midget. Note the fuel tank immediately behind the engine!

The offside of the engine bay, showing the dynamo is at the front of the engine standing vertically, and forming the camshaft drive.

other body was mounted on a chassis frame for further development of the scheme.

The original bodies had an upswept scuttle flare in front of the driver deleted from the production examples. Doors were fitted to each side and the layout of the body gave adequate room for a driver and passenger sitting side by side, while their forward vision was protected by a V-shaped glass windscreen. A wiper was not originally envisaged, but a suction wiper was provided for the driver in production cars. A hood was supplied, this being closed by removable sidescreens, resulting in a cosy driving compartment when it rained . . . the fact that most owners chose to drive with the hood left off suggests that it was a mite too cosy!

The chassis layout of the basic Morris Minor was barely changed. The rake of the steering column was lowered a couple of inches. Steering was operated by an Adamant worm and wheel gearbox. This system was one of the best fitted to an MG for many years and proved trouble-free. The scuttle was lowered, but otherwise very little was changed at all. Brakes were operated by a mixture of rods and cables, but the 8in drums were considered to be adequate. The shoes were expanded by a rotating cam against springs. During 1930 Charles re-schemed the MG brakes to

be operated by cables alone which improved their effectiveness. At the same time he did away with the impractical transmission handbrake. The parent company followed Wolseley Motors and went for hydraulic operation after 1931.

The engine and gearbox were to be lifted straight from the Minor, but as the MG was nearly 300lb, or about 25 per cent lighter in weight than the open Minor, the road performance was excellent by the standards of the day, with a top speed in excess of 60mph achievable on most level main roads. This was in days where few production cars could better 50mph on the level, whatever the engine capacity, so to achieve 60-plus from 850cc was a real landmark, and set a new standard for small sports cars. The Austin, Triumph and Singer competition was hard pressed to better the 50mph mark by a significant margin in standard tune.

All the design work was done in the space of about four weeks, and Kimber made an instant decision to send the cars to the London Motor Show at Olympia, with a price ticket of £175. Although there was no actual engine under the bonnet of the stand car, the only available unit being fitted to the demonstration car outside, over 200 orders for the car were taken. Now there was a problem: how to produce the car, not in number, but at all! The Edmund Road factory was committed to producing 14hp and 18hp cars at the rate of perhaps five or seven a week, and space was at a premium. At this stage, Morris Motors did not know much about the intentions of MG, and were probably not expecting the order for 200 chassis which was apparently placed early in November! They had taken a large number of orders for Minors at the Show themselves and were not all that certain how to produce the car in the numbers now demanded.

The little MG was in production by April, at a revised price of £185 and was duly road tested by an enthusiastic press, who stated that here was '. . . a real sports car for under £200'. It now became imperative to give the car maximum exposure at sporting events to gain the best publicity for the new car and Kimber looked for owners who might do this. One of the earliest owners was the Earl of March, who regarded it as a sports car with potential in its class. Kimber was able to persuade his friend Leslie G. Callingham to buy one. Both these men were keen competitors. Harold Parker also bought a car, and the three of them entered their cars in the Junior Car Club (JCC) High Speed Trial to be held at Brooklands in June. The three cars were given a check over at Abingdon by Cousins and his staff. Co-drivers had to be taken, so Kimber agreed that these might as well be works mechanics, and Cousins, Jackson and Frank Tayler were nominated. All three cars succeeded in gaining gold medals, the highest award available, and allowed for good copy in the press.

Following this event a car was put at the disposal of the Experimental Department, and Cousins designated Reg Jackson the job of improving the performance of the car. Jackson was, in addition to being a first-class mechanic and fitter, a very keen motorcyclist, well versed in the art of getting the best from a limited capacity motor. He therefore experimented with the M-type with stronger valve springs, polished ports and matched manifolds until he achieved an engine which was developing a good healthy output. He was surprised to find, however, that there was no valve overlap on the camshaft, which he knew would result in a useful power increase, a problem he took to H. N. Charles. Charles was able to use his influence at Wolseley to have a camshaft ground with a bit of overlap, and by carefully adjusting the cam follower angle Jackson used this to get a significant power increase, further improved by getting all four cylinders with the same opening timing. Charles started to use this car as daily transport, and was very impressed with the performance. It had earned the sobriquet 'Shinio' from the vast amount of Brasso which had been used, not on the brightwork, because the car was actually a shabby beast, but on the engine internals. Using a large SU downdraft carburettor an output of 27bhp was achieved by early 1930 which endowed Shinio with a performance which was pretty exciting, with over 50mph available in second gear, and the ability to reach over 70 in top.

M-types started to be used by enthusiastic owners for other sporting events. Reports were received from proud owners from all over the world, even as far afield as South Africa and Singapore, of sporting achievements with the MG Midget, even though it had not yet been in production for a year.

The complete car, displaying its smooth lines: placing the seat well back from the steering wheel gave plenty of room for the taller drivers, unlike many of the competitors' vehicles.

Kenneth Marsh driving his car during the 100 consecutive ascents of Beggars Roost Hill in Devon. The passenger was an RAC official, who observed that the engine was not stopped, and that nothing apart from fuel was added to the car.

During 1930 an enthusiastic owner, Kenneth Marsh, decided to undertake 100 consecutive ascents of the Beggars Roost Climb in Devon. For what reason is not altogether clear, but the Singer Company had the previous year performed a similar attack on Porlock Hill, and Kimber was taken with the publicity which

The event over, the spectators cheer the success: Reg Jackson is third from the left.

that company had gained from such a simple stunt. Reg Jackson was told to go with the car, and under RAC supervision the attempt was made. The bonnet had to be opened once, for refuelling purposes, but the motor was not stopped . . . I can imagine the contortions in apoplexy the RAC officials would have now, pouring petrol into a tank near to a running engine! Anyway the stunt was successful for the right reasons, and much good publicity was gained from it.

The MG Car Club

In March 1930 Kenneth Marsh had written a letter to *The Motor* suggesting the founding of a social club based around the MG marque. This was followed up by

the calling of a meeting of all interested parties at the Roebuck Inn on the Great North Road, near Stevenage, which was attended by over 50 enthusiasts, and resulted in the formation of a club, with John Thornley as secretary and Robin Mere as treasurer. The intention for the new club was to organise trials and other road events, as well as social events for owners and to form support crews for those participating in more serious events on the track.

The committee of the club were very quick to get the support of the MG Car Company, but this was only support in the sense that the club's existence was noted and supported. A letter from Kimber was friendly but stated unequivocally that there was to be no financial assistance, and the club was expected to be self-supporting. The club was expected to cater for the needs of the MG owner in preference to other marques, and the name of the MG Car Company was not to be in any way compromised.

Within six months it was fairly obvious that the club was going to be a huge undertaking, attracting over 300 members within a very short time. John Thornley wrote to Kimber saying that it was going to be impossible to organise it as a wholly amateur venture, and for its continued success it would be necessary to incorporate the administration into the company in some way. Kimber offered Thornley a job as a service receptionist, but keeping responsibility for the club organisation which was to be his first priority. John Temple, the Service Manager, told the newcomer that he was there to do the job of receptionist first and foremost, and the club was not to interfere with work at all! This was to be the first lesson in factory diplomacy for the young Thornley. It was obvious that the notion of a club was not going to fit into the Factory easily and it was notable that it was only to be a couple of years before the Car Club was removed from the factory environs

The whole team at Brooklands, before the race: spirits were even higher after!

The Murton-Neale car at Le Mans during practice.

and given an office in London and a full-time secretary who was allowed to earn an income from the magazine which was published. This secretary was Alan Hess.

The JCC Double Twelve Race, Brooklands, May 1930

While all this was going on, two successful farmers from Essex, Cecil Randall and William Edmundson, had bought M-types and went to Kimber with a plan to enter, not a high speed trial, but the Double Twelve Race to be held at Brooklands in May, aiming to win the Team Prize. Kimber was not all that enthusiastic, for he was committed to the Tigress project and could hardly spare the people to spend time on development. Charles told Kimber about Shinio, and it was decided to go ahead with 25 cars based on the Midget, with an initial run of five for the actual race.

Charles had got the revised camshaft drawn up, while all the other modifications were in hand. A new body style incorporating the requirements for the racing of touring cars in 1930, where scuttle height and windscreen shape were laid down, but not complied with on the standard body. Cars were fitted with the regulation Brooklands exhaust system and a full under-shield. These cars were offered 'split-pinned and ready to race' at £245.

Overall position at the finish was irrelevant, and it was wisely decided that even class honours were out of reach, since the car was to run in the 751/1,100cc class. In the event five M-types ran, driven by C. J. Randall/F.

M. Montgomery, H. H. Stisted/N. Black, R. R. Jackson/W. Townend, G. Roberts/A. A. Pollard and Miss V. Worsley/D. G. Foster. They easily took the Team Prize, finishing 14th, 15th, 18th, 19th and 20th, and all averaging around 60mph for the 24 hours. The standard car could reach this speed fairly easily, so that it was simple for the owner of an M-type to relate to this result.

The run of Double Twelve Replica Midgets was added to the available models during the summer and it cannot be pretended that they found a ready market at £245, but they were all sold by the following spring, and before the replacement model was announced.

Francis Samuelson and Murton Neale had each ordered a similar car to run at Le Mans the following month, but their runs were not blessed with similar success, with Murton Neale ruining a big end, and Samuelson breaking one of his duralumin connecting rods. Samuelson went on to Spa for the 24-hour race there and was able to finish fifth in the 1,100cc class with Fred Kindell as co-driver.

The capabilities of the Midget as a racing car were thus demonstrated, but all those at Abingdon realised that to make the car go significantly quicker it would need a better chassis, since small cars go faster by cornering faster, and the limits of cornering abilities were being reached with the M-type with its high centre of gravity. As it happens ideas for the new chassis were already being worked on, but it needed a target for the development time to be given, and was received during the autumn of 1930, however this work is better contained in the next chapter, for the dawn of the MG sports car had passed, and the sun was rising fast.

CHAPTER 2

THE LUCK OF THE GAME 1931

DEVELOPMENT OF THE RACING MIDGET, EARLY RECORD ATTEMPTS, SPORTS CARS FROM RACING CARS

The Hon Mrs Chetwynd, who was one of the early customers. Note the gauze screen and still no glass in front of the driver, let alone the passenger space.

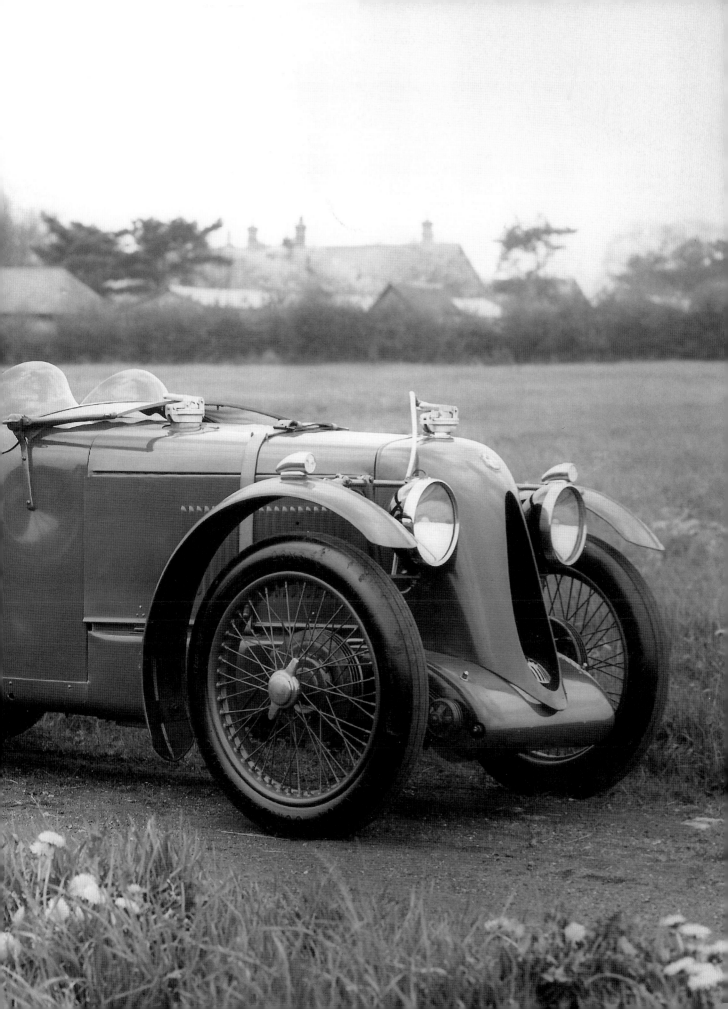

If the M-type established a new class of small sports cars, what followed in the next five years ensured that this breed would have an unrivalled place in motoring history. Although the M-type chassis left much to be desired, the engine had proved a willing horse whose possibilities were later fully exploited to the extent that the specific power outputs increased by a factor of eight or so over the original 23.5hp per litre. Obviously the chassis needed development to cope with any power increases and this chapter deals with the early work associated with this.

Before a successful MG sports car, suitable for active competition, could be developed, a new chassis was essential. During 1929 Charles was at work with possible layouts, and several cars were brought to Edmund Road to be looked at in some detail. My friend and MG historian, the late F. Wilson McComb, was able to show that one of the cars looked at was the Rally, a small sports car of French manufacture, and was keen to show that this formed the inspiration for the MG chassis, this notion arising from the fact that photographs existed in the Cowley archive showing this chassis in a background which could have been the Edmund Road factory.

However it is my opinion, after a discussion with H. N. Charles in 1968, that this was not the full story. True, Charles did look at this chassis, but quite a few other designs were considered too. Indeed there were a number of successful British designs using underslung chassis frames, and Aston Martin, Frazer Nash and other layouts had been looked at in detail. He also discussed these with others amongst his colleagues and peers. Charles was a very good engineer thinking problems out from a point of view of state-of-the-art engineering logic and linking these with success or otherwise achieved by other productions and past designs, and he brought a great deal of original thought to MG, as we will see.

It was decided at a fairly early stage that an overslung chassis such as that used by Morris was unlikely to give the ultimate handling characteristics being sought. This is rather interesting because other designers persevered with this layout for sports and racing cars right up to the coming of independent suspension systems. Even so, it was notable that Riley used an underslung chassis for its sports cars, while the touring cars were all overslung. However, after a great deal of consideration, Charles became a disciple to the cause of the low-slung chassis frame coupled with a low centre of gravity. At this stage he also seems to have considered that the possibility of obtaining a truly rigid frame was beyond the technology of the time, and rather than making a heavy frame, he decided the best route was to have a light flexible one and to couple this with very stiff springs, well damped, as a suspension medium.

Whatever the myths which have been previously told and accepted, the eventual chassis layout was not designed overnight or even in a short time. It seems that it took something approaching 18 months to get the final layout designed and constructed, which indicates that plans were probably laid as early as 1929, as the original Midget was going into production. The chassis prototype was being constructed in the development shop under the Experimental Shop code EX120 but this was not a first priority since the racing M-types and the Tigress projects were taking most of the time available, as told in the previous chapter.

The job received the breath of life in the autumn of 1930 when Captain George Eyston decided that he would like to try to be the first man to drive a 'baby car' at 100mph, a target which the Austin company had been attempting for some time then. It has not been recorded whether Eyston went to Austin first, which is quite possible, but the events of the previous May at Brooklands must have suggested to him that a reduced capacity MG might just beat Austin to the target.

Eyston and his business partner, J. A. Palmes, were prepared to buy a car, and E. A. D. Eldridge, a Land Speed Record breaker himself a few years previously, agreed to put up the money for the attempt. Jimmy Palmes had managed to obtain, from Wolseley Motors, an unbored cylinder block, which he decided could be bored to a size to give an engine capacity of under 750cc. Spurred by the achievements of the M-types at Brooklands, the trio approached Cecil Kimber with the plan during the late summer of 1930. Kimber's imagination was immediately fired, and he was able to get the support of Sir William Morris who thought the idea of beating Austin to the target was worth some effort.

Charles was duly called for to discuss the feasibility of the attempt with an MG. Eventually his prototype chassis was unveiled, even though it was far from complete and to date he had not given serious thought to a 750cc engine. The small group was sufficiently impressed to think that the project was workable, and Morris gave his blessing, provided that not too much money was spent on it by MG. One suspects that Kimber was able to persuade him that the development work would lead to an improved range of production sports cars. The Austin Motor Company was actively, and with great publicity, pursuing the target so it was decided that the fewer people who knew what was happening at Abingdon the better, but that the attempt would have to be made before the end of the year, less than three months hence!

Reg Jackson personally took on the job of preparing the engine, and it was decided that a small-bore version of the M-type unit would save the effort, not to say expense, of a re-designed crankshaft and connecting rods which the short-stroke alternative, using standard bore size, would have meant. So the block which Palmes had was used. In the event it proved possible to grind a crankshaft from the standard forging with a throw of 81mm instead of 83mm, and the bore size was decided at 54mm, and resulted in a capacity of 742.12cc. Connecting rods were machined by Jacko from unmachined steel forgings on the mill at Abingdon and polished all over. Making these enabled the deletion of the pinch bolt retention of the gudgeon pin, a bronze bush being inserted to form the small-end eye, while the ends of the gudgeon pin were plugged with duralumin, which later became the standard MG practice.

As told in the previous chapter, Jackson had been given the task of Midget engine development some time before. Working from the reprofiled 12/12 camshaft, a revised timing was already available as a prototype, giving much greater overlap than that used hitherto and using the 12/12 downdraft carburettor an output of approaching 40bhp was being achieved, from 850cc. Jacko thought that this should be enough to achieve the magic 100mph, even allowing for reduced capacity, but he freely admitted 30 years later, that he did not appreciate at the time how much aerodynamics contributed to maximum speed, or indeed exactly what an aerodynamic shape might be!

Meanwhile work to get the chassis built up proceeded under the supervision of Cecil Cousins. Gordon Phillips carried out much of this work with Frank Stevens providing additional machine shop backup as needed. The revised M-type rear axle was built up at MG, using components received from Wolseley Motors. A new front axle was designed, and the work put to Wolseley.

Since EX120 was the prototype for a range of production sports cars, a four-speed gearbox had been decided upon, and the ENV and Moss Gears companies were approached for quotations since neither Morris nor Wolseley had a suitable one on the stocks at the time. In the event, ENV gave the more attractive quotation, and an order was placed for a single unit 'for test purposes', but they were not able to deliver in time, so EX120 was fitted with a standard three-speed unit.

The chassis frame had parallel side frames joined with tubular cross members, which were fitted into cast brackets riveted to the main frames with the tubes brazed in place. In the event the whole chassis was bolted together, with the bolts then being peened over the nuts. The prototype was designed with a view to having both the Midget engine, and its six-cylinder cousin fitted, the wheelbase being increased to accommodate the longer unit. A wheelbase of 81in was decided upon for the Midget against a track of 42in, making the dimensions just short of the then-accepted 2:1 ideal relationship between wheelbase and track . . . rather interesting this, because an 86in wheelbase was eventually adopted for the much faster Midget racing cars to come following complaints from drivers about the cars being nervous at speed. The six-cylinder cars had a wheelbase of 94in which was, perhaps, too long!

Road springs were to be the standard laminated

EX120 as it appeared on the Newmarket road in December 1930, with silencer and number plate . . . I wonder if it was legal, even then?

semi-elliptic type of the period, set at a high rate, and designed to be flat as installed in the car. The front ends were formed into an eye which pivoted on a single shackle pin, with the main leaf sliding in bronze trunnions at the rear end. The principal reason for using this medium was that positive location for the springs at each end was achieved, and the axles were prevented from changing alignment as the chassis flexed. This in turn obviated the need for any additional form of axle location. Spring damping was by Andre Hartford friction shock absorbers, which were widely used at the time.

A 'hole' was left in the frame design for the engine, but the front mounting of this was arranged as a single point in the centre of one of the cross tubes, and this enabled the radiator to be carried on an extension from the engine thus stopping the cooling system hoses being put under stress. The rear engine mount was to be carried in a cross tube passing through the clutch pit. However, when it became clear that the new gearbox was not going to be available, the prototype chassis used the standard M-type rear engine mounting. Brackets were raised from the chassis frame to enable this to be done and these were riveted in place, and this mounting was to be perpetuated through the D, F, and J-series production cars.

Cable actuated mechanical brakes were used, a new master cross shaft being devised, and the cables working off pulleys placed at the outer ends of this. The drums and back plates employed the standard 1930 M-type parts, together with the now familiar sheathed cable layout originally designed for the 18/80. Charles distrusted hydraulic brakes, which were not without their problems in 1930/1: the copper pipes used then suffered from fatigue fractures early in their life, and natural rubber seals had a short life. In fact the MG brakes were always equal to the car performance by the standards of the day, and while it is now considered that the 8in brakes used until 1933 offer a poor performance, this is judged by later standards. The fact is that in 1930 drivers were used to using the gearbox to slow the car, and of course traffic density was very low.

The original intention had been to make the new Record Attempt car low slung, with a very low body, but this was not going to work out in the time available. Lack of time precluded any radical body development but Jackson, to use his own words, thought he 'knew how to make a slippery shape'. Kimber was insisting that the car must look like one of the production models, and he decided that the MG radiator shell should be retained. A modified M-type radiator was made, to fit the revised mountings, and the body was constructed by Jackson and Gordon Phillips, which was in effect a narrow M-type and 'about a couple of inches lower'. This was made in aluminium sheet which, because neither of them could weld this material, was riveted together. No frame was used apart from the firewall and rear bulkhead. The exposed edges were all wired to give a measure of stiffness. The rear of the body was raised behind the driver's head and a reversed cowl was arranged to give 'streamlining'.

At the beginning of December there was still no front axle available, so Charles decided that the standard M-type unit would have to be used. Because this was mounted under the front springs, it gave the machine a curious nose-up attitude. The car was taken out on the road wearing trade plates one evening to try, and everything appeared to be working, so Jackson opened the throttle and a tachometer reading equivalent of over 80mph came up along the fairly straight and smooth Marcham Road. Eyston was informed and asked to make arrangements to ship the car to Montlhéry, since Brooklands was by this time closed for winter repairs.

Now a short drive to Brooklands and failing was one thing, but to slog all the way to Paris and find that the car was not going to work could be something of a gamble. Eyston was not totally convinced about the road test result, so it was decided that he would try the car, under controlled conditions using stop watches and a measured distance, on the Roman road near Newmarket. The car was duly licensed, RX 7368, and then transported in a lorry with Jackson and Gordon Phillips in attendance. Eyston arrived, anxious to give the appearance of a professional driver, dressed in his linen helmet and white racing overalls. When the car was started the exhaust noise was shattering, even though an M-type silencer was fitted. Eyston did a run and reported that the car felt all right, but not fast enough. This was confirmed when the stop watches revealed that the maximum speed achieved was 87mph, but with nothing in hand. Adjustments followed by further runs failed to increase this performance.

It was decided to delay the trip to Paris and to raise the compression ratio to try for more power. Eyston, on the other hand, had an interest in the manufacture of superchargers, and suggested fitting one of these, but to Jackson, this was a very large unknown quantity with which it was better not to get involved at this stage. Kimber and Charles agreed with Jacko's more cautious approach, and in any case it would be a real slap in the face to Austin *if* they could take the record unblown, as the Austin was known to be supercharged.

Back at Abingdon, the engine was stripped and eccentric small end bushes were made and fitted, which raised the pistons by 0.064in, and filled the head gasket space. The car was back together just before Christmas, and arrangements were made with Eldridge, whose money was being used, to leave Abingdon on Boxing Day for France . . . no nonsense about long Christmas Holidays in those days! Eldridge wanted two mechanics, so Jackson and Phillips were duly sent under the wing of Cousins as their foreman. Eyston arranged for a couple of superchargers and some suitable carburettors to go with the van although no-one at that stage had any idea about what might actually be suitable. How the blower was to work he obviously had not thought about too deeply for he omitted to take any mountings or any form of coupling to drive the thing, according to Cousins and Jackson!

At Montlhéry several runs were tried, but the car would not go past 88mph, whatever tuning tweaks were applied. Different fuels were tried and it dawned on the assembled group that there was simply not enough power to achieve the 100mph target. On 30 December three records were taken at around 86/87mph, but shortly after the car had run 100km (62 miles) a valve broke, and put paid to any more running. It was agreed to fit a supercharger for future runs.

If all this appears to be a great deal of fuss about one record, consider a small fact. The maximum speed of most so-called 'baby' cars was but 50mph, so the importance of being the first in the class to achieve 100mph cannot be understated, because this was a record which could never be taken away, unlike being the fastest at any given time, which was an ephemeral achievement and always under attack. Austin had sent a very special car out to Daytona to do what both they and MG had so far failed to do. The intention was that Malcolm Campbell would drive it after taking the World Land Speed Record, thus driving the largest and smallest cars to record speeds.

Back at Abingdon, Phillips overhauled the cylinder head, and meanwhile Jackson prepared the supercharger, together with suitable chain drives, for Fred Kindell to fit. Jackson was convinced that friction was stopping the engine from delivering its full power, and arranged for roller bearings to be used as camshaft bearings. When the engine was completed it was so free that the pressure of a closing valve spring would cause the crankshaft to revolve, and a 'swing' would make it revolve for several whole turns, and this against compression!

EX120 at Montlhéry. Ernest Eldridge is on the right of the group. Fred Kindell is next to him, wearing his beret, while Jackson is pushing at the offside, wearing his white overalls.

Assembly and installation of engine and supercharger was completed by the end of January 1931. Jackson set off for Paris with Kindell who could help with the tuning. Kindell had been chief tester for the Mercedes concessionaire in London, and a mechanic for various racing people, most notably 'Scrap' Thyslethwaite, and had experience of the art of setting up supercharged engines, and had plenty of experience of keeping cars running in adverse conditions. He was also a driver of some talent.

When they arrived at the track it was very cold, and it proved difficult to get the radiator warm enough for the engine to run cleanly. The problem was exacerbated by the use of methyl alcohol in the fuel, considered necessary in view of the fact that the supercharged engine was expected to run hotter. Jackson blanked the radiator bit by bit and it soon became obvious that a cowling was necessary to shroud the radiator.

News was relayed through to the Montlhéry team that Campbell had succeeded in being the 'Fastest on Earth' by achieving a speed of over four miles a minute in *Bluebird*, but that the Austin had not bettered 94mph for the flying mile, nor could they improve upon this. All this news Eyston heard with some relief, since this now left the field clear for the MG team.

It was at this stage, during one of his regular telephone calls to report progress to Charles and

This is EX120 at the conclusion of the 100mph run, with Eyston signalling his achievement. Note the Tigress prototype car (B0251) in the background.

Kimber, that Jackson appealed for some help: he and Kindell were simply tired out, they had each worked 126 hours that week: seven consecutive 18-hour days! Cousins and Phillips were duly despatched, while the overworked pair had *one whole day* off! Cousins was able to fashion a warm-air intake for the carburettor which resulted in a better performance, but agreed with Jackson that a radiator cowl was needed.

None of those present was a panel beater, but Jackson and Kindell, using an old oil drum as a source of sheet metal, fashioned a suitable cowl using a 2lb ball-peen hammer, a block of wood, and a convenient rain gully in the garage floor, welding up the splits and joins which resulted. With this fitted the water in the radiator warmed up and the engine started to run cleanly, with a crisp bark which soon had spectators looking around to see what was causing the noise!

A little more tuning and the car was soon running at, and maintaining, 7,000rpm – equivalent to over 100mph. So an official attempt was put in hand, and records were taken at over 101.87mph, and the MG, driven by George Eyston, was thus the first car with an engine capacity of less than 750cc to achieve 100mph. Many were the congratulations received, including from Captain Waite and from Herbert Austin himself. Even William Morris declared that he was pleased and arranged for a celebration luncheon party in London.

EX120 was then put aside for a time, partly because it had served its purpose, but more importantly it was time to concentrate on putting the lessons learned into production – literally. The first manifestation was to be a racing car for the new season. Enquiries

were coming in from potential customers for possible mounts for the Double Twelve Race, and the rate of receipt of these increased dramatically after the success in record breaking.

The Montlhéry Midget

EX120 had always been seen as the prototype for the 1931 racing car and for subsequent sports models. Development of the car into a proper racing car, for sale to drivers who might provide more information to the designers, thus proceeded apace. With the success at Montlhéry being fresh in the mind, a run of production cars was put together, and a number of favoured drivers were approached to see if they would buy a new and untried car, in addition to the prospective customers actually asking about a suitable mount.

In the event no less than 14 people paid for cars to be delivered, in time for the Double Twelve Race at Brooklands, at £295 each, fully prepared. This might be compared with the Riley Brooklands which was a full £100 more in the showroom and needed race preparation, so that the new MG represented a very good offer. Extra staff were drafted to the Experimental Shop and overtime was plentiful to cope with this demand, for it was essential that all cars should be ready for the race.

The new car was styled on the record-breaking machine, indeed it was coded EX121 but was called the Montlhéry Midget. The chassis prefix was 'C'. The actual chassis layout was an almost exact replica of the prototype, but with a body big enough to carry two people, and with flares on the scuttle in front of driver and passenger. Actual coachwork was aluminium panelled on a wooden frame, and brought to a boat tail which concealed a 15-gallon fuel tank and a spare wheel. Regulations called for a windscreen to be fitted, but wily Jackson pointed out that glass was not called for, so the screens were of extremely lightweight construction with wire gauze panels. Wings and lights were required and these were strengthened versions of those fitted to the 12/12 racers of the previous year.

The general layout of the car was closely similar to EX120, sharing a matching chassis, axles and radiator, and even a copy of the cowl. The engine had a reduced stroke of 73mm for the crankshaft so that the standard 57mm bore could be used to optimise the combustion chamber design. Initially the crankshaft was made from a revised simple forging similar to the standard M-type component. The connecting rods were made similar to those of the record car, with

The engine bay of the C-type Montlhéry racing car, showing the large downdraft carburettor.

bushed small-ends. A 1¼in SU downdraft carburettor, similar to that used on the 12/12 M-type was used. The ENV four-speed gearbox was by this time available, with its cross-tube mounting through the clutch pit. Other than this, the car was mechanically identical to the record holder. Could the new car deliver the performance its specification and looks promised?

Double Twelve, May 1931

A batch of 15 cars was laid down, one being retained by the works for development purposes. The arrangement to buy was on the basis that the cars were to be paid for in full, prior to collection at Brooklands on the first day of practice for the Double Twelve.

The Earl of March, who was actually in the motor trade, had paid for three of these, with Norman Black and Harold Parker each buying one from him. Cecil Randall had guaranteed three more purchases, being paid for by Gordon Hendy, F. M. Montgomery and L. Fell, their co-drivers being Selby, Hebeler and Ron Gibson, respectively. Major A. T. G. Gardner bought one, starting a 20-year association with MG cars, and he was to share with Ron Horton who hitherto had driven Austin cars with some success, but who was ordering a car for delivery later. Captain Francis Samuelson had ordered a car, but in the event shared with Murton Neale who had also ordered one, Samuelson's car not being delivered for this event, since he had loftier targets in mind. Robin Jackson, who was building up a tuning business at Brooklands, and would later be associated with some significant achievements using MG cars also ordered a car. The Hon. Alan Chetwynd, H. H. Stisted and Dan

All the works personnel line up with the successful Earl of March team cars under Kimber's office. Cousins and Tayler are in the lead car, George Propert, the Works Manager, stands by the bonnet of the same car. (The original copy of this photograph was given to the author by Jack Lewis.)

Higgin also had cars. Another car was ordered by Hugh Hamilton, who was to prove a real driving talent with MG cars during the next two years or so.

The cars were all driven by road from Abingdon on the morning of first practice for the event in convoy. What a stirring sight it must have been, and it is not easy to think what Kimber must have felt, as he headed the procession himself. Every worker turned out to see the cars go off, and those who saw the convoy said all workers were extremely proud that their work should have contributed to the racers. The works arranged for charabancs to take as many as wanted to go to attend the race, for which privilege they had to pay, and lost a day and a half pay! This did not deter many from going, even though not many had any previous knowledge of motor racing, or indeed had taken much part in the actual building of the cars! However they all felt that this was a demonstration of what MG was all about.

The practice period passed with little incident, until Black's engine had a connecting rod decide to come into daylight. Fortunately a spare engine had been built up, and was fitted that evening at Abingdon, and Kimber himself ran it in by driving the car for 400 miles through the Thursday night!

The race consisted of two 12-hour stints, one each on Friday and Saturday. The night between the cars stood in a compound, locked to prevent any work taking place until half an hour before the start, when this year it was permitted for mechanics to drain the oil and refill with warmed-up replenishment, so that drivers could restart at full speed, if they so wished.

It was a wet grey morning on which 42 cars roared off on their odyssey that Friday. The MGs were led by Dan Higgin, and were quickly seen to be travelling at a speed which others were going to find difficult to

match. After the first six hours, Higgin led Hamilton by some seven miles, and had averaged around 70mph. The Earl's team was following at a more sedate pace, around 65mph, but even this was far higher than the handicap required, and the larger cars were forced to be driven at a much higher pace than was wise in the interests of finishing. Their drivers were hoping, and indeed saying, that the small engines would not survive the racket of hour after hour at 6,000rpm. In the early afternoon Higgin it was whose engine suddenly went off song, and then started to belch smoke from the exhaust: a piston had failed. Shortly after this more cars stopped with valve spring failure, although these were replaced, which enabled the cars to continue.

Kimber was worried about the spring failures and could see a glorious win being reduced to a total disaster. Discussing the problem with Reid Railton, they decided it was caused by valve crash, and that such was the lead that the speed of all the cars could be reduced by 5mph without affecting the likely result. Cousins and Jackson separately discussed the matter with Charles, and they had come to the conclusion that over-revving was not the problem so much as a surge period in the springs at much lower speeds. The faster cars had after all not suffered with any problems. Cousins, who was in charge of the Earl's team, therefore decided to comply with CK's wishes and display a 'slower' signal at the pits . . .

having first briefed the drivers to read 'OK' for such a signal, and to slow down if the 'OK' sign was hoisted!

The following morning, with the continued high speeds, saw the larger cars start to drop out through mechanical failures, while the Midgets howled round at unabated speed to win the race, the 750cc class, and the Team Prize for the second year in succession. They did not just win, MG dominated the 1931 Double Twelve race.

Some reporters referred to the entry having been swamped with MGs and state that the result was inevitable, but before accepting this theory let it be said that, prior to the race, the C-type was not very far removed from being a prototype, being still a bare four months since EX120 first ran up the Marcham Road. The prototype had covered barely a couple of hundred miles and had thus far not been raced. To enter a 24-hour race as a debut event is something that very few manufacturers would undertake even today with much thought of winning. To win with an undeveloped car at a speed well in excess of expectations was, I suggest, one of the great achievements in motor racing.

Following the race, modifications were put in hand to the wing stays and to the valve springs. The latter were modified from double springs to triples, but still with a comparatively low seat pressure. At the same time the method of retention was changed from the standard split cotters to spring circlips, after which there was no occasion on which a works-prepared MG suffered with a valve related failure.

It had been reported by all drivers at Brooklands that the engines ran too hot, and so all cars had their Montlhéry cowls removed from the radiators. No other problems had been reported, but Jackson and Tayler both pointed out to Cousins that only the engines had really been tested at Brooklands: what would happen when the transmissions were tested? Cousins reckoned that they were a couple of Jonahs, and they all agreed that 24 hours of Brooklands bumps had tested the general structure of the cars well, and that there was not a lot wrong with that! However the pessimism was to prove not without foundation.

Phoenix Park, 5 June 1931

As a result of the Double Twelve, four new cars were ordered, including one for F. S. Barnes, all to be ready in time for the Irish Grand Prix to be held at Phoenix Park in Dublin. This was in addition to overhauls to seven of the cars which had competed at Brooklands so once again the Experimental shop was busy.

Incidentally all customers had to pay for this service, although parts were normally discounted to trade rates.

Towards the end of practice Norman Black's car came to an abrupt standstill when the gearbox seized. A spare was wired for from Abingdon, and was fitted the following day in time for the start of the race. Meanwhile the old unit was stripped and it was found that the third speed gear bush had seized on its shaft, which could cause a sudden stop to any car in the field. Cousins decided not to say anything to anyone about the problem, using the time-honoured rule of MNH: 'might not happen'!

Like most British races of the period, the Irish Grand Prix was run under a handicap system, although this one was blessed with a particular form of Irish logic. The race was in two parts, one for cars with engine displacement under 1,500cc, and the other for cars with engines over that capacity. Each contest was sub-divided into capacity classes. Each class was set a handicap speed, and the object was to better this set speed by the largest margin. Both races had a major award, the 1,500cc race winner taking the Saorstat Cup, while the second race winner took the Eirran Cup. The car achieving the greatest improvement on its handicap speed was the winner of the Irish Grand Prix.

In the Saorstat Cup event, there were handicaps set based on engine capacity, with classes for up to 750cc, 751/1,100cc, and for 1,101/1,500cc. Ten MGs were present for the start, lined up with six Austins and several Rileys, which were considered the greatest threat to the chances of the Abingdon marque. It was a Brooklands Riley which roared off into an early lead, driven by Victor Gillow. The MGs of Horton, Robin Jackson and Black followed, to lead the 750cc class. So hard pressed was he that Gillow overdid one of the corners early on and bent his car, leaving the field clear for the MGs, most of which were well ahead of the larger opposition. Kimber, who was present, issued orders that the MG contingent should slow, and not race each other. However here his policy of supplying cars to customers backfired on him since they were not actual works entries and they were each there to try to win. So they all ignored the instruction and carried on at unabated speed!

It was raining hard, and Black was a better wet weather driver than any of the others, and took the lead to give a clean sweep for MG. This time there could be no argument, because this race was on scratch: none of the 1,100 or 1,500cc cars had been able to match the MGs for speed in the Saorstat Cup, and to complain that it was a wet race was a *non sequitur* since the conditions were the same for all! Furthermore, Black's

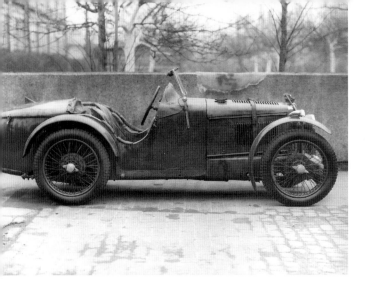

The Norman Black car after its return from success in the Irish Grand Prix. Frank Tayler was to have the gearbox seize as he drove out of Liverpool!

speed had been so high that the runners in the Eirran Cup would have to drive very hard, rain or no rain, to beat him on handicap for the Grand Prix. The following day, therefore, not even the powerful 2.3-litre Alfa Romeo of Brian Lewis could achieve a high enough speed to win the overall honours. Norman Black was announced the winner of the Irish Grand Prix, to the genuine plaudits of everybody.

The unfortunate tailpiece story is that Tayler was told to drive the race-winning car back to Abingdon for overhaul, and just two miles through Liverpool suffered with a seized gearbox!

Le Mans, June 1931

In 1930, Francis Samuelson and Murton Neale had run their specially prepared M-types at Le Mans. Samuelson aspired to a similar run in 1931, and his car was supported by the Chetwynd car, to be driven by Mrs Chetwynd and H. H. Stisted. Reg Jackson was told to get the two cars ready, but since the C-type was built with sports car racing regulations in mind there was 'little' to do other than prepare Samuelson's new car, and to complete the rebuild of Chetwynd's 12/12 car.

Samuelson had contracted for Jackson and Kindell to accompany him to Le Mans, the latter as second driver. The team was soon installed at the Morris-Leon-Bollée factory. A telegram from Abingdon informed Jackson that he needed to change the gearboxes on the two cars at Le Mans, and that the replacements were on their way. After the gearbox troubles at Phoenix Park, ENV had quickly produced a roller bearing in place of the offending plain bush on third speed and this modification was to be incorporated.

This is a good example of how all MG customers were

provided with the latest specification by the Factory as these became available, in direct contrast to those who drove some other marques, who frequently found they were being left out of the reckoning by improvements introduced, even where they were paying for the cars to be factory prepared. The gearboxes were installed in the two cars in time for the start of the race.

Once started the race proceeded without drama for the MG camp until, just before midnight, Stisted came strolling into the pits, having abandoned his car with a broken key in the timing gear on the crankshaft, but Samuelson was still charging round, driving three-hour stints alternating with Kindell. Early in the morning, Kindell was driving and became involved in someone else's accident, spinning off in the process, clouting the bank and having one of the rear springs come adrift, which caused a frantic pit stop to put things back together. In those days only the two drivers were allowed to work on the cars, but Jackson was able to advise from the other side of the pit counter.

Later in the morning, with less than an hour to run, Samuelson was not only lying third on formula, but was also fifth on scratch overall, when the engine made an ominous noise and it was obvious that a connecting rod had broken. He called into the pit, and Jackson told him that he just had to carry on with the engine, driving on its remaining three cylinders. It was essential that he drove to finish. The regulations stated that if any car failed to complete its last lap in 30 minutes it would not be classified a finisher. So Samuelson drove off on his last lap, unfortunately not checking his dashboard clock on leaving, he took 31 minutes, which resulted in his disqualification!

The coming of the supercharger

The RAC Tourist Trophy race was the next objective for MG, but it was obvious that to do well the engines would need to be supercharged for this event. This was causing Jacko some severe headaches, for although they had experience of running EX120 with a blower, the science was far from perfected: to use Jacko's own words, apart from one brief moment of glory, superchargers had brought little more than '. . . a lot of coughing and banging'. Furthermore the drive and manifolding were far from perfect, the chain drive system having been concocted in a rush to get EX120 to work rather than with a view to selling production parts to customers.

The drive problem was solved by H. N. Charles who produced a simple constant velocity joint, one of which was attached to the front of the crankshaft and another to the rear of the supercharger. A short-splined shaft joined the two together, ensuring that the blower did not suffer with variations in running speed due to minor misalignment. The Powerplus supercharger employed a set of vanes running in a drum, and was not too keen to run at the 6,000rpm or more which the crankshaft did. A neat epicyclic gearbox was constructed and attached to the blower, which allowed it to run at around two-thirds of this speed. A unit with a larger casing was then employed to maintain the desired boost of 12/14psi.

An oil supply for the blower was fed from the cylinder head of the engine through a metering valve which varied the delivery of lubricant according to the engine speed, and so ensured that the blower was properly lubricated at all times. Once set up it needed little attention and this system served for all MG supercharger installations until 1939.

The manifolding was causing some headaches, and it was Reg Jackson himself who cured the mystery. The problem was that a large diameter connecting pipe was used to allow the passage of mixture to satisfy the demands of the high performance engine. However it was difficult to get the engine to idle, or pick up smoothly when the throttle was opened. On the other hand, when a smaller diameter pipe was used, initial acceleration was improved but top end power was restricted and plugs oiled up. The solution to the problem was to use twin pipes, one large and the other small, feeding the manifold through two throttle butterflies, which were interlinked and employed according to the engine speed. The throttle linkage was not simple, but the problem was solved. In reality the poor response was probably a fault of the cylinder head design and the relatively high boost pressures being used. Until the advent of the C-type, most supercharged racing engines had run with a boost of 5/8psi.

It was anticipated that some methanol would be added to the fuel, as had been the case on the record-breaking run but no advice on this matter was available, and so the cars were initially run on a petrol–benzole mixture.

As an aside here, Reg Jackson once told me that ideally when running supercharged, one needs as much boost as possible. If petrol is the fuel, the maximum boost available is 12/14psi. Anything less than this results in less than desirable power, for racing purposes. His own maxim was that if it were less than five pounds then it was not worth fitting a blower, while seven was a practical minimum. Ten pounds should produce a worthwhile power increase and I must say that my own practical experience has shown the truth of this theorem.

Nürburgring: German Grand Prix, 19 July 1931

Suffice to say that a working package was available by July, and a chance enquiry from Czechoslovakia gave the opportunity to test the blower under race conditions. Samuelson had entered his car for the German Grand Prix, to be held at the Nürburgring. An amateur Czech driver, Hugo Urban-Emmerich, wrote to Kimber asking to be loaned a car. Kimber did not approve of this sort of thing, but Jackson thought it would be an excellent opportunity to try the new blower away from the eyes of E. V. Ebblewhite, the famous Brooklands timekeeper, who was in the process of checking performances of all likely TT competitors before setting their handicaps. In effect, this gave two bites of the cherry. The Factory test car was therefore despatched to the Nürburgring, with Jackson and Kindell in attendance, having been paid for to help Samuelson. Samuelson's car was also provided with a blower installation.

For practice the weather was exceptionally hot, and the MGs could not be made to run properly. Jacko realised that the fuel mixture was wrong, but, not speaking German, was finding it difficult to get a supply organised. It was none less than Dr Porsche who introduced Jacko to the local Shell representative, and they got some alcohol fuel mixed to suit the MG. Using this the cars were very fast indeed. Unfortunately, when it rained, Urban-Emmerich refused to practise, and of course it rained on race day, with the result that, having no experience of driving in the wet, he soon disappeared into the scenery and bent the car

'Hoodoo', at the Nürburgring after Hugo Urban-Emmerich ran off the circuit in the rain, not having practised in wet conditions, which he did not like. Fred Kindell, in beret, is at the front, with an even more disconsolate Reg Jackson just behind. The others are German track marshals.

The 1931 TT. Charles Fiennes, who did not finish, leads Robin Jackson, who was fifth in class, somewhere along the Ballystockart section, leading to Dundonald.

considerably. Samuelson, on the other hand, drove with great speed and good sense, and despite a long stop caused by a broken fuel union, finished a good fifth in the 1100cc class and easily fastest of the 750cc cars.

RAC Tourist Trophy, 22 August 1931

The RAC Tourist Trophy race was the premier race for sports cars held within the British Isles at the time. Although dating back to 1905, the current series of races held on the Ards Circuit, to the south-east of Belfast, had commenced in 1928. It was a road race in the true sense of the words. The circuit was on public roads, closed for the occasion, and took in up and down grades, level crossings, bridges, and hairpin bends. It started just east of the village of Dundonald, and passed through Newtownards and Comber. A lap of over 13 miles, the races were designed to last for six hours, and for the first few years the distance was 30 laps, some 400 miles. The races were open to catalogue models in series production, which included the C-type Midget, now officially advertised as the Mark 2 model, with supercharger, at £595, and in unsupercharged form the price had leapt to £495.

Very strong that year were the Alfa Romeo team, who virtually assumed that they would win for the second consecutive year with their new 2.3-litre cars. Riley were also strongly fancied with a good team of five Factory-entered Brooklands models. Austin had entered a similar-sized team of supercharged cars. No less than 13 MGs were entered, however, and from the very start of practise it was obvious that these cars were strong contenders.

The Earl of March had entered his team, to be driven by Harold Parker, with the Earl himself as second driver, Norman Black had his car again, with which he had won the Irish GP, while the third car was to be driven by C. W. Fiennes. Goldie Gardner entered three cars, driven by himself, Ron Horton and Robin Jackson. Lone

entries were received from Stan Hailwood, father of Mike, Stan Crabtree, Eddie Hall, Stanley Barnes, Freddie Montgomery, Hugh Hamilton, and Dan Higgin.

One or two of the cars were provided with lightweight aluminium body shells with a rectangular tank at the rear in place of the boat tails. With the supercharged engines this was giving the cars a top speed near to 100mph, with wings and lights fitted, and most impressive acceleration.

Montgomery had decided to run unsupercharged, in the interests of reliability, and was to be partnered by R. G. J. Nash. Crabtree, a motorcycle racer of great repute, was to be partnered by Charlie Dodson, another great motorcyclist, who was later to become a great racing motorist as well. Both Norman Black and Hugh Hamilton had nominated G. K. Cox as their second driver, but since they were all involved with University Motors in London, and this firm was probably sponsoring both cars, it may have been a way of keeping the firm interested, for Cox was one of the directors!

The method of handicapping was to give credit laps, and a small time allowance. The latter was seen in the starting order, while the credit laps were shown on a master scoreboard near the start line. The larger cars effectively had to drive four laps further than the MGs to win, which on known performance was feasible. The Rileys had to make up a lap on the MGs, which again was possible. However, the handicapper is seldom able to make an accurate forecast of the result, any more than a punter can forecast the result of a horse race. A race of six hours' duration has too many imponderables for this to be an accurate science.

All cars had to carry a riding mechanic, and only the driver and his mechanic were permitted to work on the car during the race. It was permissible for a car to have two drivers sharing, but only one mechanic per car was allowed. In a race of 400 miles, it would be expected to stop for fuel and tyres, but only the two in the car could do the work. All MG mechanics arranged to practise pit stops, and while these were not lightning fast, Reg Jackson told me that, during practice, he did not expect any car to be stationary for more than three minutes when changing two wheels, pouring in ten gallons of fuel, and meanwhile checking engine oil, gearbox and rear axle levels, and having a sandwich to eat while they got going again! A long time compared with modern grand prix stops, but that is with a veritable army of mechanics to help!

During practice Stan Barnes spun off and overturned at Ballystockart and bent the chassis of his car, and did not start, the unlucky 13th! The grid of 44 starters lined up, and were despatched in their handicap groups.

The race soon settled down. As at Brooklands, Dan Higgin managed to break a valve spring, since, so Cousins told me, he had not yet bought any of the triples now being fitted by the works. Two laps later, Eddie Hall had a connecting rod break. Next to disappear was Goldie Gardner, who had a nasty crash as Davis in the Mercedes tried to pass him near Carstrand Bridge, the two coming together. Hugh Hamilton was driving with wild abandon and keeping everything under control until lap 19 when he had a cam follower break.

As the race proceeded it became apparent that it was between the MG cars, which were just about ahead of their handicap, and the Alfa Romeo team, which were near to theirs. Fortunately for the home side, the Italians were strongly involved with their own race for the first place causing failures amongst themselves, and soon it was seen that the MGs were getting stronger. This caused a response from the Italian team, and Borzacchini was seen to be making progress. At the end Black won from the Italian by 72 seconds, with Crabtree third, five seconds behind after 5¼ hours of racing. Montgomery finished a creditable 16th, at a speed only some 5mph slower than the winner, quantifying the difference between supercharged and unblown performance.

Once again the detractors of domestic racing were heard to be complaining about the unfairness of it all, but to extract a performance increase over expectation of 10 per cent, less than eight months after its prototype had first run is no small achievement. It has to be said that if all the cars had achieved a similar increase then the MG would have been no better than seventh. However there are no 'ifs' in motor racing, it is the performance on the day to the rules applying that counts.

The '500', 3 October 1931

The last important race of the year was the BRDC 500-mile Race held at Brooklands on the Outer Circuit. Effectively a flat-out race, it was the fastest race in the world until after the Second World War, when Indianapolis finally became the fastest, although by then Brooklands had ceased to exist as a motor track. What chance would the small cars have in this race would be determined by performance against handicap, but all cars needed to be driven flat out, so that reliability would play a large part in the result. The previous year Sammy Davis and the Earl of March had won in their Austin Seven at 83.4mph, while the fastest finisher had been Dudley Benjafield and Eddie Hall in a Bentley at 112.12mph.

For 1931 the handicap for the blown 750cc class was set at 93.97mph, a figure of some 10mph more than for 1930, and a measure of the improvement which MG had brought during the year in the smallest class. Urban-Emmerich's crashed German GP car was rebuilt

in the space of four days into a single-seater and given to Kindell to drive, almost certainly a direct factory entry taking the place of the cancelled entry of Eyston, whose car was not yet built. Eddie Hall had the Factory rebuild his car as a single-seater too. The Earl of March again entered his three cars, with himself, Parker and Black driving, the last named going for his third major win of the year. Gardner was entered, as were Dan Higgin, Stan Crabtree and Jeffrey Clover. Against these MG entries were ranged five Austins to complete the 750cc class.

Forty starters came to the line, but it was Clover in the unblown MG who made a solitary start and was to run for 25 minutes before the blown cars started! Gradually all the starters left the line, the blown Mercedes entries some 1hr 20min after Clover. The unique aspect of the 'Five Hundred' was that all cars had to cover the full distance, and the first to do so declared the winner. Although there was a speed differential of some 40mph between the fastest and slowest entries there were no incidents, but mechanical unreliability was to rule out several entries as the race was run.

The race was over with Dunfee's six-litre Bentley winning at 118.39mph, Lewis was second in a 2½-litre Talbot at 112.9mph, and Hall third in his ¾-litre MG at a slightly disappointing 92.17mph . . . but still 9mph quicker than the previous year's winning speed! The MG team of Hall, Crabtree, who was fifth, and Kindell who just failed to complete the distance before the track was closed, took the Team Prize, vindicating the reliability of the small cars against the heavier metal.

Production derivatives

With the success of the C-types, the M-type's days were numbered, although still in production at the end of 1931. Using a slightly lengthened C-type chassis, a four-seat touring car called the Long Chassis Midget, or D-type, was introduced, and alongside it came a six-cylinder engined car on the longer chassis, and called the Magna, or F-type. Both models were at the 1931 Motor Show, with the two-seater M-type Midget continuing, although now offered with steel panelling in place of the fabric covered body. A C-type was also on the stand to complete a colourful array of cars.

All of this did not quite finish the season, but the last details are better given in the next chapter. Suffice to say that MG cars really dominated the smallest capacity class in racing and record breaking during 1931. All in all a satisfactory first full racing season, which fully rewarded the policy of Kimber to encourage private entries to race his cars with Factory support, rather than entering a full works team.

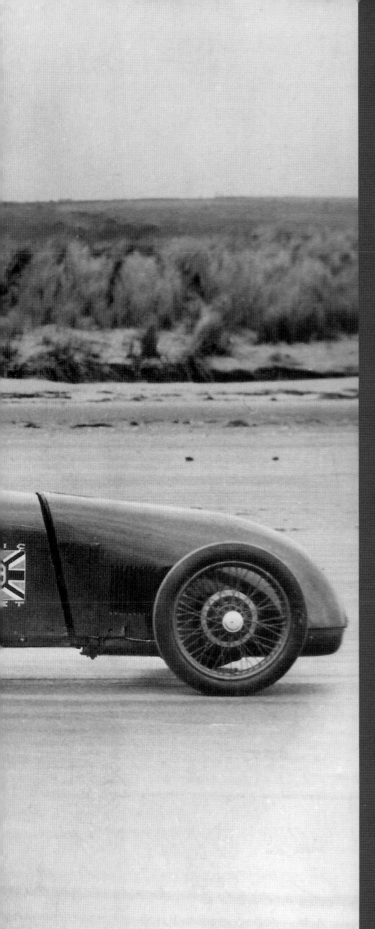

CHAPTER 3

THE LUCK CONTINUES
1932

SUPERCHARGING,
MORE RECORD BREAKING

Push starting was the order of the day in 1932: a
wonderful action shot at Pendine.

During 1931 not only was the Experimental Department involved in keeping happy the customers who were racing, preparing cars, carrying out modifications and attending race meetings when required, but they were also progressively producing modifications to improve the cars and developing the next series of both production sports cars and racing car derivatives. If the order of statement here sounds wrong, I can assure you that it was not – parts were designed for the production series of cars, and then incorporated into racing cars which improved the performance of these. Any faults found during racing were fed back to Experimental, and went towards the improvement of the product, thus ensuring the truth of the dictum: 'racing improves the breed'.

As an example of this system working, it was decided during 1931, that with increasing performance of both road and racing cars, and increasing weight of the former, it was desirable to increase braking efficiency. A 12in diameter drum system was therefore developed with a view to putting it into the six-cylinder F-type. Parts became available during 1932 and were put into the F-type model during the autumn of that year. They were then made available to those with racing C-types at the same time.

In order to ensure the smooth operation of this system, responsibility for running the Department was moved to H. N. Charles, as Chief Designer and Engineer, while Cecil Cousins was made Works Manager, with responsibility for production cars. He, of course, became involved when racing cars went into production. Charles remained as Chief Engineer, while Reg Jackson was in charge of Experimental, and his staff at this time consisted of Tayler, Kindell, Phillips, Robinson, and a youngster called Sydney Enever, who was starting to make a name for himself as a capable fitter, with a line in original thought. Others were drafted in as required to enable the workload to be completed, some of whom stayed on to become permanent.

Work on the small six-cylinder engine

The six-cylinder engine in standard Wolseley tune was not noted for its high output, but on the other hand the power it did produce came smoothly and over a wide torque band. This did not stop Experimental looking for ways to improve the engine. There were a number of basic problems with the engine of which the most serious was the cooling around the valves. The cylinder head design was identical to that of the M-type, and one of the problems with that layout was

that water in effect had to run the whole length of the head to get out to the radiator, getting ever hotter as it made its way forward. The extra length of the six-cylinder engine merely ensured that the front two cylinders ran hotter than the other four. While it would be possible to improve power along the lines followed in the C-type, this would almost certainly emphasise the fact that the head was poorly cooled.

A certain amount of work in this direction was carried out, and early in 1932 an engine was rigged up with larger inlet valves, 12/12 M-type valve timing and higher compression, and with an extra water pipe on the head to carry the water away. This showed an increase in power of some 27 per cent, but with work being carried out on the Midget crossflow head it was decided to suspend work until the new design was finalised in four-cylinder form.

Meanwhile, over at Brooklands, Robin Jackson was carrying out experiments of his own with the F-type engine, and was supercharging it. He found, not surprisingly, that the cooling water was boiling in the head, and that this work was a blind alley. He therefore took the engine to the works and tried to get them interested in producing a revised design of water flow. Charles did not want to get involved with this however, having already done this work himself, and at this stage could not let Jackson (Robin, not Reg) know what they were doing with a revised head.

This blown Magna engine was eventually sold to Richard Bolster, who fitted it to his GN-based Special. It went well at hill climbs and sprints, but eventually suffered a broken connecting rod and was scrapped. Another make of engine was fitted to the car, which survives, but it is now fitted with a blown MG N-type engine, proving that the development of historic cars never stops!

Crossflow head

In pursuit of more power, H. N. Charles had schemed ideas for an opposed port layout in the cylinder head. Wolseley Motors committed his ideas to paper, and the development work had started late in 1930. During 1931 work proceeded but it was not until the end of the year that work started in earnest with actual running prototypes.

There were two reasons for this; the first was that so long as the C-type was unsupercharged, the power available was more than enough to satisfy the demands of the racers. It was only when they ran supercharged that the deficiencies in the cylinder head design became really apparent, and this was not until the latter end of the season. The second reason was that MG was in business to sell sports cars to the general public, and development time for these products was taken up in producing the D and F-type cars: as in any business the primary objective was to produce a profit, and this was less likely to arise from the sale of 20 or so racing cars than from the 1,500 or more sports cars sold in the same period.

The problems of the cylinder head design centred mainly on cooling, but obviously if a new head was to be designed then it should have separate ports for each valve which should result in less hot-spots within the head. The result was a very good example of what can be achieved by engineers who get on with the engineering, unhindered by accountants. Not only was the new head a good design for the next generation of racing cars, but it was also brilliant in use in road sports cars, which were after all keeping MG alive in the financial sense. It was, moreover, no more expensive to produce than the earlier head.

Ports were kept short, and there was plenty of coolant around the exhaust valves. If there was a propensity to crack between the valves, this was a result of running the fuel mixture too weak rather than an inherent design fault.

The cam follower was redesigned along the lines of that decided for EX120 while it was found that the C-type camshaft timing gave excellent results both blown and unblown. The desired 50bhp unsupercharged was achieved with alcohol-based fuels, while in basic road tune 35/37bhp was achieved on petrol. Upwards of 70bhp was available initially on alcohol fuel when blown. Actual claims of power outputs were on the conservative side of these figures when the head eventually went into production, but we anticipate work was to be carried out.

Magic Midget

As 1931 came to a close, work was proceeding at Abingdon on a new record car, Project EX127, to the order of George Eyston. Closely based on the C-type, it was intended that the car should be lower in profile, because the work carried out with EX120 had showed that the smaller the frontal area which a car presented to the air, the faster it could be propelled for a given power output. Work was be carried out on ideas which H. N. Charles had from the engineers at Adderley Park, as already outlined. However it was also anticipated that boost pressures would be raised, and that power

The end of EX120, a burnt-out wreck. From the left are George Propert, George Eyston, Reg Jackson, Cecil Kimber and Jimmy Palmes.

outputs approaching 100bhp, from three quarters of a litre remember, would be attained in due course. All this was heady stuff, but Eyston had now set his eyes on a target speed of 120mph, as well as covering one hundred miles *in an hour*.

Around June 1931 Eyston therefore commissioned a C-type with this latter aim in mind, essentially a single-seater car, but based on the technology available so that costs would be kept within bounds. At this stage support from the Factory to Eyston was increasing, and while he ordered the car, and had to pay for it in advance, all the development work was provided free by the Factory. Reg Jackson was personally responsible for liaising with Eyston and translating ideas into metal.

Gradually plans came together, and by September 1931 the car was taking shape. Using a C-type chassis frame, front axle, engine and gearbox, it was decided that the maximum desirable height of the car would be that of the engine. The driver's head would need to protrude above this in order to keep the driver as low in the car as possible, the engine was turned through an angle of six degrees from the direction of travel, and the rear axle banjo was offset to the nearside to compensate. This enabled the car to be kept both narrow and low. It had been hoped that the new cylinder head would be available right from the start, but this proved optimistic, and the car was initially fitted with a 1931 specification supercharged C-type engine, developing something around 60bhp.

The car, together with EX120, was shipped to Montlhéry. So far as EX120 was concerned it was decided that this would attempt to take the longer distance records, up to one hour, while the new car would go for the sprint records.

At first the new car did not want to play. The radiator was too small, and the grille aperture at the front was not letting enough air in. Furthermore, at the insistence of Ernest Eldridge, the old chain drive to the supercharger had been retained, and on this car resulted in the blower masking the radiator. Jackson wanted to substitute the standard C-type drive and thus drop the line of drive to the blower, but Eldridge wanted to be able to vary boost pressures by changing the drive ratio. This obviously rankled with Jackson, for whom changing the supercharger for a larger unit was a much simpler operation, and a cleaner one!

To overcome the overheated engine, Jackson used tin-snips to open the radiator aperture, and then tried raising the rear of the bonnet to improve the airflow, but still the engine ran hot. Eldridge rushed off to Paris to buy an aircraft-type surface radiator which could be mounted on the body, in front of the supercharger. The plumbing necessary to fit this was not of the highest order, but at least it proved the point by keeping the coolant below 90°C. It was soon possible to prove that the car would be fast enough for the objectives. Modifications were put in hand to get the car in a state to perform its task, but meanwhile EX120 was put on the track for the hour run.

The old car ran faultlessly, and comfortably took

the hour record, covering 103 miles, but then disaster struck after passing the line for the last time. Eyston had not seen the signal to stop, and kept going at full speed, not being sure whether the hour was complete or not. As the car entered the banking a connecting rod broke, and the oil which poured out of the resultant hole in the cylinder block caught fire, flames licking around the driver's legs. George was, in his own words '. . . quite keen to get out at this stage', and so he killed the engine, turned off the fuel, and steered the car to the inside of the circuit, where he ejected himself as quickly as he could, with the car still moving at around 70mph.

It so happened that the Citroën Company was performing some tests on the track at the same time, and one of their cars arrived on the scene just as Eyston baled out – the French driver picked him up and rushed him straight to the local hospital for treatment for burns and bruises. The Frenchman was obviously a strong man, for George was generously proportioned, and admitted to being nearly 200lb at the time, and yet he was picked up bodily and carried from where he lay to the back of the car.

However the MG pit crew knew nothing of this. Jackson and his men were leaping with joy, shaking each other's hands and generally celebrating, when it became obvious that EX120 had stopped working. They were not too worried at first, thinking he had cut the engine to coast back to the depot, until someone pointed out that it was a full three minutes since he had last passed, and he had been lapping at not much over a minute. Then Kindell spotted the smoke plume! Jacko jumped into a car and drove as quickly as he could, with Kindell hanging on the windscreen and running board in the style of the contemporary Chicago gangsters, to the source of the smoke, to find EX120 blazing away. They quickly decided that George must still be in there, so with nothing to put the flames out apart from a travelling rug, rushed to the car and started to hack their way into it using a pickaxe. Apparently Kindell objected to the rough handling of the car, but Jacko responded 'Let the b***** burn, where the devil is George?' Of George there was no sign!

They searched high and low, before the Citroën team foreman came over, thinking there must have been a collision, and in a great state of apoplexy! Putting two and two together, they decided that the Citroën driver must have rescued George and taken him to hospital, and the Citroën pit crew were able to direct the MG men there, and everyone was relieved and happy, except George Eyston who was in no condition to drive EX127 in his heavily bandaged state.

Incidentally the remains of the older car were returned to Abingdon, where Jackson broke her up, her job done, retaining the broken rod and piston in his personal collection. The second unbored block survived and formed the basis for a recreation of the car some 30 years later, but the actual car had ceased to be.

Eldridge decided that the attempt on the sprint records must go on, and volunteered to drive the car himself. It proved something of a squeeze to get him in the cockpit, but he was soon driving the car fast enough to take the 5km record at 110mph, when the new radiator burst, and this put paid to further runs.

On return to Abingdon, Jackson made the unilateral decision that the standard MG blower drive would be installed, and that if more boost was required then a larger blower would be fitted. The surface radiator was discarded, and Morris Radiators man, 'Whip' Howard, hand-made a new unit to fit the space, and with ample spare cooling capacity, allowing the use of the original cowl which incorporated the MG monogram.

With these modifications in place, and several more, the car was christened *Magic Midget*, and sprayed green with large union flags being painted each side of the body, and the car was despatched to Montlhéry in December. Eyston was back to good health, and still dearly wanted to be the first to '120' in the small car class.

The weather was very cold, and delay followed delay. Eventually, on 22 December, even though a thick coating of ice lay on the track, he decided that it was now or never. He got in the car and drove as fast as he could under the conditions and took four records at over 114mph, before the team packed up and returned home for Christmas, but not satisfied that the car had performed to its full potential.

After the holiday, Kimber decided that, with all the publicity surrounding the attempts, the sooner the magic 120mph was in the bag the better, but the problem was where to do it. Montlhéry was not approved for the sprint records, and Brooklands was closed. Jackson reminded Kimber about Pendine Sands in South Wales, where many speed records had been taken in years gone by at speeds in excess of the MG target, and so he was charged with the job of setting up an attempt there.

A run along the sands in an M-type showed that the windscreen was quickly obscured by sand. On removing the screen, Jacko was soon convinced that salt and sand in the eyes was uncomfortable at 60mph – at twice that speed it was going to be a serious problem, and devised a special windscreen

EX127 at Pendine; this car became known as Magic Midget. Reg Jackson is at the nearside front wheel, and Frankie Tayler is at the offside rear. The pusher with the cigarette is Morgan, the adviser of tidal conditions at Pendine.

to overcome it. Basically it allowed the driver to look through a split in the screen while the air and sand was deflected over the driver's head.

At the end of January 1932 the equipe made its way to Pendine, setting up headquarters at the Beach Hotel. During his earlier foray, Jackson had befriended local man Wilfred Morgan, adviser to the great Parry Thomas, and who could read the weather and tide signs. It was said that he could predict the state of the sands as much as two days ahead. On 8 February, after many trials and tribulations Eyston made an attempt and reckoned to have reached well over 120mph, only to find that the time keeper's recorder had run out of ink. By this time the tide was infiltrating the sand and further runs were undertaken at great risk, taking the records, but 'only' at 118.39mph.

On return to Abingdon, the car was cleaned down, and the engine and supercharger were given their customary overhauls. At the Brooklands Whitsun meeting it was taken for a parade lap or two. However during this 'parade' Eyston managed to take the Class Outer Circuit record at 112.93mph, nearly 10mph better than the previous one held by Driscoll in an Austin. *Magic Midget* was then put in wraps, as the new racing season got started.

The 1932 season

The new cylinder head was available for the start of the 1932 season, and was offered to racing customers at a package price of £30, fitted in the car for an extra £10 if desired. Because the inlet ports were now on the offside of the engine, the inlet pipe was led over the top of the rocker box, so that the blower installation itself was not changed, keeping costs to a minimum.

The fitting of the new head brought about a couple of new problems, of which the worst was repeated blowing of the head gasket with 16SWG copper being tried in place of the copper and asbestos standard gasket, but it was still prone to burn, especially when using petrol fuels. Studs of ⅜in diameter were specified, as used with the old head when superchargers were fitted. It took a little time before a revised gasket, made of 20SWG mild steel was specified, and fitted after the head and block had been carefully, not to say laboriously, lapped by hand. Gas-filled rings were used as combustion chamber seals in conjunction with this gasket. After this no gasket failed on a racing MG prepared by the works.

Another problem encountered was the use of the then new 14mm sparking plugs, for which there was as yet an insufficient heat range to suit all purposes. However this would only take a short time to put right. This does put into perspective the fact that we are very lucky that there are so many plugs available today that there is now little problem finding one to suit any engine or fuel combination.

A keen C-type owner, Lord Edward de Clifford, decided that he would run in the famous 1,000-mile Italian road race, the Mille Miglia. With no real preparation this undertaking was started, and the little car ran for three quarters of the race without drama until it stopped. The Italian crowds gave de Clifford a hearty welcome wherever he went, chiefly, one suspects, because there is nothing nationalists like better than the good loser, and the Italians are nothing if not good nationalists! Amongst those who were present at the event was the English racing peer, Earl Howe, who was another great nationalist. This little-heralded event was to signal consideration of something far more grand the following year.

Brooklands 1,000-mile Race, 3/4 May 1932

The first important domestic race of the year was the 1,000-mile Race, to be held at Brooklands, and which took the place of the 'Double Twelve'. Whereas the 12/12 race had been designed for Le Mans-style sports cars with full touring impedimenta installed, the new event was to be for stripped sports cars. Cars were required to be started on the self starters, presumably to prove they were sports cars as opposed to racing cars. All cars were required to be actual catalogue models, offered for sale, but the interpretation of this rule seems to have been very liberal. Alcohol fuel was not allowed, and the cars were to be impounded overnight as they had been in the older race.

Cars were handicapped by capacity classes, by way of time, which meant that slower cars started well ahead of the faster ones. The race was to be divided into two sections, each of 500 miles. Finishers all had to complete the full distance to be classified, and the track was to be closed half an hour after the winner completed the distance. The race did not seem to capture the imagination as only 28 entries were received.

The success of the supercharged MGs in the previous year's '500' had caused a considerable change in required handicap speeds. This virtually ruled out any chance of a supercharged car winning, and so all the MGs ran with twin carburettors where the new head was fitted. Unfortunately, this being the first extended run with the new head also coincided with the discovery of the gasket problem, mentioned above, and all the cars suffered, both in practice and in the race itself. So adept were the works mechanics at changing head gaskets that less than half an hour was lost at the pits for this task!

Unfortunately, it was at this meeting that the first MG fatality occurred when, just a few laps from the start, H. Leeson lost control of his car as he approached the bend taking the road from Railway Straight to the Finishing Straight, and struck a bridge parapet, which shot the car off the track to fall 20ft to the entry road below.

Meanwhile the other cars were lapping at speeds of up to 85mph, and within their handicap, when the gasket problem started to hit. The Black/Gibson car managed to salvage third place, in spite of the fuel tank cracking and developing an increasingly serious fuel leak. It was Enever who eventually devised a plug which stemmed the leak, using a wooden bung wrapped with sacking. Black's speed for the 1,000 miles was 75.5mph inclusive of stops, which was 10mph faster than the winning speed the previous year, such was progress in the smallest class. The race was won by the Talbot of Brian Lewis and John Cobb, with a Riley second driven by Elsie Wisdom and Joan Richmond, the first time that ladies had figured in the results of an open race.

Le Mans, 18/19 June 1932

Francis Samuelson had once again entered the Le Mans race, hoping that his bad luck in previous years would be at an end. He arranged for Norman Black to be his co-driver, and the car was prepared at Abingdon, with Jackson and Kindell once again being employed as support crew. The little MG ran well, Samuelson finding no problem cornering as fast as, if not faster than, the larger-engined entries. Black, during the second spell, had worked the car into seventh place on the road, and after Samuelson took over from him it was obvious that they were leading the Index of Performance.

Early in the morning, Samuelson took over for his last spell, still leading on handicap, but after just nine laps, he found that the fuel level was low. The fuel tank had split. Although a repair was possible, the rules would not allow any fuel to be taken on for another eleven laps, so they had to retire.

For Samuelson, the race had not proved third

time lucky, and at Abingdon, revised tank fixings were devised, which put the problem finally to rest. Hitherto the tank had been secured by studs soldered to the base of the tank, and it was these which were breaking away, and tearing a small piece of the tank with them. All MG tanks were afterwards fixed in place by encircling them with straps and resting them on wooden blocks, with a rubber strip interposed, yet another example of racing improving the breed!

Nürburgring, German GP, 17 July 1932

Hugh Hamilton wanted to make a name for himself in Continental racing and had got backing from University Motors to run in the German Grand Prix. Thompson & Taylor of Brooklands prepared his car, and it was they who shortened the inlet pipe, by inverting the supercharger and leading the pipe around the offside of the radiator: this put the carburettor on the nearside, but resulted in the deletion of Jackson's somewhat complicated twin pipe induction system with no loss of tractability. Never too proud to learn from others, MG quickly adopted this layout in the Factory-prepared cars, and offered it to customers!

Hugo Urban-Emmerich again asked Kimber for the loan of a car for this race, and once again Jackson took the works experimental car, the same one as in 1931, over with Kindell as support. This car was fitted with all the latest parts from the Experimental programme, including a larger supercharger, and was the nearest that MG had got to a works entry at this stage; mind you Emmerich paid for the use of the car, its transportation to Germany, and for the expenses of the mechanics!

Hamilton started with a standing lap, which bettered the existing flying record, but stopped to reset his shock absorbers. After which he started to go fast! Urban-Emmerich, on the other hand, complained that his car was misfiring badly and kept on stopping. Jackson could find nothing wrong, and eventually did a lap of the circuit himself faster than the Czech to report that there was no misfire but that the car was too fast for *his* comfort!

Jackson had been instructed by Kimber to look after Hamilton's car, but Hamilton was trying not to get involved with Jacko, which might have proved embarrassing for the T&T crew. One evening after practice he and Kindell were being entertained to dinner by the Czech. They had just been served with coffee when a very dirty and dishevelled Hamilton appeared at the table with a newspaper-wrapped package under his arm. He bowed formally to

Emmerich, and then said to Jackson: 'What the devil do I do with this, Jacko?' simultaneously unwrapping the parcel onto the table to reveal the disembowelled supercharger from his car! This had obviously seized, but not from lack of oil. The hotel management were not too pleased as oil and fuel poured from the casing over the white table linen, but Jackson was able to salvage the situation, and after working all through the night got the car mobile again.

Against the MGs in the 800cc class was the BMW of Kohlrausch, this being in reality an Austin Seven car produced in Germany, and the Longbridge-built Ulster Austins of Baumer and Marquis de Belleroche. In addition there were other entries driving two-stroke DKW cars, which were not expected to give much opposition. At the same time were running the cars in the 1,500cc class, which included the ex-GP Delage of Earl Howe, a couple of Frazer Nashes, an old C6 Amilcar and an eight-cylinder 1,100cc Maserati driven by Ernesto Maserati himself. The unlimited capacity class was also starting with some very fast machinery to lead the way. The Grand Prix Formula at the time was for two-seater cars, virtually run on a *Formule Libre* basis.

As the cars lined up on the grid for the start, there was inevitably a moment when things went fairly quiet. This stage had just been reached when there was a short sharp expletive, unmistakably English, using a then seldom heard 'F' word: Hamilton had managed to shear off a sparking plug flush with the head! Jacko heard this, as indeed probably did most of the people in Nürburg that day, but was tending to the car of Urban-Emmerich. So it was left to George Thomas, Earl Howe's mechanic, to salvage what remained of English dignity: he quickly appraised the situation, and was able to extract the remains using an 'easy-out' tool and thus save face for Hamilton, who was a strong follower of the 'do it up tight' school of engineering. However, the lesson was learned, and from that date, Hamilton left race car preparation to the professionals, except for one more occasion some 12 months later.

At the start of the race, the MGs quickly outstripped their class competitors, with Hamilton leading Urban-Emmerich not far behind Earl Howe and the big Alfa of Tauber. Kohlrausch caught, but could not pass, Hamilton, while the Czech dropped behind unable to sustain the pace. The German driver soon also started to lose out to the Irishman, who was really motoring very quickly and pressed home his advantage to pull well clear of the opposition, and keeping close to Earl Howe in the Delage.

Urban-Emmerich stopped a couple of times with alleged plug problems, and then finally spun off the circuit for the second year running. Meanwhile, by the end of the race Hamilton went so far ahead of the 800cc opposition that he was given orders from the pits to slow down, but still won the class at 59.08mph, faster than the 1,100cc cars of the previous year. He was no less than 24 minutes ahead of Kohlrausch who was second in the class. This result was significant as it was the first Continental race victory for MG, and at a speed only 3mph slower than the first three in the 1,500cc class, and ahead of the rest of the field.

The Emmerich car was returned to Abingdon and repaired. Although it was the Experimental hack, and had been from new, it became known in the Factory as 'Hoodoo' because each time it was raced it seemed to bring bad luck. It was taken to Ulster to act as the practice car again. However, before that race, Kimber himself drove the car in the Craigantlet Hill Climb which was held the weekend before the TT. In this event he was able to post the second-fastest time of the day and win three first-class and four second-class awards, running, as was common in those days, in every class. This showed that there was nothing really wrong with the car, which was actually the fastest C-type at that time, as one might expect of an Experimental hack.

The Ulster TT, 29 August 1932

Nine MGs were entered for the TT, held as the previous year over 30 laps of the Ards course. However it was the race which signified to those at the MG factory how, in motor racing, last year's car is history, and that each year a new model must be produced. It was largely because time was being spent in the development of new models that the C-type was beginning to show its age, but the new models were the sports cars rather than new racing models which would follow in natural progression.

The event was notable mainly for Hugh Hamilton's high speed motoring in practice than for the finishing order of the race, but this is not to belittle the result achieved by those who finished, in particular Eddie Hall in his Midget. The winner was Cyril Whitcroft in the 1,100cc Riley Brooklands, at 74.23mph with George Eyston second in a similar car at 73.9mph while Hall's speed in third place was 69.93mph, enough for him to have won the previous year. However Hamilton had put in practice laps of up to 75.5mph, before putting himself in hospital. Had he raced, the result might have been different, but 'ifs' do not count in racing results. His entry was taken up by Stanley Barnes, who was given the dubious distinction of driving 'Hoodoo'.

Of the other MG entries, John Low finished second in class in his unblown car, 10th overall. The rest retired,

Scrutineering queue for the 1932 TT. The cars are: 34 E. R. Hall, who is to the right in overalls; 33 Stan Hailwood, who is in a leather jacket to the left of the car, and 32, Goldie Gardner, who is tightening something up on the right. The last car crashed badly during this race, but the car survives and is racing to this day.

Black suffering with rear axle failure, while Crabtree retired with a punctured carburettor float, Stan Barnes was, almost inevitably, eliminated in an accident, Cyril Paul ran a big end bearing, Goldie Gardner crashed very badly, and Stan Hailwood retired with a burnt valve. Geoffrey Manby-Colegrave did not even get to Belfast.

BARC Autumn meeting, 10 September 1932

This meeting followed the normal course of Brooklands meetings with a miscellany of short races on each of the circuits then in use. Ronnie Horton had had his car rebodied with a narrow and offset single-seater, built by Jensen of Wolverhampton, and which improved its performance by an unbelievable amount. In its first race it lapped the Outer Circuit at no less than 107.80mph, winning at an average of no less than 104.47mph.

Hamilton was there with his car, now painted black and entered for the Mountain Race which supported the main event. His car was equipped with the new 12-in brake gear, twin rear wheels and a closer ratio gearbox, these items on test for the following season, and with it Hamilton managed to achieve a lap of 69.28mph which broke the class record. Unfortunately even Ebblewhite had seen the potential of this car and driver team, and Hammy had to be content with a good second place, a mere 5.8 seconds behind Eccles's 1.5-litre supercharged Bugatti.

This result followed an amusing incident at the Factory, although no one thought it particularly funny at the time. The car had been prepared by Jacko, with a low rear axle ratio for the Mountain Circuit, and sent to Brooklands a couple of days prior to the meeting. On the Friday it was returned looking as though it had been bombed: the propeller shaft having broken. Kimber was incensed, for Hammy had been very lucky not to be hurt, and had Cousins, who was working late, on the carpet for a dressing down for not ensuring that the car was better prepared. Cecil Cousins was not over-pleased, partly because Experimental was no longer part of his responsibility, and partly because the reason he was late was that production was not running too well and matters in the Factory needed his undivided attention. He knew that if he said anything, Jacko would get the full force of Kimber's fury, so he decided to handle the problem.

Cousins had already seen the car, and had removed the tachometer and brought it to the office with him. As Kim drew breath, Cousins asked if *he* could have a few words, and pointed out that the tell tale was stuck at 8,600rpm! 'If Mr Hamilton was going to treat

engines, prepared by Mr Jackson taking hours of careful work to get right, in this way, he could jolly well go back to Thompson & Taylor and let them repair them!' Now Hammy was very good in respecting the rev limits in the gears, although he seldom looked at the tacho once he was in top: so it was obvious that the eight thousand-odd revolutions was achieved on *top* gear! Hamilton owned up and had of course been on the Outer Circuit with the car, and done some flat-out driving! A fresh engine and a new propeller shaft were installed and the car ran as already told.

In the penultimate race of the day, Horton was back, heavily re-handicapped. However like all good competitors in handicap events, he had something in hand and was able to lap the Outer Circuit at 115.29mph to take that class record, a speed higher than the 1100cc Class Record at the time, to take third place in the race.

The Brooklands 500, 24 September 1932

The last major event of the year was the BRDC 500-mile race at Brooklands, commonly known as the 'long blind' by the works mechanics, and for which George Eyston entered *Magic Midget*, sharing the drive with Bert Denly. Ron Horton had entered his Jensen-bodied offset single-seater. The other MG entries were more or less standard C-types, with Jeffress driving his unblown car, with Low, Black and Hailwood to keep him company in the unblown class. Black was to share with Ron Gibson, who prepared the car himself, as a 'homer', and caused a minor disciplinary problem at the works, since he was employed by them! Hailwood's car was prepared by Bill Lacey, better known in the motorcycle world, but very good at the job.

Hall, Dennis Evans, and Letts had their blown C-types there to add to the numbers, keeping the single-seaters company. Vic Derrington had somewhat optimistically entered an F-type Magna. The entry was a strong one, but practice times showed that if *Magic Midget* kept going there was going to be no contest, because it was lapping at well over 100mph, well in excess of its required handicap speed, 95.78mph, which practically no-one else could match. Not to be outdone, Horton started to go fast too, as befitted the record holder.

When the race started at 11.30am the unblown 750s, less Jeffress who did not come to the line, went off with Black taking the early lead. When the blown 750s went off, Horton got off to a cracking start, leaving all the others for dead for a few laps, before Eyston's 'slow' signal was withdrawn and he speeded up, soon

The 1932 BRDC 500-Mile Race: EX127 receives pit attention. Tayler is in front of the car, while Bert Denly, the driver, is behind. The car had the cross-flow head fitted, but the charge was carried over the rocker cover, and the carburettor was on the offside.

to catch and pass Horton, lapping at over 103mph. Just remember that this was a 500-mile race, so the drivers were expecting their cars to keep going for five hours at this pace! The other classes started in order, until all the entry was going.

Hall had elected to run with the Montlhéry cowl fitted, but, as predicted by Jackson, found that his radiator water boiled, and had to stop to hack pieces off. Eyston and Horton were pulling ahead of the rest of the entry and it needed a super human effort by someone to catch them, if they kept going. Denis Evans was in third place, and going well in the car he had recently bought from University Motors, having had the somewhat dubious pleasure of having it demonstrated by Hugh Hamilton, when a piston broke putting an end to his run.

Eyston stopped for fuel after two and a half hours, letting Horton take the lead, and Denly took over, still in second place. Vibration from the rough surface of the track was such that Hall's car dropped a small piece off, possibly a part of the hacked away cowling, which Black managed to pick up in his rear tyre, resulting in his spinning into the retaining wall along the Railway Straight.

At 14.30 *Magic Midget* was back in the lead, having averaged 100.51mph, inclusive of stops, with Horton

second. Letts' Midget holed a piston to retire around this time, and Derrington's Magna had a con-rod break at much the same time.

Denly was just rounding the Home Banking keeping fairly low down, when the Dunfee Bentley, passing Howe's Bugatti, roared past right on the upper rim: Denly saw to his horror one of the front wheels go over the edge, and the whole car reared up and overturned amongst the trees, killing Clive Dunfee, whose body was on the track. Denly not unnaturally shut the throttle on seeing this horrific accident, and steered down the banking, but in so doing probably got a hydraulic lock in a cylinder, which resulted in a piston breaking and the demise of the car.

Ron Horton's Jensen-bodied single-seater car bounces over the notorious Brooklands bumps on his way to winning the BRDC 500-Mile race outright.

Horton was still in the lead, with Hall travelling strongly, when his car broke a half shaft. Horton, whose car was fitted with an ultra-high axle ratio and had not seemed to run clean right from the start, was obviously playing a waiting game, for at this stage he started to go faster, and the exhaust sounded really crisp. Paul in the Riley was still going strongly as was the Cobb/Lewis Talbot, but the MG was just too fast for them, and Horton came home the winner on handicap at 96.29mph.

The Black/Gibson car finished, as did the Wright/ Couper car, and Low/Balmain, while Hailwood was flagged off when the circuit was closed. MG took first place, the Team Award and Class H, so it was a good end to a mediocre racing season for the Abingdon marque.

Two miles a minute

If the racing season was over there was still some unfinished business on the record breaking front. As a result of its foray in the 'Five Hundred', *Magic Midget* had engine problems and these needed to be attended to at Abingdon before any further running could be done. Also it had run for nearly three hours round Brooklands, which was hardly likely to improve the reliability of the chassis for record breaking, so Jackson set to on a complete rebuild of the car.

At the same time, the new J-series of cars had been announced, and this was to include a proper road going supercharged model, known as the J3, which in effect was a civilised version of the C-type racer, equipped with windscreen and doors as well as other creature comforts. The real racing car for 1933 was to be the J4 model, which was equipped with a larger supercharger, a fully counterbalanced crankshaft, and with 12in brake gear as tried by Hamilton at Brooklands in August, and looks which at first sight were identical with those of the road car except that the body was doorless.

Work on the J-series cars had been progressing through 1932, and when the press first tried the cars, a mildly tuned J2 was given to them, and they were able to report an 80mph top speed. Actual production examples would barely exceed 70mph comfortably, and this caused MG quite a few warranty problems, but in the end the car gained a deserved reputation for being a nicely mannered car on which performance could be improved for competition if required.

It was November before *Magic Midget* was rebuilt, by which time a J3 was also ready, the plan being to take International records in Class H up to and including 24 hours. On 1 November, Eddie Hall used his C-type to take the British and international standing start mile and kilometre records at Brooklands.

During the rebuild a celluloid dome had been made for the cockpit of *Magic Midget*, but in use Eyston found that his head contacted this, and to add to his discomfort, found the fumes in the cockpit were all too much. He tried safety straps to hold him down in his seat, but to no avail . . . this could be an early use of seat belts, although not for the reasons they are used now, being to keep the driver from being thrown out of the car in normal running, rather than in the event of an accident! In the end, a hole was cut in the dome, and this was found to eliminate both complaints.

The front offside corner of a J3 Midget, showing the layout of the supercharger for this car. All the racing cars carried the charge around the radiator, but on this more mundane car, the induction pipe is carried under the chassis cross-tube and inside the bonnet.

By the time the car was ready to make the record attempts, Brooklands was closed, so once again the team made its way to Montlhéry early in December. It was decided to make the first runs on the 13th, but the track was wet from overnight rain. Jackson was in charge of the service crew, with Nobby Marney, Fred Kindell and Gordon Phillips to help. Each time Eyston tried a run, the weather seemed to be against them, but eventually, late in the afternoon, things seemed to be right, and Eyston tried a timed run. The ride was so bumpy that he could not read the instruments, so he just drove flat out. From outside the car sounded really terrific and after three laps George came in to see what had happened. He had taken the mile and kilometre records at 120.56mph, with longer-distance records being taken at slightly less than the 120mph mark. Once again MG had achieved a benchmark speed for the Class H – the first in class to achieve two miles a minute. It was time to turn attention to the longer distances.

The J3 was made ready. Starting on the 19th, the run was to be shared between Eyston, Denly and Tommy Wisdom each taking a three-hour stint in rotation. The car had, according to the Factory notes of the time, been fitted with a J4 engine. I think it was probably only fitted with the engine itself, for the speeds actually attained were comparatively modest, so it was unlikely that the larger supercharger was used. The J4 engine, of course, had a fully counter-balanced crankshaft against the J3's 'bent wire' type, as used in the original C-types.

The car was given a set lap speed of around 75mph, and shortly after the first driver change Wisdom had the misfortune to have a fuel line break, and was forced to push the car back to the pits. This coupled with the repair time delayed the car, but it was soon cracking round again at its pre-set 75mph and took all the records up to 24 hours at speeds of up to 70.62mph, inclusive of stops! This with a car which was a Factory model, and of which replicas could be bought for £300.

Two days later, and starting at six in the morning, using oil lamps to mark the trackside, *Magic Midget* was again wheeled out to attempt the intermediate distance records, so that MG could claim to have all the class records at the end of the season. Running for a total of 12 hours, sharing with Denly, all the records were taken at speeds of up to 95.52mph, the 12-hour going at 86.67mph. This enabled MG to claim all the 750cc records, a feat which had never before been achieved by one make of car in any capacity class at one time and was especially satisfying since less than two years previously speeds of 60mph were rarely attained for the class. Now this speed had been handsomely surpassed by a catalogue model, with double the speed being attained by a purpose-built racing car.

Not only that, but the marque had taken honours in most of the prestigious races of the time, always using cars owned by the drivers, even if they were prepared by the works. In the history of motor racing this had never before been achieved.

The more rugged J4 for 1933, with full road equipment, displaying the fact that the cars were sports-racing cars. In fact, it is doubtful if any were ever raced in this form!

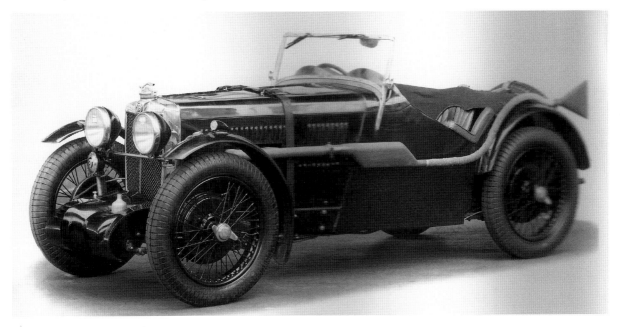

CHAPTER 4

AS IF BY MAGIC

1933

DEVELOPMENT OF THE MAGNETTE

R.A. Yallop in the second prototype K3 during the Mannin Beg race. (National Motor Museum)

As the 1932 season was progressing, the plans for the road cars in 1933 were unfolding. The MG alphabet had reached the letters D and F so logically the next models should be G, H and I, the letter E having been reserved for use in the experimental cars. It is a mystery why these letters were not used, but the next models were in fact J, K and L. The J-types were dealt with in the previous chapter, and much of what follows is related to the six-cylinder cars, the K and L types both featuring small sixes to follow on from the F-type Magna.

The six-cylinder engine is developed

As already related, the development of the six-cylinder engine was slowed during the development of the crossflow head for the four. Needless to say, work did continue, and it is reasonably certain to surmise that Charles wanted to build an engine which was suitable for the next capacity class up from 750cc, namely the 751-1,100cc Class G. The 1,271cc F-type unit was too big for this, so with the agreement of Kimber, but probably without the knowledge of Sir William Morris, the Wolseley people were approached to see what could be achieved by redesigning the 750cc C-type unit as a six-cylinder, using as much of the technology of the F-type as feasible, but taking into account the way things were developing. There can be little doubt that Kimber saw this as a minor redesign exercise, and work must have started during 1931, and by early 1932 it was drawn up. By this time, work on the crossflow C-type head was well under way, and the deficiencies of the small diameter camshaft were becoming apparent. It was decided to double this dimension, and rework the layout of the head in proportion, and it was quickly realised that this would cost no more than using the Midget layout when put into production, and could logically be incorporated into a four-cylinder design with a minimum of complication when required.

The cylinder block was revised in respect of water flow and oil supply. It had been decided to shorten the stroke for the new engine and to maintain the cylinder head shape, as well as to allow higher crankshaft speeds to be used. A few details were changed, the crankshaft journal dimensions were increased by one eighth of an inch, and the connecting rods were altered to the C-type pattern and uprated in the matter of dimensions all over to give greater strength. Full flow oil filtration was fitted for the first time to an MG engine. The front main bearing was replaced by a white metal bush, with end float thrust taken by steel discs bearing on a white metal washer, which was much cheaper in fitting time than the ball race option used thus far.

There can be no doubt that the design was made on the assumption that the unit would be supercharged, and develop a lot of power, because quite a bit of the detail betrays elements of over-design. Valve porting, in particular, was extremely generous, even if the valves themselves were rather on the small size by present-day thinking. The basic bore of 57mm was retained, and the stroke came out at 71mm to keep the engine below 1,100cc, rather than the 73mm used on the racing Midgets.

Rather interestingly Wolseley Motors were redesigning their own OHC engine used in the Hornet, and decided to opt for a chain drive to the camshaft, and eventually changing, for 1934, to a completely different valve gear based on that used in the Morris Isis engine, as fitted to the obsolete 18/80 MG. At the same time they went for increasing the capacity to 1,650cc. Unfortunately they compounded their problems by adhering to the eccentric bush adjustment of the rockers, which resulted in drastic changes in valve timing when the bushes are moved, and thus ensured the perpetuation of the worst feature of both engines!

Why they went a different route is not clear, and how Sir William Morris allowed this independence of thought to be carried through will never be known. Of course, Frank Woolard, the Morris Motors engine designer, was Chief Engine Designer at the period, but then why would he allow a line of independent thought to come from Abingdon? Certainly Wolseley Motors were more interested in producing up-market cars, but these were little better than modified Morris's so far as chassis and body design was concerned. The route taken by MG was to try to appeal to the genuine sporting motorist, and to build cars which had a dual personality for road and track. All this forms the basis for very interesting conjecture about the in-house politics which existed in Morris Motors at the time, and which were apparently not only condoned by WRM but actually encouraged by him.

To return to the revised MG, now code-named the K-type, the chassis frame was a much more robust unit than that used on previous small MG cars, and the axles were of a wider track. The steering arrangement deployed a split track rod in an attempt to overcome the effects of kick-back in the steering affecting the steering wheel. The brakes were 13in Alford & Alder units, featuring magnesium alloy (called 'Elektron') back plates and shoes, and were unique to the K-type, and not used on another model in the Morris group.

The K-series of cars, which was called the 'Magnette'

right from the start for all its variants, was therefore announced at the 1932 Motor Show, as a '1933' model, and appeared alongside the J-type Midget range. The name Magnette presumably meant that it was a small Magna but, even if it had a smaller engine capacity, the car was physically much larger than the F-type had been. The new engine was also more powerful than the older unit.

The K1 was the tourer version, based on a 9ft wheelbase chassis and offering open and closed four-seat bodies, the saloon being especially good looking and featuring pillarless construction which was then in vogue, whereby the front and rear doors were front and rear hinged respectively and came together when closed, but offered a huge opening for easy entry and exit of the passengers. The open tourer featured a conventional two-door four-seat body of the period.

The K2 on the other hand had a shorter wheelbase, the same as the Magna, and was fitted with a sports two-seater body with a slab tank, similar to that fitted to the J2, although the K-type cars all had long flowing mudguards in place of the cycle wings used hitherto on both the Midget and Magna models. The whole car was much larger in concept and looked like a large J2, but was out of proportion and failed to make a mark.

Alongside these offerings was announced a K3 which was to be a supercharged competition car, based

The prototype K3, as driven by F. M. Montgomery in the 1933 Monte Carlo Rally, and which succeeded in taking FTD in the Mont des Mules Hill-climb event.

on the K2, featured in the show literature, but a car was not on display at the 1932 Motor Show, probably because there appears to have been a problem deciding on what it should look like!

All these cars featured the 1,100cc engine. Originally the sports and touring K-type engine was offered with three SU carburettors and BTH magneto but this set-up caused quite a bit of trouble with warranty claims and not a few were subsequently changed to twin carburettors and coil ignition.

There was a choice of manual transmission using the Wolseley gearbox used in the J-type, but with a different remote control, or an ENV-built Wilson-type preselector gearbox, the latter for an additional £25. The preselector was gaining considerable fashion as a solution to the problem of those who could not change gear in the ubiquitous sliding dog box of the period, often colloquially called a 'crash box'. Designed and patented by Major Wilson, the preselector used an epicyclic geartrain in which ratios were changed by applying a brake to one of four internally toothed drums. The virtue of the system was that a gear selected could be engaged at will later than the selection process, and removed the need for co-ordination of arm and foot movements. The MG featured a small selector lever mounted on the gearbox extension, just like the change-speed lever of the manual gearbox, and around which were clustered other controls making a neat arrangement.

Along with the K-type Magnette was announced an up-dated Magna model, thus falling into the trap which

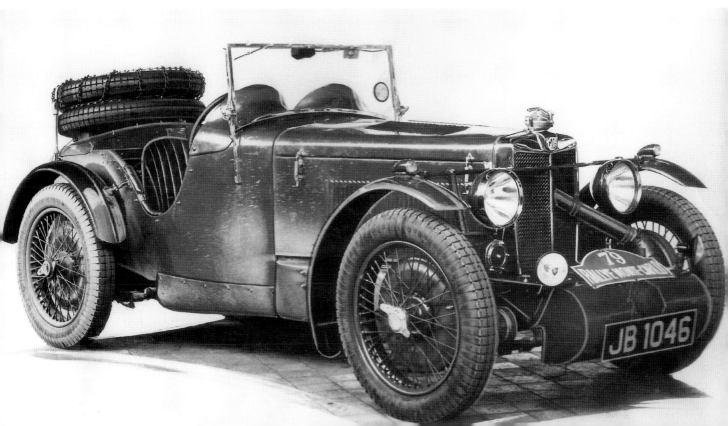

so many manufacturers suffered around this time of producing a confusing array of models. Dubbed the L-type, the new Magna featured the 1,100cc engine, but with two carburettors and coil ignition, and the Wolseley manual transmission similar to that used on the J-types. The L1 was the four-seater, offered in open and closed forms, and the L2 was the open two-seater. While the four-seater models were not especially attractive, the two-seater was very good looking, featuring long swept wings which were to be a feature of MG design for the next 20 years or so. The chassis layout was closely similar to that of the F-type which had the merit of being light, but even in its own time the L-type was not renowned for its ability to steer a straight line at high speed! The brakes used the 12in drums which had first appeared during 1932 on the later F-type cars.

Pricing policy was something of a problem, but it was resolved that the J2 models would be around £200, while the J3 would be around £100 dearer than the J2 at £300. The L2 was offered at £250, and the K2 was considerably dearer at £310. The L1 was offered at just over the £300 mark and some £50 dearer than the J1, while the K1 was around £400, the pillarless saloon being the dearest at £445. The J4 racer was to be £500 and the K3 was priced at £795: not far off the figure for which the ill-fated Tigress had been offered. All these prices must be taken in the context that very few people earned more than £200 per year at that time, and that the men who actually built the cars were earning £100/150 per annum! Reg Jackson had told me that he considered himself one of the elite at the time, for he was being paid 1s 4d (about 7p) per hour as the foreman of the Experimental Department in 1933 for a 48-hour week, or just over £166 per annum!

Development of the K3 Magnette

By the end of 1932 an entry had been made to the Monte Carlo Rally by F. M. Montgomery to drive his C-type, but Kimber was able to persuade him to use the prototype K3 Magnette instead. This was an expanded C-type in conception, using a modified body and the ENV gearbox from this model, but using the new K-type chassis and engine, which was supercharged. Alongside this entry was entered Walter Belgrave in a J3.

Late in 1932, probably during the London Motor Show, Earl Howe had approached Kimber with a plan to enter the Mille Miglia the following year using a team of Magnettes. The team would comprise of Howe, Bernard Rubin and George Eyston, each of whom was in a position to buy a car, but Howe wanted

works assistance. Sir William Morris was brought into the discussion, and in the end it was agreed that the three cars would be loaned, but the entry details and expenses would be borne by the entrant, and MG would offer assistance by way of supplying a practice car for testing and reconnaissance, as well as three mechanics for servicing the cars during the race.

The other team drivers were to include Sir Henry Birkin, who only the previous year had derided the hordes of small cars taking valuable track space from the cars which are nowadays described as 'vintage', and Hugh Hamilton, who was a new star in the racing world following his brilliant drives in a C-type at Nürburgring, Brooklands, and Belfast. The last team driver was to be none other than Count Giovanni Lurani the Italian ace driver, whose local knowledge was to prove invaluable. Such a plan was exactly what Kimber needed to get the Magnette programme off the ground, and to have the tacit agreement of Sir William would stop sniping from those in Morris Motors who thought that Kimber was altogether too big for his boots.

A second prototype car was in the process of being built up by Jackson and his men in Experimental, and Kimber urged early completion, no doubt with pressure from Earl Howe, so that the car would be available to the team for reconnaissance work prior to the event due to take place in April, less than four months away. This car was completed and shipped from Newhaven so that Jackson, driving in convoy with the noble Earl in his Alfa Romeo, and followed by his personal mechanic, Thomas, driving Howe's SSK Mercedes, could reach Milan to meet the rest of the team on 10 January.

Jacko and Thomas made their way in convoy, while Howe visited Molshiem to see Ettore Bugatti. Reg told me that he did not meet Bugatti, nor did the MG go there, which puts the lie to the story that Bugatti had said that the front axle was not strong enough.

Jackson always said that he was not much of a driver, but personal experience suggests that this was not true, and while he was not a competitive driver in any sense of the word, he was well able to press on safely when required. At this stage he had not been driving cars for long and he had never driven a car on ice previous to this trip and somewhere just after crossing the Italian border they had their first experience of driving on an autostrada. They were travelling at between 60 and 70mph when, after a few miles, he was somewhat alarmed to see the Mercedes suddenly swinging to right and left as Thomas fought for control . . . then Jacko learned how to control the K3 on ice the practical way, but was able to come to a standstill. After this experience they both drove more sedately!

During the testing it became obvious that the standard gearbox ratios were too low, but a wire to Abingdon elicited information that ENV were providing closer ratios for the race cars. Apparently it was Birkin who ventured the suggestion that the front axle beam was wanting in strength, since he could actually *see it flexing* under heavy braking, and work started back at Abingdon redesigning this item. The car gave surprisingly little trouble, but having the practical Jackson present on the scene helped considerably in solving problems as they arose. He averred that it was hard work and that sleep was taken when possible in the passenger seat of one of the tender cars after all-night rebuilding and design sessions.

Howe had arranged for the team to visit the King of Italy, and of course Benito Mussolini, a rising force in Italian politics at the time, was involved in this meeting. Jackson remembered him as a bumptious and excitable man of no real charm, nor much knowledge of motor racing, despite contemporary reports. Jackson met Nuvolari, the great racing driver who was then at the height of his fame and fortune, where the two became unlikely friends, neither speaking the other's language. This meeting was to lead to other things as we will see.

On return to Abingdon the car was stripped completely, and thoroughly inspected. The three team cars, plus three more for early customers were already laid down, but detail modifications were added as a result of the experiences in Italy. Altogether some 3,500 miles had been covered, and the car had been driven by several different drivers: it says much for Charles's basic design that so little reworking was actually necessary.

The three team cars were ready, fitted with coach-built ash-framed bodies, by the end of February. The driver pairings were to be Earl Howe with Hugh Hamilton, George Eyston with Count Lurani and Bernard Rubin with Sir Henry Birkin. The last car had already been sold to Rubin, who had decided to take it back with him to Australia. Eyston was going to buy his car on his usual terms, while Howe had taken an option to buy after the race. All these sales were made on the basis that the cars were put into roadworthy condition after their return from Italy.

Sales of K3 Magnettes had been made to Ronnie Horton, Eddie Hall and Robin Mere, following the Motor Show. Horton and Hall had already done great things with their MG cars, while Mere was a keen amateur, and prominent member of the MG Car Club, who had run a C-type in trials and rallies in 1932. Orders were also being processed for others who had

Enid Riddell, who was one of the first customers for a K3. She seldom raced, but was a frequent competitor in rallies.

expressed interest in the new car, including the lady rally driver Enid Riddell. The future of the K3 seemed secure before the car achieved anything at all, when news came through that Montgomery had made the fastest time in the Mont des Mules hill-climb event at the end of the Monte Carlo Rally.

The inaugural Donington meeting: 25 March 1933

Shortly before the Mille Miglia, the Donington Park track in Derbyshire was opened, and it was actually at this meeting that a K3 won its first race. The car used was the first prototype car, still owned by the works and travel-stained from its excursion to France, but loaned for the day to Ron Horton for this meeting, since his own car was not ready in time. The programme of six races was listed and open to two-seater cars with a capacity of less than 1,500cc, at that time described as 'light cars'.

Eddie Hall won the very first event at the meeting, for cars with a capacity of less than 850cc, in his C-type, beating Turner's Austin by 21 seconds after a close-fought race which resulted in the Longbridge car's

Ron Horton, driving the K3 prototype at Donington Park, where he scored the first victory for the model in a racing event, at the first meeting ever held at that circuit.

supercharger seizing. The second event was in two heats, with aggregate results to decide the winner, and this was also won by Hall. The third race was for unblown 850cc cars, and was won by Alf Langley in his J2. The fourth race was for unblown cars up to 1,500cc, and no MGs took part in this which was won by Hutchison's Type 37 Bugatti.

The fifth race in the programme was for supercharged cars up to 1,500cc capacity, but only Horton and Hall came to the line, the former winning by over six seconds to give the K3 its first actual race win.

In the last race of the day, however, the clutch on the prototype failed on the fifth lap when easily leading Dixon, leaving the latter to win in his Riley. Rayson was second in another Riley, with Robin Jackson third in his C-type, described as the 'noisiest car ever made' in one report!

The meeting was hardly the big-time, with probably only 30 competitors present altogether, but it was important as a showcase for MG cars to be seen in this first event at the Derbyshire circuit.

Preparations for the Mille Miglia

There were far bigger fish to catch in the wider world and so to return to the arrangements for the Mille Miglia. Hugh McConnell, the famous Brooklands scrutineer was appointed by Kimber to act as team manager for the event. There were two principal reasons for this. First such a function was going to be necessary, and secondly he spoke fluent Italian. MG of course had a proven race manager in Cecil Cousins, but his mastery of foreign tongues was limited to, in his own words, 'the King's English, which I certainly didn't normally speak!'. McConnell was well known to Howe, who arranged for the necessary fee to be paid.

McConnell studied the route map, and decided that pit stop areas would be needed at Bologna, Siena and Perugia. He also suggested the idea of a travelling service crew using Howe's Mercedes and running as a competitor. C. Penn Hughes the amateur driver was conscripted for this job, with George Thomas as co-driver. This car was loaded with spare wheels, a dynamo, starter motor and boxes of nuts, bolts, washers and sparking plugs, as well as heavy lifting gear and the tools which Jackson thought might be necessary to keep the cars going. The three MGs were ready for shipping on 10 March.

It was decided to take the cars direct by sea to Genoa, so that they covered as little road mileage as possible before the event. In these days of regular Channel crossings it is difficult to imagine a time when drive-on/drive-off ferries were not operating, but 1933 was such a time. The only way that could be found to take the cars to Genoa was to ship from Fowey in Cornwall, which, although a regular port for this journey, had never handled a car previously. The shippers had decided to take the cars as deck cargo in a boat, 'ship' would be too grand a title for the small vessel used, carrying a normal cargo of china clay and fish! Such was the state of chaos at the docks that the cars had to be loaded onto railway wagons to get them into the docks, and then Jacko had to arrange to borrow a crane to lift the cars onto the deck of the SS *Florentine* from the Southern Railway Company, and brought all the way from Folkestone. This apparently called for great powers of persuasion, since Fowey was a competitive port operated by the Great Western Railway Company! Once loaded the journey took 12 days, through some very rough seas. Apparently Jackson and Marney went to Genoa by train, while Bert Denly travelled with the cars. He was sea-sick for the whole time they were afloat, and hardly remembered the journey at all . . . which was probably just as well. The cars, however, were none the worse for their sea trip, and they were driven in convoy to a garage to await customs clearance. None of the mechanics could speak Italian, and the Italians spoke no English, but they were very friendly because it was known that

the cars were to run in the Mille Miglia. Eventually they were all transported by rail to Milan for the final preparations to be made before the start.

For official practice, it was decided that only one of the Magnettes be used, and that the drivers did the bulk of their testing on Howe's Alfa Romeo 2900C. It was long enough to find that the brake drums were cracking on the Magnettes. Frantic phone calls to Abingdon were made, and some midnight oil burned. The drums consisted of rings of cast iron, shrunk into outer drums made of Elektron. Charles carried out his sums, and decided that during the early tests, in cold weather, the drums had not been subjected to great heat and that now they were being used to their full advantage excessive heat build-up was causing the failure. New drums, in which the friction drum was made of steel and shrunk into the magnesium alloy outer, then screwed in around the periphery, were made and sent out to Italy for fitting to the cars. These were wholly successful, and not redesigned during the life of the model. H. N. Charles's genius for design has been mentioned before, but this experience underlines the truth of the matter. The new drums were actually taken by road in the old practice K3 prototype all the way to Brescia. Who undertook this journey is not known, but it was probably Kindell, who was able to report to Jackson that the new drums had worked well on the way there!

The production K3, with Mille Miglia body. This is one of the 1933 racing cars, driven by Earl Howe and Hugh Hamilton. Note that there is no silencer fitted!

The Mille Miglia: 8/9 April 1933

So arrived the start of the race. Official technical scrutiny of the cars produced a problem with the exhaust systems, which were not provided with silencers. They were deemed necessary, and Jackson drew up a design, which was executed by an Italian blacksmith in double quick time and fitted to the cars to satisfy the officials. Jacko told me that there was nothing in the can, and he thought that all that was wanted was something that *looked like* a silencer – certainly the noise was, if anything, louder, although the pitch was a tone or two lower!

The object of the expedition was to take the class win and hope for the Team Award. Although there was a host of Fiats entered, the main class opposition was considered to be provided by a team of four-cylinder Maseratis, with twin OHC supercharged engines and which had been extremely successful in the previous season. These were out-and-out racing machines, and driven by some of the best Italian drivers of the period, headed by Tufanelli. They were very fast, and McConnell, after conference with Howe and Lurani, decided that the best plan would be for Birkin to drive as quickly as he could. This was wise, because Birkin would probably have done that anyway! With any luck, the Italians would attempt to stay with the leading MG, and they would be likely to suffer mechanical breakages as a result.

At the start the green MGs were causing a great hit with the enthusiastic crowds. Their engines sounded purposeful, with the glorious crisp exhaust bark which only a supercharged 'six' can give. Cheers of 'Viva! Viva gli Inglese!' resounded around the cars, and even the black shirted *Fascisti* were cheering the foreigners.

It will seem ridiculous now, but the roads were not closed, and ordinary traffic had to be contended with. Cars were started off singly at one-minute intervals, starting with the smallest. The shortest elapsed time for the distance was declared the winner, but results might take time to complete, since all finishers had to complete the distance before times were fully known. The MGs were away after the first 40 cars had left, and Birkin was soon passing those ahead of him, and setting a really fast pace. Tufanelli responded and although he was soon going all out he could not match the Englishman's pace, try as he might.

At Bologna, 130 miles from the start, Birkin was ahead of all others, and had set new records for every part, averaging over 87mph for the first section. Next came the Raticosa Pass, where the MGs with their preselector gearboxes made a great impression, and it was here that Tufanelli fell out with gearbox problems. By the time the MGs reached their first service point at Siena, it was obvious that they were in some trouble with sparking plugs oiling when the engine went onto overrun, due to the supercharger oiling system not cutting off. Birkin's engine broke a valve, which put his car out, its job done, but the other two were still in good heart. All the Italian opposition in the class was in severe trouble, the MG tactic having worked, the remaining Fiat team being so much slower as to be of

Harry Robinson, generally known as 'Robby', was the chief engine tester, and is here seen setting up a K3 engine on the Abingdon dynamometer.

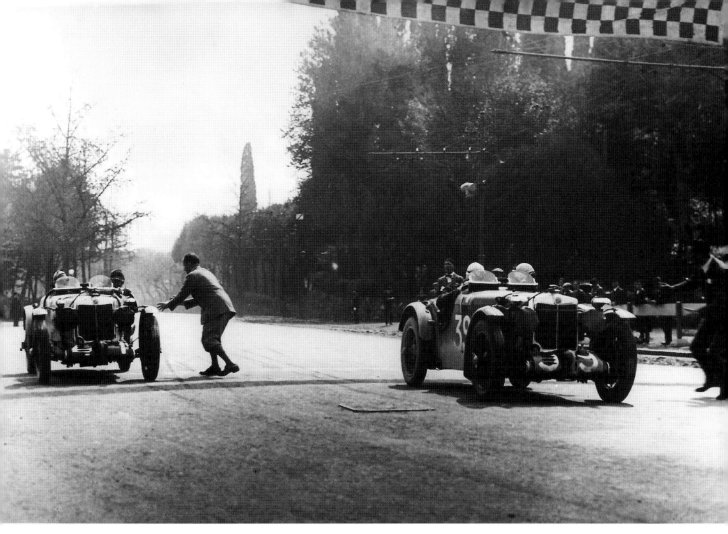

A wonderful action shot, taken during the Mille Miglia. Eyston/Lurani check in on the right, while Howe and Hamilton do so on the left, at the Sienna checkpoint.

no threat in the Team Prize, provided the remaining MG entries survived.

At Rome, Eyston checked in having covered the 380 miles in 6 hours 18 minutes, easily breaking the previous record, and they were followed by Howe and Hamilton 20 minutes later, but still five minutes inside the previous best! The former car was suffering with a non-charging dynamo, and with brakes which were beyond their best, but again the preselector gearbox came in handy as an emergency brake!

Shortly after the halfway stage, Eyston started to complain that the steering of the car was odd. In reality he was exhausted, and when Lurani took over, he confirmed that the chassis was *not* broken after all! In this period, Howe and Hamilton caught up, and by Ancona, 606 miles from the start, were only ten minutes in arrears. It was now dark, and the headlights were needed. In many of the towns spectators standing on the road, actually in the path of the cars, made

driving even more hazardous than it already was.

At Bologna, for the second time, McConnell had set up the pit, only to be told by the local police that he had to move. Jackson, Marney and Co. soon moved everything, but less than two minutes passed before Eyston and Lurani appeared! The crowd swarmed around the car, making it impossible to work on, or even for the drivers to get out, but Marney got a length of rope, an end of which was tied to a tree and herded the people away from the cars, shouting 'Get back, you silly b*****s', in English of course, and they all moved aside like a flock of sheep! A new battery was fitted to the car, and it was soon fuelled and serviced, while drivers ate a sandwich and had a drink, and then away for the last leg of the race. Seven minutes later the other car arrived and got similar treatment. The actual pit stops overlapped by a few minutes, which proved reassuring for both teams of drivers, who were able to exchange stories and encourage each other. During the service of the second car, it was found that one of the headlamp stays had broken. Fortunately Denly had arrived in the practice car from Siena, where he had been running the pit, and it only took a few minutes to remove one from this car and fit it to the race car.

Howe left the service area just 12 minutes after Eyston.

A Fiat was the first car in Brescia, having started an hour before the MGs, but Eyston followed him home right at his tail, and it soon became apparent that the two MG cars were first and second in class, easily outpacing the Fiats, while all the Maseratis had failed. Italian face was saved by Nuvolari who won the event outright in his 2.3-litre supercharged Alfa Romeo, at an average of 67.45mph. The Eyston/Lurani car had averaged 56.90mph, while Howe and Hamilton were close at 56.82mph! When all the finishers had arrived, the MG team learned they had won the Team Prize too, achieving all they had set out to do, with the bonus that they had set new class records all the way.

The race had lasted 18 hours for the MG drivers, and they had covered 1,005 miles, and at the end they were only one and half minutes apart. The problems which they had experienced were not too serious, and all are mentioned above, although Eyston maintained that they had changed 157 sparking plugs along the road! The truth of this story was held in question by Jackson, who merely said it was a lot, but that it was unlikely that the *whole team* used that number in the race. Certainly sparking plug oiling was a problem with the car, which used a Powerplus blower which needed a generous supply of oil to stop it from seizing. Bearing in mind that the cars were largely untried before the race, the result was far better than could fairly have been expected. Troubles were not serious and the cars were still serviceable at the end of the race, and all three were actually driven home through France and shipped back via the conventional route from Calais.

Whatever the problems it was a truly exciting and great achievement, and received considerable coverage in the British press, which at that time was most unusual. Amongst the ex-works memorabilia I have is Kimber's complete file of press cuttings for this event, given to me by Grace Lewis who had compiled it for him, and it does make most interesting reading.

Brooklands International Trophy Race: 6 May 1933

There was no let up in the schedule for the Works Experimental Department. Jackson, Marney and Denly drove the cars back via Calais arriving around 15 April, and then all three cars were stripped down in preparation for the first major Brooklands meeting of the year. The practice prototype car had been sold to R. A. Yallop, who had been racing one of the old 12/12 M-types during 1932, and wanted more performance for 1933. The Rubin/Birkin car was to be prepared for

Bernard Rubin to take back to Australia later in the year. Howe and Eyston had decided to keep theirs for a time, but were both needed for the International Trophy, and in addition new cars were to be ready for Horton, Hall, Mere and Geoffrey Manby-Colegrave.

Extra staff were drafted into Experimental, from the main factory: among them Alec Hounslow, Henry Stone and Herbert Wirdnam, generally known as 'Ginger' for his shock of red hair. Those of us who got to know him in later years found this difficult to believe, since he was near bald and what hair remained was white – we knew him as Bert. There was always very stiff competition to get into 'Racing' as it was known, and a principal factor was whether or not Reg Jackson had noticed you. Anyone drafted in knew that the position was at best only temporary, but the work was very glamorous, often spending days at Brooklands. Pay was standard rate of 9d (3.75p) per hour, but it did involve a lot of overtime, which was probably not all paid for, or even claimed, as well as weekend work, which certainly was not! One of the attractions was that satisfied customers would often give a generous tip to the mechanics for work well done, and if they won or were placed, this could be a couple of pound notes or, sometimes, a 'blanket', the sobriquet for one of the large white five pound notes of the period, or even ten pounds on some occasions. Eddie Hall was remembered with affection for being especially generous in this way.

For the event, Eyston elected to drive his *Magic Midget*, but his Magnette was driven in the Trophy race by Elsie Wisdom, the noted lady driver of the day, and wife of Tommy, the driver and journalist. Howe decided to drive his car in this race. Horton's car was still not ready, but Hall's was, wearing a lightweight body with a long-tail which had originally been offered as an optional add-on extra: this had proved impractical, and the long tail body was a shell made of aluminium, and suited to the racing track. The bodies could be switched easily and quickly (within two hours in fact) and Hall ordered his car with both bodies. Mere's car was not finished, but Manby-Colegrave got his, owing mainly to the fact that Adrian Squire worked in the MG Drawing Office and was able to keep things moving for his friend.

In addition to the Magnettes, there was a good entry of six Midgets. Eyston's has already been mentioned, but alongside him were the J4 entries of Hamilton and of Elwes and Watson, MG dealers from the Bournemouth area, the single seater C-type of Ron Horton, the C-type of the Evans brothers, and the similar cars of Donald Letts, Goldie Gardner and Stan Crabtree.

The race was designed to replace the 1,000-Mile

Race which had not proved popular the previous year. It was styled the International Trophy, a race of 250 miles for racing cars in any trim and all engine sizes. A novel approach to handicapping was found and the race was run on a circuit comprising the Byfleet Banking and the Finishing Straight, with three channels being marked on the latter. One of these, for the fastest cars, caused competitors to turn an acute bend, while cars with engines of less than 3,000cc unsupercharged or 1,750cc blown had a less severe turn to make, while the smallest cars, with engines smaller than 750cc supercharged or 1,500cc unblown, drove a straight path. The race was therefore run on a straightforward scratch start, with the first to cross the line being declared the winner. The idea was superb, and provided some good close racing, and surprisingly no-one appears to have taken a wrong path or tried to cheat. Of course, such handicapping was only possible because the track at Brooklands was so wide.

Hamilton put himself out during practice when he crashed the J4 on the final lap! The rest of the 28 starters lined up, and when flagged away Yallop was left standing with a broken half shaft, which put him out before he turned a wheel. Elwes got off to a cracking start, but went too fast and slid off the circuit to bend his front axle beyond immediate repair before he had completed a lap! Three laps later, Eyston lost a rear wheel from *Magic Midget* due, Jackson said, to using wheel discs which would not allow the Rudge-Whitworth hub-nut to seat on the cone of the wheel properly. Horton was going fast enough to worry the heavy brigade, lying fifth overall, but his sparking plugs gave up the battle against heat, and the engine was soon misfiring badly, causing him to stop for a change of plugs.

Meanwhile, Kenneth Evans broke his crankshaft,

'Jock' Manby-Colegrave bought a K3 (K3004) from the factory, which was pushed through for delivery by Adrian Squire, who worked in the drawing office at Abingdon. Squire later left MG to make a few cars under his own name at the roadside garage near Henley where this photograph was taken.

and things did not look very good on the MG front. However all was not lost, for the Magnettes were going very well, all four driving in fairly close formation. Hall was forced to stop for fresh tyres at the rear, and while he was stopped, Manby-Colegrave rather carelessly hit a marker tub at one of the chicanes, bending his front axle and putting him out of the running. Mrs Wisdom was going well, as was Earl Howe.

After his stop, Hall was soon charging around and was in second place, to Brian Lewis on his blown 2.6-litre Monza Alfa Romeo, with Elsie Wisdom a close third. So it worked out at the end with Lewis winning at 88.07mph, Hall second at 82.77mph and Elsie Wisdom third at 81.24mph. Earl Howe came in fourth. MG did not win, but again the new Magnette had proved itself capable of excellent results, and this time on the racing circuit, as opposed to the roads.

It was after this race that further staff changes were made for the Competitions Department. Reg Jackson was still foreman in charge of the Experimental Department, but Kimber decided that a Competitions Department had to be set up, and this was done under John Temple as manager. Temple was a Service Department receptionist up until this time, and John Thornley was transferred to take over his old job. Cecil Cousins was retained as a team manager, as was Jacko. Other personnel would be recruited as required.

Avusrennen: 21 May 1933

One of the few good things that came from Nazi Germany was the completion of the first motorway system in Europe. An early manifestation of this and no doubt its inspiration, was the building of a two carriageway road outside Berlin, with a sweeping banked turn at the city end, and a wide radius turn at the outer end, which was actually built after a study of the Brooklands Track and came into use in 1913. The idea was to create a test track for the motor industry, for the testing of cars at high speed in safety. Inevitably this road became used occasionally as a racing track, which was in fairly constant use until well after the Second World War.

The Avusrennen was held annually, but attracted little interest outside Germany. However in 1933 both Horton and Hamilton entered, partly because there was a class for 800cc cars, but chiefly because the prize money on offer was £750; an enormous sum then, when race prize money was seldom more than a few pounds, if any, and the concept of starting money was barely known! In the event, due to his accident at Brooklands, Hamilton could not go, so Horton made a lone trip.

Horton's car was prepared, as ever, by Thompson & Taylor, and shipped to Berlin a week early. Soon after unofficial practice started the crankshaft broke. His mechanics were amazed at the extent of the damage, but had no spares so Horton telephoned the works who said a replacement would be available there. Horton himself drove to Abingdon, day and night, to pick up the unit, which was barely finished as he arrived. He then drove back with it and then left the mechanics to fit it while he caught up on his sleep! However he was met at the circuit with the news that the engine was not to be started, because it was found that a batch of water pumps had been wrongly assembled. This was a simple thing to correct, so after issuing the necessary instructions to a German machinist, Horton retired to his room.

His troubles were not over, because when it came to starting the engine, it was apparently seized. Stripping down revealed that a piece of piston ring from the original engine had somehow got stuck in the supercharger, and when this was removed all was well again. All in the best traditions of motor racing!

Even that was not the end, because at pre-race scrutiny the officials decided that the car should be green, for red was the Italian racing colour, not that anyone could accuse the terse 'Brummy' of being anything but a Briton! However the car was the 'wrong' colour and there was no alternative but to get it re-sprayed, which was achieved quickly with Teutonic efficiency at a hefty cost of 96 reichmarks, or some £50. Eventually, testing the car revealed that the new engine was rather tight and needed considerable running in; truly poor Horton thought this was an expedition he should never have started!

The race was due to run for 120 miles, so there was not much by way of latitude for playing a waiting game, but he decided to just keep everyone in sight for the first 50 or so miles, and then make a decision of what to do. Opposition in the class came from Austins and a couple of DKW cars. Macher in a DKW and Barnes in an Austin made the running with Horton close to. Their speed was such that they were still within half a lap of the 1,500cc machines leading the race. Macher was the first of the trio to run into trouble, and slowed with a persistent misfire. As they swept into the last lap, Horton opened up to full throttle and eased past Barnes, who had no answer to the flying MG, and Horton won the 800cc class of the Avusrennen at 90.9mph. He also won a large bag of reichsmarks, which was nice. He was not too sure about the plaudits of the uniformed officials, which even in 1933 he found a little sinister! However, some 40 years later he said it was an experience that he enjoyed at the time, and that the German people were very friendly and even excited that someone from abroad should have done well at their race.

Nürburgring – Eifelrennen: 28 May 1933

If Hamilton missed the Avusrennen, his car was ready for the Eifelrennen held a week later on the Nürburgring, that fabulous man-built circuit in the Eifel Mountain region, not far from Cologne. He had of course won the previous year in his C-type, and so expected to do even better in the J4 this year. The car was shipped to Cologne by train, and then driven to the circuit!

There were three classes, one for cars with engines of over 1,500cc, one for 800/1,500cc and the class for engines of less than 800cc. Hamilton was in this smallest class, along with Kohlrausch and Baumer in Austins, four front-wheel drive DKW entries and three BMW entries, which were actually Austin cars built under licence in Germany. The DKWs were powered by supercharged two-stroke engines, and were obviously very powerful, but they smoked a great deal, and this obscured the starter's flag from Hamilton who was slow away in consequence. However at the end of his first lap Hamilton led Kohlrausch, and gradually improved his position.

After four laps, the race leaders in the larger cars headed by Nuvolari in the 8C Alfa Romeo, swept by. When Howe in the Delage went past, Hamilton found it fairly easy to stay with him through the twistier parts of the long circuit, and allowed him to pull further away from Kohlrausch. Hamilton easily won the 800cc class at 59.7mph, a lap and a half ahead of the Austin of the German driver, and the first significant win for the new J4 Midget.

Le Mans: 16 June 1933

Once again, MG cars were to make a foray to Le Mans. Sadly the persistent Francis Samuelson was not able to make the trip, but two entries were made. One was the J3 of Gordon Hendy, who was to be partnered by Harold Parker, while the other was J. Ludovic Ford who had entered his C-type to be shared with his business partner Maurice Baumer. Ford and Baumer had driven at Brooklands events during the previous 12 months, and had both driven at Le Mans on previous occasions. Both cars were prepared by the works, Hendy's being the car which had run the successful 24-hour record attempt the previous winter, while Ford's was a car

which had apparently only raced once before in a short Brooklands event.

Kimber was asked if works support could be given and in the end Jackson and Kindell went, fares and hotels paid by the entrants, and they were each paid £1 10s (£1.50) a day, and had to pay for their own meals if the entrants omitted to provide this service. Reg said that they would probably have gone even if they had had to pay their own way!

An amusing story told by Jacko arose from practice, when Hendy complained that his car was not steering correctly. Since Parker had made no complaint, Jacko drove the car himself, and pronounced it fit and well. Hendy tried it again, and said it was hopeless, so Jackson went out for a lap with him, and found to his horror that he gripped the steering wheel with an iron hand and literally steered it all the time, not relenting when the suspension kicked as the wheels went over bumps and holes in the road, of which there were plenty! Jackson took over and demonstrated to him the art of letting the car steer itself, merely correcting major deflections, after which Hendy was *much* happier. Many people to this day try fighting the steering of the lighter 'vintage' cars and grow to hate the steering characteristics as dangerous . . . *not so friends, and I have the word of those who drove the cars when they were new to support me!*

Once the race itself started Baumer was well placed in his C-type, while Hendy was also going well, both averaging 100kph (62mph), as planned. After three hours, Ford took over the C-type, but the J3 was starting to misfire, and kept stopping for changes of sparking plugs. Then after Parker had been driving for about an hour the car was stopped because it was using a lot of fuel according to the gauge. A quick check showed that a fuel tank seam was split. Jacko estimated that they should be able to keep the car running until the next routine fuel stop and, not for the first time in MG history, got the whole team chewing gum. Those who think the habit came with the American GIs during the Second World War can think again!

As the car pulled in, Jacko had prepared a cardboard and chewing gum sandwich, which was applied, using more gum, to the offending seam, and strapped into place. The fuel tank was refilled, and no further fuel was lost during the whole race. Ford meanwhile was still circulating exactly to his planned schedule. What those in the pits were not aware of was that the dynamo had stopped charging, which was all right so long as daylight was with him, but would prove a problem when it got dark.

Ford continued to drive with lights off, until finally instructions were received from the officials that it was essential that his lights were 'on'. It was another two laps before he was observed to have the lights on as he passed the pits. What was not realised was that, as soon as he was out of sight, Ford turned the lights off again, restoring them after passing the infamous White House corner!

Using this subterfuge, and only using the headlights on the darker parts of the course, Ford and Baumer drove through the night, gradually moving up to ninth place, out of 19 still running. Hendy and Parker were further behind, but still going, and with others falling by the wayside, there was a chance they might yet finish well up the order. Then, when the Ford/Baumer team had reached sixth place, they were saddened to see Parker pulling up at l'Hippodrome, it transpired with big-end failure.

At the end Ford and Baumer maintained their sixth place, a very respectable position for a car with a 750cc engine in a 24-hour race, at a race average of 99.5kph, the first finish in the Le Mans race for the Abingdon marque, and a very creditable placing.

Empire Trophy Meeting, Brooklands: 1 July 1933

The Empire Trophy at Brooklands had not yet grown to be the important meeting it was to become, and at the 1933 encounter was to be run off in three parts. The India Trophy was for the small cars and of 50 miles, while the Canada Trophy was a similar 50-mile race for the heavier metal, while the Empire Trophy itself was a 125-mile final for the fastest cars from these two races.

The India Trophy was contested by four each Midgets and Magnettes and six other marques, and was won easily by Michael Watson in the J4 he shared with Jim Elwes, at a remarkable speed of 101.23mph. Kenneth Evans was second in the family C-type at 98.70mph. Horton, who could not beat his handicap, was third in his Magnette, but broke the 1,100cc lap record at the truly magnificent speed of 115.55mph.

In the Empire Trophy Manby-Colegrave came in third, at 106.88mph, when most of the heavy metal failed, and Horton's hard pressed engine developed a misfire, dropping him to fourth place, at 106.76mph.

LCC Relay Race, Brooklands: July 1933

The Light Car Club ran a relay race for amateur drivers of a total distance 250 miles to be run with teams of three cars in relay, each taking a 30-lap stint, and a sash

being carried by the driver of the car performing to be passed to the driver of the next car before it could start. The new secretary of the MG Car Club, Alan Hess, decided that he would enter a team of three cars, and sought support from Kimber, but was not met with great enthusiasm.

At this stage it should be recorded that the unblown Magna engine was disappointing in power output, and that H. N. Charles, Reg Jackson, and just about everyone else in the Factory who thought that they knew about engine tuning were giving gratuitous advice concerning increasing the power. A revised compression ratio coupled with a wider spacing of the carburettors was giving a good spread of power on the test-bed, increasing the output from 41 to 50bhp, which was not bad for an unblown 1,100 in 1933. Further increases were available by careful selection of petrol, and without resorting to special racing brews. Therefore the cars were built up using the revised tuning mods, and were run stripped of wings, lights and touring gear, but naturally carried the compulsory Brooklands silencer.

Hess's team, with G. W. J. H. Wright and Charlie Martin as the other two drivers, ran reliably and outstripped the opposition to finish first at 88.62mph, a very good performance when it is remembered that the standard L2 had been road-tested to achieve 80mph flat out!

One owner who benefited from all this work was Aubrey Ashton-Rigby whose L2 was becoming faster and faster as the season progressed, by being told what the works were doing, and allowing his car to be an unofficial test-bed. The Factory of course had the free publicity from his exploits, as well as the use of a free test-bed for their latest thinking, which was to stand them in good stead in due course when unsupercharged engines became fashionable once more!

Alpine Trial: July 1933

A full team of three cars was entered for the Alpine Trial. At the instigation of W. E. C. Watkinson, a team of L2 Magnas was prepared, mildly tuned and driven by Watkinson and Ward-Johnson, the brothers Welch, and by husband and wife team Wisdom. These cars appear to have been direct works entries, loaned for the event, in direct contradiction to Kimber's normal persuasion. It was apparently Cecil Cousins who pointed out that there were three Relay cars, with no immediate prospect for sale sitting in the Factory, and these were prepared with proper road silencers and full road equipment.

All three cars took a Glacier Cup, and the team won the Team Award, which was an excellent performance. At one stage, at the end of a day's running, Watkinson complained that his engine was down on power. It did not take long to realise that compression was missing on number five. No Red Queen gave the order, but off came the head, to reveal a 5⁄16in nut on top of the piston, having left ample signs of not liking this position, and its unsuccessful trail of escape. No one could explain how it got there, for one was not missing from the engine, but after a night's work the car was ready for the exertions of the following day.

Mannin Beg: 12 July 1933

Road racing in the British Isles has always been a bone of contention, and with the very idea of roads being built at all it is probably understandable that there is inevitably pressure on authorities not to allow the closing of roads for car or motorcycle racing. Fortunately within the British Isles there are a small number of autonomous administrations who can please themselves, including Northern Ireland and Eire, where the fabulous Ards TT and Phoenix Park, among other races, occurred in those days. Then there is the Isle of Man, where each year motorcycle road races are held which are acknowledged as the ultimate test of rider and machine by all but a small number of people who wish to impose a 'nanny-state' for the somewhat dubious benefit of all.

In 1933 the Manx authorities, in collusion with the RAC, put up the idea of road races on the streets of the town of Douglas for cars. It was decided that two races would be run, one for 'light cars', with capacity less than 1,500cc, and the other for unlimited capacity cars. These would be known respectively as the Mannin Beg and the Mannin Moar, implying broadly and respectively the little and large Man races. There was to be no pussy-footing with spoof races for road cars, these races were intended for real racing cars. The racing fraternity was soon galvanised into action, and a good entry was received for both races, not quite the International entry which was hoped for, but nevertheless an excellent entry of all the best names on the domestic racing scene.

The MG owners were more interested in the Mannin Beg race, and Magnettes were entered by Eyston, Hall, Yallop, Mere, Rubin, who had not yet gone home to Australia, and Hugh Hamilton. Rubin's car was to be driven by Kaye Don. Hamilton had entered his J4, which was still on its way back from Germany, but was able to borrow Enid Riddell's K3 for this race.

Midgets were entered by Ludovic Ford, Stan Crabtree, Ernest Gardner, all in C-types, and Denis Mansell in a J4. Ford and Baumer were involved in an epic rebuild of their car after Le Mans, sending the engine to Abingdon for overhaul, and preparing the chassis themselves. Mansell was a new recruit to the MG racing scene, having previously raced and trialled motorcycles and cars, but somewhat jumping in at the deep end in this road race.

Eddie Hall actually came to the island a month before the race with his Midget, and with Jock Little of the MG factory to help. They drove round the course several times, taking films with a ciné camera, which is an early example of such preparation before a race. The films were then made available through Abingdon to all the MG entrants which enabled them to know what to expect.

All the Magnettes were equipped with lightweight racing bodies, rather than the coach-built ones used previously, these being known in the Factory as 'skimpy' bodies. These offered a saving in weight of around 2½cwt, and gave the cars a considerable increase in acceleration. The final drive ratio was also lowered to 5.78:1, since there were no long straight sections, and speeds of 100mph would probably not be reached, acceleration between the corners was of prime importance, but this proved to be a serious miscalculation. Other than this the cars were in the same tune as they had been at Brooklands.

Practice was somewhat fraught with most of the cars in trouble one way or another. Hamilton found his brakes spongy, and wanted them relined, while Eyston had a persistent plug oiling problem. Mansell had a supercharger drive shaft break, while Eddie Hall, who had one of the first large capacity oil sumps, was in trouble with an oil surge! Then to cap it all Kaye Don had his rear axle fail. All this resulted in a large amount of work for Jacko and his men, keeping them busy until the early hours of the morning. The rear axle failure was a major problem, since no spares for this component had been brought in the MG van. Don Finlayson, Sir Henry Birkin's former mechanic, was able to pirate a complete axle from a Magnette saloon, the owner of which was fortunately a friend of Kaye Don. This, if nothing else, showed that the racing car parts were shared with the touring cars! However this problem in practice was to prove prophetic.

After the final timed practice, Freddie Dixon was fastest, but there was really little difference in speed, and the Magnettes were obviously going to be a force to be reckoned with. Not surprisingly it rained in the morning as the cars were lining up, but this did not stop hundreds of spectators lining the circuit, often literally on the roadsides, in doorways, on and behind stone walls, and hanging from windows overlooking the course.

At the drop of the starter's flag it was Kaye Don who took the lead closely followed by Crabtree in the Midget, with Hamilton on his tail. Dixon was slower away with his unsupercharged engine, but was soon up with the leaders. Eyston and Hall were close behind, and spectators were excited by the closeness of it all. At the end of his second lap Hall stopped to change a plug, and then got going again at enormous speed – too great for as he turned into the bend at the end of the Promenade a tyre burst, and the car careered off over a kerb, bending the front axle too severely to continue. While this was going on Hamilton took the lead, with Don seemingly trying to hold onto his tail! Then a lap later Eyston had a connecting rod let go, and he was out.

Crabtree was having the race of his life, hanging onto the two Magnettes and not giving an inch, with Dixon following. After ten laps, Hamilton led Don by half a mile. Dixon had a moment which appeared to eliminate him, but he was too strong a character to give up with a bent rear axle, and after quick repairs on the roadside got going again at unabated speed, but two laps behind the flying Hamilton. Then Crabtree tried to take Onchan hairpin at a speed which can only be described kindly as optimistic, and he spun and crashed. Although he got going again, the supercharger was deranged, and he was forced to retire.

Surprisingly Mere was now going nearly as fast as Hamilton when his rear axle emitted a shriek; the pinion bearing had failed, and the car ground to a standstill. Still Hamilton led from Don and Yallop, with Gardner and Ford in the next places, followed by Dixon and Mansell, the rest having now retired. Gardner stopped for fuel, but when he restarted he fell off the track, which put him out of contention. Baumer took over from Ford, and then Don stopped with magneto drive failure. This was at the halfway stage, and only five cars were still running.

Shortly after Yallop stopped with rear axle failure, which left Hamilton leading Dixon, Baumer next up and then Mansell. At 38 laps Hamilton's axle also failed. Dixon and Baumer were the only two now travelling at full speed, although Mansell was encouraged to try harder now he was officially third! Then Baumer stopped, his instrument panel having come apart! The two remaining cars motored on to the finish, and, in fact Baumer managed to wire up the ignition and get going again to run through to the finish, ending what

had started as a most promising race as something of a damp squib. Oddly enough, if the race had lasted one more lap Dixon would not have finished either, for his oil sump was bone dry at the finish!

The problem with the rear axle was that a two-star differential, as used in the production Magnettes, was used and in each of the four failures this had proved unable to put up with the stresses imposed, severely increased due to the use of the low ratio crown wheel and pinion. Needless to say, Hubert Charles already had a four-star unit drawn up, and this was put into production. Once more racing was able to contribute to the improvement of the breed.

Freiburg: 16 July 1933

After the busy time in the Isle of Man, one might have expected drivers to take a rest, and perhaps get some work done. Hamilton's J4 was already in Germany, having not been returned since the Eifelrennen, and the local agent, Birch, had arranged an entry for him in the Grosser Bergpries von Deutschland, at Freiburg, near Breslau. This hill was 7½ miles, and presented a real challenge, not that Hamilton thought much of hill-climb events, at least not in the UK! Freiburg was a real challenge, however, especially since the competitors had only one shot at it.

In the event, Hamilton excelled himself, not only winning the small car class with an average speed of 59mph, but ending up third-fastest overall, which was reward enough for Robert Birch, and another indicator of the growing ability which Hammy was developing.

Craigantlet: 28 August 1933

Eddie Hall decided that it might be a good plan before the TT race to enter the Craigantlet Hill Climb, and so get a little familiarisation of the Ards circuit before any of the other competitors arrived. He approached Kimber to see if there would be any works support if he entered both his Midget and Magnette cars, and so be able to try for a clean sweep of the classes, with the exception of the road-going sports car class, which was specifically for unsupercharged cars. Kimber was only able to offer the services of a mechanic, and the use of his personal K1 tourer car to try for the remaining class.

'Ginger' Wirdnam was the mechanic who was seconded to the job, and many years later he told me that it was a lot of hard work keeping three cars on the go, with only the help of Jock Little, who was Hall's personal mechanic. In the event Jacko was present too, delivering Kimber's K1 and taking a short holiday before the TT to check on that circuit without drawing too much attention to himself!

Craigantlet is a hill on the public highway which was, and still is, closed on occasions for the hill-climb meeting, and consists of a run of some 1,200 yards of fairly wide macadam road with an average gradient of 1 in 12, and a selection of right and left-hand bends. The finish was taken at a reasonable speed, and there was a good pull-up area in which to stop the car. The climb, although very similar to this day, is actually now about 70 yards shorter in the interests of safety it is said . . . and I thought modern cars had better brakes!

Jackson had been working for some time on an improvement to the SU carburettor, and had found that a two-choke layout gave better power at certain speeds. The idea was wholly Jacko's and was not followed up in the pre-war period, but the SU Company did produce a two-choke unit after the Second World War. Prompted by the desire to improve gasflow at smaller throttle openings, Hall very quickly found that the K3 accelerated much quicker using the special unit than with its standard carburettor.

The exercise was a complete success, for Hall won all five classes for which he was entered, and set the unlimited class record for the hill, previously held by R. G. J. Nash in his Frazer Nash car, beating the previous mark by some *eleven seconds*.

Coppa Acerbo: 15 August 1933

One of the early customers for a K3 was Whitney Straight, an American who had attended Cambridge University. He was bitten by the racing bug, and being financially able to indulge his passion, he ordered a K3 in chassis form. To this he had a boat-tailed lightweight shell body fitted. Straight had entered the car for the Mannin Beg, but it was not ready for him, and his first real race was to be in Italy, the Coppa Acerbo, held as part of a week-long speed festival on the Adriatic Coast held in memory of a local First World War hero, Capitano Tito Acerbo.

Few knew Straight was going, even those at Abingdon, but when it was reported that he had won the Junior race, beating all the Maseratis at record speed, the result so surprised the Italians that one of the Maserati supporters called for engine measurement! Naturally the engine was within capacity limits, which impressed the Italians considerably, especially the great Tazio Nuvolari, who was to race in the GP which formed the major event of the week. Kimber was well pleased, and a new star was made.

Nuvolari and Hounslow climb Mill Hill on their way to eventual victory in the 1933 TT. (National Motor Museum)

RAC Tourist Trophy: 2 September 1933

Kimber dearly wanted an MG to win the Tourist Trophy race again. Jacko had met Nuvolari in February, and the famous racing driver had expressed an interest, possibly encouraged by Johnny Lurani, in driving a Magnette in the TT. Of course Jackson had no real influence, and it was obvious that the Italian would want paying if he was going to drive. It was Whitney Straight who provided the necessary spur, for it was impossible for him to get his car back to Northern Ireland in time for the start of the TT, so MG had a 'spare' entry available, if only a car could be provided. This was done when George Eyston said that with the building of a special K3, which he had recently ordered, he had no further use for his old Mille Miglia car, this having been taken as the down payment for the new car. Jackson suggested offering this to Nuvolari, but Kimber was not too sure. Sir William Morris was approached, and surprisingly he agreed to the loan of the car, and to paying £100, from his personal bank account, to the great Italian as a fee. I understand that this was not really enough for Nuvolari, but he dearly wanted this drive and agreed to his Lordship's offer.

The car was to be prepared and fitted with a skimpy body, and with less than two weeks in which to do it! Jacko assembled the engine himself, while Alec Hounslow did most of the chassis work. When the car was completed they took it for a test run on the roads, using the long test route out to Wantage and back. The car had no mudguards or lights fitted, but it was found very much to their liking and declared fit for the race.

The race distance had been increased for 1933 to 35 laps, or 478 miles, round the same course used since 1928, the idea being to keep the race time at between five and six hours. Cars were to be two-seaters, run in capacity divisions, with time penalties being applied for supercharged engines. The cars could, however, run stripped of weather and road equipment. Mechanics were to be carried, and as in previous years only the driver and riding mechanic could work on the car. Jackson wanted to ride with Nuvolari, but this idea was vetoed by CK who said that he was much too valuable an asset to the company to risk losing, so Alec Hounslow won the lottery amongst the mechanics to take the ride which was based on their own weight. Those of us who came to know Alec in his later years were always amazed to hear that he weighed only eight stone in 1933! It is to Alec that I am indebted for many of the recollections in this part of the story.

MG entries were, in addition to the 'Straight' car, Manby-Colegrave, Eddie Hall, Ronny Yallop, and Ron Horton, all in Magnettes, with Stan Hailwood, Luis Fontes, Tommy Simister, Hugh Hamilton, Denis Mansell, all on J4 Midgets, and Stan Crabtree, Hubert Attwood, and John Ford in their older supercharged C-types, while John Low was there again with his unblown C-type. Apart from the Nuvolari entry, all the cars were privately owned.

The Magnettes were starting with the powerful unsupercharged six-cylinder 1½-litre Riley Grebe cars entered by the Riley works, but not in the same class, but if they kept going they could be a threat for overall honours. The Riley Brooklands entries were being spoken of well, probably as the previous year's winning car. Considered by MG to be the biggest threat, however were the Alfa Romeo entries of Earl Howe, Brian Lewis and Tim Rose-Richards. In fact entries were down this year, and for the first time in several years there were no entries of Talbot, Frazer Nash or Bentley cars, no doubt due in large part to the depressed car sales figures, although 'noises' were made from some quarters about cars running stripped not being 'true' sports cars, whatever that meant! There were even those who said that superchargers were not a 'fair' addition to an engine, which was even more fatuous in handicap racing! At least the MGs were catalogue models, and could be bought by customers. Many of the products of those who complained were far from series production cars, and could certainly not be bought!

Oddly enough, those at MG expected the Magnette to win, and did not give a second thought to the threat that lurked in the J4 Midget of Hamilton, whose own local knowledge was second to none. The Magnette teams of Hall and Nuvolari practised pit stops. Nuvolari showed Jackson how to make a quick-lift jack from steel tubing that lifted one end of the car in a single movement, which speeded up the wheel changing operation. All this was done until it was possible for the driver and mechanic to get out of the car, change two rear wheels, put in 15 gallons of fuel, and check the engine oil and gearbox level, as well as top up the radiator, all within two minutes . . . those used to seeing today's lightning pit stops in grand prix racing might do well to remember that this was with only two people working, and that they had to get out of the car before any work could be done!

Along with the other MG drivers, Hamilton watched all this activity but did not take note, which was to prove a serious mistake. Hamilton's pit was being supervised by Goldie Gardner, with Robin Mere, who had decided against entering his K3 since he did not think he had sufficient experience to drive in a race of this distance, instead acting as lap scorer and timekeeper.

Pit work was slick. At the Ards circuit for the 1933 TT, Hounslow is jacking the rear of the car while Nuvolari pours fuel into the tank from a churn. (National Motor Museum)

Pit mechanics were from the MG factory, but the riding mechanic, whose identity I have not been able to find, was a Belfast friend of the Hamilton family, who apparently thought that all he had to do was ride in the car. Unfortunately, Hamilton, who was always short on words, said nothing to disabuse him of this opinion until during the race, and then, by all accounts, everyone in Belfast got to know that Hamilton could use some very picturesque, if rather rude, Anglo-Saxon!

Before practice, Nuvolari sat in the car and got the feel of the driving position, set the aeroscreen angle, and the mirrors, and checked all the controls. He stated that he wanted a special seat made, and drew his requirements for Jacko to execute. This done, he then pronounced himself happy for an exploratory lap. When practice started on the Wednesday at around 6am, he was away at high speed, and Alec Hounslow was wondering if his life insurance was in order, and whether this ride was a good idea or not! Apparently the great man had not listened to his instructions regarding the preselector gearbox, via the omnipresent Hugh McConnell attending once more as interpreter. He was therefore selecting a gear but omitted to push the foot pedal, and so practically the whole lap was done in top gear! There were a couple of near misses at high speed, and a spin or two, but on return to the pit matters were put right. Nuvolari quickly accepted that it was he who was at fault so far as the driving was concerned.

He felt that a few adjustments were necessary to the car before resuming practice. Firstly Jackson was prevailed upon to re-adjust the shock absorbers to a recipe given by Nuvolari. Jacko told me how to perform this task, and it does give a better method than the traditional 'bounce-the-chassis' method which so many use to this day. The method involves supporting the chassis on stands, and then adjusting each damper until the weight of the wheel just stays suspended against the spring. In this way it is possible to get each axle pair of dampers to give the same resistance.

Next tyre pressures needed adjusting to give the car the handling Nuvolari wanted. With the benefit of hindsight, Hounslow said that Nuvolari obviously liked a car that understeered on a trailing throttle, and converted to oversteer as power was applied, as opposed to the majority of British drivers of the time, who if they asked for anything merely wanted the tyres run as hard as possible! Both Jackson and Hounslow were amazed that the Italian wanted pressures adjusted *exactly the same* for each pair of tyres, front and rear, which was certainly an unusual demand for the period: within a 'couple of pounds' was OK for ordinary drivers, most of whom were not driving fast enough to notice any irregularity, said Alec.

Nuvolari was also critical of the seat position and rake angle, and requested that it was reset an inch and a half higher at the front, and four inches further from the wheel. Jackson moved the seat back, but, thinking that Nuvolari would not notice, ignored the former instruction, which raised the temper of the Great Man, and had Jacko do as he was bid! At this stage, even if he had not admitted it before, Jackson realised that he was dealing with a true professional, knowing *exactly* what he wanted. Jacko himself then became the professional mechanic he was and did not try to outsmart *il maestro* again.

When all was done as required another practice lap was tried. This time Alec was a little less alarmed about the speed, since the Italian had taken on board his instructions regarding the gearbox, and approaches to the sharper bends at least were taken in third speed . . . but now with very little use of the brakes, indeed Alec said that although the car slowed, he was not aware of the brakes being used, and certainly the wheels never locked. On returning to the pits at the end of this lap, Nuvolari pronounced that the car felt to his liking and that he would now like to try some fast laps, which took Alec by surprise, as he thought he had been going fast! Three more laps were done, and Alec was able to record that at no time was he frightened, but he was amazed at the way in which Nuvolari positioned the car within inches of walls and kerb-stones with great precision. To use his words, 'I felt as if, had I put a penny anywhere along the circuit on his line, Nuvolari would have driven over it each time around.' In addition, Hounslow reported that the car was not slid at the rear end as most British drivers cornered, but the whole car seemed to be moving sideways around the bends, but under complete control. We now recognise this as four-wheel drift, but Nuvolari was probably the first driver to exploit this technique, which the MG mechanics were able to marvel at.

At the end of six laps, plus of course the previous two, Nuvolari pronounced himself satisfied with the car. His speed was very good, causing comment from all the other teams, with the exception of Hamilton. Hamilton knew the circuit very well indeed and had put in some very fast laps, which was worrying Nuvolari! Hammy was content not to keep on practising, because he knew the circuit so well, and watched other drivers at various points around the circuit. Jackson was worried about tyre wear on all the Magnettes, while Nuvolari seemed to be using more rubber than the other drivers. He told McConnell that it might be necessary for two pit stops for tyres, one of these for a four wheel change. Nuvolari replied that, while he could not speak for the other drivers, practice periods were for wearing out tyres, and that during the race he would use much less rubber!

Meanwhile, tragically, Maurice Balmain, driving Low's unsupercharged Midget, crashed at Ballystockart, the accident killing their mechanic, and the two had no further heart to continue with the race.

The race day dawned dry, which was unusual, and it brought spectators in tram, train and bus loads from Belfast. Many people came over from the mainland to watch and the race was to be attended by none other than Sir William Morris, that well known motor sporting enthusiast! Ramsay Macdonald, the Prime Minister, was also present, perhaps indicating that motor racing was becoming acceptable to the British Establishment, or perhaps, being an astute politician, he was taking note that he might be recognised by the estimated half a million spectators lining the circuit . . . politicians are ever the same!

Ebblewhite had decided that the handicaps were such that the Midgets had three laps' start, two more than the Magnettes, the rest of the starters up to 2 litres engine size being separated only by a small time allowance. Those over 2 litres had no credit lap – the race could be considered wide open at the start; since it was to run for such a long distance and time, almost anything could happen.

The four-cylinder Rileys were first away, followed 13 seconds later by the Midgets, but the Midgets had a lap in hand. A minute and a half later started the six-cylinder Rileys and MGs, but a lap in addition behind the smaller Rileys. Then a minute later started the Alfa Romeos, followed half a minute later by the huge low slung Invictas, and then the start area was all peace and calm. Less than ten minutes later the early starters were streaming through, but Fontes had over-revved his engine and had a connecting rod break on his J4 and was missing. Hamilton was ahead of the pack, going like the wind, and indeed was found to be leading on handicap at the end of the first hour, from Nuvolari with Hall third, and the larger Rileys following. Hamilton was lapping at around 75mph and Nuvolari at 78mph, while the large Alfas were 'only' managing 83mph, which demonstrated how quick the small cars had become, and how difficult the task was going to be to beat the fleet MGs and Rileys.

After just over 2½ hours Nuvolari, some ten seconds behind Hamilton on handicap, stopped and his pit stop was a model of co-ordination, changing two rear wheels, taking on ten gallons of fuel, checking oil and water, eating a sandwich and having a quick drink and out again in three minutes and nine seconds. On seeing the

Italian stopped, Hamilton went a little faster, and even broke the class lap record. He came into the pits after three hours' running, with some six minutes in hand.

This pit stop demonstrated the importance of planning. Robin Mere was sitting in the pit recording laps and times. He was a solicitor, not at all used to rough words used in temper, was shocked, then mildly amused by what went on. He wrote me a letter about it, from which the following is taken. Hamilton shouted to his mechanic who became flustered while pouring in the fuel and spilt quite a bit, necessitating taking on another churn, but only half of that went into the fuel tank, the rest, about two gallons, being spilt over the rear of the car. There was no quick lift jack, just an ordinary screw type which should have been simple enough to use. But the mechanic had not used that pattern of jack previously and an irate Hamilton pushed him aside to operate it himself and it was an age before the wheels were clear of the ground. The work completed, they were both in the car, and the starter would not operate, so out jumped the mechanic to short the solenoid, but he used a spanner which arced to earth and set his petrol-soaked gloves on fire. Once the fire was out, near pandemonium was the order in the Hamilton pit, and it took the calm Jackson, coming from the Nuvolari pit, to smooth things out, and get the mechanic to short the solenoid using an insulated screwdriver, so now at last the engine was running, and Hamilton positively screamed at him to get into the car. He leapt back into the car, but the bonnet strap was not done up, causing Hamilton, far from politely, to ask whether he was from a settled home and requesting that the poor chap get out again and do it up! The whole fiasco lasted over seven minutes, by which time Hamilton was beside himself with rage, and took the best part of half a lap before he started driving properly again.

This allowed Nuvolari into the lead on handicap, but he knew that he had to go really fast from here on, because Hamilton would 'catch up' if he resumed his previous speed. The Great Man pushed his lap speed from 78 to 79 to 80mph and then put in a lap of 81mph. Hamilton was responding by pushing his speed up to nearly 78mph! Truly the battle must have been exciting to watch, the green Magnette against the blue Midget, with the smaller car just getting back into the lead on handicap. The rest of the runners were nowhere in comparison.

During his penultimate lap, Hamilton discovered that the reserve fuel pump would not work and realised that he would need to stop. He did so, taking Goldie and the pit crew by surprise, but this time at rest for only 20 seconds, his mechanic not stirring from his seat!

While he was stopped, Nuvolari roared by, Alec noting the Midget in the pits, and gave a 'thumbs up' sign to his driver. They carried on at unabated speed, with the Midget chasing hard, when as they swooped through the fast Ballystockart curves, the engine cut out, and Nuvolari raised his hands in despair: knowing they were short of fuel! Alec switched the fuel tap to 'reserve' and the engine picked up again, and they had enough to get them to the finish line, to win by 40 seconds after nearly six hours' racing. There was not enough fuel in the tank to complete a complementary lap, indeed Jackson said that there was barely a tea-cupful left!

Nuvolari's race average was 78.65mph, the fastest speed at which an Ards TT was ever won, and his fastest lap was 81.42mph. Hamilton's speed was 73.46mph, with a fastest lap of 77.20mph. Tim Rose-Richards was third in a blown 2.3-litre Alfa at a speed only 0.06mph faster than Nuvolari's. Eddie Hall was fourth in his Magnette, while Manby-Colegrave was the only other MG finisher in eighth place in his K3. The winning speed was to remain the fastest speed at which a TT was won until 1950, when it required a little over three times the engine capacity to beat it!

This was an epic race that is still talked of as inspiring even by those who could not have seen it! Kimber was delighted with the outcome, as was Sir William Morris, who could not disagree that the publicity was worthwhile for MG, and therefore good for Morris Motors Ltd.

Reg Jackson was delighted with the performance of the car, which needed very little work to make it ready for a 'road test' by Sammy Davis. He fitted a new set of sparking plugs, and some replacement tyres, put some fuel in the tank, but the engine oil did not even need topping up, and Davis produced a nice piece in *The Autocar* to show that the car could still be driven with ease. Alec Hounslow never forgot his ride, and was forever in awe of the truly great racing drivers, but for him, Nuvolari was the best of them all . . . and who could argue?

Czech GP, Masaryk Circuit, Brno: 17 September 1933

Following his performance in the TT, Hamilton was keen to race again on the Continent, and was able to arrange through Zdenek Klika, who held the MG agency in Prague, to get an entry for the 1,500cc Czechoslovakian Grand Prix. It was touch and go getting the car ready, but the engine was rebuilt at Abingdon, and the chassis was prepared by Hamilton in London, and the body re-sprayed green, before the car was transported by rail.

Nuvolari celebrates his victory in the 1933 TT with a well-earned glass of orange juice… Hounslow enjoys the first of many glasses of beer that night, with an arm around Reg Jackson, who was not allowed to ride in the race by edict of Cecil Kimber, and modestly checks the shine on his shoes!

Somehow everything was done in time, and by flying out he was able to run in the three practice sessions set aside.

The circuit was a road circuit near to Brno, and was some 29km (18 miles) long, rather like the Ards course in character. The existing lap record for 1,500cc cars stood at 16 minutes 46 seconds, some 65.1mph. The Midget had the smallest engine in the race, most of the competitors running the full 1½-litre allowance. It was not too long before Hamilton was well inside this time in practice, and it was suggested that he should run the extra two laps for a place in the grand prix itself, which was being run concurrently with the 1,500cc race. At this time the Germans had not yet formed their fantastically successful and thoroughly dominant teams, and most of the cars running were sports car derivatives.

Race day, Sunday, dawned wet, and Hamilton thought it might be a good idea to wear a poncho-style raincoat, belted at the waist to keep his overalls reasonably dry.

One can imagine what he thought of Earl Howe, who had his umbrella held over him, by the ever present George Thomas, until the last minute before the start! When the starter's flag fell, Hamilton took an immediate lead over most of the other 1,500cc cars, by lap five he was actually passing the slower grand prix cars, third in class and fifth in the grand prix overall!

At the end of lap six, he was fourth overall, when he had to stop for fuel, but restarted immediately behind Landi in a 1,500cc single-seater Maserati, who was leading the class and lay third overall. Landi made a mistake and fell off the track, allowing Hamilton through, who then started making up ground on Fagioli who was second. Landi had not given up and was chasing hard, slipping by in the faster part of the circuit. At this stage, fate intervened, and Hamilton found that his poncho belt had broken, and that the cape was billowing up but he managed to keep it under control. Then, suddenly, as he went into a corner, it blew up over his head and at the same time wrapped itself around the steering wheel and column, making it impossible to correct the direction of the car, even had he been able to see. The J4 then took control and went bounding through the scenery, rolling over three times with Hamilton still sitting in.

He was quite badly knocked about, and was rushed off to the hospital. It was a few days before he was fit enough to travel, and in the meantime the car was returned to Abingdon. In fact Hamilton's drive received far more attention than he expected, indeed more than if he had actually won the grand prix. Landi was generous enough to say that he thought that he would not have been second if Hamilton had not crashed, and even Louis Chiron, the winner of the grand prix, praised the Ulsterman's driving prowess.

BRDC 500-Mile Race: October 1933

As ever at the end of the season, all the British drivers went to Brooklands for the final 'blind', 500 miles of flat-out motoring around Brooklands Outer Circuit. This year there were to be 38 starters, with MG entrants driving Midgets, Magnas and Magnettes. All cars were required to have lapped the Surrey circuit that season in excess of 90mph.

Amongst the smaller cars, there was Eyston in *Magic Midget*, Brackenbury in Horton's offset Midget, while Elwes and Watson were to share their standard J4. Kenneth Evans and Stan Hailwood, had entered their C-types, as had Maurice Balmain, in the unblown car he shared with John Lowe.

Hess had entered the same three L2 Magnas as had run in the Relay race, to be driven by himself, Charles Martin and Lewis Welch. It is interesting that Alan Hess was by this time secretary of the MGCC and treated as normal the fact that MG would put his requirement for a team of cars at his disposal. It was said that Kimber was not too pleased with this, and was hard pressed to explain to Leonard Lord why Hess, or his fellow team members, had not paid for the cars. Hess was replaced by 'Mit' Harris as club secretary during the winter of 1933/34!

In addition to the three works L-types, Aubrey Ashton-Rigby was entered in his own similar car, which had been going so well during the year. Magnettes were entered by Horton, Hall, Manby-Colegrave, Whitney Straight, and Yallop, but Horton failed to make the start.

The event was unique in that all cars had to complete the 500-mile distance, handicaps being applied by way of starting times, and the unblown Midget of Low had been running for 81 minutes before the 4.9-litre blown Bugatti of Kaye Don started! As the race unfolded, it was Freddie Dixon in his 1,800cc Riley who led from Eddie Hall's K3, the latter lapping at almost 110mph, but unable to catch the unblown Riley. Don was making up time well, but the

strain on his engine proved too much, and the car slowed and then stopped.

As Don stopped, Hall made his scheduled pit stop for fuel and tyres, and was soon away again, still in second place. Jim Elwes stopped his J4 shortly after this, and handed over to Michael Watson, but the latter had barely got going when the car went out of control and rolled, killing the likeable young Brighton man. While the track was being cleared of debris, Dixon blew his head gasket, which effectively put him out of the running, although he went ahead and changed it. Hall took the lead, which he did not again lose. Martin in the Magna went into second place.

Only eight cars were running at the end, with Hall coming home first at 106.33mph, Martin second at a remarkable 92.24mph. Yallop finished fifth, and Welch brought home the remaining Magna just failing by one lap to complete the distance in the time allowed. For the Hall equipe it was their first major victory with an MG car, and I am indebted to Joan Hall for her first-hand experience as pit manager for the details above.

1934 Model road cars at the London Motor Show

At the London Motor Show, for the first time there was really nothing new from MG. The J-type range was kept on, with the J2 and J3 being offered with swept wings similar to those used on the Magna and Magnette ranges. The L-types continued, with the addition of the all-time lemon, even yellow in colour, the Continental Coupé. The car was neither attractive to look at, nor particularly fast, but it was actually a forerunner of the modern GT car in concept. The K-types were improved with a re-vamped long stroke engine reverting to 1,271cc, and being blessed with twin carburettors and coil ignition. These two modifications together made the cars much more driveable, and had in fact been introduced during 1933, but this was the first motor show at which they had been exhibited. The preselector gearbox was supplemented with a flywheel-mounted external clutch operated by the gear-change pedal. This overcame all the objections of the previous year's confection which was apt to give rise to severe judder at low speeds. There were vague suggestions of revisions to the racing Midget and Magnette cars, but nothing was on show, while the ex-Nuvolari TT Magnette was starting to do the rounds of the MG dealers around the country.

All in all this was not one of the more exciting motor shows for MG buffs. However better things were to come as the new year started.

CHAPTER 5

THE MAGIC CONTINUES 1934

UNSUPERCHARGED MAGNETTES, HIGH-PRESSURE SUPERCHARGING FOR MIDGETS

Mannin Beg, 1934. Here, Eyston in EX135, fitted with the road-racing body, leads Hamilton in the rebodied Mere car, K3009. Eyston finished third, but Hamilton's race ended when he hit a telegraph pole. (National Motor Museum)

Early in 1934, a very unusual time of the year for motor manufacturers, MG announced a revised programme of cars for the 1934 season, with two new models, showing quite a degree of model rationalisation. The P-type Midget to replace the J-types, and the N-type Magnette which was to replace both the K-type Magnette and L-type Magna models. Alongside the N-type was to be a KN Magnette, which was basically a K1 saloon fitted with the N-type engine and gearbox, but with other improvements to the specification. Revisions to the racing models were now finalised, with the introduction of the new K3 and the Q-type Midget.

The P and N-type road cars

The P-type engine was to have the same bore and stroke as the J1/J2, but the crankshaft was supported in three main bearings, with all journals increased in diameter by ⅛in, and the camshaft increased in diameter to that of the K/L series and it also had an additional bearing. Full flow oil filtration was incorporated, and the whole unit looked more purposeful than the J, but it was considerably heavier. The 12in diameter brakes were featured on the new model, benefiting from racing experience. The chassis frame was similar, but the bodywork, either two or four-seater to choice, was better made and offered improved weather protection over the earlier cars. The whole car was heavier, this being countered by the unfortunate measure of lowering first and second gear ratios, which resulted in a noticeable 'gap' between second and third gears. The prices of the cars were not altered from those of the J-types, and they were well received by all but the dyed-in-the-wool traditionalist, who felt the cars were becoming 'softer'.

However, it was not long before everyone acknowledged that the new Midget was everything that the J2 had been with undeniable improvements in comfort and handling, and the capability of bringing the car to a quick stop. Such was their faith in the strength and durability of their new car that the company took the unusual step of stating in the sales information that the guarantee was not invalidated if one of the approved supercharger kits was added to the car, provided the boost did not exceed 5psi.

The N-type Magnette was a completely new car, with a chassis frame which was wider at the rear than the front, and used much deeper channels than used previously, as well as larger diameter cross tubing. The very heavy cruciform member of the K-type Magnette chassis was no longer necessary, while the body was mounted on a rubber-bushed subframe which isolated it from the excesses of chassis deflections. The engine was a completely revised KD unit with a new cylinder head designed which shared its layout with the P-type engine. Unfortunately it also shared the P-type gearbox, but the torque output of the engine was such that second gear was only seldom needed when driving the car. Many components were shared between the new models, including the brake gear, in an honest attempt to bring some sanity to the spare parts departments.

The N-type was available in two and four-seater forms, employing an enclosed fuel tank under a sloping tail, thus modernising the shape of the car considerably. Clamshell swept wings were featured, and the N-type was one of the nicer pre-war MG touring cars. Its stiffer chassis than previous models allowed good use to be made of the really good road performance with the added bonus of it being comfortable to ride in.

A slab-tanked addition was unofficially built as the NK tourer, later called the ND, using up the stock of remaining K2 bodies, and these cars were offered to trials drivers as a competition car, often with a tuned engine, and higher first and second gear ratios.

The 1934 programme must therefore be viewed as an attempt to rationalise production, to which goal Charles, with his protégé Enever, was working. During 1933 they had started work on drafting the previous models, since at this stage not many drawings had been made, and this work was to continue for the next two years.

The Q-type

By the latter part of 1933 the limitations of the chassis of the J4 Midget had become apparent – no matter how clever the driver, the plain fact was that the car was just too fast. Its power output was high enough to cause the car to be unstable, and within the known technology the only way to increase stability was to increase the track and wheelbase, which would naturally increase the weight of the car, which meant that it needed more power, which would again start the circle from which it was desirable to escape! Charles had, of course, taken note of the direction the German Grand Prix contenders were going, and quickly learned the lesson.

Not only were racing cars leading the way, but various Continental manufacturers were also producing models with independent suspension for sale to the general public. Similar experiments were coming from across the Atlantic and, for Charles, this seemed the way to proceed for the long-term future in road cars, giving

The production Q-type as sold to the public: note no wings, lights or windscreen – this car is no longer a sports-racer. It is tuned to run on alcohol fuel, running as it did with 24/26psi boost, and developed over 110bhp from a displacement of 750cc.

at the same time comfortable ride characteristics and much improved handling. Work in Experimental had therefore started, late in 1933, on the development of independent front suspension, HN giving expression to his ideas of a really stiff chassis and a very supple suspension – not at all the notion accepted as the 'last word' by those who thought they knew about cars.

As a stopgap it was decided that the racing Midget for 1934, although not announced until May, would be very closely allied to the Magnette, which was in itself a stable car, with good roadholding and unimpeachable handling. Necessarily this would mean an increase in power. Potential buyers found that the new Q-type racer was claimed to have a power of over 110bhp, and this from 750cc! The engine was a short-stroke version of that fitted to the P-type. The power was derived by increasing the supercharger boost to no less than 25psi, or 2.67 bar, using a Zoller vane-type blower. The Experimental shop had bench-tested engines with boost pressures of up to 3.25 bar, but had decided that with 110/115bhp the new racing Midget was going to be quite exciting enough.

As with the Magnette, an ENV-built preselector gearbox was used in the transmission, but unlike the Magnette, it was decided that an intermediate clutch was necessary. For the Q-type, this took the form of a two-plate clutch for which no withdrawal mechanism was called up, but the springs were carefully adjusted so that the clutch would slip if more than 70lb/ft of torque was applied, this being the load limit of the gearbox. In practice the clutch could not slip in top gear, and increasing degrees of slip were available as the gear ratio lowered, which stopped the overloading of the gearbox bands. This, in turn, protected the rear axle from any nasty surprises, and virtually eliminated crown wheel and pinion failure, a fairly common fault with racing Midgets hitherto. Coincidentally this device also protected the preselector gearbox bottom gear band from excessive slipping, which was proving a problem on the Magnette.

The bodywork of the new Q-type Midget was closely similar to, but not identical with, the new K3 body for 1934. As for the Magnette in 1934, wings and lights were not offered, and even a windscreen was considered an extra, only a single driver's aeroscreen ever being fitted to these cars by the works. The Q-type was designed to be a racing car, and with passengers no longer being carried even in sports car events after 1933, no provision was made for a passenger seat in the original design. Since the engine was so highly supercharged, it would only successfully run on alcohol based fuels, with the works specifying a mixture of 60 per cent methanol, 30 per cent benzole, and 10 per cent acetone, with 1 per cent castor oil added after mixing and prior to pouring into the tank: this mixture being known as MG1.

The Q-type quickly gained a reputation for being very noisy, which it certainly was, even when its twin Brooklands exhaust system was fitted, and for being a fractious beast, which according to Henry Stone it wasn't really. Oil supply to the vane-type supercharger was critical, but with the introduction of a new type of

metering unit, with a ratchet control, this was proving to be quite simple. This metering unit was known by the mechanics as a 'fuff-fuff' valve for some reason.

However the engine certainly needed a range of sparking plugs to be available, and the normal routine was to start the engine using a hard road plug, and keep the load and engine speed down until the water was hot. Then the engine was changed to its racing plugs, although these would differ for various types of events, harder (colder) plugs being called for when there were longer straights than for sprint races, where the amount of full throttle work was restricted. When the engines became worn, it was not uncommon for a particular unit to require four different heat ranges in its four cylinders! The big problem was that the operating heat range of plugs available at that time was restricted, and owners were not always keen to have a selection of plugs for different circuits and weather conditions which might be experienced. Even in 1934, three sets of racing plugs might typically run to £30, which was a considerable sum of money then, representing around 5 per cent of the purchase price of the car!

However for whatever faults it may have had, the Q-type was a very fast car, but suffered during the season for the reputation of its predecessor. Eight cars were built, one setting the seal on the career of Bill Everitt, others being sold to Eddie Hall, the Evans family, the Dutchman Harry Herkuleyns, and the Brooklands racer A. R. Samuels. In due course one was sold to a Frenchman, Jacques Meunier, another to an

Australian and the last one went to another Brooklands specialist, Dudley Folland, but not until early 1935, suggesting that racing Midgets were getting too expensive at £595.

The 1934 K3 and EX135

For the 1934 season the K3 was offered with a lower pressure supercharger than used the previous year, a Marshall-built Roots-type blower delivering 10/12psi boost. This was introduced to overcome the chronic over-oiling problems experienced using the Powerplus blowers. At the same time the new cylinder head, developed for the N-type road car, was introduced, which improved gas-flow and allowed for the use of higher compression ratios without necessarily resorting to the need for alcohol fuels. In fact, most cars did use alcohol fuels, and produced very similar power outputs to the old Powerplus blown engines. Normally MG1 was used, since this allowed the engines to run cooler, and valve burning troubles were not then experienced.

Additionally, the brakes were improved by the adoption of twin lever application of the shoes, one lever for each shoe, one lever being operated by the pull of the cable, while the other was pushed by the opposite reaction of the outer cable covering. This allowed for a much lighter application pressure of the driver's foot being necessary, but ignored the improvement which might have been enjoyed if two leading shoe applications had been used. Apparently

The 1934 K3 was similar in style to the Q-type, and was not offered with wings and lights. As riding mechanics were finally banned from January 1934, no windscreen was provided for the passenger position either. George Eyston is here seen testing the car at Brooklands.

the original idea for this modification had come from Cousins, who had noted that the outer cables moved whenever the pedal was applied. Jackson had been working on the twin leading shoe system with his friend Enever, but this was never put into use, as ever, HN having to make the decision as to which system might end up in production.

The only other improvement offered on the K3 was the racing body shell, with an external fuel tank incorporated into the shape. The body was, in reality, an attempt to improve on the original 1933 long-tailed offering, which was a pretty hideous removable item, and heavy into the bargain, and the slab-tank racing 'skimpy' which was functional, but not good looking! Built to the then current sports car regulations of the ACIAR, the new body was a great improvement, even if it was slab sided, and gave the car another lease of life. A single aeroscreen was provided for the driver, and only the driver's seat was supplied with the car. The price remained at £795, but no wings, lights, other road or weather equipment were offered. Even the battery was an extra, since the fuel was now fed from a pressurised tank. The car weighed some 4cwt less than the original 1933 model, which gave it a much better

potential performance. *There was absolutely no doubt that this car was for racing!*

Mention has already been made of a special car ordered from Kimber by George Eyston, along the lines of the successful *Magic Midget*. Charles and Jackson were involved right from the start, the idea being to have a car which was suitable for track and road racing, and for record breaking too. The experiment was coded EX135, since work was progressing on the 1934 K3 under EX134, and development started in July 1933, the car being completed in time for the International Trophy Race in May 1934.

Like EX127, the Magnette was to have an offset drive line, but engine and gearbox were to be as for the standard K3, only the rear axle being different. The engine and drive line were inclined from the straight-ahead by some six degrees, and the axle nose piece was mounted well to the nearside of the car, resulting in that drive shaft being shorter than the other. The engine was built up to 1934 standard, with N-type head, and Marshall supercharger, but Eyston also requested an alternative blower be supplied for higher boost pressures when required.

Two alternative bodies were supplied, one an open single seater for road racing, which had no aesthetic value at all, and was scathingly called the 'coal scuttle' by Jacko's men! The car was finished in a two-tone brown over cream, which did not enhance its appearance. The other body was a more streamlined shell, with an enclosed radiator and a longer tail, which was eventually painted in parallel stripes of chocolate

Eyston commissioned a special single-seater car, known as EX135, but based on chassis K3023, with off-set transmission, and to be fitted with two interchangeable bodies, one for track racing and record breaking, and the other for road racing. Here is the chassis in its original form, fitted with pre-selector gearbox.

The track racing body for EX135. This was painted in brown and cream stripes, and was known at the factory as the 'Flying Humbug', after a popular candy of the time. The front brakes have been removed to reduce unsprung weight.

and cream colours, and called the 'humbug'. Like the *Magic Midget* it carried a large MG motif ahead of the radiator, and it was natural that it became officially known as *Magic Magnette*. This car was to be developed into the fastest pre-war MG.

Mille Miglia: April 1934

As in the previous year, Earl Howe sponsored a team of three cars in the Italian road race, the cars being driven this year by Howe with his personal mechanic George Thomas, Hall with his wife Joan, and Lurani with Penn Hughes. Although the cars were all new, the whole expedition was scaled down, with no works mechanics being in attendance. In the event the Halls suffered engine problems, and Howe crashed, leaving Lurani and Penn Hughes, who could only succeed in being placed second to Taruffi in a Maserati, even though they were 2mph faster than the previous year's winners. The lesson had been learned by the Italians, and taken to heart!

Although the cars were all bought by the entrants, none of them was kept. The Howe car was afterwards sold to George Hartwell, his Lordship finishing his association with the Abingdon marque. Eddie Hall still had his older car which he retained, and the Mille Miglia car was sold on to G. W. J. H. Wright, while the Lurani car was sold to Goldie Gardner, who was keen to start racing again, and was about to make a spectacular comeback in due course in *Magic Magnette*.

International Trophy, Brooklands: 28 April 1934

The first major event at Brooklands attracted a good entry of 42 cars, of which 16 were MGs. This race followed the precedent set the previous year and was to take the form of a race for stripped cars running with the unique form of handicapping, using three channels for each of the three capacity groups competing, which was really only available in the wide open spaces of the Weybridge circuit. Cars were to cover 500 miles, and to classify as a finisher the full distance had to be covered.

The race proved that the handicapping system was 'fair', for although it was one of the fastest cars which won, Straight in the 2.6-litre Maserati, the smaller cars were not outpaced to a degree that made the race a walkover. It was not a great day for Abingdon, however, with Dodson's K3 in seventh place being the best of the bunch.

Mannin Beg: 30 May 1934

The annual light car races around Douglas had been a disaster for MG in 1933, but they more than made amends in this year's race. The 1934 model K3 Magnettes were there in force, with teams entered by Kaye Don and by George Eyston. In Don's team, the drivers were Dudley Froy, Norman Black and A. P. Hamilton while Eyston's drivers were himself, driving EX135, and Wal Handley and Charlie Dodson driving

George Eyston in the 'coal-scuttle' bodied EX135 is harried by Hamilton in Mere's K3009 on the drive from the promenade. Mannin Beg, 1934. (National Motor Museum)

standard 1934 cars. Independent entries were Ashton-Rigby, driving Donkin's 1933 car, and Hamilton, driving Mere's similar vintage machine.

At the end of 1933, Robin Mere had concluded that he would not make a racing driver, and therefore offered the loan of his car to Hamilton. Hamilton was pleased to accept, and rebodied the car as a single seater, without the permission of the owner, which caused friction at first. However the Ulsterman proceeded to drive the car to great effect, which pleased Mere considerably. The MG works were sufficiently impressed to treat Hamilton as a special case driver, and made sure that the car was kept as up-to-date as possible, supplying many parts at low rates . . . paid for by Mere of course!

Most unfortunately, Don had an accident on the road, which resulted in the death of Frankie Tayler, and stopped the carrying of riding mechanics in racing events for ever. The race went on and proved an overwhelming success for Abingdon, with K3s filling the first five places. Celebrations at Abingdon were muted, however. More than 30 years after his death, Frankie Tayler was genuinely missed as one of the characters of the racing gang.

It was around this time that the racing mechanics became known as 'Jacko's insomnia gang' because of the long hours they put into the preparation of

Charles Martin in his newly acquired K3025, takes the Broadway turn off the sea-front during the Mannin Beg. Martin retired, but six of the K3s finished the race, taking the first five places.

the cars, often with little pay. Apparently if they were working late at the Factory, Kimber himself would appear, thanking the men for carrying on working, and after he took his leave, there were always plates of hot food, sandwiches, and a crate of beer for consumption.

British Empire Trophy Race: 23 June 1934

For 1934, the British Empire Trophy Race was held at Brooklands, on what was described at the time as a simulated road course. The intention was, of course, to distract some of the attention that the Midlands upstart track at Donington was enjoying, and also to try to get the grand prix cars of the period to raise interest in the Surrey track. So a course was laid out on the concrete bowl with artificial corners constructed using sand banks and straw bales. The result was, according to those drivers I have spoken to, a poor substitute for the real thing, but on the other hand, this race did provide an excellent one for the competitors, and some good entertainment for the small crowd which attended as spectators.

To attract a wider range of entries, a large prize fund was organised, including £1,000 donated by

Lord Nuffield. The race was scheduled for 100 laps of the three-mile course, as ever, in class handicap, determined by engine capacity settled by the International Class groups. There were nine genuine GP cars entered, three each from Alfa Romeo, Maserati and Bugatti, but of the German cars there was no sign. A wide range of British cars were entered, with, of course, good representation from the MG marque. Raymond Mays was present with the ERA, this being the first official outing for the car at Brooklands.

Samuel, Evans, Everitt and Hall were entered in their Q-type Midgets, with Ron Horton in his single-seater C-type completing the entry in the 750cc class. No less than ten Magnettes were entered, including George Eyston in EX135. The Midgets all suffered with problems, but Eyston won at 80.81mph from the GP cars of Straight (2.9 Maserati) and Eccles (4.9 Bugatti). Magnettes filled five of the first ten places, which was a satisfactory result. Apparently, when he was flagged in, Eyston asked what the result was, and on hearing he had won said 'Well, that's nice, I've been racing for about a hundred years, so it's about time I won something!'

LCC Relay Race

Following criticism that the Tourist Trophy race had degenerated into an event for racing cars to the exclusion of touring cars, during April the RAC had announced that the Ulster TT race in 1934 was to be for unsupercharged cars only, and that these were to be Factory models, of which at least 100 had been built and sold to the public. Several manufacturers complained that this was not possible, indeed firms like Aston Martin and Frazer Nash had no standard models, building cars to order for customers at a rate of perhaps a car or two per week. Within a couple of weeks the rules were changed to the extent that re-bodied factory cars were to be permitted and that mild tuning was to be allowed. The replacement bodies were to conform to the current ACAIR regulations, which ruled out of contention most standard bodies, due to the maximum width requirement! Cecil Kimber was vociferous in his opposition to the new rules, and many well known people were heard to voice the opinion that lack of superchargers would make the race boring, and would serve no useful purpose.

At MG however, work went ahead to produce a suitable car to run in the TT, arguably the most important race on the calendar for a sports car manufacturer, and it is quite likely that the ND model was at first thought to be ideal. However, it was actually too wide in the body to meet the regulations, and so another model was developed.

Following experience during 1933 with the L-types, the new N-type engine was developed to run with a compression ratio not far short of 10:1, and to use a revised camshaft timing. This was so satisfactory that an output of 74bhp at 6,500rpm was seen on the test-bed, and it was fairly obvious that this was probably enough for a successful car, provided it could be made light enough. A body shape was developed on the N-type chassis which was attractive, and it only remained to test the car in action, preferably without drawing attention to the fact that the cars were a TT contender.

As a sponsor of the TT team, George Eyston proposed that a team of lady drivers be entered in his name for the relay race, and this was done, the drivers being Irene Schwendler, Margaret Allen and Doreen Evans. They were supposed to be chasing the Ladies Award, but went so well that they annexed third place overall at an average of 87.86mph, thus losing the former special cup! There was no doubt for Reg Jackson that the new Magnettes would do well at the TT! Equally there was no fooling the opposition that MG could not produce a successful unblown car.

Coppa Acerbo: 15 August 1934

Following Whitney Straight's success the previous year, MG entries were present in force for the 1934 Coppa Acerbo Junior race, with entries for Richard Seaman, in Straight's old car, Hamilton, in Mere's single-seater,

and Rafaele Cecchini in a car of his own, also in single-seater form. The latter was a wealthy Italian, who had raced Fiat cars hitherto, and who was so impressed by the performance of the K3 that he had ordered a car for himself, fitting it with a single-seater body, and using it to great effect in the 1934 season, winning his class in the Italian racing drivers' championship.

In the race, Hamilton stalled at the start, and was last away, but responded magnificently and soon caught and passed everyone else in the race. He led Cecchini home, with Seaman a little behind to complete a clean sweep for the Abingdon marque. If Hamilton's speed was not quite as good as Straight's the previous year, this was explained by his poor start, and by the fact that it was sufficient for the win!

RAC TT: 1 September 1934

Much has been made of the supercharger ban, a great deal before the actual race, but by common consent, the 1934 race was one of the best held at the Ards circuit. Certainly a review of the handicaps made the race fairly open, with a favourable edge being given to the larger engined cars. Most favoured were probably the Aston Martins, for their group had only to equal the times put up by the previous year's 1,500cc cars, whereas most of the others had to improve on previous performances. Classes were to be sub-divided into capacity classes of 200cc increments, each group having a separate handicap, thus the MG group, with 1,271cc engines, were to be given a 2 minute 16 second start over the Aston Martin, Riley and Singer group, all with a full 1,500cc displacement. However since the race was of six hours' expected duration, a couple of minutes was reckoned to be not enough by the Abingdon teams . . . after all the Rileys had chased the K3 Magnettes hard the previous year, but had succumbed to mechanical unreliability; if they, or the Astons or Singers were reliable this year who could tell?

Cars were entered by George Eyston, for himself, Handley and Dodson. Independent entries were made by Black, Everitt and A. P. Hamilton, no relation of the late lamented Hugh. Since the cars had only the TT to perform, for almost the first time they were all loaned by the works to the entrants for the race on a 'Bend it/mend it' basis. Entry fees, tyres and fuel, and mechanics' services were all to be paid for by the entrants. Bill Everitt took over the Nuvolari entry, when the Italian's financial aspirations could not be met, while Hamilton took over the intended Kaye Don entry.

In practice it quickly became evident that Eddie Hall driving a privately entered, but highly modified, Bentley

The NE was a TT car, built to conform to the 'no supercharger' rules for the race in 1934. Four of the cars leave the start of the race, the Ulster RAC TT, Black leading, with Eyston just behind, followed by Handley and eventual race winner, Dodson, bringing up the rear.

was going to be difficult to beat. He dearly wanted to win a TT race, and tried very hard, being one of only two drivers to compete in every Ards event. With MG cars he had done well, but had decided early in the year that MG would not provide a winning car, but that, in view of the supercharger ban, a large engine would offer the best chance, and certainly during practice it seemed if he might be right. Not only did he go well but so did Brian Lewis (Lagonda) and with John Cobb and John Hindmarsh for support the team from Staines looked formidable.

So the stage was set. The MG camp felt that they could do well, but were far from confident. Spirits were high when they left the pits, actually the first group to leave that year, followed some two minutes later by the rest of the 1.5-litre class, and over the next seven minutes by the rest of the field.

At the end of the first lap, it was Eyston who led, closely followed by Dodson, Handley, Black, Everitt

and Hamilton. Almost as soon as he cleared the pit area, Black's engine started to misfire, and he stopped at Comber with, of all things, a defective rotor arm. He borrowed one from a spectator's car, presumably with permission, and carried on for a few laps before stopping to confess that he had broken the rules!

Dodson found that he could out-run the supposed pace-maker, Handley, and started to go quick enough for the faster cars to hang out 'speed up' signs from their pits. Handley was having problems with the gearbox in his car, while Bill Everitt had a wheel collapse. It appears that at the last moment it had been decided to paint the wheels of all the cars silver, in place of the normal black colour used for racing cars, and in consequence the specially tensioned competition wheels got mixed up with some standard road wheels, some of which were fitted in mistake to the racing cars. No-one, according to Cousins, knew how the error had occurred or had any idea how many cars might be affected. Jackson thought it was only the Eyston team which was concerned, but Everitt was not part of it, so all the remaining cars were to be called in, Eyston first. A full four-wheel change had not been practised, but Jackson worked out a routine for two mechanics, which were allowed this year for the first time. This was talked about with

Eyston leads Handley up Quarry Hill.
(National Motor Museum)

Stone, Hounslow and Scott, until they knew what they would do.

At the signal, Eyston arrived, but found that Handley was already there of his own volition, complaining that he could only use third and top gears. Jackson despatched him with short shrift, and proceeded to change Eyston's wheels with the help of Henry Stone. Next in was Dodson, who was attended to by Jackson and Bob Scott. Then came Hamilton to complete the task, with Hounslow and Jackson, for when Handley arrived he had demolished the gearbox, and retired in a huff!

The race continued with Dodson slowly improving his margin, but this was continually under attack by Eddie Hall in the 4-litre Bentley. Then Hall got involved in a dice with Brian Lewis in the 4-litre Lagonda which lasted for some time, and had the effect of slowing him down. Eventually the duel broke up, but at the end, it was a sprinkling of rain at Comber which put paid to any hope that Hall might have had to catch the fleet MG. Dodson was able to come home the winner by the margin of 17 seconds, at a speed of 78.65mph. That this was only 4mph slower than Nuvolari's speed the previous year was remarkable enough, but when it is reflected that it was achieved with an unsupercharged car which

was also third-fastest finisher overall, regardless of capacity, it speaks volumes for the achievement.

After the race Dodson was able to report that the drive had been largely uneventful, with the car behaving impeccably throughout. He remarked that he even had time to spot a lovely young lady amongst the crowd at Dundonald, which reminded him to readjust his mirror! As a dig against the organisers, no doubt, he also wistfully commented that the car would have been just as safe had it been fitted with a supercharger!

The last comment may have been true, but the fact was that, apart from MG, by 1934 no large-scale manufacturer was producing a supercharged sports car for sale and it was important for the race organisers to make sports car racing representative of cars available for sale to the public.

Racing in France: 9 September 1934

At the French Grand Prix, held at Montlhéry on 9 September, Dutchman Harry Herkuleyns won in his Q-type MG at 69.85mph, with Maillard-Brune following in the J4 of Meunier 3rd, just over a minute behind.

Czechoslovakian Grand Prix: 30 September 1934

George Eyston decided that he would take a car out to compete in the Czechoslovakian GP at Brno towards the end of the year. He was able to get support from Dick Seaman in this venture, and so took two K3s with him, including the car which Jackson was developing as the new powerful model for 1935. Eyston was able to keep pace with the 1.5-litre Type 51 Bugatti entries of Burggaller and Sojka, but not able to pass them, while the race was won by Farina in a 4CM1500 Maserati, almost a minute ahead of the dicing trio. Seaman followed Eyston home, a couple of minutes down.

A Czech driver, Zdenek Pohl, asked if Eyston's class-winning car could be bought, and the deal was done, thus losing Jackson his development twin choke carburettor which had proved something of a success. This car went on, in the hands of Pohl, to race until well after the war, and has recently been rebuilt in Switzerland.

The BRDC 500-Mile Race: 22 September 1934

Goldie Gardner used his ex-Penn Hughes Mille Miglia K3, which he shared with Benjafield. It was assumed that Gardner was having a final fling in a racing car, when, right at the end of the season, he came out of what everyone had assumed was retirement, following his dreadful accident in the 1932 TT. He found that he was still enjoying his racing however, and as the season progressed he bought the ex-Horton single-seater K3, which he had prepared by Robin Jackson at Brooklands. The younger car he sold to John Smith of Mitcham, who did many great things with it over the next few years.

One of the driving sensations of the season had been Bill Everitt, who hitherto had driven a J2 in minor races at Donington Park, but who at the beginning of 1934 had bought a Q-type. In this he was possibly sponsored by Kaye Don or George Eyston, since he drove during the season for both those teams as already recorded. However, he was the only driver consistently successful in the Q-type during the 1934 season culminating in taking the Standing Start Mile and Kilometre class records at Brooklands.

Dodson takes the flag at the end of the race, winning by just 17 seconds from Eddie Hall's Bentley after six hours of racing at an average speed of 76mph.

CHAPTER 6

MAINTAINING THE BREED

1935

INDEPENDENT SUSPENSION, THE CESSATION OF RACING, BUT COMPETITION CONTINUES

Eddie Hall, although he still had his C-type and the K3, wanted to try for the outright record at Shelsley, and commissioned a car based on an N-type chassis. This was fitted with a highly supercharged, 25psi, Zoller blown 1,271cc N-type engine, and nearly achieved the target, knocking 0.6 seconds off his own time of 44.4 seconds in his K3, but was beaten by Mays in the ERA with a staggeringly fast time of 39.6 seconds. (National Motor Museum)

Sir William Morris had been ennobled as Lord Nuffield, and decided that he would rationalise his business interests. He formed the Nuffield Group, around Morris Motors Ltd, and sold his personal interests in Wolseley Motors (1927) Ltd, the SU Carburettor Co. Ltd, and the MG Car Co. Ltd to this Group. Into it were also grouped Morris Motors, Morris Commercial, Morris Engines and Morris Bodies, and which in due course also included the Pressed Steel Co. Ltd. Leonard Lord was appointed Managing Director of the Group, with Nuffield himself as Chairman. None of this appeared to affect the working of the individual companies at first, but the wind of change had started to blow.

So far as MG development was concerned, the way ahead from the Q-type was undoubtedly to improve the chassis. By now, the racing car development was really driving the production car improvements, and each new model was certainly far better than its predecessor. Charles was certain that the road cars of the future would have independent suspension, but the problem was the development of a suitable chassis.

So far as the racing cars were concerned, the limit of road holding for the power available had undoubtedly been reached for the 750cc-engined car let alone the more powerful, but very much heavier, K3. Cart sprung axles were all very well but as speeds increased the effects of the axles bounding and rebounding at high frequency set up all kinds of unpleasantness for the drivers of the cars, and the faster the potential of the car the worse the effects became. The Q-type should have been a very fast car, but in fact it was not possible to realise the full potential of the performance. The power achieved from the 750cc Q-type engine was only a few horsepower short of that produced by the 1,100cc K-type unit, but the car was so skittish, that the K3 was the faster car. Charles reasoned that the lighter Q-type *should* have been quicker than the Magnette.

From around the middle of 1932 HN, aided and abetted by Jacko, had been working on various forms of independent front suspension, even building up a J2 with a rudimentary system fitted, which was worked on throughout 1934. The standard MG chassis frame was not notably rigid, and any independent suspension system needs a stiff base from which to work effectively. This car had poor handling and Charles was convinced that the chassis frame needed to have no built-in flexibility, unlike the older cart-sprung designs, for which chassis flexibility was an essential part of the road holding equation, at least with small light cars.

The work was given greater impetus when the fabulous German grand prix cars appeared. By mid-1934 Syd Enever was working alongside Charles on this project and after a lot of trial and error eventually it was decided that the ideal chassis was a 'Y'-shaped frame, in which the engine and front suspension were mounted in the diverging front facing arms, while the rear suspension was bolted on a subframe to the long rear-facing single arm. The patents for the original chassis and suspension layout are in the names of Charles and Kimber, and are dated late 1934. Work was continuing through the winter of 1934/5.

The R-type Midget development

Listed as EX146, the chassis frame itself was made of 12SWG sheet material formed into square section tubes and electrically welded. The result was notably rigid, showing virtually no deflection when loaded, even though it weighed a bare 56lb. This compares with the weight of the Q-type frame of nearly 80lb, and of the K3 at around 120lb! Frank Stevens, one of the pioneer MG staff, was the man who carried out this work, and he told the following story. Charles had a routine of jumping on the frame each time he came into the

The R-type chassis undergoing fettling after the plates have been electrically welded. This picture was given to the author by Frank Stevens, so it might be him who is working.

Experimental Shop, and exclaiming 'Like standing on a floor'. This inevitable routine was eventually stopped when Charles enquired as to the meaning of the considerable row of chalk marks on the shop wall; one for each time he had said this over some two weeks!

While the chassis was fairly large in construction, the suspension arms were not, being built up of 5⁄16in diameter high tensile alloy-steel bar. Even Enever was constrained to ask if he (H. N. Charles) really expected a racing driver to entrust his neck to 'a set of knitting needles'!

To call the cars revolutionary is understating the case. The new MG was the first British car to feature all-round independent suspension, as well as being the first MG to be offered for sale built as a single-seater racing car. The engine and gearbox were almost identical to those of the Q-type, although a closer ratio gear-set was used in the preselector gearbox. These units were well proven by this time, and power shortage was not a problem with the older car, but it was the inability to transfer this power to the road when cornering which caused the greatest problem for drivers of the older models. The supercharger was a Zoller instrument, as on the Q compressing at 24psi.

The suspension and chassis were the really radical aspects of the design. The suspension medium was torsion bars, and the movement was damped by Luvax hydraulic shock absorbers. Compared with previous MG models suspension movement was huge, at around six inches from bump to rebound. Steering was by a unique Bishop-Cam gear which employed two connected worm gears, one right-hand and the other left, which relayed movement of the steering wheel to right and left-hand front wheel independently, and thus there was no track rod between the front wheels. The whole suspension had the ability for variation of suspension geometry static settings, which pre-dated work by Cooper and Lotus in this direction by 20 years.

During the building of the original car it was decided that all prototype work would be carried out at Abingdon to try to keep costs down, and this gave rise to a number of amusing stories. One of the more repeatable concerns the making of the first differential housing. Since there were suspension mountings designed into this, a new casting needed to be developed: attempts to make a subframe to carry the suspension mountings had resulted in the structure being far too flexible. Eventually a design was finalised, but no one knew if it would work or be strong enough. It was decided by Jackson that the prototype should be made in house, so that modifications to the pattern could be accomplished cheaply and quickly. A pattern-box was made up by Harry Herring, and it was decided

The R-type chassis, front offside view, showing many of the features of this advanced racing car.

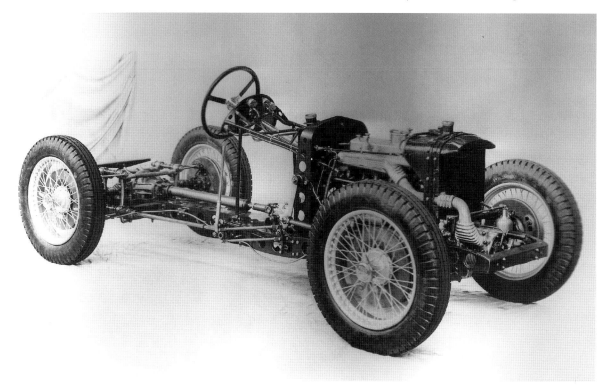

to make the casting, using sand in the pattern box, in aluminium, in the interests of lightness, and due to the fact that someone said that this material melted at a much lower temperature than iron. It was doubtful whether the small furnace at MG would have been able to sustain the higher temperature needed to melt several pounds of iron anyway.

To buy aluminium a minimum order for 56lb was required, which was far more than was needed, even for the complete batch of the first ten cars. Jacko said that he had several boxes of scrapped pistons in the racing shop, so these were cleaned down, and put in a large crucible, which was heated in the furnace. Eventually, after a great deal of time, the metal started to melt. No one in the shop, Jackson, Enever, Robinson or Stone had any experience of sand casting of large patterns. When the material was judged to be melted, and able to be poured, the slag was skimmed off the top, and then carefully poured into the pattern box. Of course, the sand was nowhere near dry enough, and immediately the hot material was forcefully ejected! Everyone took cover, except the luckless Jackson, ever the good foreman, who was holding the crucible steady (almost!), while faces appeared from under benches. There were holes in the tiled walls, but fortunately no one was hurt.

Incidentally, in later years, the Experimental Shop became the Apprentice School, and the chips in the tiled wall could still be seen, and Jackson was not above telling the story against himself to the new recruits, possibly as a salutary warning, about the hazards of home castings!

Having learned the need to dry the sand out thoroughly, and this being accomplished using a battery of welding torches, a second run was attempted, this time successfully. When it was judged cool enough, the pattern box was opened, and there inside was revealed a perfect casting, ready for machining, and to everyone's surprise was free of blow-holes. Jackson duly machined this successfully and Charles was delighted to see the result of the home casting, and when he was asked what the material was, Jackson evasively, but strictly truthfully, said it was aluminium. Charles was too good an engineer to be satisfied with this, but when he pressed the question to find which alloy was used, and suggesting 'duralumin', Jackson had to say that it was not, but was a special alloy they had concocted for the pouring, which he named 'pistominium'. Eventually, Charles got to the bottom of the story, and congratulated Jacko on his ingenuity. The name stuck, and the other nine units were made of the same material: although the specification sheet attached to the drawing is not able to record the exact composition of that alloy!

Back to the R-type itself. The other major change of policy was to adopt Girling brakes, in place of the Alford & Alder systems used hitherto. The newer system relied on a much stiffer backplate assembly, coupled with an

Rear nearside view of the chassis showing the gear lever below the steering wheel, where it could be operated by a single finger without the need to remove a hand from the steering wheel.

The front of the R-type chassis, displaying a supercharger which is similar to a Q-type. Note the starting dog to the upper right of the blower, to which could be engaged a portable electric starter motor. The thin section of the wishbones is well shown here, but remember these were twice the diameter Charles had calculated them necessary to be!

expander which multiplied the mechanical advantage and improved both the braking performance and the feel to the driver immeasurably. The actual operation was still by cables, Charles holding firm to his belief that fluid operation was not the way to go. He even rejected the idea of using rod operation, which Girling brakes normally employed, stating that such operation needed a multiplicity of bell cranks and clevis pins, which only caused wear points and possible failures!

The gear change selector was placed to the left of the steering column under the steering wheel in the position this control is more commonly found, and enabled the driver to select gears without removing a hand from the steering wheel. Many drivers facetiously commented that a problem when racing at Brooklands was knowing which gear stick one should actually use to change gear, so great was the vibration in the car!

Instrumentation was complete, with tachometer, water and oil thermometers, oil pressure gauge, and fuel pressure and supercharger boost pressure gauges. The whole car was given a very attractive single-seat body with a full cowl to cover the radiator and supercharger, with a delightful 'MG' grille on the front which doubled as a trap door to gain access to the latter. This cowl was known at the time as the Jersey Cow, and was generally unloved, but it was as ahead of its time as the rest of the car. The car was equipped with the double Brooklands exhaust system . . . as with the Q-type one could hardly refer to this as a silencing device! The new model featuring the chassis, and called the R-type, was announced to the world in the April of 1935, and cars were immediately available for customers to use in the International Trophy Race at Brooklands.

Rear view of the R-type chassis. The cylindrical rear Luvax shock absorbers, which contributed to the failure of the suspension on the early outings of the car can be seen. They were simply not designed to run at the amplitude of the R-type torsion bar suspension.

At an all in price of £795, the car gave fantastic value for money, and there can be little surprise that nine of the first batch of cars were sold as soon as the model was announced. George Eyston placed an order for three cars. The Evans family ordered a car through their Bellevue Garages sales outlet, while a young driver by the name of Bill Esplen, who had been doing well in a Talbot for the past couple of years, also ordered one. These cars were entered for the International Trophy Race.

Interest had also been shown by Jacques Meunier in France, and by Bobby Baird in Northern Ireland, while Ian Connell, Douggie Briault, Reggie Tongue and Ron Horton had all expressed interest in the new model. The first five named all eventually placed firm orders.

International Trophy Race, Brooklands: 6 May 1935

The first important race of the year was the International Trophy Race to be held at Brooklands, and it was intended that the R-type would be there in force. Eyston's team of three cars, with himself, Handley and Black driving were the 'official' team. Private entries were received from Kenneth Evans and Bill Esplen. Following a successful press release of the car, Kimber had managed to talk Malcolm Campbell into driving one, coming out of retirement for the purpose. The Campbell

An R-type cornering during the British Empire Trophy Race at Brooklands, 1935.

entry caused a small problem, since it was obvious that he did not expect to put any money up for the pleasure, so the development car was made available for the race. According to Alec Hounslow the car was prepared in works racing cream, like the Eyston cars, but without the brown body-length stripes. However, a 'coloured' photograph purporting to be Campbell driving showing the car in Bluebird blue exists. The Evans car was painted in their shade of blue, while Esplen's car was white.

The race itself was not a notable success for the R-type. All the Eyston cars retired, as did Kenneth Evans, but after a good run the Campbell/Everitt car finished a reasonable sixth place, at 82.96mph. Eddie Hall was third overall in his K3 however, to save MG honour, behind Fontes in the GP Alfa Romeo and Dixon in his two-litre Riley Six. Doreen Evans, meanwhile, was seventh in her Q-type now modified with a very nice narrow single-seater body fitted.

Mannin Beg: 20 May 1935

Baird had his R-type in time for the Mannin Beg, and the Eyston Team and Kenneth Evans were also entered in theirs for the race. Eddie Hall was entered in his K3, and he kept the flag flying for the Abingdon marque, leading for the first lap, until Raymond Mays in the ERA finally found the power of the larger car and swept into the lead. However, it was Fairfield who won in his ERA from Dixon in the Riley Six, with Hall following in third, and Baird taking fourth place, but some seven laps in arrears. All of the R-types had suffered with suspension problems, the shock absorbers losing damping ability as they warmed up, and rendering the cars difficult to keep on the road. This was hardly the start the new model needed, with none of the Eyston team in the money.

In fact it was at this race that the limitations of the Luvax dampers became apparent to all, for they were overheating and ceasing to function for their designated purpose. The cure for the problem was to change to dampers, and Charles had put plans into action for this by the time the cars were returned to Abingdon.

An R-type victory

In fact it was Maillard-Brune who, on 2 June, gave the R-type its first race win at Montlhéry when he came home at 74.25mph in the GP de France. This car had been bought by Jacques Meunier, the chocolate magnate, and Maillard-Brune was also successful in it at the Bol d'Or race that year. Jackson had been on hand at the delivery of the car, and no doubt gave some useful information about how to set it up.

The PB at Le Mans: June 1935

If all the work on the R-type was exciting, there were developments on the production car front as well. For some time it had been apparent to those at MG that there was some sales resistance to the small high revving MG engine, when for much the same money one could buy the Singer 'Nine', with an engine of 972cc displacement and a much better torque characteristic. This enabled the car to be driven at lower crankshaft speeds, and to remain in top gear at 30/40mph, a speed range in which the MG cars needed to be in third speed to ensure smooth acceleration. The answer was for MG to produce a similar size engine, and this was possible by the simple expedient of boring the cylinders to 60mm, giving a capacity of 939cc.

The resulting power was at first disappointing, but after experiments with different widths of piston ring the desired power increase was forthcoming, and the new model was introduced as the PB in March 1935.

An entry was submitted for the Le Mans race at around this time, in the name of George Eyston who nominated a team of six lady drivers to take the three cars and endeavour to get the first stage of the Rudge-Whitworth Cup completed, with a view to winning it the following year. The team became known as Eyston's Dancing Daughters in the press, such was the novelty of lady drivers taking part in an important international race. The three cars ran almost faultlessly, performing their intended task, with only one rear lamp bulb being replaced apart from fuel, in a total of 72 hours' running, in which the cars covered an aggregate of 4,500 miles.

The RB chassis design

After the International Trophy Race, a considerable amount of information came back from drivers regarding the handling of the R-type. The cars rolled on corners, and, as a result, were inclined to break away under acceleration away from bends. The roll effect was disconcerting to drivers, because the body and wheels moved in unison, due to the use of equal length wishbones at the rear. One thing was certain, that the rear suspension needed altering to have shorter wishbones at the top. It seemed likely too that some form of radius rod might be needed for the rear suspension. Charles worked out a scheme for a roll-resisting linkage as EX152 and, in due course, a patent was filed for this in his and Enever's names. Work started on modifying the development car chassis, and a set of parts was ordered.

Urged on by Kimber, Charles wanted to produce a K3

replacement car based on the R-type, which was coded EX147, and it seems that around the works this was referred to as the S-type by May 1935. Jackson said that they had tried a six-cylinder engine in the R-type frame, and established that the forward legs would need lengthening by six inches, if the standard supercharger layout was preserved. Charles wanted to mount the supercharger nearer to the engine, under the bonnet, and was scheming ideas for this.

Kimber, impetuous as ever, decided that the car was worthy of higher things and had thoughts of moving to 1,500cc, no doubt encouraged by the introduction of the ERA of Raymond Mays and his team. He even had a letter published in the press on the subject of grand prix racing, and of the validity of restricting engine capacity to 1,500cc.

At this stage it appears that Leonard Lord, who thought that racing was a total waste of money, was getting worried about the levels of expenditure which had been put against the R-type development, and wanted to know more about where this was leading. Miles Thomas was sent by him to investigate, and while Kimber was insistent that a road car could easily be developed from the racing car, even Lord Nuffield was not convinced by this. It seems that the final nail in the coffin was the sight of an engine at the works which was clearly not an in-house product, and which had twin overhead camshafts. Various stories are told as to what this might have been, but Cousins was clear that it was a Blackburn unit. Kimber was no doubt influenced by the two camshafts, and probably a similar unit to that used by Frazer Nash in one of their models. But, in all likelihood, Kimber did not appreciate that this particular unit was not an ideal engine for a racing car. Thomas reported to Lord, who made the decision that all development projects at Abingdon would cease forthwith. Apparently his words were: 'He has finally overstepped the mark, I've got him!' Lord ordered Thomas to tell Kimber, and close the Experimental Department forthwith, also that all support for racing would cease immediately.

If this was not the true story, then I can only say that Cousins did not contest it, and Jackson was always tight-lipped about the subject. In 1968 Charles simply would not talk about it, but said that he would neither confirm nor deny it, but from where had my information come?

Whatever the truth of the six-cylinder story, work continued with the 750cc car. The upshot of all this is that the chassis still exists, and has stamped on the number RA0260, which is that of the 'Campbell' car, and still has all the modified parts for the revised suspension which had been designed and made. Another car, which I now believe is probably the ex-Handley repaired car, has the front suspension from the Campbell car, to bear out the story which I was told in 1968 when the modified one first came to light.

Racing is stopped

Late in June 1935 Kimber called all the staff into the canteen and read a formal statement issued by the recently formed Nuffield Group which said that forthwith all activities associated with motor racing will stop, and that the Department would be closed down with immediate effect, and that in future all design work would be done at Cowley. Charles and Enever were to have jobs there, and as many of the staff as possible would be absorbed into the Factory. Kimber added that no one would be left without work, but that it might not be what they actually wanted to do. Beyond this nothing was said, he merely left the room. The announcement had taken barely three minutes, after which Kim never said another word on the subject in public.

Everyone was astounded: MG had without doubt the most successful British racing team by 1935. It was well known that most, if not all, of the actual racing was paid for by customers. The Experimental Department, known unofficially by this time as 'Racing', felt as though they had been kicked in the teeth, but they had to wind up all the activities and put their toys away. In the press there were various comments regarding an agreement between Austin and MG that a moratorium on racing was called for since racing had served its purpose for the foreseeable future. This failed to hold water when Austin not only carried on racing, but did so in higher profile, producing the famous twin-cam racing cars in 1936, each of which reputedly cost £10,000 to build, which was rather more than the cost of the first ten R-types all together!

While it seems likely that a principal reason for the rationalisation within the Nuffield Group caused the end of the MG ohc unit, and the Wolseley one too come to that, it was one of commercial sense, but there is very little doubt that the antipathy that existed between Lord, Thomas and Kimber was a major factor.

It was very difficult for the MG people to understand the reasoning behind the stoppage of the racing, let alone anyone from outside the Nuffield Group. Indeed, right up to the time the various people retired there was a certain amount of rancour regarding the way in which it had all been ended suddenly. The original run of R-type cars had all been sold, and there were firm orders for more on the books. The 'Campbell' car, in reality the works development car, had been dismantled and was undergoing modifications for future racing, but this work was incomplete, and the parts were shipped to Cowley.

One of the Eyston cars, driven by Handley, had been involved in an accident at Brooklands, while testing damper modifications. Eyston had just agreed a sale of this car, so it was in the process of being straightened out, very much on the QT, and parts of the front suspension were transferred from the development car to complete the latter. There was some hope that a production prototype car could be cobbled up quickly, using the independent suspension chassis, and a little work was done in this direction during June and into July by Charles and Enever, even mounting a small saloon body on it.

Although the Evans Bellevue Garage equipe bought an R-type, they updated their Q-type with a narrow single-seater body and raced this with some success. This is Kenneth Evans at Donington Park. The original car disappeared during the 1950s, and a replica of it is being built in England.

Kimber argued his corner, using his personal special relationship with Lord Nuffield. He even asked Thomas, Lord and Nuffield to see the prototype S-type saloon, EX150, which was under construction at Abingdon. A quick mock up had been made by Jackson and Cousins, using a Morris 18 engine, possibly an Isis unit, on the R-type chassis. The resultant car was called *Queen Mary* by the factory hands, and the whole thing was not well thought out and was obviously a ploy to buy time. Lord was unimpressed, and conveyed his feelings to Nuffield very forcibly.

Kimber's wings had been severely clipped, and it is probable that it was the fact that he was a special favourite of Nuffield, coupled with his personal high standing in the industry at large that saved him from being dismissed . . . that would have been too difficult for even the Nuffield Group hard men to account for!

The reasons for stopping the development of the highly sophisticated chassis were probably more complex than the simple one that MG was not making money. In fact the sports car market was declining, and there can be little doubt that the close alliance of sports cars with a racing image caused insurance companies to raise premiums, which in turn caused some people to reconsider buying an MG.

This new conglomerate, although under the Chairmanship of Lord Nuffield, was really run by a board of directors, which included a number of business hard-nuts. They may have been able to read balance sheets, but did not have much of a clue about motoring, let alone sports motoring, which was, and is, in reality driving for the sake of itself, and so were out of tune with the very customers which Kimber had been courting with his cars for the past ten years and more. That they regarded Kimber as a maverick to be distrusted there can be little doubt, and this as much as anything else probably affected the future of the MG Car Company.

However, there was some sound economic sense behind the decision, and this Kimber fully understood. If MG cars could be made from the Morris Motors parts bin, then MG cars might be cheaper to build, and might therefore be more profitable. This, in turn, should lead to higher sales which could only be better for the future of the MG image. Certainly it was arguable that the buying public were not yet ready for the complication of independent suspension on everyday cars, and the trade almost certainly was not!

After all the excitement of racing, it was difficult to believe that it was all over. Reg Jackson and his men had thought that it would carry on for ever, and Jacko

in particular was hard hit. His friend Enever was kept on the design side, and went to Cowley to continue to work under H. N. Charles, until he finally went his own way leaving Enever the liaison man between Cowley and the MG factory.

Most of the other competition people were absorbed into the Factory. Alec Hounslow, however, eventually left the Company, while Jackson himself was tempted to go, but with a young family to support he wanted something more secure in terms of career prospects. His difficulty was that, as Head of Competitions, his seniority put him into the unemployable category . . . there were simply no vacancies! Kimber therefore created a new position for him as an itinerant trouble-shooter, equipping him with a small van and a stock of parts, and sending him off to various dealers and good customers to sort out their problems at first hand in the field, a job he found very much to his liking. He was also always available to answer questions about the tuning of the old racing engines, which he often carried out on behalf of those still running the now obsolescent cars. He eventually got called back to the works on a permanent basis during 1937 when it was decided that, with the increasing likelihood of a war, ministry contracts might require a formal engineering inspection department to be set up, and Reg was given the job of organising it.

London Motor Show, 1935

A new 2-litre model was announced at the London Motor Show, based on the Morris 18, becoming the official SA model, all thoughts of independent suspension, let alone the single-seater, now forgotten! This car was put into production alongside the PB Midget and the N-type Magnette which had revised bodywork and was now called the NB at the Factory. By the end of 1935, at the Factory, the overhead camshaft cars were being talked of as old-fashioned, even though they were still in production in the PB. The last N-type was built right at the end of 1935, but the depressed market ensured that these models could be bought well into the following year. Sadly it took until well into 1936 before any customers got their 2-litre models, and it was the growing SS Company of William Lyons which copied the idea and got it into production first, proving that the small factory could always outstrip the larger multi-plant operations.

At the same time work was progressing at Cowley, on EX151 under H. N. Charles, a new Midget was based

Dennis Evans on the Bellavue R-type at Brooklands.

on the Morris 10/4, and called the T-series when it was introduced the following April. This car was to feature hydraulic brakes and a pushrod overhead valve engine, giving the car a much lazier performance than the old PB. Gone was the high revving engine, with the constant need to be in the right gear, and in its place a large displacement low speed engine of quite different character. The new car quickly endeared itself to the buying public, which is what really mattered to the 'bean counters' at Cowley.

The wind of change was indeed blowing across the Thames Valley into Abingdon, but it did ensure the survival of the MG marque.

Racing carries on!

Of course the official racing ban did not affect the majority of owners, at least at first, because they still had their cars, and they could still race: it was just that the works could no longer provide facilities for preparation of the cars. MGs continued to be raced, but with diminishing successes right up to 1939. Robin Jackson, in particular, offered a good reliable preparation service, and kept several cars in the results. It was notable that the cars were able to keep pace with most cars throughout this period, underlining the fact that the MG racing cars represented state-of-the-art racing practice when they were new.

RAC Tourist Trophy: 7 September 1935

Although there was no official entry for the TT, Graham Evans, on behalf of Bellevue Garages, had bought the three Eyston team cars from the 1934 TT for Kenneth and Dennis to drive, and Richard Seaman was invited to drive the third car. Bobby Baird had purchased a fourth car, and entered this. Then, it turned out, Ian Connell had bought a car, and this was entered under the Evans banner, bringing to five the MG entry.

Mention is made of this race only because Evans actually equipped his three cars with 'pits-to-car' radios, and a great deal of publicity was gained by so doing. So far as I am aware this was the first use of radio for such a purpose, which is now considered commonplace. In fact the experiment was a failure because the radios of the time, using thermionic valves, could not stand the buffeting and failed. The drivers wore clumsy headphones under their leather helmets, but it was difficult for them to hear their instructions above the noise of the cars anyway!

Seaman finished in tenth place at 73.68mph, much down on Dodson's winning speed of the previous year, but won his class, with Baird and Kenneth Evans the other finishers.

CHAPTER 7

ESTABLISHMENT AND RETRENCHMENT 1935–39

SPORTS CARS FROM TOURING CARS, MORE RECORD BREAKING, TRIALS AND RALLIES

First time out for the now-named Cream Cracker, and Three Musketeer teams, here running in line astern, Crackers leading, MacDermid, Bastock and Toulmin, followed by Welch, Hounslow and Nash in the Musketeer cars. Abingdon Trial, 1935.

This chapter reviews some of the many activities which the MG Car Company were to get involved with after the official activities were stopped. Inevitably with some 130-odd racing cars having been sold over the previous six years there was still a sizeable number of active competitors, and that these would still need to be supplied with parts to keep the cars active. Quite a few competitors carried on being successful, and there can be little doubt that these were given support by way of bonuses right up to 1939, but the cruel fact was that there were to be no more MG racing cars built. There have been several stories about new cars being supplied by the Company, but these must be taken with a sizeable pinch of salt. Factory sales records show that no racing cars were sold after 1935, although a few redundant chassis frames, axles and engines were sold off, all as 'second-hand, of no further commercial value'. However parts do not make a complete car, and any car built up from such spares can only be regarded as post-factory built 'specials'. As far as I am aware, having studied the Factory sales records, none were officially sold as complete cars.

The original MGCC 'A-team' of 1934, from the left: R.A. MacDermid, always known as 'Mac', J.A. Bastock, always referred to by his friends as 'Jack', and J.M. Toulmin, normally referred to as the 'Colonel'. MacDermid and Toulmin here have P-types, while Bastock is still using his J2. The team later that year became the 'Cream Crackers'.

Rallying

The car rally in the pre-war era was a somewhat different type of event to what it has become. Rallies were essentially a means of proving that a car could transport its occupants to a given destination within a prescribed time limit. Events were organised both nationally and internationally on this basis, but they were regarded as gentle events for older people to take part in, or those who were not interested in who won. As time passed, it became obvious that any form of competition became a vehicle for publicity, and as the third decade of the century closed so a closer interest in rallies was growing.

MG as a company was never much attracted to rallies. Reg Jackson, more than once, said that it was a lot of hard work to get a car to the finish, and then one did not know the result for a day or so, while these were being worked out. Although this was said tongue in cheek one can be sympathetic with the view. The real attraction to rallies must have been that at that time one could enter with a more or less standard car. This, in turn, allowed the Factory to support entries from privateers, as well as a number of thinly disguised entries of factory-owned cars.

A few previous forays into the rally world have been mentioned, the Alpine being an event which MG cars figured reasonably well in, but the truth was that the standard car was never going to be a success in results terms when other companies were building special cars

with specially prepared transmissions and engines fitted. The only time MG seems to have tried this semi-officially was when the noted journalist Humfrey Symons asked Kimber for a car to run in the 1935 Monte Carlo Rally. He had already run an N-type in the Alpine Trial in 1934, probably as a result of writing up the N-type well in *The Motor*, and was rewarded with a drive.

Monte Carlo Rally: January 1935

Symons thought that a suitably prepared MG might just pull off an outright win since, given a clean sheet on arrival at the Principality, one only had to put in a good time in a final, but long, driving test to win. He had competed in the Monte since 1928 but usually in large touring cars, so could be assumed to have plenty of experience in getting cars through difficult winter terrain against the odds. He had noted how well the winners of previous events had performed with near-racing cars, and decided that this was the way to go.

He told Kimber that he wanted a car with reasonable comfort, but with a supercharged engine and pre-selector gearbox, and thought a Mille Miglia specification K3 would do the business. Kimber had long since decided that the road specification competition car had had its day, and was, by mid-1934, moving towards the idea that racing cars were for racing, and that there was little else worthy of consideration. Moreover, Symons had let him know that MG were going to foot the bill! After some discussion with Reg Jackson, Kimber said that it was possible to prepare an N-type, actually the car he had used on the Alpine, to the specification he wanted, and that provided Symons paid the expenses of the trip in full, it would be conceivable to loan him a car. So it was agreed, with Temple Press probably footing the expenses bill.

For some time competitors in the rally had experimented with small diameter wheels and large section tyres, and Symons stated that this would be a good thing to add to the N-type. Jacko, having discussed the matter in detail with H. N. Charles, eventually decided that 16in diameter wheels were right, using 5.50in section tyres, so as not to alter the final drive ratio too drastically. Several other modifications were carried out, the car being equipped with an accurate speedometer in place of its tachometer, but after driving the car it was decided to fit a rev counter in the centre of the dash, since it was alarmingly easy to get to 6,000rpm, even in top gear! The rear axle ratio was raised to 4.89:1, which meant that at 6,000rpm on top gear, the car was travelling at around 100mph!

Fred Kindell was to be the second driver, principally because, as well as being a first-class mechanic, he was something of an expert at driving cars in confined places, and he said that the steering was better with standard 18in wheels at the front. It was decided to carry these on the side of the car specifically for the final driving test, which Kindell was expecting to drive. Symons had wanted a heater to be fitted, but this was not carried out, because when Jackson drove the car he found the preselector gearbox kept the occupants quite warm enough!

When completed the car was taken to a weighbridge and found to scale 23cwt complete with tools, luggage and the snow chains which Symons thought it so important to take. Hardly a lightweight car for 1,300cc but it was a real performer: Jackson had recorded 100mph on the road near East Hanney in the Vale of the White Horse, and had ascended Chain Hill out of Wantage in top gear, where most cars ground their way up in second at that time. However highly modified, it was still nowhere near the standard of some of the cars which took part, which used special parts straight from the factory development shops or tool-rooms. As ever, all parts used in the MG were available to customers, and were drawn from production stock.

It would be nice to record that the MG was successful and won the rally outright, but fairy stories do not happen in reality, being the preserve of fiction. In fact Symons and Kindell successfully drove all the way to Monte Carlo without penalty, one of four teams to achieve this in a notably cold rally where quite a few cars got stranded in snowdrifts, and many more failed utterly due to mechanical problems. After the hill-climb section the MG had the only clean sheet, and only had to complete the final driving test without penalty to win outright. Symons decided that he would do the driving test, even though part of the agreement with Kimber had been for Kindell to do this part. Symons made a complete porridge of the thing, first forgetting to turn on the battery master switch, and then trying for a fast time roared along one of the longer sections, and mistimed the braking spot and ended up crashing the car heavily into some sand bags, with the result that they were placed 98th!

Post-event checking revealed that the steering column was broken, and Symons arbitrarily and unilaterally decided that this was what had caused the accident. Kindell was sure it was a result of the accident and not the cause, which was later confirmed by Reg Jackson back at the Factory. Symons never drove another MG, but Kindell was to do more driving in works-prepared cars.

Happily the car still exists, owned by the author since 1961.

Other rallies

As the SA became available, various drivers felt that it should do well in the RAC Rally, and later the Monte, and even the Mille Miglia. However the model was never much of a success in competitive events, being on the whole rather too heavy. Modest successes were seen in domestic events, but not internationally. However, it was in the uniquely British sport of the reliability trial that the MG marque was to make further headlines.

The Cream Crackers

Since on road competition activities with motor cars was not viewed with any enthusiasm by the police or the magistrates' benches, it was a more gentle form of motorsport which blossomed in the British Isles in the early half of the century. Originally designed to show that cars could climb well known hills, as cars became more powerful and more reliable, the main road hills became less of a challenge, and side roads and out-of-the-way tracks were used increasingly as the tests in motor trials. The hills which became used were of uncertain surface, often with loose or muddy surfaces, where cars needed to be low geared or very powerful to climb. These trials had become known as Reliability Trials, for good reason, and it was found from 1924 onwards that MG cars performed spectacularly well in these events. This was not because the cars were low geared or particularly powerful, but more a function of the all important high power-to-weight ratio that they enjoyed. Thus many MG owners took their cars at weekends to these events, of which there could be several every weekend, and these were often to be found in the results lists.

Early in 1930 a group of MG enthusiasts had got together to form the MG Car Club, and this had been given the blessing of recognition by the MG Car Company Ltd, which even gave small support by way of trophies and limited financial support to help with administration. The MG Car Club was not only one of the first single marque motoring clubs to be established, but soon became a leader in the organisation of trials and rallies in its own right.

Meanwhile at the Factory in late 1935 all was not quiet on the competition front. The Cowley ban was specifically on racing, and many customers were involved with rallies and trials. The J and then P-type Midgets were particularly successful, although most models had successes. There was even a group of enthusiasts who had entered as a team under the banner of the MG Car Club, calling themselves the

'MGCC A-Team'. This team had received a small amount of support from the Company, mainly by way of bonuses and free parts. For 1935 the team was formally called the 'Cream Crackers', and the cars were painted in the livery of George Eyston's MG racing team, although they were privately owned by the drivers.

Although several people have written about the name of the team, few seem to know the origin of the title. It appears that when the three cars, owned by Toulmin, MacDermid, and Bastock, were taken to Abingdon for painting, no one knew what colour they should be painted. Up until that time they were standard paint jobs, but with a brown and cream striping along the side of the car at waist-level, to represent the colours of the MGCC.

John Thornley told me this story many years ago, which I repeat here, chiefly because Jack Bastock told me that he was present on the occasion. It is generally thought that Kimber decided the cars would be cream with brown wings, like the racing cars. The fact that the cars were privately owned and that the owners might not have taken kindly to having their cars sprayed a works colour was not really discussed. However, it seems that the paint foreman of the time assumed that the cars *were* MG works cars, and, having no other orders, painted them in the same scheme as the 1934 K3s of the Eyston team.

The finished cars were lined up outside Service waiting to be picked up by their owners. When Toulmin arrived he exclaimed that they looked 'real little crackers'. Bastock liked this idea, and labelled them Cream Crackers, ' . . . because they are cream', and the name stuck. One wonders if a well-known biscuit manufacturer was approached for sponsorship, but this is very unlikely, since ideas of that type did not occur in 1935.

Development of the Three Musketeers Team

During 1934 a team of ND Magnettes had been entered in a small number of rallies and trials. The team became known as the 'Three Musketeers' following a comment from one of the Factory wags when the three cars were lined up at the fuel pump before the start of a rally. Originally the drivers were Russell Chiesman (who had run MG cars in rallies and trials since the earliest days of the company, and was a personal friend of Kimber), Lewis Welch (an Abingdon garage owner active in trials on his own account) and Fred Kindell (who was supposed to keep the cars going, usually successfully). The NDs were sold off during 1934, but the idea of running a team of Magnettes refused to die off.

Sam Nash driving the ex-Dancing Daughter P-type, in 'Three Musketeers' livery. This is at the top of Simms Hill, on the Torquay Trial.

Kimber had, by now, realised that a team of Midgets and a team of Magnettes running in rallies and trials was good for publicity. The events were well covered by the motoring journals. The Evans family was running a team of NA specials built at their own London workshops, so that another team seemed superfluous. However, towards the end of 1934, the Evanses sold their cars on, and the Three Musketeers were therefore reborn using three of the ex-TT NE Magnettes, which were rebodied with ND-style bodies and cycle wings, in time for the Lands End Trial in March 1935. The drivers used under the captaincy of Lewis Welch included at various times Fred Kindell, Alec Hounslow and Sam Nash, all works employees. The team ran through the early part of 1935, getting a really good win in the Welsh Rally, which finished on 20 July. George Eyston then announced to Kimber that he had sold his NE cars to Graham Evans for the 1935 TT, since, by this time, it was obvious that there would be no new racing cars. This caused a problem!

Four of the seven NEs had been sold already, including two of George's, leaving only the three trials cars. George pointed out that there were the three Le Mans P-types, which he, George, was having a problem

disposing of and which would be suitable for trials, while he had actually done a deal with Graham Evans for the NEs. The NEs were therefore hurriedly returned to standard, and passed to Bellevue Garage.

The PAs were used as Three Musketeers for the Torquay Rally on 26 July, but the Factory sold these shortly afterwards. This left the team car-less, but some rather spectacular special cars based on L-type frames were built up, but powered with oversized N-type engines, and supercharged. These cars continued to be run by works employees, until, at the end of 1935, they were turned over to a new team of MacDermid, Bastock and Langley, who owned the cars on similar terms to those of the Cream Crackers.

This came about partly because there was some criticism of 'professionals playing in an amateur game', which was largely unjustified, as both Singer and Austin were fielding teams of works employees in special cars, whereas the MG cars used were standard cars using modifications available to anyone caring to buy them. In any case, the works personnel would have been paid to go on these events, even it was only subsistence. The cars with their supercharged 1,408cc engines were formidable adversaries, and enjoyed considerable success.

In 1936 the Cream Crackers and the Three Musketeers carried all before them and more or less monopolised the trials scene. The Magnette team won

the MCC Team Championship, and the three drivers a considerable amount of the silverware for individual success. When the Musketeers were not winning, the Cream Crackers did so.

It was shortly after being deprived of his drive in the Three Musketeers that Alec Hounslow decided to leave the MG Car Co., and went to work for the Brooklands tuners, Thomson & Taylor. Alec told Jackson privately that messing around in muddy fields in bottom gear was no substitute for the former passenger of Nuvolari, and what is more he felt that the fun in motoring started when top gear was engaged and the foot went to the floor!

While all this activity was going on, it was inevitable that in an active car club, other teams should lay a claim to favours from the works, and so the Highlanders Team was formed in Scotland, and the Norwesters in the Lakeland area. These teams were favoured with parts subsidy allowances in much the same way as the Crackers and Musketeers were, but there were no special cars for them. However, both these teams, and an unofficial Midlands team, were told when the previous year's cars were being sold off, and these came at agreeable terms. The Midlands team included

Austen May, who wrote up his experiences so well in his book *Wheelspin*, published just after the war, and which inspired so many later enthusiasts to try their hand at the sport.

Le Mans

There was no official racing in 1936, but the MG Company had qualified at Le Mans for the Biennial Cup. Dorothy Stanley Turner entered a fairly standard PB to take up this qualification, and ran with some distinction. Her old car still exists.

More Crackers and Musketeers

The Musketeer team had won the MCC Trials Team Championship in 1935/6, after which it was decided that both the Cream Cracker and Three Musketeer teams should use a more up-to-date model of MG. During 1936 the PB had been replaced by the T-series Midget, powered by a pushrod OHV engine of 1,292cc, larger in displacement than that of the old six-cylinder Magnette, and the car which was a much larger vehicle than the Midget had hitherto been, featured hydraulic brakes and hydraulic suspension dampers. The engine was based on the new Morris Ten model, and both Wolseley and MG were required to use the new range of Morris designed power units and transmissions in their

For 1936, the Cream Crackers had supercharged PB cars. Toulmin climbs Simms Hill on the Exeter.

vehicles, although both were actually manufactured at the old Wolseley factory.

Although apparently a retrograde step from the engineering point of view, there was no doubting that the new engine gave the Midget a very useful turn of speed, even if it could not match the N-type Magnette! The larger body made the car much more comfortable, and the ride of the car was improved immeasurably by using the wheelbase and track dimensions of the N-type. The transmission was by way of a Morris oil bath clutch and a four-speed gearbox. The former was not in the least sporting, being attached to a very heavy flywheel, while the latter was of reasonably close ratios . . . but the torque curve of the engine was such that gear changing was less essential than it had been on the earlier cars! All in all it was a good road car, but an unlikely contender for honours in the sporting world. Just how wrong this notion was came to be proved over the following few years.

The Magnette meanwhile was to be replaced by a new series of more luxurious cars, known at the time as the 'One-and-a-half litre', although powered by an engine of more than that capacity. It was a four-cylinder pushrod OHV unit of 1,548cc, and this car featured a full synchromesh gearbox for the first time in an MG.

The range of cars was actually preceded by the announcement of the 'Two-litre MG' called the SA type, announced at the end of 1935, but not in full production until later the following year. This car offered a six-cylinder engine of 2,233cc and a very

luxurious body styling very much in the character of post-war Jaguar cars. Indeed it is significant that the SS Company brought out a very similar car very shortly after the announcement of the new MG, but that it was MG who first used the sales slogan 'For Grace, for Space, for Pace'. This model was only to feature very slightly in sporting events.

Kohlrausch and Magic Midget: EX154

During 1934, George Eyston sold the *Magic Midget* to Bobby Kohlrausch, the German driver, who had performed very well in loaned J4 and K3 cars. These cars were loaned through the Factory on the basis of a rental agreement, and when they came back to England, Kohlrausch stated that he was looking for something faster. An agreement with Kimber allowed for the car to be maintained at the Factory. During the winter of 1934/35 it was completely rebuilt at the Factory.

Alongside the old record-breaker, Kohlrausch commissioned the building of a special P-type car, fitted with a J4 style body, and powered by a new Q-type engine. The car was built under Project EX154. This car was used in road racing events, while EX127 was used for track racing, and even to set a new standard of 130mph for the straight mile and kilometre.

During 1936, the cars were run by club drivers, who had bought them. Here, MacDermid almost literally flies through the gate at Worthy Lane.

At the end of 1936, both cars were returned to Abingdon for overhaul. However, Kohlrausch stated that he wanted to get the speed up to 140mph, but, after consultation with Enever, Jackson said that it would not be possible to increase the power of the old two-bearing engine to achieve this speed. The idea was then hatched to amalgamate the two cars, working under EX154 to hide the activities from the Cowley 'bean counting' department. As it turned out this work was complex, and it was some time before it was delivered. The work was more far reaching than originally planned, and the project must have cost quite a lot of money. Some of this came from Kohlrausch himself, while Jack Woodhouse, the German MG agent in Frankfurt was also said to have sponsored the project, which was felt to be worthwhile.

The chassis side rails were changed to P-type, which resulted in the car being longer. An N-type front axle was fitted, making the car crab-tracked, and because of these revisions, a new body was made, complete with a cowl similar in concept to that used on the R-type.

The engine was a specially built R-type unit using a cylinder head cast in bronze, to help dissipate the extra heat produced from the use of higher boost pressures than had been previously used. It is not completely clear how high this went, but certainly over 30psi was used for short bursts, and Laurence Pomeroy Junior told me that up to 40 was tried. I do not think that this was at MG, however, as all the power curves which I saw related to absolute pressures of up to 50psi, or 3.3 bar, that is 35psi boost . . . still high pressure by anyone's standard and not equalled until the immediate post-war era of grand prix racing.

The engine eventually gave up to 164bhp on test, while when supplied to Kohlrausch it gave a reliable 140mph. Much of the development of the engine was done under the supervision of Reg Jackson, once more working on this activity in his own time. Arthur Baldt, Kohlrausch's personal mechanic, was doing the actual handwork on the dynamometer at Abingdon, and apparently, at one stage, was having endless problems if the engine was held at maximum speed for more than a minute, with a bad misfire. Jacko realised that in the bronze head, the valve guides were too short. These were also bronze, and there was no suitable bar stock in Abingdon. As it was a Sunday, none was to be had, so Baldt cut the guides in half, and used a piece of cast-iron guide ⅜in long as a spacer, and pressed all three pieces into the cylinder head. This modification was successful, and the engine ran cleanly.

So far as anyone at Abingdon knew these were never removed, and the engine took the car in this form to win a few races, but achieved immortality for being the first 750cc car to better 140mph at Gyon, Hungary, in 1936. It was, of course, coincidence that Reg Jackson was on holiday there at the time!

The 750cc Outer Circuit record

George Harvey-Noble bought two Q-type MG cars, and proceeded during 1937, with the help of Robin Jackson at Brooklands, to make a very fast single-seater, primarily with the view of attacking national British records. The car was actually built up from two, one being the ex-Dudley Froy car, which provided the basis and chassis frame. The ex-Dudley Folland car had been written off in a racing accident, and it provided various spares for the car. The chassis frame was standard,

The modified Q-type used by George Harvey-Noble to take the Class H Brooklands Outer Circuit lap record at over 122mph.

but a K3 front axle was fitted. The engine was a fairly standard Q-type unit, although a bronze cylinder head was obtained for the car, apparently from the works, where a spare existed from the Kohlrausch car. The preselector gearbox was done away with and an ENV crash box, as fitted to the J4, was used. A narrow single-seater body was constructed, and the car started to run at Brooklands meetings.

In this he was very successful, culminating on 18 August in taking the Outer Circuit Class Record at a resounding 122.42mph. Not bad for a three-year-old racing car powered by an engine of 750cc!

Twin cam R-types and K3

An interesting diversion was the production of a twin cam cylinder head for use on R and K3 models. This was produced by Michael McEvoy, with some technical advice from Lawrence Pomeroy Junior, and in fact three of the four cylinder heads were made and sold to Graham Evans. These were fitted to three R-type cars, but the project was not well thought out, and cannot be described as successful. The works had nothing to do with these at all.

The six-cylinder head was sold direct to Reg Parnell, and fitted to his ex-Hamilton K3. This project proved more successful, and although still only a 1,100, it frequently ran ahead of 1,500cc ERAs but more often than not failed in the longer distance events. Nevertheless the car scored some worthwhile results right up to the outbreak of the war, and even a couple after!

12-Hour Sports Car Race, Donington 1937

In this event, which has not been written up for a long time in any detail, a team of MGs was entered by the works, and featured the three team cars of the Three Musketeers driven jointly by the drivers of both the Cream Crackers and the Three Musketeers. The cars were the TA Midgets, with superchargers removed, and were team managed by John Thornley.

The intention of the organisers was to provide a competition in which standard sports cars would run, and had it been run to this strict format may well have been repeated. It was almost certainly seen at Abingdon as an event they could justifiably take part in. However, the race itself was marred by a tragic incident in which a driver of an AC car was killed, but from the MG point of view it was a success. They ran reliably, and finished eighth, ninth and 17th and won the Team Prize for the event. This proved to be the only time T-types were raced by the works until after the Second World War.

Record breaking: the 200mph light car

Goldie Gardner had bought the ex-Horton single-seater at the end of 1934, but for various reasons had not used the car during 1935. During 1936 he had taken the Brooklands Outer Circuit lap record for the 1,100cc class at 124.40mph which now stands for all time. Making an attempt on the outright Hour record at Brooklands, he was unsuccessful, but formed the opinion that he should stand a chance of achieving international class honours for the short distance records, if only a suitable venue could be found.

It was Jack Woodhouse, the resident distributor for Morris and MG cars in Germany, who suggested that Goldie try to get an entry in the annual Frankfurt Speed week. Each year the autobahn near the city was closed, and various manufacturers and would-be record-breakers made attempts on speed records. Gardner was enthusiastic to get permission, and formed a team which included Robin Jackson, who was responsible for the preparation of the car, and Reg Jackson, who was officially there on holiday! The two Jacksons were not related, neither were they the best of friends being quite different temperamentally, the one commercially minded and something of an egotist, while the other the archetypal Company man, anxious that the name of MG should do well and not minding who did the work or got the credit, so long as it was successful. Reg knew Woodhouse quite well, and it was the latter who kept the peace!

In the event, the car went well enough to take the Flying Kilometre Record at 142.2mph (228.8kph) and the Mile at 148.5mph. Clearly the next target had to be 150mph, but both Jacksons were of the opinion that the Horton car would need some drastic modifications before it would be suitable to go faster.

In the meantime Gardner took the car to Montlhéry and took some of the longer distance records at around 130mph, and also was awarded a coveted 200kph badge for lapping in excess of that speed. While at Montlhéry, the engine had started to misfire quite badly, and Robin Jackson had changed two of the pistons in an unsuccessful attempt to eradicate the problem.

October saw the car back at Frankfurt, again with Jacko in attendance, but officially once more on holiday, again chasing the 150mph mark unsuccessfully, but narrowly beating his previous records. The engine still suffered with its misfire, which had started at Montlhéry, and which Robin Jackson was unable to cure. Unfortunately Reg was unable to investigate this

but thought that the valve seats had cracked, since the head casting had by this time seen considerable work. This caused further friction between the two, because Robin was unable to accept this view, and refused to comment. However the trip confirmed the two Jacksons' previous conviction that the car was not really suitable for higher speeds.

On returning to England, Gardner therefore approached Kimber at Abingdon to see if he would build a suitable car to achieve 150mph. Kim would like nothing better than to get back into the racing world, but his instructions were that he was simply not to, and the idea of using an obsolete model to break records would not have appealed to Morris Motors at all. The notion of using one of the current models, S, V or T-type was out of the question, since they were not suitable.

Reg Jackson was asked for his opinion, and he pointed out that the old EX135, which had been sold by George Eyston to Donald Letts, was currently on sale at Bellevue Garages, who had been responsible for the car's preparation during Letts' ownership. Jackson reasoned that this car should be able to break 150mph quite easily with suitable preparation and tuning. Furthermore, at Frankfurt, Jacko had had a conversation with Eberan von Eberhorst, the Chief Engineer of Auto Union, who had suggested that the MG should be fitted with all-enclosed bodywork, like the record-breaking Auto Union and Mercedes cars, which might allow the car to achieve really high speeds.

Back at Abingdon, Jacko consulted with his friend

The most famous of all K3s: EX135 in its final pre-war guise. This is one of the few pre-war pictures of it taken shortly after raising the flying mile record in Class G to over 200mph.

and colleague, Syd Enever, who stated straight away that if the car was equipped with a suitable, properly streamlined, body then he thought that even with a standard K3 engine fitted, 170mph or more should be possible. On hearing this Kimber started to get really excited, and suggested that Gardner go himself to Lord Nuffield for official support for the project.

This was done, and Nuffield was sufficiently impressed to say that the project could proceed, and that Kimber at MG was to facilitate the attempt and so things were set up. Gardner was to buy EX135, and turn both cars over to Kimber for preparation to be carried out. Robin Jackson was to continue to develop the engine. Kimber ordered that Reg Jackson, assisted by Enever, was to run the overall project at the Factory seeking whatever outside help might be needed.

Jacko had a deal of unfinished business to complete with the six-cylinder engine, reasoning that having made the 750 produce around 180bhp/litre, it should be possible to obtain 200hp from the 1,100cc unit! Syd voiced the opinion that with this power, then 200mph might be possible. All heady stuff! There was the problem that Robin Jackson was doing all Goldie's engine work, and Reg and he did not see eye-to-eye in this matter, possibly with some justification, for Robin Jackson's patent inlet manifold had failed on each of the previous runs . . . and Jacko was doubtful whether this produced any worthwhile power gain over the Factory manifold anyway! The Jackson manifold fed the charge from the supercharger to the centre of the cylinder head manifold instead of to one end as on the standard MG layout. There was also the problem of the disagreement during the second Frankfurt trip regarding the engine misfire. Jacko felt that there was some merit in making the manifold adjustable to overcome some of the problems they had suffered, but Robin J did not agree with this at all.

Profiting from the MG experience with *Magic Midget*, a bronze cylinder head had been cast for the engine, and the camshaft modified to give a lot of overlap. This should have allowed the engine to run successfully with very high supercharger pressures, but this was not the case, and hence more cause for disagreement between the two Jacksons. Jacko said that the formula should work, and Robin said it did not on his test-bed!

The problem was solved by Syd Enever who was able to show that Robin Jackson's test-bed was unsuitable for the work in hand, there being insufficient air available there to service the needs of the high output engine running at very high speeds. The engine was therefore brought to Abingdon, where it quickly

became apparent that the misfiring experienced now was due to two causes. First the exhaust valves were going incandescent at the very high crankshaft speed being used, and secondly, there was a water leakage across the cylinder head gasket face.

The head was removed, and following R-type practice, the water passages were sealed on both faces of the cylinder head joint, and it was arranged for the water from the pump to feed the block in the normal way, and then be fed from the back of the block to the back of the cylinder head using a one-inch bore transfer pipe. No cylinder head gasket was to be used. Meanwhile hollow exhaust valves were made, and the space in them was part filled with sodium metal, which when the engine ran would melt and give a better heat transfer from the head of the valve to the stem. The idea for this had come from contacts at Rolls-Royce who had used sodium-cooled valves in the engines of the Schneider Trophy Cup aeroplanes. Phosphor bronze valve guides were fitted at this time too. The Robin Jackson camshaft was retained.

Syd Enever was getting intrigued with inlet manifolds again, and decided that it might be better to have two feeds into the cylinder head manifold instead of one, and built up a suitable unit from steel tubing. During the various test-bed runs, Syd also came up with a rule that the total volume of the inlet manifold of a supercharged engine needed to be close to five times the swept volume of the engine, and made sure that the new manifold complied with this. When the engine was re-tested, it ran clean right up to 8,000rpm, and was found to be developing a peak power of around 180bhp at 6,700rpm. A Centric supercharger giving a boost of 26psi (2.75 bar), when running at 0.6 times crankshaft speed, was used.

While all this was going on Reid Railton had been consulted regarding the development of a suitable body to mount on the car. The shape of this had to be known before much development of the chassis could take place. Railton came up with a design with a frontal area of less than 11 square feet, and which was a bare 22 inches tall. It was, however 16ft long, and enclosed all four wheels. Calculations showed that with 180bhp, it should be possible to exceed 175mph, and that 180mph was a realistic goal – *three miles per minute*. Jacko was now able to say with some confidence that he thought it might be possible to get 200 horses from the 1,100cc engine, which for the first time made 200mph seem an attainable target, as opposed to a pipe dream.

Now work could proceed with the preparation of the chassis. The transmission of the old car was offset at an angle of six degrees, which allowed the driver to sit low beside the propeller shaft. The standard K3 preselector gearbox, which had been fitted to both Horton's car and EX135, was replaced by a racing ENV unit, as fitted to the C-type and J4 models, and a Borg & Beck clutch was designed and used, bearing on the thin K3 flywheel.

The driver's head had to protrude from the body, of course, but was to be enclosed in a Perspex dome of the type then being recommended for fighter aeroplanes. In the event the top was removed, to give ventilation, but the screen ensured that the driver's face was not directly buffeted by the air flow.

At the end of the year, in November 1938, the car was shipped to Frankfurt, where permission had been gained to close the autobahn for a couple of hours on each of four days for a record attempt to be made. Inevitably the weather took a hand in things and more permission had to be obtained before the conditions were deemed safe. The engine had not been run since its test-bed activities, but it started up straight away, Jackson driving it to warm up engine and transmission before fitting the hard plugs. He had driven perhaps 300 yards, when the engine died, and refused to restart.

Stripping down the carburettors revealed a sliver of wood in the fuel line, which had jammed into one of the float bowl inlets, and cut the fuel off. This removed, everything behaved as it should, and Jacko drove off in Goldie's SA saloon to the other end of the prescribed run, some eight miles away, to establish a turn around pit for the return run. It was two hours before Goldie was ready, and Jacko eventually heard the MG approaching, obviously with a lot of revs on, and then it cut out, and the car arrived, with Goldie in a state of some agitation. The ENV gearbox had a 'back-to-front' gear-change, and he had become confused as to which gear he was in, and had seen 8,000rpm. Jacko telephoned the timing box who confirmed that the one-way speed was some 288kph (179mph) . . . clearly Gardner had been in top!

The fuel tank was refilled, sparking plugs checked, and Jacko said 'Go back with your foot on the floor, and see what it will do'. Gardner did just that, and the return speed was recorded at 196mph, giving a mean speed for the attempt of 187.61mph! Not only were the theoretical calculations proved to be correct, but they were cautious to some 5 per cent . . . 200mph was merely a matter of getting the axle ratio right!

Jackson remembered that somehow Goldie's SA had gone back to the start, and so he was left alone at the end of the road with no transport. It was nearly an hour before Gardner realised this, and sent Kimber and Laurence Pomeroy off to fetch the now very cold, and

understandably irritated, Jackson. Kimber insisted that Pomeroy give Jackson his nearly new overcoat to keep him warm! Jacko said that he got the impression there was £100 in one of the pockets, because Pom never let Jackson out of his sight until the coat was duly returned an hour or so later!

There was considerable partying at all levels, which carried on until well into the autumn at the London Motor Show, and Gardner received a special trophy from Lord Nuffield, while Jackson and Enever were each presented with a pair of silver cufflinks. Cecil Kimber presented Gardner with a new Tickford-bodied WA car, with the blessing of Lord Nuffield.

For his efforts, Goldie Gardner received the Segrave Trophy from the RAC. However, Syd Enever was not happy. He felt that 200mph was easily within the compass of the car, if the gear ratio of the final drive was raised. He also pointed out that the speed achieved was well in excess of anything achieved in the 1,500cc class, but when the appropriate records were claimed, it was pointed out by the officials at the RAC that the class was for capacities of 1,101–1,500cc, and that the car was ineligible because then displacement was too small! It was necessary to do two separate runs with different engine capacities to annex both records.

Syd was livid, but Jackson jokingly suggested that they could always rebore the engine between runs, and then take the 1,500cc class records! This was not considered seriously at this stage, but as the plans for 1939 were formulated with Gardner, Jackson convinced himself that there was no harm in taking a portable boring bar and a set of +0.020in pistons in the lorry.

The whole car was stripped at Gardner's garage in Croydon, Jackson and Enever going down each weekend to do the detailed and more specialised work. When the supercharger was taken apart it was found to be full of aluminium particles, which had got into the engine, and done quite a bit of damage. It was obvious that the vanes had taken a liberal bite off the casing. Chris Shorrock was contacted and he redesigned the whole unit and its oiling system.

The chassis and body were considered to be OK, and apart from a few nuts and bolts nothing was replaced. The engine was rebuilt at Abingdon, and when mated to its new supercharger was found to be giving the expected power output. The shaft speed was increased, and a new fuel was tried, and the power went up to 202bhp at 7,500rpm . . . remember this was from 1,100cc in 1939!

The news from the international front was causing grave concern and it had become increasingly obvious to all concerned that so far as motorsport

The office of the revised EX135, which Goldie Gardner used to such great effect. The steering wheel pre-dated modern F1 practice by some 50 years, although the gear gate would almost certainly baffle the present day drivers!

was concerned 1939 was going to be a short year, and things passed a crisis point when Neville Chamberlain waved the infamous piece of paper bearing the signature of Herr Hitler at the newsreel cameras at Croydon Aerodrome. Things, it seemed, might calm down again, and plans were made with the German authorities to use the newly opened Dessau Autobahn for a spot of record breaking.

There was a general feeling of uneasiness when the party arrived in Germany. The people themselves were as friendly as ever, but to Jackson and Enever it was clear that behind the organisation was a mighty military machine. Everything was conducted to a timetable, and everything happened on time! The Dessau police put their garage and yard at the disposal of the MG team, while the army provided support crews for everything from mobile canteen to weather forecasting. The actual setting up of the road was a model of efficiency, for some 13km of dual carriageway were closed to traffic, the centre reservation removed, and a black line painted along the centre, all in the space of a couple of hours. Things were then ready to start! In such a comfortable and relaxed atmosphere, even the record breaking appeared to be a formality, with the 1,100cc class records for a flying kilometre and a flying mile being taken at over 203mph.

As soon as the records were in the bag, the car was returned to its garage, and Jacko set about preparing to rebore the engine to attack the 1,500cc class records. Now Jackson assumed that Enever knew how to operate the Van Norman boring machine, but Enever was quick to point out that he only dealt with new parts: in his view, it was Jackson, now the officially accepted field expert in reconditioning MG cars who should know all about the use of the machine. Fortunately, it was a new machine they had brought with them, and in its box were the complete operating instructions.

The first problem was that they needed a 440-volt three-phase supply, and the Dessau police used the 110-volt single-phase supply, standard on the mainland Continent. A word to the foreman of the garage got a military 'obergruppen-something-or-other', to quote Enever, who was able to run a cable from the railway station, and the supply was assured with the correct number of volts. The machine, at this stage lying on the floor, was plugged in whereupon our heroes found that it was already switched on and it proceeded to move off across the floor and try to demolish everything in the garage, while they chased after it!

Jackson had already removed the cylinder head and

the sump, and pulled the pistons out, and checked the bearings for wear. Once the reboring machine was under control, it did not take too long to fix it to the top of the engine, and take the appropriate safety measures to ensure that swarf did not get where it was not wanted. The cutter was set in accordance with the instructions, and the machine turned on . . . the result was a fairly coarse screw thread right down number six cylinder! The feed of the machine had not been correctly set.

Further reading of the instructions put right the matter, and after a slight flutter in the cardiac department, they found that the bore cleaned up on the second cut. The piston fitted perfectly, so it looked as though everything was to be all right. However, the cutter had to be re-sharpened, which was not a problem, but Syd managed to fit it back to front, and the second bore also had a poor finish at first. In spite of all this the six bores were completed, and the pistons were shown to have a perfect fit, and assembly of the engine was commenced. However this was not the end to the troubles for our heroes.

On checking the valve gear, Jackson found that the front camshaft stand was broken, and no spare had been brought. The foreman of the police garage was again contacted, and he pointed out that the official in charge of the inspection on behalf of the ADAC was also a director of the nearby Junkers aircraft factory. Strings were pulled, and Jackson was taken to the works. There he was put into a room, and plied with coffee while a weld repair was effected. Jackson did not

see anyone apart from the director, and was not aware of any aircraft activity, but he was not surprised at this, only the fact that he was taken there at all!

Believe it or not, the engine was not tried before the actual record run. Jackson opined that the mixture and ignition settings should be the same as for the 1,086cc engine, since the increase in capacity was to 1,106cc, at less than 2 per cent, not a significant increase for a supercharged engine.

After consulting the weather oracle of the German Army, Gardner was contacted, and everything was put in hand for the 1,500cc class runs. The engine was started and warmed up, after which Gardner got in and carried out his runs, covering the flying mile and kilometre at around 204mph, and the five-kilometre mark at over 200mph.

Gardner had already expressed the opinion that he should attempt the 750cc class records, using a linered down block as early as 1938. There was no precedent for using such a small capacity six-cylinder engine, and Jackson had said that they might be better off using an R-type engine, but by this time these were not to be found at any price. Lord Nuffield gave his blessing to MG producing a one-off six-cylinder 750cc engine, and plans were laid down for this.

Jackson stated that the combustion chambers of the cylinder head were too big to work with a very short stroke engine, something that Enever was inclined to agree with. In the end it was decided to use a 53mm bore with a 56mm stroke, which gave a total capacity of 741.1cc. This, Enever argued should work with an N-type head, provided the pistons had extra crown height to compensate for the lower resultant compression ratio. A final compression ratio of 5.1:1 was achieved, and everything was well under way for an initial assembly and test of the engine, when war broke out and put a stop to any further work.

Early in 1938, Jackson had been recalled to the works from his itinerant 'field fix-it-man' job, and was told to set up an inspection and production system which would meet the demands of the War Department, and enable them to undertake work for the military in the case of war becoming a reality. As soon as war was declared, the works started work on ministry contracts, some of which Kimber went out and got independently of the Nuffield Group. It was this that finally gave Miles Thomas the excuse to sack Kimber, something he had tried to do many times in the previous ten or 15 years.

Goldie Gardner poses with EX135 outside the works.

CHAPTER 8

POST-WAR RECORD BREAKING 1945–54

THE END OF THE OVERHEAD-CAMSHAFT CARS

Unloading the car at Ghent in Belgium... the ramps look rather precarious for a professional record attempt team!

Strictly speaking, the story of the pre-war works cars finished in 1939, but after the fall of Germany Goldie Gardner was keen to put his dormant pre-war plans into operation, and take the records in the 750cc class with EX135. His car was put away into storage in Abingdon. Regrettably many of the spares had been destroyed in a fire during the war, and it seemed that a new supercharger would be needed.

After he left MG, Kimber had gone to work for the Specialloid Piston Company, and was killed in 1945 in a railway accident near London's King's Cross station. Almost immediately upon leaving the station trains enter a tunnel, in which there is an uphill gradient. Many of the wartime, overloaded, trains had problems following the start of the journey from here, and in the smoke-filled darkness it was difficult for the driver to judge his speed or actual direction of motion. In this case, the locomotive stalled and ran back on to its coaches, crushing the front one and killing three of the occupants, one of which was Kimber.

Without Kimber, there was no obvious leading light who was enthusiastic to promote frivolous speed events. However Gardner was nothing if not a national patriot keen to wave the flag, and was able to get Jackson and Enever enthusiastic about getting the car running again. Jacko had been at MG throughout the war and needed little encouragement to get the harness back on, to do something really useful again. Syd Enever was also available and raring to go. There was no question of either of them being able to do the preparation at the works, since the factory was virtually ruled by civil servants and their piles of paperwork in triplicate stopped any serious production and development work being completed, let alone any frivolous activities such as record breaking. The car was removed to a secret location, which I believe was Gardner's Croydon garage, and in the evenings and at weekends was stripped down and refurbished.

Those who accuse me of being anti-socialist might be right, but in this case the criticisms recorded here are those of the people I spoke to at the Factory some 20 years after the event. Whether one likes it or not, the fact was that in the period immediately after the war there was a dire shortage of raw materials and what there was could only be obtained through the 'right channels' which involved piles of paperwork and endless letters being written. There was rampant inflation, and to quote a fixed price for a job was a way of signing a death warrant on a business, because materials prices might increase by factors of three to five between order and delivery time. I personally remember little of all this as I was a schoolboy, and only learned of the worst excesses of the socialist state later, and oddly enough from people who were at the time declared socialists!

The car, of course, was Gardner's property. All work was to be financed by him personally in whatever way he could. Lord Nuffield put up an undisclosed sum, probably £1,000, and the promise that Jackson and Enever's overtime payments would be paid by the MG Car Company. These two were not allowed to handle the car in working time but Gardner would not have to pay for the use of facilities within the Nuffield Group, or for parts supplied if these were standard production parts from stock.

Enever had stated that it would be necessary to run the 750cc engine to over 10,000rpm to achieve the sort of power they were looking for. The standard MG valve gear was not all that good once 7,500rpm was passed. This was designed in 1932, remember, and the origins of its layout went back to a 1916 aero engine, designed to run at around 2,000rpm! Attempts were made to improve the scheme and various test rigs were built in an endeavour to overcome the problems of running it at five times the original design speed. Without a really radical expenditure of money, which was not available, and resources, which could not be bought even if there was any money, it was decided that a few minor changes would have to suffice, and the crankshaft speed would be limited to 9,000rpm.

The supercharger was one of the items destroyed in the fire. The Centric Company, which had been responsible for the design, had disappeared during the war, but Chris Shorrock designed a new improved unit, which he called the Clyde for some reason. This was to be fed by two 2.1875in SU carburettors. It was decided that the very large blower running at around one third times engine speed would be preferable to running at the very high crankshaft speeds envisaged. Even under these conditions a boost of around 30psi (3.0 bar, approximately) was found to be available on test, which was giving something approaching 130bhp at 8,000rpm. This was actually a disappointing figure, since the pre-war four-cylinder engine had given in excess of this figure. Jackson realised that a new cylinder head was needed, since the combustion chamber shape was not ideal for the short-stroke engine. He tried to find an unmachined casting, but one was not available and the best had to be made of what there was.

Surprisingly the car was almost ready to run by the early part of 1946, with the war still not having been 'over' for much more than six months at this stage.

It says much for Gardner's powers of persuasion that so much was accomplished in such a short time, but Jackson told me that Gardner knew all the right people to contact. Apart from being a successful racing driver, he was also a war hero from the previous conflict, having the MC and bar to prove it. He was not afraid to use the morale-boosting or flag-waving cards to achieve what he wanted, or to bypass the official paperwork channels if he thought it possible to get what he wanted by talking to those he knew in the Government and the Opposition.

Having got the car ready, the next problem was where to make the attempt. German *autobahnen* were not going to be available for some time, due to war damage, but Gardner, through his old friend Giovanni Lurani, discovered that the Milan-Brescia Autostrada could be made available. Preparations were made, the necessary licences to move the car were obtained, and the bid was started in July. Things did not go to plan. The road was not straight, and there was a problem in building up the speed to the required level and the run was called off when the supercharger seized solid.

The car was returned to England, and once again it was Jackson who found a suitable solution to the problem. A friend of his had recently returned from Belgium, and said that there was a stretch of motor road at Jabbeke, not very far from Gent, which might be suitable for straight line records, and why had they gone all the way to Italy '. . . to blow the car up, when they could have done it in their own back yard, so to speak!?'

Gardner was told, and he contacted Jean Simons, an official of the Royal Automobile Club of Belgium, and he reported that this looked a good venue, because, although it was built as the first stage of a trans-Europe motorway, at this stage it was not being used as a road at all! After a check by Gardner, Jackson and Enever, the RACB was contacted officially and the necessary paperwork was completed to make an attempt in October.

Although the Belgians were not equipped at this stage for motor speed record attempts, they made up for the deficiency in a willingness to learn, and everything went well, culminating in Goldie taking the 750cc class records for the flying kilometre, mile and five kilometres at speeds in excess of 150mph, comfortably ahead of the records set by Kohlrausch in 1936 using *Magic Midget*.

This seemed to Enever to be the end of the road for the old car, which had started life as *Magic Magnette*, but Shorrock had suggested that it might be fun to disconnect two cylinders and see how the car went as a 'five-hundred'. This was prompted by the fact that Lurani had been attempting the small capacity records himself, in his motor cycle engined, twin-boomed car '*Nibbio*'.

Enever prepared a couple of pistons with holes in the crowns and had these fitted to cylinders 2 and 5. He also arranged for the cam followers to be omitted

The unsuccessful 750cc attempt in Italy, but I think the car is passing the army lorry!

on these two cylinders, and tried the engine on the test-bed. Not unnaturally, it sounded dreadful, but it did produce over 65bhp at 8,000rpm, at which speed it sounded fairly crisp! It was fitted to the car, and Goldie achieved over 100mph, but this was some 6mph slower than the record.

Enever was worried about the lack of power from this engine as it was much lower than he had anticipated. He sought help from Shorrock and Kesterton, of the SU Company, and between them they concocted a revised blower using 1.625in carburettors, and eliminated the Woodruffe keys from the vertical drive, substituting splines, which allowed for vernier adjustment of the primary valve timing. All this resulted in an increase in power of around 5 per cent, which should have given a maximum speed for the car of 130mph. An attempt was made at Jabbeke in July 1947 using this engine, but 'only' 118mph was achieved. This was enough for the record, but disappointing and was aggravated by the fact that Lurani raised the records to 129mph later in the year.

At this stage Goldie decided that, since Nuffield could not be persuaded to pay for the further development which the engine required, it was time to earn some money, and made the car available to the Jaguar Company in 1948, fitting their prototype four-cylinder XK engine of 2-litre displacement, and taking records in the 2-litre class at 177mph. This was not considered a friendly move at Cowley, but the car was Gardner's and he should be able to make it earn a living if he so wished!

Meanwhile Enever worked on the problem with the 500cc unit, and came to the conclusion that the six-cylinder 750cc was not a well-found engine, so two thirds of it was unlikely to make a good 500cc. On the other hand, a three-cylinder version of the original 1,100cc, with a suitable reduction in stroke might just deliver the power required. Accordingly, Laystall were contacted to make a 64.3mm stroke, three-throw crankshaft to utilise cylinders 4, 5 and 6 of the six-cylinder block, with the front part of the crank replaced with a plain bar, although running in the main bearings.

Syd Enever giving Gardner the instructions as to which switch is used!

The Lucas Company was asked to produce a three-cylinder magneto, which appeared in a surprisingly short time. The lead time was so short, that after the attempt, Lucas had sheepishly to ask for it back so that they could make a drawing of it! The cylinder head layout reverted to standard, missing the operating mechanism for number 1, 2 and 3 cylinders, and flat-top pistons were used. When the engine was tried on the test-bed, and after changing the carburettors for 1.75in units and lowering the boost pressure, something approaching 100bhp was achieved and the engine was running cleanly to 8,000rpm and beyond.

By September 1949, Goldie was brought back to the fold and the car was fitted with the engine, and the now usual party of Gardner, Enever and Jackson went to Belgium to take some records. This time, over 150mph was achieved, which elicited congratulations from Lurani who made no further attempts.

This might have been the end of the story for the car, but Syd decided to try a two-cylinder version, running in the next smaller class: for 350cc. Number

6 piston was replaced by one with no crown, and the whole process was repeated, but the speed achieved with this two-cylinder car was too slow at 92mph to disturb the record.

The engine was further modified for the two-cylinder layout, and eventually was persuaded to give something approaching 50bhp, nothing by current motorcycle standards, but when one considers that this was an engine that started life as a six-cylinder 1,100 and was now a 350cc 'twin' with all the attendant iron still in place it was a reasonably acceptable power!

In July, Goldie succeeded in raising the records for the class to over 120mph. At the same session Goldie drove a standard Y-type saloon, owned by Dick Benn, and equipped with a low-pressure supercharger and achieved 104mph, proving that the new breed of post-war MG cars were just as effective as their pre-war ancestors! This sounded the death knell for the

The 750cc records are in the bag, at significantly more than 150mph.

*Reg Jackson tends to the engine, while Syd
Enever doesn't really want to hear, and looks
despondent. Meanwhile, others are looking on,
trying to be helpful.*

overhead camshaft unit, at least so far as the works
were concerned.

By this time production was under way with the TC
Midget, derived directly from the pre-war TB model,
and then in 1949, the TD was introduced. However
good the pre-war overhead camshaft designs had
been they owed their roots to the Wolseley engines
designed in the 1920s, and the chassis design was by all
standards not a way forward.

The XPAG engine was a Nuffield product unit which
powered the Morris Ten and Wolseley 10 models of
the immediate pre-war era. After the war the engine
continued in the TC MG and the Morris Ten, from
which the new model MG saloon, the 1¼-litre, or Y-type,
was developed. This car featured independent front
suspension, and a high degree of interior appointments,
and was a highly regarded car in its time.

Starting with the chassis of the Y-type saloon, a new
breed of sports car was developed which was to carry
the marque forward until well into the eighth decade,
and beyond. The TD Midget was a good basis, featuring
independent suspension at the front and a supple rear
suspension with a live axle. The frame was rigid, and
if the power unit was rather modest, it was cheap to
produce, and was able to develop a good power output
when tuned. The resultant car was competitively
priced, and available in numbers to satisfy the demand,
while offering 'Safety Fast' in a more modern guise.
What more could the aspiring sports car owner ask for?

Three TD cars were raced by enthusiasts with
modest Factory support in production car racing
events in 1949 to 1951, but then events overtook the
TD, and the project never really developed. The cars
were driven by Dick Jacobs, Ted Lund and George
Phillips, generally achieving good results while the
competition came from other car manufacturers,
notably HRG, and Jowett. However cars of a different
nature started to appear which were nothing more
than cars built to meet racing regulations, and with

The chassis of EX135, fitted with the highly supercharged XPAG engine, for the runs in 1952 which culminated in two runs in excess of 180mph in Class H (1,101–1,500cc).

hardly a thought given to how these might go into production. For a time some of these were powered by the XPAG engine, but then capacity classes were changed, and the MG name started to be denigrated in certain sections of the press for not meeting the challenge. The challenge that MG did meet however was in the sales place, and a notable heritage was in due course carried forward as will be seen in the next section.

In many ways it was a pity that racing catered for the specialist car to the exclusion of genuine, if modified, road sports cars.

The heritage handed on . . .

A plan was formulated to supercharge the XPAG engine, to see how this would perform. The reasoning behind this was that while MG could claim to hold the class records at prodigious speeds, this was using a more sophisticated power unit than in actual production. Various people were racing T-type cars using this engine, and were able to obtain around

70bhp fairly easily, and Syd Enever suggested that at least double this output might be available if the unit was supercharged. He felt that a speed of 210mph might be available for the car using such a unit, in the 1,500cc class. Additionally he pointed out that the one-hour record for the class stood at a fairly modest 119mph, and might be taken using rather less power.

The plan was put to the Morris Motors board, and they gave qualified approval, on the basis that the publicity was worthwhile, and the costs were fairly modest. The latter because the car was, of course, owned by Gardner!

Two engines were prepared, both using the standard capacity of 1,250cc. One had a 9.3:1 compression ratio, running with 30psi boost using alcohol fuel, and developing 213bhp at 7,000rpm. This represented the final, most powerful version of the XPAG engine, and was developing 170bhp per litre – not bad for a stock pushrod valve engine! The other unit was a Stage III modified unit, as described in the official Factory Tuning Book, but running with a 10psi boost, and giving around 90bhp at 5,500rpm, on 80 octane gasoline fuel.

It had been decided to run on Bonneville Salt Flats, Utah, the reasoning behind this being the increasing American market for MG cars made it essential to impress the local market on their home ground with the achievement of records . . . if any!

The car was sent in the summer of 1951, with the lower powered engine installed, and the other in a crate. The whole consignment was carried across the Atlantic by ship, and then across the USA by train, to a place called Wendover. Nuffield Exports, who arranged all this, had faith in the ability of the railroad companies to behave like their British counterparts and deliver the goods on time. However, in the US rail was not particularly well organised, and the shipment was 'lost' for three days, actually arriving some 100 miles away in Salt Lake City! Once found it was a simple matter to get the shipment correctly delivered, and as soon as it was uncrated, the attempt could be made.

A suitable circular course was laid out and marked on the salt flat, giving a lap distance of around five miles. This was scraped flat, and picked clear of sharp objects and stones near the surface.

As ever, Reg Jackson and Syd Enever were in charge,

performing their double act. Gardner was driving, and the targets were all distances up to one hour, both international and national United States. In this, everything went well, with speeds of up to 139mph being recorded, and much celebration following. Jacko said that he thought that they knew how to celebrate, but the Americans taught them a thing or two!

After that it was back to work, and the final drive ratio was raised, and the high output engine and supercharger installed. It seemed but a matter of an hour or so to take the high-speed short-distance records. A new track some 14 miles long was marked and cleaned as before, and then it was hoped to start.

For various reasons, things did not happen as smoothly for this part of the proceedings, and eventually the rains came before any proper attempts could be made, turning the salt flats back into the shallow lake it became at this time of the year. The team packed up and returned home, while the car was taken on a tour of the USA for show purposes.

Back home there seemed to be little to do, although it was decided that to attempt the one record was a little wasteful of machinery and manpower. Thoughts as to other possibilities for the car turned to the 1,500-2,000cc class, which records were held by the car but using the Jaguar engine. The only engine at that time available which might have been near the capacity was that fitted to the Wolseley 6/80 car, used by most of Britain's police forces at the time. The engine was actually too large at 2,215cc, but such a detail had never proved a barrier to the people at Abingdon before!

A new crankshaft, with shorter stroke (77.5mm in place of 88mm) brought the capacity below two litres, and work started in finding ways to get a power output of 240bhp+ from it . . . in standard tune it developed just under 80bhp! All the usual modifications for high pressure supercharging were carried out, and the engine modified so that it would fit under the bonnet of the car. On its initial test the output was well short of the expected levels, and it was obvious that the head was lifting, allowing oil and water to mix in the sump. Furthermore, the engine started to misfire badly as soon as power was sustained.

It took some time to realise that the misfire was

In 1952, when Goldie Gardner retired, he made presentations of thanks to Reg Jackson and Syd Enever at the MGCC Showtime dinner-dance, remarking in his speech that without these two none of the records would have been possible – nor possibly would any of the pre-war racing and record breaking successes.

a direct result of the cylinder head having siamesed exhaust ports, which of course none of the MG engines had. It was the detonation which caused the head to lift, and water to get into the oil. The supercharger had suffered quite a bit, and had bent vanes, so a very large Roots-type blower was substituted. However, in due course the engine was found to reach 249bhp at 5,400rpm, and it was decided that this was sufficient for the job in hand.

The low-powered, blown Stage II MG engine had meanwhile been overhauled and tested, and refitted to the car, and the whole lot was shipped out to Wendover once more in August 1952. The plan was to raise all the US national records once more, if possible, to around 150mph.

This was achieved in short order, collecting three international and eleven American national records at the required speed, when disaster struck, and Goldie actually spun the car on the barren salt flats, and collected one of the marker posts, throwing it into the air to land on his own head! It was a chance in a million, but it shook him up quite a bit. The car was only superficially damaged, and overnight the high output XPAG engine was fitted to the car. With this unit installed Gardner achieved 190mph, but a piston collapsed, and the attempt was called off.

Next, the 2-litre engine was fitted and speeds of up to 202mph were recorded which were good enough to take records, but not to beat the speeds of the old 1,106cc unit running in the class below! The reason was put down to wheel slip, but equally, Enever told me many years later, they were reaching the end of the road for the 1937-designed body shape, which needed large increases in power to go beyond the speeds so far achieved. The engines by this time in use were not capable of being developed to achieve this level of power, and so it was that EX135 was finally retired from active service.

It held records for being the fastest car ever in international classes E (1,501-2,000cc), F (1,101-1,500cc), G (751-1,100cc), H (501-750cc), I (351-500cc) and J (251-350cc), some of these still standing to the present day. The works bought the car back from Goldie and it is now on permanent display at Gaydon. If ever a car earned retirement this is the one. Fortunately, other cars remain in private ownership, and these continue to demonstrate the race-worthiness of the pre-war MG design . . . if such proof is still needed. A fine linear heritage has been passed on to future generations, which was upheld for the rest of the time that the Abingdon works produced cars.

PART TWO

THE
POST-WAR
CARS

INTRODUCTION TO PART 2

The opportunity to tell the competition story of the post-war works MGs completes a personal ambition as I have already documented in *The Works Minis* and *The Works Big Healeys* the achievements of the two other major marques campaigned by the BMC Competitions Department at Abingdon. Graham Robson has completed the 'set' with his story of *The Works Triumphs*.

All of these titles, published by Haynes Publishing, have relied heavily upon the official Competitions Department records maintained and later well documented by the former and long-serving Deputy Competitions Manager, Bill Price, in his book *The BMC/BL Competitions Department*.

Inevitably the post-war competitions story of the works MGs and these other marques covers much of the same ground. It all takes place during the same era of motorsport, involves many of the same drivers and co-drivers, the cars were prepared by the same mechanics and they often competed side by side on the same events. Despite this, I believe that the individuality of the cars themselves, not to mention strong marque allegiance amongst enthusiasts, justifies these individual publications.

With all three titles I have tried where possible to see that the personalities involved tell their own story, either first-hand or from articles which have appeared previously. Although I was personally involved with the works MGs as Competitions Manager for many of the events, first-hand accounts by those who crewed the cars are, I feel, far more valuable than my own recollections.

I am thus indebted for personal contributions from Raymond Baxter, Willy Cave, Tony Fall, John Handley, John Fitzpatrick, Den Green, Paddy Hopkirk, Cliff Humphries, Timo Mäkinen, Don and Erle Morley, Pat Moss, Brian Moylan, George Phillips, John Rhodes, Peter Scott-Russell, Len Shaw, Mike Sutcliffe, John Sprinzel, John Thornley, Chris Tooley and Tommy Wellman. My thanks also go to those who have allowed me to rifle their photographic collections: Harold Brooks, Den Green, Malcolm Green, Neill Bruce, Bill Price and the MG Car Club.

As probably more books and articles have been written about tuning post-war MGs than any other marque, I have confined the technical topics in this story to specific details of the works competition car specifications. These are generally very brief because usually the works cars followed closely the factory Stage Tuning recommendations which were published in tuning manuals for most models and which are still available today.

An apology may be due to those readers disappointed not to find in these pages detailed records of the whereabouts of ex-works MGs today. But, as mentioned at the beginning of the book, attempting to authenticate ex-works cars is probably best left to their current owners, many of whom have dedicated an enormous amount of time and effort into researching the post-Abingdon history of their cars.

While I have tremendous admiration for those who have rescued genuine ex-works cars and painstakingly restored them to original and authentic condition, there are, I fear, some cars around today whose only claim to ex-works fame is little more than the cherished registration number!

Mike Allison and I recall an incident when we were both working at Abingdon when, descending the steps from the canteen after lunch and approaching the area outside the hallowed Competitions Department, we happened to see three works MGBs. One was cut up into sections in a refuse skip having been written off, one was just leaving the factory on road test, and the third car was being built up from a new bodyshell in the Competitions shop. The strange thing was that all three cars carried the same – and one of the best-known – works MGB registration numbers! The Competitions Department were often the worst offenders at confusing history!

More significant than any debate about the authenticity of ex-works cars today is the fact that there remains a growing interest in the background stories, the history and the achievements of the post-war works cars.

I hope that today's followers of MG history find interest in the following chapters which are dedicated to those designers, mechanics, drivers and co-drivers who made the stories possible.

Peter Browning

The MGB victory in the 84-Hour Marathon de la Route at the Nürburgring in 1966 was one of the marque's two outright international post-war wins. Andrew Hedges (left), the most successful of the post-war MG works drivers, is seen with his Belgian Marathon team-mate Julien Vernaeve.

CHAPTER 9

POST-WAR REVIVAL

MGs RETURN TO
MOTORSPORT, WORKS
SUPPORT, COMPETITIONS
OBJECTIVES, RACE AND
RALLY CAR DEVELOPMENT
AND PREPARATION

The Magnette was the first MG model to be entered in international rallies by the newly formed BMC Competitions Department in 1955. Driven by Geoff Holt, this is one of the three team cars entered for the 1955 Tulip Rally.

In his account of the pre-war works MGs, Mike Allison had a more difficult task than I in determining which cars should or should not be included as works cars in this story. The post-war situation is somewhat easier in this respect as I have chosen to be guided by the official and well-documented records of the BMC Competitions Department which was set up at Abingdon at the end of 1954. I have therefore concentrated only on the factory-entered MGs which competed alongside the other BMC, and later British Leyland, marques in international races and rallies.

However, as motorsport slowly recovered momentum in the immediate post-war period there were, as in pre-war years, a number of private MG owners who received various levels of works support, principally through personal contacts with friends at Abingdon and particularly those in the Development

Doug Watts (left), the long-serving Competitions Department Foreman, was responsible for moulding the unique team spirit amongst the Abingdon mechanics seen here with (from left) Johnny Organ, Gerald Wiffen and Doug Hamblin testing the 1960 Sebring MGA Twin Cams at Silverstone.

Department which, until Competitions was established as a separate unit, also handled the preparation of some competition cars. Where appropriate, I have included mention of these entries.

Works support to private owners in the immediate post-war period, when finance and resources were limited, was usually restricted to helpful technical advice, perhaps the loan of one or two special parts or, on rare occasions, the provision of a chassis upon which private owners based various MG specials. Sometimes, a private owner's car would be given the 'once over' at the factory before an event.

Unfortunately, the often commendable efforts of these private owners were not at the time well chronicled in the press (mainly because the cars only gained modest class awards) while there are very sparse factory records available (probably because senior management at the time did not approve of such activities). Nevertheless, the pioneering efforts of these private owners during a period when considerable personal resources and enthusiasm were required to make a serious return to motorsport, were notable – particularly as the MGs of the day were not really very competitive in international events.

In later years, for political reasons within the factory, or perhaps due to particular aspects of event regulations, various MG competition activities took place which were not officially recorded as works entries. Some were 'back-door' projects which ran under the guise of a private entry, probably because Competitions' budget approval had not been given for that specific sortie, which nevertheless the Competitions Manager at the time felt had a sporting chance of bringing some success. Many projects were handled by the Development Department, perhaps again for budgetary reasons, or the fact that the cars may have been running with some experimental modification considered too risky to be seen on an official works-entered car! These projects have, where appropriate, been included in the story.

It has been hard to avoid mentioning the many private MG entrants and drivers who achieved considerable success without any works support,

The works Midgets won their class on the 1961 RAC Rally (Derek Astle), the 1962 Monte Carlo Rally (Peter Riley) and the 1963 Monte Carlo Rally (Rev Rupert Jones).

both in international and club motorsport, at home and overseas. They certainly did as much for the world-wide sporting reputation of MG as the works achievements in international events. Unfortunately, if you mention one it is difficult not to offend others who may consider that their efforts were equally worthy. Our story, therefore, with one or two exceptions, has to be confined to the officially listed factory-entered activities.

I have not featured in this story the post-war MG record-breakers, other than outlining their relevance to the background to the works MGA competition cars. The record-breakers were exclusively the preserve of the Development Department and, furthermore, their history has been fully chronicled in so many articles and other books.

This post-war story has ended with the last works entry by the Competitions Department of Abingdon-built MGs – the MGC-GTS cars which ran in the 84-Hour Marathon at the Nürburgring on the eve of the closure of the Department by British Leyland in 1968.

I have not included the MG Metro 6R4 Group 'B' rally project which was run from the resurrected but short-lived British Leyland Competitions Department based

The Abingdon-built Midget coupés run by Dick Jacobs in 1962–64 achieved a well-earned reputation for immaculate preparation, reliability and often giant-killing results in the hands of Alan Foster, Andrew Hedges and Keith Greene.

at Cowley in the mid-1980s. At the risk of offending those who were involved with this wildly extravagant, adventuresome and prematurely aborted project, I am sure that the majority of 'octagonal' enthusiasts do not really associate the marque with this venture, for the only relevance was the adoption of the MG badge purely for marketing purposes.

Winning ways

In my two previous books in this series, *The Works Big Healeys* and *The Works Minis*, it was easy to get quite euphoric about the chequered competition success story of those cars. In the case of the big Healey, this was developed at Abingdon to become the first car with which a British manufacturer could seriously challenge the opposition of the day to win European Championship rallies outright. Later came the works Mini-Coopers which of course became the most successful competition cars of the era and which buzzed their way around the world to win the most prestigious rallies and racing championships outright.

Against this, when you compare the international race and rally achievements of the post-war works MGs, the marque can actually only claim two outright 'wins' – the Guards 1000 Race at Brands Hatch in 1965 (which was really a 'club' event in which the works should actually not have been involved) and the 84-Hour Marathon at the Nürburgring in 1966 (which some may claim was neither a race nor a rally but a rather strange regularity trial).

Judged, therefore, against its rivals, the post-war works MGs may not have scored too well in terms of outright victories but, perhaps more significant from a marketing viewpoint, MGs in competition (just as they did in the hands of everyday motorists) did establish a splendid reputation for reliability. By careful choice of events and selection of classes, the works MGs did collect a reasonable array of international awards.

Most enthusiasts, and certainly the motorsport press at the time, appreciated that while other manufacturers often entered seriously modified cars, the policy at Abingdon was to compete with models which generally only used factory recommended tuning parts available to any owner. The magic touch of the Abingdon team, and the quality of the works drivers, did much to produce worthwhile results.

The MGC-GTS project was an attempt to produce a more competitive race car and a possible rally winner, but its potential was never realised when British Leyland closed the Competitions Department in 1969 just when the project was starting to show potential.

Post-war entries

The first of the post-war MGs to be entered by the works, the Magnette, was a typical example of how the team coaxed results in the mid-1950s from a car with seemingly little competition potential. The Magnette was a gutsy, tough saloon, over-weight, under-powered and often over-laden on events, but it was reliable enough on rallies in the hands of drivers like the redoubtable Nancy Mitchell to win the Ladies' European Rally Championship – an achievement which may not have done much to promote MG sports car sales but certainly rubbed off on the overall image of BMC engineering. In those days a Ladies' win was always very promotable.

Next came the TF, really only entered for British rallies of the period, where it performed quite well as the results were usually decided upon driving tests for which it was well suited.

The MGA, with its stunning styling, was not only beaten into the showrooms by the Austin-Healey 100, when BMC favoured the Warwick-designed sports car against Abingdon's offering, but it was later also eclipsed in international competitions, and certainly in rallying, by the sheer speed of the works big Healeys – confirming the maxim that in motorsport there is generally no substitute for power. The MGA Twin-Cam, however, was a better proposition, and racing successes in particular did something to redeem the car's poor reputation for engine reliability.

The MGA, and its successor the MGB, both suffered from being around at a time when the Appendix J international motorsporting regulations were not kind to production cars in competition and MGs usually had to compete against the specialised lightweight sports racing machinery of the day. Furthermore, MGs invariably found themselves in the same 2-litre class as the most expensive and competitive production sports car of the era – the Porsche. While enthusiasts generally appreciated that MG versus Porsche was not a fair contest, it was significant that the works MGs in long-distance races were seldom beaten by their commercial British rivals – Sunbeam, Lotus, Austin-Healey, Triumph and even Jaguar.

The MGB arrived on the competition scene at the

end of the big Healey's reign, and by this time the Mini-Cooper was spearheading Abingdon's competition entries. For rallying, therefore, the works MGBs were only used to compete for the occasional GT category award. On the race tracks, however, the MGB fared well at Le Mans and particularly at Sebring where it achieved the important objective of promoting US sales.

Because of the agreement that the Donald Healey Motor Company at Warwick would handle all works Sprite racing activities, Abingdon's only involvement with the Midget was a brief rally programme on the RAC Rally and the Monte Carlo Rally where the cars ran well in the GT category. The highly competitive and successful Dick Jacobs' Midgets racing programme was one of those private entry projects that nevertheless evolved through Abingdon and is therefore included in our story.

Finally, there was a glimmer of hope that MG could have an outright winner on rallies, and possibly be more competitive on the race tracks, with the works MGC-GTS project which was starting to show promise in the late 1960s, but this arrived on the scene just as the British Leyland axe was about to fall on Competitions.

Competitions policy

Whatever the model entered by the works, the overriding objective of MG's post-war international competition programme, was really to demonstrate reliability rather than 'winning' potential – more effectively achieved in racing than rallying. The policy was to compete with cars which closely resembled the production model and which the customer could buy and race or rally himself. With the MGA, Midget and MGB, a complete range of works-approved competition parts and tuning manuals were available to the private owner. The works cars were usually presented externally in 'showroom' trim, running with standard hardtops, bumpers in place and fully-trimmed interiors. Very seldom did technical modifications stray much beyond the works-approved stage tuning kits.

There was no doubt that there were those qualified within MG's Development Department who could

The first of the three single-car MGB entries for Le Mans in 1963, with the aerodynamic 'droop-snout' nose.

THE WORKS MGs

have designed and built a 'racer' with a chassis that could have been as good as the opposition of the day. There was probably also the expertise at Longbridge and Coventry to provide an equally appropriate competition power unit. More than one such project was on the drawing board at MG but none saw the light of day. These 'specials' might have produced a few more class wins, and possibly achieved what in today's grand prix parlance is called a 'podium finish'. But this would have cost a fortune, there would probably have been little feedback to production and certainly such projects would have diverted valuable design resources and expertise from production work. Whether it would have actually promoted the sale of more cars is always questionable.

My most vivid memory of the value of MG's style of competition during the period was at Le Mans when the British contingent of spectators who braved an all-night sitting in the lonely grandstand, gave a hearty cheer and waved a Union Jack every time the red and white MGB with its distinctive exhaust note bumbled by on yet another lap. The MG was really the only true production car entered for the race, keeping going to finish well-

placed while so many Ferraris, Porsches and other exotica failed to last the distance. The hat-trick of Le Mans finishes with a single car entry was a worthy effort.

Development

In comparison with today's works race and rally teams, there was really very little development and testing done on MGs by the Competitions Department. The works MGs, however, perhaps did receive a little more attention than other BMC and later British Leyland marques from the Development Department next door because of Abingdon's infectious enthusiasm and pride in the cars. MG marque loyalty was demonstrated after Paddy Hopkirk's momentous Monte Carlo Rally victory with the Mini-Cooper in 1964 when the victorious team returned to the Abingdon factory to find all the flags flying. Some were convinced that amongst the MG workforce this was more to celebrate Don Morley winning the GT category in an MGB than the remarkable Monte Mini victory!

Under-bonnet view of the 1965 Le Mans MGB.

Pre-event testing of the works cars in those days was pretty basic. Cliff Humphries, Abingdon's resident engine tuning wizard who was responsible in later years for all of the engine development of the works cars, typified the situation with his comments on the pre-rally testing of the first works Minis.

'We took the cars up the road by a local golf course, gave them full stick along the flat, starting opposite an AA box. If they pulled 5,800 in top by the end of the straight, that was good enough. If they pulled any more it was probably a faulty rev counter!'

It was not until the mid-1960s that Competitions was allowed the use of a rolling road at Abingdon and very seldom was it possible to make use of the limited and pretty primitive MG engine test-bed facilities.

Tony Fall, a regular member of the works Mini-Cooper team in the mid-1960s and who drove a works MGB on the Monte Carlo Rally in 1966, once commented that a typical Abingdon pre-event shakedown for a rally car at the time was little more sophisticated than allowing the legendary Timo Mäkinen a quick burst around the car park, up and down the rows of shiny new MGs and Austin-Healeys awaiting their pre-delivery check. If Timo brought the car back in one piece and did not say anything it was considered good enough!

Development as far as the works MGs were concerned was really aimed at seeking continued reliability rather than a search for more performance. Post-event job sheets were usually confined to finding a solution to any problems that occurred on the event and making sure that this was applied to the preparation of the cars next time out. As far as the chassis and suspension was concerned, development was minimal, even on rallies. Any engine improvements were extremely conservative and seldom went further than updating with the latest tuning manual recommendations.

The preparation of the Sebring race MGs presented its own problems. With the race being run in March, and allowing time for the cars to be shipped across to the United States by boat, unpacked by BMC in New York and taken down to Florida by trailer, the MGAs and MGBs were usually built around the time of the Monte Carlo Rally which was always the most hectic time for the Department. Preparing race cars in the depths of the British winter to be raced in the tropical heat of Florida presented its own difficulties. More than once it was hard to find British circuits which were open for testing at this time of the year and, more often than not, the best that could be arranged was one or two days at Silverstone on a freezing, wet or damp track. Often the mechanics had to run the race cars in themselves at night driving around Abingdon's often snowy and icy lanes.

Mechanic's magic

In complete contrast to the preparation of works competition cars today, where a whole army of highly-qualified specialist technicians individually handle various aspects of the car's build, all of the Abingdon works cars were hand-built by one mechanic responsible for the complete car. This included all chassis and body modifications, suspension tweaks, brake modifications, complete engine assembly and

Generally the works-entered MGs ran in near-showroom form with bumpers in place, standard hardtops and full interior trim. Engine modifications were usually in line with the Stage Tuning Manual recommendations. This is Tony Fall's car for the 1966 Monte Carlo Rally.

tuning, transmission assembly, testing the car and running it in. Wherever possible the mechanic who built the car also went on the event so that he could look after 'his' car.

Mechanic Brian Moylan recalls that they had to be quite inventive.

'Reclining seats were a luxury item not found in BMC cars of that period and we were instructed to make a passenger's seat fold back so that the crew could rest when not driving. We were not given any more specification than that and were left to do the job in the best way that we could. Ron Bettles, one of the fitters that joined the Department when we broke away from Development, came up with a device which incorporated the use of the long screw part of a wind-up jack. The seat frame was cut at the joint of the back of the seat and bolted together to form a hinge, a bar was welded across the bottom of the seat back with the nut from the jack in the middle. The screw with its handle was fixed to the front of the seat for the occupant to wind the back up or down. It worked a treat.'

In the case of the preparation of MGAs and MGBs, the mechanics usually started with a complete standard production car off the line, unlike the works Mini-Coopers which were usually built up from trimmed body shells. The reason for this was that

The extreme British winter meant that pre-race testing for the MGB's race debut at Sebring in 1963 had to be carried out on a snow-covered airfield. As a result an oil surge problem under race conditions did not show up and both works cars blew their engines.

body and chassis-wise the MGs were little modified and starting with a complete car off the line was easier than working from a bare shell because the mechanic had available all the production parts that he required. It was often more difficult, for example, to raise a purchase order for a standard window winder or a piece of trim than for a special competition component.

Finally a word about the all-important Abingdon mechanics. Surprisingly very few of them actually started with any specific experience in competition car preparation. Most of the team's top mechanics began as tea boys or served time in Competitions as part of their general MG apprenticeship. They started by washing the cars, perhaps changing wheels, stripping an old recce car to be written off and then learning all they could from working alongside the more experienced members of the team. It was amazing that as individuals they all became brilliant and resourceful mechanics while collectively the team was acknowledged worldwide as the best in the business.

Their efforts were to win post-war international fame for MG just as their predecessors had done pre-war in racing and record breaking.

CHAPTER 10

T-TYPES AND MAGNETTES 1949–55

SUPPORT TO PRIVATE OWNERS, TCs AND TDs AT SILVERSTONE, RALLYING Y-TYPES;

THE COMPETITIONS DEPARTMENT IS FORMED;

WILLY CAVE AND MAGNETTE ON THE 1955 MONTE CARLO RALLY, PAT MOSS AND TF ON THE 1955 RAC RALLY, NEW RECRUITS

Two drivers who were to play a significant role in the future of MG in competitions – George Phillips (20) and Dick Jacobs (19) in the works TDs entered for the 1950 Silverstone Production Car Race. Phillips's enthusiastic Le Mans ventures with a T-type-based special led to the birth of the MGA while Jacobs was to run successful MGA Twin-Cam and Midget racing teams.

M otorsport in Britain immediately after the Second World War took some time to recover. There was a serious lack of suitable venues although enthusiasts did discover various disused airfields for illicit race meetings and speed events while hill-climbs became very popular. Most enthusiasts could not afford much, there was a severe shortage of petrol and spares while manufacturers were too busy trying to get back to full-time production to even consider either works entries or supporting the more determined private owners in competitions.

The MG marque, however, was amongst the first to rekindle some of the pre-war motorsporting spirit, obviously a lot of enthusiasts who had stored MGs through the war were anxious to get them running again. The post-war sales of the TC were picking up and providing a whole new generation with their first sports car ready to be used in competition.

Silverstone first echoed to the sounds of serious motor racing with the running of the RAC Grand Prix in 1948 and, in the following year, the circuit pioneered the first One Hour Production Car Race – a popular novelty complete with Le Mans-style start.

Three MG enthusiasts – George Phillips, Dick Jacobs and Ted Lund (each of whom were to play a significant role in MG's post-war motorsport revival), persuaded Abingdon's General Manager, John Thornley, that MG should be represented with a team of TCs at Silverstone. Thornley instructed Alec Hounslow from Development to provide three cars and these were to finish fifth, sixth and seventh overall, averaging 70mph running in completely standard trim, even to side-screens in place. Everyone was impressed with the result but the cars were returned to Abingdon and not seen again.

For the same race at Silverstone the following year the persuasive trio pressed Thornley to compete with the newly announced TD and Abingdon provided three cars prepared to Stage 2 tune. The TDs finished second (Jacobs), third (Lund) and fourth (Phillips) in their class behind an HRG, Phillips losing what could have been a class win when he spun off into the infield. The drivers, however, complained that the cars were not much faster than the TCs from the previous year. Works support was verified by the presence of Thornley, Hounslow and Reg Jackson, MG's legendary tuning wizard who features in Mike Allison's pre-war story.

The same TD team contested the 1950 Tourist Trophy at Dundrod, all three cars finishing a very wet race in 1-2-3 class formation. Phillips, with co-driver Raymond Flower, returned with a TD to Dundrod in the following year and won the production car class.

Rally revival

Post-war rallying was slow to be revived but amongst the first events to be run were the Monte Carlo Rally, the Alpine Rally and the very tough Liège-Rome-Liège Marathon. Apart from these classic events there were few internationals where British crews and cars competed.

One of the first recorded MG private owners to receive unofficial works support for post-war rallies was Terry Heath who entered the 1948 Lisbon Rally in a Y-type. He blew the engine up but at least won the Concours d'Elegance and, as a result, the local dealer was reported to have taken orders for a few extra MGs which must have justified Abingdon's support.

The redoubtable Betty Haig was another driver to receive a certain amount of works support at this time, winning her class with a TC on the Alpine Rally and competing regularly with a Y-type on the Monte Carlo Rally. Len Shaw, later to drive in the official works Magnette team, campaigned a works-supported Y-type with some success.

The 1949 *Daily Express* Rally, forerunner of the RAC Rally, was the first serious post-war British road event attracting some 499 entries. Len Shaw came third overall and won his class in a Y-type provided by Abingdon and he teamed up with Geoffrey Holt (TD) and George Phillips (YA) to take the Team Prize. The revived RAC Rally in 1951 was won by Ian Appleyard in a Jaguar XK120 while Len Shaw's Y-type came third in the under two-litre class.

By the early 1950s, the vast majority of TD production was going to the States where the little car started the motorsporting careers of such stars as Phil Hill, John Fitch, Ken Miles, Carroll Shelby and Richie Ginther. The first running of the Sebring 12-Hours in 1952 saw TDs driven by local Americans win the Team Prize and one car was sixth overall, fourth on handicap.

In 1952, John Thornley, ever keen to see MG formally back in motorsport, sanctioned the construction of three hand-built YBs at Abingdon at a cost of £1,000 each. One of these was raced by Dick Jacobs, who also campaigned a ZA Magnette for the Production Saloon Car race at Silverstone. Len Shaw drove one of the YBs on the 1953 RAC Rally scoring a class win and finishing sixth overall. At the end of their competition life these works Y-types were rebuilt and offered to their drivers at a discount.

While the TC and the TD had introduced countless enthusiasts to the delights of sports car motoring and competition driving, by now the 'square-riggers' were becoming somewhat outdated. Abingdon had already made plans for its replacement with what was to be the MGA but the newly formed amalgamation of the Nuffield Organisation (Morris and MG) and Austin into the British Motor Corporation favoured Donald Healey's Austin-Healey 100. Clearly there was not room for two very similar sports car models at the time from the same group and plans for the new streamlined MG had to be shelved, much to Abingdon's frustration.

The stopgap TF did not really fill the bill as far as many MG enthusiasts were concerned and certainly in competitions it could not hope to compete internationally with the Jaguar XK120, the Austin-Healey 100 or the Triumph TR2.

Standard Triumph were to win the RAC Rally first with the TR2 and later with the little Standard 10 and, having set up its own Competitions Department at Coventry, John Thornley needed no encouragement to push his new bosses at BMC for a more formal and organised competitions programme. It was entirely due to his personal efforts that in October 1954 he gained permission for the BMC Competitions Department to be formally established at Abingdon.

Competitions Department opens

Initially, competitions activities were set up as part of the Development Department under MG's Chief Designer, Syd Enever and foreman Alec Hounslow, a stalwart competitions man who had been Nuvolari's MG riding mechanic. The preparation of competition cars was carried out alongside the work being done on the MG record-breakers and the development of the MGA.

Later, the Competitions team was to be re-established in its own building and Marcus Chambers was

Marcus Chambers, BMC's first Competitions Manager, came from HRG and had wide experience of racing at Le Mans and European rallying.

appointed as the first Competitions Manager. Marcus came from HRG, one of the most forceful teams of the day, and he came to Abingdon with much experience of racing and rallying with production cars across Europe.

Moving into the new Competitions shop came people like Doug Watts, Tommy Wellman and a nucleus of staff. As shop supervisor Doug was a man whose personality, drive and shrewd judgement of character, was to mould the team into a talented and dedicated unit. Tommy Wellman originally came from the MG Service Division and was to serve as Doug's long-standing foreman – a fatherly figure and a clever schemer when it came to solving even the most challenging technical problems. Den Green was later to join as Deputy Foreman and became one of the most respected and resourceful members of the team. On the management side, Bill Price was to enjoy a long career with the Department, serving as faithful assistant to all three Competitions Managers, Marcus Chambers, Stuart Turner, and myself.

The brief for the new Competitions Department from BMC was to go rallying and racing – and win – with the pick of the marques and models within the BMC range. That was initially a pretty tough assignment because there was certainly nothing capable of winning events outright and the best that the team could hope for were class awards, possibly a Ladies' Award or the Team Prize.

The early strategy was to see the various marques represented as widely as possible to try to please the Austin and Morris factions within the Company. Early sorties, when resources were limited and servicing on events was virtually non-existent, led to some disappointing results and Marcus was quick to change the policy to concentrate on a more restricted programme with fewer but higher quality entries aiming for more consistent and meaningful results.

First Monte sortie

The first official event for the new team was the 1955 Monte Carlo Rally for which the entry of three Abingdon-prepared Magnettes and three Austin A90s built in the Longbridge Experimental Shop had already been made when Marcus arrived at Abingdon.

Following the traditions of the 1935 works NE Magnettes, the Abingdon cars carried the Three Musketeers' names: Athos, Porthos and Aramis. The MGs ran in the Special Touring Category allowing some modifications and they carried twin spare wheels which required a specially reshaped floor pan, two cans of petrol, a set of chains, de-ditching

First entry for the new Competitions Department was the three-car Magnette team for the 1955 Monte Carlo Rally. Seen here, from left, are Reg Holt, Willy Cave, Alan Collinson, Len Shaw, Freddie Finnemore, Ben Brown, Geoff Holt, Stan Astbury and Harold Brooks.

gear and a large box of tools. To cope with the extra weight, the rear leaf springs were bound with cord but, when this was found to adversely affect the handling, it was hastily removed.

Austin's motorsport adviser, Sammy Davis, famed for his Le Mans Bentley drives and later a motorsport journalist but who nevertheless knew little about rallying, had suggested that all the BMC crews went three-up. So with some 5cwt of extra gear the Magnettes turned the scales at one and a half times the design weight and with only 60bhp the performance was not brilliant.

Willy Cave, one of the team's earliest navigators who was to become a regular works co-driver, was invited to join one of the Magnette crews and recalls his Monte experience.

'The original plan was that the three MG team cars would run together each with a driver and co-driver, and the leading car would carry a third crew member who would be a specialist navigator. This master navigator would devote himself to any major problems that arose during the rally, and would work out the course to be followed for all three cars.

So I came to be invited to join Reg Holt and Alan Collinson in the leading MG. But when the entry list was published, all the three team cars were separated – Len Shaw was drawn 36, Geoff Holt got 49 and we were far behind at 58. So the master navigator idea was out and each crew had to do its own route finding.

In 1954 there were few British factory-entered rally teams. Daimler, Ford and Aston Martin had experienced crews but these were all signed up for the Monte. MG therefore turned to the flourishing MG Car Club and selected three successful drivers from the North-Western Centre, all operating around the Manchester area. The starting point for the MGs was to be Glasgow.

Nancy Mitchell, twice Ladies' European Rally Champion, with her favourite Magnette.

We all had some romantic vintage idea that the equipment required was courage and determination, snow chains, snow shovels and a long wire cable with a contraption of pulleys and spikes known as de-ditching gear. We had all read about the Rally and we were all familiar with the legend that Sidney Allard would never have won in 1952 if he had stopped to help his wife when he came round a corner to find her in a snow drift. It was just a question of getting the chains on quickly and not stopping for anybody or anything. Regular turns at the wheel, regular spells of sleep and we would soon experience for ourselves that very special moment when one descends from the last snow-clad Alp into the warm Mediterranean sunshine.

The modern reader should not laugh too much at all this. Our ideas may well have been a bit quaint, but rallying was still pretty different in those days from the state of play today.

One paragraph that has never appeared since, I particularly marked in the regulations. "Competitors will have complete freedom of choice as to the route between any two consecutive controls."

The vital classification test too would have horrified today's authorities. "On leaving the control at Gap, competitors will be issued with a form which will specify the route which they are obliged to follow, the positions of the time controls and the maximum and minimum time allowance, given in seconds per kilometre".

So the secret route would be chosen from a number of possibilities at the last moment, the roads would not be closed to the public, the location of the controls unknown and the set average speeds could be anything. Moreover, 20 minutes late anywhere between Gap and Monaco entailed automatic exclusion from further tests.

Many people scarcely noticed another article and a complicated mathematical calculation which basically started the era of the secret check. But as nobody had heard of a secret check before, most people ignored the warning. For the classification tests, Marcus produced a unique secret weapon for the navigators. A set of *calibrated aluminium rings which could be fitted over the clock made the minute hand show how many kilometres should have been covered. As the speeds would be given in seconds per kilometre, the rings were stamped accordingly. All you had to do was to select the right ring and fit it on the clock to give a sort of do-it-yourself average speed meter. The idea became known as "Sammy" – Short Answer to Much Mathematics.'*

A rubber pipe carried some air from the heater to my feet at the back. It did not seem to warm my feet which soon froze in their boots, but a degree of warmth could be felt by putting the end of the pipe up my trouser legs!'

The MG crews reached Dover after a fairly adventurous 18-hour drive from Glasgow, icy and snowbound roads and disconcerting decisions about which route to use to cross the Pennines. There was an easier run across France and to the Belgian frontier while in Brussels the local MG Car Club provided pilot cars.

'On the second night we completed a loop of the Low Countries, first north to cross the Rhine by the Nijmegen bridge and thus to Arnhem and the Dutch motorway, the first time I had ever been on a motorway. At Amsterdam there was service by the local Nuffield dealer where the starters from Stockholm, Oslo and Munich joined the common route. Entering Rotterdam a police motorcycle escort took up station, the Magnette keeping up with difficulty at 120kph.

It dawned fine as we crossed back into Belgium and with clear roads and the going good at Reims there was an hour to spare allowing the off-duty crews time to lunch and enjoy free champagne. As we headed to Paris, the first of the Monte Carlo and Lisbon starters were approaching the town, the vast rally convoy was joining up and took five hours to pass a single point.

We romped into Paris with a great blaring of horns and blowing of whistles. Here there were notices of flooded roads, everyone was searching anxiously over the next set of maps, the moment for the master navigator was at hand.

I decided to stick to the original route and rely upon my map reading to make a quick local detour if floods stopped us. Then I discovered that the likes of Ian Appleyard, George Hartwell and Gregor Grant had all opted for the long way round. The choice was a miserable one, but this

was the reason for my presence and I had to make the decision.'

Willy's decision paid off for, apart from some minor flooding, the roads were clear and they completed the section without drama.

'As the third night approached, I suppose we were doing quite well. We had seen people crashed, and people dropped out, people in trouble and people late. Our car had given no trouble, we were without penalty, and there were only another 12 hours to go. But the mountains were ahead and we were tired.

From Chambery the survivors from Athens and Palermo had now joined in and everyone was now on the common route, our own slot just under an hour from the front and with perhaps 40 surviving cars ahead. From Grenoble we were hell bent on building up time for the hills ahead. I grappled with the navigation and remembered the article in the regulations that was there to stop us doing just this. We slowed down and immediately were overtaken by one or two competitors anxious to have plenty of time in hand at Gap.

When the road became snow-covered our average dropped below the set speed. Slowly the time we had built up began to slip away. Suddenly we were aware of the dreaded red glow of many tail lights ahead. Cars were slipping and failing to climb a steep incline. We stopped too and tumbled out to push and shove and coax the Magnette. People were fitting chains, letting air out of their tyres and pushing and levering. Eventually our chance came and Alan Collinson, who was nearest the wheel, leapt in and got us on the move again.

We reached the top of the Col Bayard and began a slow descent into Gap. Everyone was tight for time and many immediately raced away on the downhill only to discover too late that the surface was like a skating rink. Cars were off the road in all directions. It was the most expensive five kilometres of the rally but we scraped safely past the graveyard into Gap.

We managed to refuel and began to dither about whether to fit chains or not to start the classification test. The roads in Gap were clear so we decided not to use them. Alan took the driving seat and we hurried off on the first special stage as a faint trace of dawn began to appear over the mountains to the east.

For a few kilometres "Sammy" showed that all was well. I counted down the distance anxiously because we had to turn right off the main road and the slot would not be easy to identify in the dark. As soon as we turned we began to climb a very steep narrow route. The speed dropped back, the car slipped all over the place. Down into the next valley briefly along the bottom and then off and up again, this time the gaining light showed there were dizzy drops on the right-hand side and no retaining wall of any sort. I think we were all terrified and there were murmurs of slowing down. I had certainly never been on such a frightening road.

The clock pointed a harsh finger at the aluminium ring. We were losing time rapidly. Halfway up the Col St Jean, which was only the first of the three 4,000ft passes on this stage, we were again on deep packed snow with a polished ice surface. In Seyne-les-Alpes we could stand it no more, and "Sammy" revealed that unless our speed was substantially increased there was no point in continuing. Several cars with chains fitted had already clanked steadily by us and their advice was obvious. Crouching and lying in the slush, we fitted our chains, more miserable as each car went by rubbing home the fact of our increasing lateness.

At La Javie, where the first special stage ended and the next immediately began, Reg stamped the card and handed it to me to make the calculations. Alan pressed on down the road towards Digne and the Col des Leques. In the slithering car I turned back the map to look for the next junction. I had not realised it but our rally was over.'

The Magnette was excluded for being six minutes over the time allowance but the crew did not fully appreciate the situation and continued determined to reach Monte. Later they were to learn that they had not done well enough to make the top 100 and thus qualify for the final 325km mountain circuit test.

'Only six of all the Glasgow starters in fact qualified including one of the Austin A90s. The three Magnettes were placed 178th (Holt), 202nd (Shaw) and our car, 237th. Experience and ability counted. I resolved to seek both.'

It had not really been a very good debut event for the new team. Marcus, in search of a more competitive car, proposed a special touring version of the Magnette with twin cam engine, disc brakes, knock-on disc wheels and close-ratio gearbox but this was rejected on the grounds that it was not practical to consider producing the minimum of 600 cars for homologation. There was also talk at the time of a special competition version of the Austin A90 to be called the Austin Abingdon and perhaps it was just as well that this politically controversially-titled project never happened either!

The three Magnettes were entered for the 1955 RAC Rally run in March, Geoff Holt winning his class but the event was more notable for the international rally debut of one Pat Moss driving a works TF.

Pat Moss joins team

After a successful show jumping career, it was inevitable that Pat should follow in the wheel tracks of her famous brother and, having failed to woo the new Triumph Competitions Team for a TR2, Pat's father persuaded John Thornley that she was worthy of a trial event with the BMC team. Starting with the TF and then the Magnette, Pat was to drive every car in the BMC team with equal determination and skill, finally winning the Ladies' European Rally Championship. She was unquestionably the fastest lady driver of her era, some would say of all time, especially those who drove against her in the formidable big Healey.

Pat recalls her first works drive in her book *The Story So Far*.

'I was as jumpy as a wild pony while I prepared for my first big rally; not frightened or anything, because I was sure I would enjoy it, but worried that I might forget to do something and excited about the whole idea of a rally like the RAC. Altogether, it made me feel nervous.

The car arrived from BMC and I liked it. The MG TF handled well and was quite fast for those days, but it was stark. There was no heater and this rally was in March so I was sure we would freeze to death. I told the MG people and they put one in and added a couple of fog lights which made me quite happy.

I knew nothing much about this particular rally or any sort of rallying, when I set off from home in my shiny red MG which had been christened "Tiffy". The weather was bad and there was ice about and I took it gently on the drive up to Chester to pick up co-driver Pat Faichney.

At Aynho, near Banbury, the road was really icy

Pat Moss made her international rally debut with a works TF on the 1955 RAC Rally with Pat Faichney.

and I came round a bend to find a queue of cars right in front of me. Somebody was stopped further up the road and all the cars behind were lined up back to the bend. There was one coming towards me as well, so I could not go round and there was a ditch on the left, a really nasty one, and all I could think of was, "Oh my beautiful rally car."

I decided to leave the ditch well alone and, as it was impossible to stop, I hit the car in front. There was not much damage because I was going about 20mph but I lost my nice new fog lights. It did not make me feel very happy about the rally, having a shunt on the way. Besides, our number was 193, which is not a nice number as the digits add up to 13. I felt twitched as we got closer to the off.

The start that year was in Blackpool and the finish at Hastings but the route, of course, went via Scotland and Wales. I had new lights fitted at Chester, picked up Pat and then went to the start. On the way the weather really clamped down. By the time we started the Rally it was as snowy as anything. We were using ordinary snow tyres as this was in the days before studs. I had never driven properly in snow before and Pat had not

done a lot of navigating, so we were a right pair.

Pat's map-reading was not all that good and, as a lot of the sign posts were covered in snow that had stuck to them and frozen, we were lost within a couple of miles of the start. We kept getting lost and the falling snow got worse and worse so that we could hardly see through it. It stuck to our lights too and we had to keep clearing them to pick out anything at night and, my word, it really got cold – in spite of the heater.

In every rally there comes a time when you say to yourself, "What the blazes am I doing here when I could be at home in bed?" That feeling came a lot on this Rally and the whole thing now has blended into a vivid memory of urgent despair with a long, twisty white road in front that never seemed to be the road we wanted and my ears throbbing from the roar of the engine that altered pitch incessantly as I made thousands of gear changes. The car slithered so much that my arms and shoulders were stiff and sore from correcting almost constant skids. The poor car must have been a bit sore as well as I banged and thumped and hammered on the rocks and ruts of the crazy tracks as I tried to make up the time we lost through mis-routing by hurrying over tiny twisty mountain roads.

The weather was so bad that section after section was cancelled and we were cold and usually lost and nobody knew what was happening. Half of Scotland and a lot of Wales was impassable and a lot of tests were ruled out. In those days the RAC used more racing circuits than now and they were really slippery.

One of them was Cadwell Park, which was a motorcycle track, and the snow was so deep that it had to be cleared with a snow plough. They cut out a circuit that was just one snow-plough wide and in the low-slung MG the snow alongside was far higher than the car.

The tests I enjoyed because it was not so easy to get lost and my times were fairly good. On one we had the fastest time in the whole Rally and I was terribly pleased. There were a lot of manoeuvring test in the RAC then and they suited the MG, which was a very manoeuvrable car.

All our times for the special bits were pretty good. In fact years later Sheila Van Damm told me that she got fed up with the sound of my blasted name. She arrived at test after test and asked them who was the fastest lady and they kept saying it was me.

We finished third in the Ladies' in the end and might have done a bit better if we had not lost ourselves so much on the road. Still, I was happy and BMC were quite pleased. They told me that I could hold on to the car to use it for any competitions I wanted, although of course they would not pay expenses or anything.'

Pat immediately went on to win her first race in the TF, a Ladies' Handicap Race at Goodwood, despite her competition number being 67 which again added up to unlucky 13. Pat was sure that everyone said that she was bound to win because she was Stirling's sister and generously acknowledged that she was given a very kind handicap time for the race.

Competitive TF

Although spurned by certain MG enthusiasts, the TF was actually quite a suitable car for the UK rallies of the day. Events like the RAC Rally, the Scottish Rally

Ann Wisdom helps to provide more rear-wheel traction for Pat Moss's TF in the London Rally, September 1955.

and the Circuit of Ireland, all followed a similar pattern with results decided upon short speed tests and what today are called autotests. Road sections were not too demanding and penalties were more likely to be lost through poor navigation than driving errors. These were the days when crews set out with bundles of Ordnance Survey maps as against the use today of fully-illustrated and detailed road books.

The TF was quite a good car for these 'rally of the tests' being small with a snappy gearbox, fly-off handbrake, adequate off-the-mark acceleration and firm road holding. Above all having an open car offered excellent visibility especially when, for many of the tests, the driver spent more time motoring backwards than forwards.

Other successful works TF entries during the 1955 season were on the Circuit of Ireland where Ian Appleyard won the class, while on the Scottish Rally, TFs took the first three places in the class and the Manufacturers' Team Prize.

Tulip Magnettes

Following the RAC Rally, Pat was invited to join the three-car Magnette team for the 1955 Tulip Rally along with Len Shaw and Geoff Holt.

Again Pat was unlucky with her competition number.

With the aid of a possibly generous handicap, Pat Moss wins her first ever race at Goodwood in the TF.

'Our rally number was 139 which should have been a warning to me because once again the digits added up to 13. And once again I had a shunt on the way to the start. This time it was in Holland and it happened because I had never driven on the Continent before and forgot which side of the road I should be on. I did some very silly things in those days.

We were on our way to Noordwijk, where the Tulip starts, and I pulled over to the left to read a signpost. I forgot to go over to the right again afterwards and just after we moved off there was this car in front, coming towards me. There was no time to get over to the right. The footpath was wide and clear and I swung up on to it to get out of his way, but he decided to do the same thing and came with me. So we met head on. He was right, of course, but I wished he had just stayed where he was on the road.

Nobody was injured, thank heaven, but the front of each car was damaged. On the Magnette, the fan was hitting against the radiator and the bonnet was jammed shut so we could not mend it. I was going to have to tell Marcus Chambers that we were stuck, broken and in need of a tow – at two o'clock in the morning. In fact I never got through to Marcus because the owner of the hotel very kindly turned out himself and towed us in. I broke the news to Marcus next morning and he was quite sweet, considering.

The partnership of Pat Moss (right) and Ann Wisdom was to blossom into one of the most successful ladies' crews in European rallying.

The mechanics had the car ready again for the start but during the first day a big end went at Frankfurt and we had to retire. I was rather cross with myself because it may have been as a result of something which happened during the shunt. And I was getting a reputation for being rather a mad driver!'

Fellow Magnette driver Len Shaw remembers two incidents on this event.

'Firstly, at the end of the second day our engine seized solid, after the radiator blind control failed and the cooling was impaired. As a result the cylinder head warped and frantic messages were sent out to locate Pat's abandoned ZA. The Stuttgart concessionaires worked wonders, they found the car, removed the sound cylinder head and brought it back to the hotel where the team were staying. We spent what was left of the night fitting it to KJB 909.

Secondly, the excitement of driving round the 14.5-mile Nürburgring circuit at night against the clock when we managed to catch up Ralph Sleigh who had started one minute earlier in a Ford Zephyr.'

Thirdly, the elimination test going down the Ballon d'Alsace where brake fade resulted in a very good time!'

After progressing to an MGA on the RAC Rally, Pat Moss was loaned a modified Magnette for her personal transport, a car which she used for a number of events. The first car delivered to her (surprise, surprise!) had 13 as the registration number so that had to go back – the replacement Pat described as an 'awful' car.

'It was a bright, scarlet modified Magnette – everybody called it the fire engine – but it was so troublesome it was unbelievable. In less than a year it had three engines, two back axles, two or three gearboxes and the brakes were always fading. It really was one of those cars.

BMC wanted us to get more experience in Continental driving so in May they sent us to France for the Dieppe Rally, which lasted a weekend. We used my modified Magnette, which was about 5mph faster than standard, and we were in the same class as TRs and Porsches so we did not have a hope.'

Navigated for the first time by Ann (Wiz) Wisdom, who was to become Pat's regular partner, the girls managed to come second in the Ladies'.

Experienced racing and rallying driver Jack Sears (left) was among the early recruits to the BMC team and is seen here with Johnny Organ and Doug Watts while testing the 1960 Sebring MGA Twin Cams.

New policy

By the end of the first season, it was realised that the new BMC team had to develop cars that were more competitive, step up the level of support service on events and, above all, recruit more teams of internationally experienced drivers and co-drivers. The result was to see the driver strength enhanced with former HRG team members Bill Shepherd

and John Williamson, tough competitors and well-experienced on European events. They were joined by fellow Scot, Johnny Milne, whose wealth and enthusiasm perhaps sometimes outshone his skill but who nevertheless became a loyal member of the team.

Gerry Burgess was a big man who liked big cars and his style was well suited to the Austin Westminsters and big Healeys. Jack Sears was one of the star drivers of the day who started his competition career with a TC and drove various MG-engined Coopers and Listers, was equally happy racing or rallying and went on to win the British Saloon Car Championship first in an Austin 105 and later in a Ford Cortina.

As far as MG was concerned, the most successful recruit from HRG was Nancy Mitchell who was to prove the most consistently successful lady driver of her era, stringing together a series of Ladies' awards, principally at the wheel of her favourite Magnette, to win the Ladies' European Rally Championship titles in 1956 and 1957. 'Mitch' went on to be equally competitive with the MGA and the big Healey.

Support for the re-organisation of the team came from the new Team Captain, John Gott, one of the most experienced drivers on European events at the time. John, who was later to be appointed Chief Constable of Northamptonshire, introduced more methodical planning for events and post-event

With his police training and a lot of European rallying experience, the new Team Captain, John Gott, brought fresh discipline into the BMC team while his detailed analytical reports of events were to prove invaluable.

analysis of results while his police background brought a new style of discipline and professionalism to the team.

While the Competitions team was building up its driving strength, next door, the Development Department was working on a new model which was to begin an important new chapter for MG both on and off the track.

CHAPTER 11

MGA'S SPORTING HERITAGE 1950–55

GEORGE PHILLIPS' SPECIALS, MGA PROTOTYPE, 1955 LE MANS AND TOURIST TROPHY

The new MGA made its debut at Le Mans in 1955 when the cars finished a very creditable 12th and 17th overall.

I f ever motorsport inspired the creation of a new production car, the well-chronicled story of the MGA is a perfect example. Whether or not Abingdon's new sports car would have happened without the involvement of George 'Phil' Phillips we will never know, but certainly he played a key role in the car's inception.

Phil was a tough, chubby, cheerful character who worked as a despatch rider in London's Fleet Street before taking up photography. Later he was to become chief photographer for *Autosport* magazine and was very much a part of the 1950s grand prix and European Rally Championship scene.

John Thornley aptly summed up his character.

'He was a rabid MG enthusiast, if ever there was one; bluff, genial, endowed with almost unlimited powers of invective and an entirely synthetic bad temper.'

Phil started competing with a standard TC after the war and in 1947 stripped the car and fitted a Lester lightweight two-seater body and, without any great engineering knowledge, set about tuning the engine himself. He competed successfully in various events at home and overseas and as a result received an invitation to compete at Le Mans in 1949.

Phil had built up quite a relationship with John Thornley by this time and for Le Mans teamed up with Curly Dryden, who had raced a Q-type, and who ran The George at Dorchester-on-Thames, a pub close to Abingdon that in later years was to become the regular watering hole for the works race and rally drivers.

The MG special was running well at Le Mans until it suffered an elusive electrical misfire and finally stopped out on the circuit. Dryden was driving at the time so Phil gave instructions for his mechanic to take a replacement magneto out to Curly but under no circumstances was he to touch the car because

Tommy Wellman joined the Competitions Department when it moved from Development; he hand-built the MGA racing prototypes and remained an enthusiastic and talented supervisor of most of the MG race and rally projects, including the last of the line, the MGC-GTS cars.

all spares had to be carried on the car and only the driver was allowed to work on the car on the circuit. However, not only did the mechanic touch the car when he reached it, he actually fitted the magneto himself and, to Phil's total amazement, Dryden gave him a lift back to the pits in the car! The MG was, of course, instantly disqualified and Phil's vocal fury had to be heard to be believed!

For the 1950 Le Mans race Phil entered the little MG special again, this time with co-driver Eric Winterbottom, a leading 500cc driver of the day. The car ran faultlessly averaging 73mph and finishing second in the class to a works Jowett Jupiter.

Phil lost no time in approaching Abingdon for support for the 1951 race.

'During the winter of 1950/51 I went to the factory to see John Thornley to try and sort out what we were going to do about the 1951 Le Mans entry. Having finished in 1950 I was automatically accepted for the 1951 race driving any car I wished. I still wanted it to be an MG. The trouble was there was only the TD so we had long discussions – John Thornley, Syd Enever and myself – as to what could be done.

It was decided that the works would build, albeit unofficially, a special-bodied lightweight version of the TD. Work was started over the winter in the Development Department. As the project (EX172) grew, more care had to be taken to keep it out of sight of a Director by the name of Smith who used to come down to the factory every Tuesday. The day finally came when the car was completed and the man had to see it. There was some apprehension in the works as to how he would react, fortunately he liked it, so everyone from John Thornley down breathed a sigh of relief.

Although the company had been good enough to build the car and gave me £150 towards my expenses, their help finished there. They never sent a mechanic or anyone from the works and I was entirely on my own. That year I had as my co-driver Allen Rippon. He used to race a 500cc Cooper Norton. He paid the same as my previous partners which was £100 towards the many expenses incurred in a venture of this nature.

I must say that when I went to collect the car from the factory, I felt very proud and very pleased with the look of the car. The body was, for that time, a very pretty and workmanlike job, with its low flowing lines that looked really efficient. At scrutineering the car created a lot of interest.

There had never been a road-going MG that looked anything like it before, although in some aspects one could detect its ancestry to the Gardner record-breaking car that Syd Enever had designed. The only snag was that the driver sat on it rather than in it. This was dictated by the chassis of the TD.'

During practice for the race poor fuel was discovered from the circuit's refuelling system and to try to cure pinking Phil decided to lift the cylinder head off the works-prepared engine and fit a second head gasket. The MG performed well in the race, topping 120mph, but then dropped a valve through the piston.

There were some recriminations back at Abingdon after the race about the failure of the engine, recalls Phil.

'If I could build an engine in my kitchen that would last for 24 hours and was used daily doing other events, I would have thought that the works could have done the same. They in turn blamed me for being lead-footed so nothing really came of that.'

Despite its retirement, the Le Mans car's outstandingly pretty bodywork prompted highly favourable comments at a time when MG was seen to be falling behind in the design stakes. Clearly the time had come for Abingdon to move on the from the traditional 'square-rigged' concept and a new modern shape was desperately needed.

Phil's Le Mans car was clearly the catalyst for a new design and after the 1951 race Enever, who was personally not happy with the very high driving position of the car, modified the design with a wider chassis where the driver sat between the side members. This was to be the first of the MGA prototypes (EX175). Alongside this on an identical chassis was built a new MG record-breaker (EX179) which, powered by a TF engine and driven by Capt George Eyston and Ken Miles, set new records at over 150mph at Utah Salt Flats in the summer of 1954.

Birth of the MGA

With very little modification or re-styling a final prototype (EX182) was built and was offered up as the MGA to the new combined Nuffield and Austin BMC management at Longbridge. The timing was unfortunate for MG because Donald Healey was already in negotiation with Austin for the production of the Austin-Healey 100; clearly there was not room for two very similar rival sports cars from the same

One of the special-bodied MGA Twin Cam race cars with modified front bodywork.

manufacturer. The Healey design won the day and the MG prototype was sent back to Abingdon, the disappointed MG team being told to produce the stop-gap TF.

It was not until 1955 that MG got the go-ahead to put their new car into production. John Thornley had planned to give the new MGA to be announced in June a publicity boost with a three-car entry for Le Mans but the launch of the new car had to be delayed because Morris Bodies Branch at Coventry could not complete the tooling in time and production cars were not expected to be available until September. Thornley persisted in going ahead with the Le Mans plans – a brave move for a manufacturer to enter an undisguised near-standard production car in such an event before it had been officially launched. Because of this, the Le Mans MGs had to run in the prototype category, not as GT cars, but at least these regulations allowed the benefit of running with lightweight bodies.

The chassis and suspension for the race cars were from the proven 1954 EX179 record car. Alloy body pressings were made by Morris Bodies Branch on the new production tools but assembled at Abingdon and hand-built by Doug Watts, Tommy Wellman and Harold Wiggins. There was a metal tonneau panel covering the passenger's seat and a small driver's aeroscreen. The cars ran a full-length undershield to aid the air-flow. A 20-gallon fuel tank was fitted and a single long-range driving lamp recessed into the radiator grille. A small oil cooler without a pump was piped to the differential casing with cold air ducted via an air scoop on the undershield. Suspension was standard production MGA but stiffened, the drum brakes had special competition linings and the cars ran with centre-lock wire wheels. The racing MGAs weighed 1,600lb.

Le Mans debut

Power unit was the unproven 'B' series engine, tuned by Abingdon and Weslake in Sussex. The bottom end was standard except for lead-bronze shell bearings but a Weslake experimental cast-iron head was used. The 'B' type cylinder block did not have oil galleries suitable for fitting a full-flow oil filter so Doug Watts and Tommy Wellman set up a radial drill in the tool shop and drilled the extra holes. The engines were built without head gaskets which involved plugging the waterways in the head and the block with dural plugs which then had to be refaced. Special pistons were used and the engines ran with a compression ratio of 9.4:1. A special camshaft was fitted and carburation was by twin 1 3/4in SUs. The Le Mans engines (of which 12 were built) produced 82.5bhp at 6,000rpm. The 'B' series gearbox was used with close ratio gears and a 3.7 rear axle was fitted.

The cars made their first public appearance for a shake-down test at Silverstone in April when Dick Jacobs and Ken Wharton did the driving and there were few problems. For the race the three cars were driven to Le Mans with the spare car in the transporter.

Driver line-up was Ken Miles (an ex-pat who raced a T-type special in the States and who was unbeaten in national racing) paired with racing motorcyclist Johnny Lockett. Northern MG enthusiast Ted Lund was paired with Hans Waeffler from Switzerland while Dick Jacobs partnered Irish TC racer Joe Flynn.

Mechanic Brian Moylan recalls the Le Mans trip.

'Alec Hounslow and Dickie Green were in joint command of the other mechanics to travel to the race – Doug Watts, Jimmy Cox, Cliff Bray, Gerald Wiffen and myself. Besides the six drivers and their wives, the rest of the party comprised various timekeepers, technicians, journalists and advisers numbering 15 in all.

A car transporter had been bought and kitted out for its role as a mobile workshop offering sleeping accommodation and a catering unit when not transporting the car. The spare car was carried to the race in the transporter, the other three cars were driven down by Jimmy Cox, Doug Watts and Alec Hounslow. Jimmy had a fright on the way to Dover when he spun his car out of control and shot up a bank, fortunately causing no more damage than a bent number plate.

The team's headquarters were in the Chateau Chene de Coeur by courtesy of Captain George Eyston's friendship with the Lady of the Chateau, Comtess de Vautibault. Here the stabling provided an excellent workshop and the forecourt was adapted for use as a training area for the drivers to perform their Le Mans start technique. The mechanics also came in for their share of training, un-strapping the bonnet, checking the oil level, wheel changes, cleaning lights, refuelling.'

The MGs put up a creditable performance, Ken Miles and Johnny Lockett having a virtually trouble-free run finishing 12th overall, fifth in class, behind three Porsches and an Osca. The car averaged 86.17mph and put up a fastest lap at 93.72mph while the MGAs were timed at 117mph on the Mulsanne Straight. The MG camp were pleased to have beaten the highest placed works Triumph TR2 in 14th place. Ted Lund and Hans Waeffler were unlucky being delayed when their car collected a stranded Jaguar at dawn but they managed to make it to the finish in 17th place.

Unhappily, the achievements of the team were over-shadowed by the terrible accident involving Pierre Levegh's Mercedes which killed some 80 spectators, and by Dick Jacobs' near fatal crash in the third MG. The cause of Dick's accident has never really been explained but it was thought that as the car approached the very fast White House Bend before the pits, where the main accident had happened, Dick was perhaps distracted by the plume of smoke from the Mercedes accident ahead. The MGA left the road at high speed and Dick received serious injuries which were to finish his racing career.

The Le Mans tragedy had widespread implications for the sport in France, one of which was the cancellation of the Alpine Rally to be held in July. Marcus Chambers had planned to run the Le Mans MGAs on the Alpine in rally tune and, rather than waste the budget that was now supporting the MGA competition development programme, it was decided to carry out an Alpine test run.

EX182, along with a standard MGA, was taken on a stiff test on the Alpine Cols, also visiting the Nürburgring and Montlhéry with drivers John Gott, Bill Shepherd, John Milne, John Williamson and Syd Enever. A Magnette fitted with one of the Le Mans engines was also tried out.

TT races

The competitions programme for 1955 had included an MG entry for the Tourist Trophy Race at Dundrod in Northern Ireland, and the two surviving Le Mans cars and the Le Mans spare car (replacing the Jacobs crashed car) were prepared for this event.

It was originally planned that the three cars would run with different specification engines, one with a Gerald Palmer-designed Morris Engines twin cam (which had an 80-degree head), the second a Bill Appleby-designed Austin twin cam (with 66-degree head) and the third car was to be fitted with the production 1,500cc ohv pushrod engine.

Before the race, Tommy Wellman and Henry Stone from Development took one car to Ireland for a test session, Mercedes kindly allowing the MGs to share the course which they had booked for exclusive testing. Ted Lund was to do some of the driving along with local man Ronnie Adams. During these tests the twin cam cars had fuel surge problems running with twin choke Solex carburettors. Later testing at home (late at night on a nearby stretch of the dead-straight Bicester road) saw the cars converted to Weber carburettors with new manifolds. The Austin twin cam engine was generally found to have a low rev limit offering no advantage over the race-tuned 'B' series Le Mans engine.

On the eve of leaving for the Liverpool ferry, when the cars were fully prepared and run-in, last-minute instructions came through from Longbridge that the Austin engine was not to be used.

Foreman Tommy Wellman recalls the occasion.

'I had just got home for dinner ready to pack my bags for an early start in the morning when Alec Hounslow phoned to tell me to get back to the shop and change the Austin twin cam for a production unit. This was not exactly a straight engine swap as there were a lot of special plumbing bits and pieces that we had rigged up for the prototype twin cam unit which were now not wanted for the standard 1,500cc engine. Anyway, the job was done, the Austin twin cam unit was sent back to Longbridge in a box and never seen again.'

In the race the lone twin cam driven by Ron Flockhart and Johnny Lockett retired at half distance with hairline cracks in the Weber manifold. This car took advantage of the prototype regulations and ran with a one-off front end which had lower wings with lower and smaller headlight units. Of the two 'B' series engined

cars, Ted Lund and Dickie Stoop retired with a split fuel tank while Jack Fairman and Peter Wilson averaged 71.07mph to finish fourth in class behind a trio of Porsche Spyders, nevertheless beating the works TR2s.

Sadly the Tourist Trophy was to witness another fatal accident which, after the Le Mans tragedy, prompted the BMC management to decree that there were to be no more works racing entries. This was clearly a bitter blow to the Abingdon team who had been making good progress with the race development programme of the prototype MGA.

Montlhéry records

With no further racing opportunities, Abingdon obtained permission to stage a record breaking attempt at Montlhéry near Paris to coincide with the Paris, Frankfurt and London motor shows where the MGA was to be officially launched. The idea was to take a group of BMC cars including Austin A90, Riley

The three MGAs in the 1955 Tourist Trophy (opposite page) Ted Lund/Dickie Stoop, (above) Jack Fairman/ Peter Wilson (No. 35) and Ron Flockhart/Johnny Lockett (No. 34) in the Twin Cam prototype.

Pathfinder, Wolseley 6/90, Austin-Healey 100 and two MGAs (one production car and one Le Mans car) and cover 100 miles in the hour with each one.

In heavy rain throughout the run, Ken Wharton averaged 102.54mph in the standard MGA and John Gott in the Le Mans car achieved 112.36mph after a re-start following a puncture at three-quarter distance. All of the other cars achieved the objective.

Tommy Wellman proudly claims that during testing back home on the MIRA banked track beforehand, he and Doug Watts 'unofficially' achieved the same results with all the cars, Doug bravely covering 500 miles at 100mph in an Austin A90!

This was to be the last appearance of the Le Mans MGAs.

CHAPTER 12

MGA IN RALLYING 1956–62

Pat Moss on the
1956 RAC Rally,
1956 Mille Miglia and
Alpine Rally;

Chris Tooley on the
1956–57 Liège;

Twin Cams on the
1958 Liège, 1959 Tulip,
Acropolis and
Alpine rallies;

Rauno Aaltonen's
1962 Tulip Rally

Don Morley tackles the round-the-houses race at the finish of the 1962 Monte Carlo Rally, on which he won the class and was runner-up in the GT category.

The first full season of rallying for the new BMC Competitions Department was 1955 and into 1956 but had not been particularly successful. The policy and the programme which Marcus Chambers had inherited was to try to achieve results with the widest variety of marques and models which made car preparation, and particularly servicing on events, extremely difficult.

The team was also trying to support far too many entries – on the 1956 Monte Carlo Rally for example there were no fewer than 12 works cars – Austin Westminsters, Austin A50s, Riley Pathfinders and MG Magnettes. With so many entries there were probably not sufficient top class crews available and this was often reflected in one or two less than worthy results. Nancy Mitchell's programme with the MG Magnette was really the only one which consistently produced promotable results. The team's first major rallying award did not come until the 1956 RAC Rally (run in March in those days) when the team of Austins won the Team Prize.

The RAC Rally of that year was Pat Moss's first outing with the MGA.

'With "Wiz" as my co-driver BMC provided a red MGA. The event started from Hastings and Blackpool, we naturally chose Hastings as it was so much closer to London. The car was nice and our rally number was 79, so having got rid of numbers that added up to 13, I did not have a shunt on the way to the start.

At both starting points the first test of the Rally involved a short, quick burst to a pylon, reversing round it and forward to a flying finish over a line, but cars had to be stopped before another line, and this made it tricky. The fastest car in each class set the standard time for the class at the starting point, which was just as well for us as the Blackpool starters had dreadful wet and windy weather which made their times slow.

After that cars from both points had a fairly easy road section to Prescott for a fast and difficult hill-climb and then we all went to the West Country and had an hour's rest at Bridgwater before starting on a hard night of tough driving and really difficult navigation around the twisty lanes.

There were over 20 controls that we had to check in at during the night and we could take our own routes from one to another, but each had to be approached from a specified direction, which can be remarkably difficult on those sort of

roads. The average speed always had to be 30mph and that is not easy either on those lanes.

One control was on an airfield and it was really easy to come unstuck there, because unless you left by the right exit there was no hope of reaching the next control on time – and airfields, of course, do not have signposts to guide you.

Ann navigated well and I managed the speed all right. On one or two sections we had enough time in hand to refuel or to have a quick cup of coffee from our vacuum flasks but, well before morning, we were tired and sagging mentally with the strain of rushing through the night, peering at maps, glaring through the darkness to find junctions that were so tiny they were almost invisible, and always with the loud exhaust noise beating into our brains and the jolts as the car jumped and bumped over the rough bits of road rattling the very teeth in our heads. Because of this in the early morning, Wiz booked us in a minute early at one of the controls and we lost 40 points.

After that hard night we went to Castle Combe race circuit, then to Matcham's Park stadium and on to Goodwood and Brands Hatch for tests of speed and manoeuvring on the tracks. After Brands Hatch we went to Hastings for acceleration and braking tests and were almost ready to drop asleep where we stood when we started the 12-hour mid-Rally break.

The car was still running nicely after the break when we headed up to the Midlands and a speed test at Silverstone, which was the circuit I knew best because of Stirling's driving lessons there. After that we ran across the country to Cadwell Park for a sprint ending in a braking test and then north to Yorkshire for more difficult speed and navigation tests during the night. Fortunately, that was not a snowy year so I was able to use the speed of the MG to make up the points we had lost and we took over the lead in the Ladies'.

Next morning in the West Riding of Yorkshire, we were behind Ken Gregory and decided to follow him, which is much more restful than having to work everything out yourself. Unfortunately, Ken went off the road and, like a clot, I just kept following him!

We were going at quite a lick, about 75mph or maybe even 80mph, on a narrow road and at a bend Ken went straight on. His car shot up a low bank which gave it the lift to jump right over the ditch and he landed in a field. We went the same way and must have been at least ten feet in the air in the middle of the jump.

The front, with the weight of the engine, dropped well down in the air and we landed with a terrible bang. I thought for an instant that we were going to somersault right over. Then the back wheels landed and I realised that the car was still motoring. We were clear of Ken so I drove straight on in a big loop and went out through the open gate of the field and rejoined the road. We stopped and examined the car, but everything was all right. Poor Ken was less lucky because his car was stuck in the mud. We gave him a hand out and drove on, none the worse for the flight. This time we led, however.

The rally carried on through the north of England and into Scotland for a while before turning back to Blackpool for the last driving test. We had made up for all our mistakes and were leading the Ladies' by 77 points, which delighted both of us. BMC were cock-a-hoop because they thought we had it in the bag. Then I did something terribly stupid – I really have made some awful booboos on the RAC. That year I made one of the worst.

The Blackpool test involved driving fast round an elongated figure of eight and then braking to a standstill before a penalty line. This made sure that the cars were still fit to go quickly and to manoeuvre, and had brakes that were still efficient.

Our MG was running perfectly so the test could give no possible trouble. BMC were all ready to announce my win and I was fairly confident too – perhaps too confident – because on the way round the simple course I passed a pylon on the wrong side and that stupid mistake cost 100 points.

So we came third in the Ladies' behind Angela Palfrey who won and Mary Handley-Page who was second. If I had not made that mistake or "Wiz" had not booked us in a minute early in the first part of the rally, we would have won. We would also have been fourth in the sports car class instead of fifth, which was just so annoying.

Mille Miglia

Despite the ban on racing, John Thornley sneakily approved the entry of two MGAs on the 1956 Mille Miglia in April on the basis that this was a rally and not a race (which is why it is included in this and not the next chapter!).

Two new 1,500cc cars were prepared to be driven by Peter Scott-Russell, an enthusiastic MG privateer

later to become well-known as Silverstone's regular race commentator. Peter was partnered by MG's chief test driver Tom Haig and the second car was driven by Nancy Mitchell with Pat Faichney. The cars were virtually standard except for big fuel tanks, high axle ratios and oil coolers.

The 1,000-mile road race around northern Italy was run that year in torrential rain for the 12 hours, the event being dominated by the Ferraris which took the first five places with winner Castelotti averaging 85.39mph. The MG crews did well, finishing second and third in the 1,500cc prize category averaging 65mph. Nancy Mitchell was the highest placed lady driver and was presented with a special trophy by the local MG dealer. This was probably one of her greatest drives.

It was on this event that Peter Scott-Russell laid the first of many claims as to who persuaded BMC to run their rally cars in red rather than the traditional British racing green. Apparently on the Mille Miglia the partisan followers tended to ensure that level crossing gates just happened to be left open for red (Italian) cars while trains always seemed to be expected for the French (blue), British (green) and German (silver) cars. Whatever the source of the story, BMC Competition cars from that time ran in bright red with white hardtops or roofs.

The team drove the cars back to England after the event and Peter Scott-Russell organised a celebration drink in London's Steering Wheel Club where he phoned John Thornley.

'I told him we had the two MGs there, all covered in Italian mud, racing numbers and a big trophy that Nancy had won for being the fastest woman driver around the Mille Miglia. I asked him if he wanted us to put them into the big BMC showroom in Piccadilly just around the corner – they would have looked marvellous there.

"God no, don't do that," replied an anxious Thornley. "Len Lord does not even know there were two MGs in the Mille Miglia. Bring them back to Abingdon and we will put a cutting torch through them!"'

Strategy change

By the summer of 1956 the team's strategy for rallies was changing, due in some respects to the influence of team captain, John Gott, who favoured channelling efforts into the development of one or two marques and models, doing this more professionally, recruiting more experienced crews and concentrating on finishes

By 1956 the team concentrated on the development of one model rather than the previous multi-marque entries. This is the MGA team for the Liège-Rome-Liège (from left): John Milne, Richard Benstead-Smith, Gerry Burgess, Sam Croft-Pearson, Nancy Mitchell, Anne Hall, John Gott and Chris Tooley.

and thus the likely chance of the Team Prize rather than trying to score class wins with a mixed bag of cars.

Entries for the 1956 Alpine Rally reflected this policy when Abingdon's works team was an impressive line-up of five MGAs to be driven by Gott himself along with John Milne, Bill Shepherd, Jack Sears and Nancy Mitchell.

The cars performed well and gave no trouble after an early problem with porous oil cooler pipes later traced to a faulty batch and cured by removing the oil coolers. Jack Sears proved an early pacesetter, lapping the Monza circuit at 83mph to worry the class-leading Porsches. Jack, however, was later to crash on the descent from the Col de la Croix-de-Fer when the car hit the rock face and turned over with all four wheels dangling dangerously near the edge. Sears and co-driver Ken Best finally got the car back on the road but were out of the event.

John Gott hit a stone pillar at the side of the road when overtaking another car in dusty conditions, bending the axle casing, breaking the rear spring and leaving a broken half-shaft wedged within the differential. By freewheeling down the Col, the crew reached a hotel where co-driver Ray Brookes borrowed some kitchen knives and managed to extricate the broken shaft. Ray then took a school bus into Annecy and found a garage to weld the half-shaft together again, and with this repair they managed to drive the MG to the finish at Marseille, albeit out of the rally. This was a

lesson in determination and initiative to get the car to the finish at all costs, something which you probably would not experience with today's World Championship Rally contenders who may abandon the car at the side of the road and take the next plane home!

Earlier, Doug Watts, in attending to John Gott's stricken rear suspension, dislocated his knee and after hospital treatment spent the rest of the rally as a frustrated spectator with his leg in plaster in the back of Marcus's service car.

Bill Shepherd and John Williamson lost a certain Coupe des Alpes when they booked out early at a control. John Milne went off the road when trying to overtake another competitor in the dust but was able to regain the road with the assistance of a tow from Jack Sears but lost a lot of time. Nancy Mitchell, driving her Mille Miglia car, was the star of the event and won the Coupe des Dames and a Coupe des Alpes with assistance from Bill Shepherd who helped her replace a smashed wheel and John Milne who attended to a broken throttle spring.

Liège Marathon

There was now growing confidence in the MGA back at Abingdon and it did not take long to put the Alpine Rally lessons into practice for the next event on the programme, the tough Liège-Rome-Liège Marathon. This was one of the most prominent events of the period and certainly the toughest on both car and crew. Run over some 3,000 miles virtually non-stop for four days and nights, the average speeds were demanding and the roads appalling.

Chris Tooley, who was to become a regular co-driver with the team and who later owned and raced an ex-works MGA, was to have his first outing with John Gott. First, he explains how the team's Liège route notes were marked.

'All of the sections would be colour-coded, some 60 pages detailing the map numbers, distance, time allowed, maximum kph, maximum and minimum estimated margins. The sections were coded blue – easy, green – don't panic, red – ten tenths and there is a chance of being on time, red plus – no chance really! The coding took into account things like the time of day when the section would be run and the tiredness factor of the crew. These notes were prepared by John and made available to all the BMC crews.

No recce or practice took place in those days – the information really all came from John as no-one else in the team at that time could have put this together. John's own notes on the sections gave intermediate times at various points along the section, there were no pace notes as such and only major hazards would be marked. Anyone who had an accident by ignoring any of John's warning notes was in trouble!

One of the problems was that John knew the country so well that we would come into a village and he would say that we turned left at the end of the main street because this was the route on the last event; I would have to correct him and say that we went right on this event! He had an amazing memory for the roads.

Unlike today's rallies where the whole route is detailed in a road book, all you got on the Liège would be a list of place names and road numbers between controls. We therefore had to mark up about 50 maps before the event; we did not dare use strip maps because there was always the possibility of last-minute diversions. You seldom knew where the controls would be in the villages and towns and quite often they would be changed at the last moment from one side of the town to another.

Nineteen fifty-six was not too long after the war and the Italians, for example, were still rebuilding towns and roads, signposts were missing and the last thing they were worried about was making things easy for rally crews!'

After the event John Gott would write copious team notes, one of his Alpine Rally reports was reputed to have run to some 20,000 words! He also wrote lengthy reports to the organisers of the events, offering constructive criticisms if, in his opinion, the organisation or the route had not been up to scratch. But he was always generous with his compliments if it had been a good rally. All of this John typed himself on an old machine in the police headquarters at Northampton – as Chief Constable he must have had his team well organised to be able to spare so much time!

Chris Tooley recalls John's briefing notes for the Liège.

'John's strategy was to run four identical cars (four MGAs) not to hot up one car to break up the opposition but concentrate on all four finishing, hoping that the best three could go for the Team Award.

Our car was now in British racing green (for some reason it had been the only white car on the Alpine) and quite a lot of work had been done since the Alpine.

The MGAs used the standard 8.3 compression ratio and 4.5 axle ratio, long-range tanks, oil cooler and wire wheels. The cars also ran with ventilated brake drums which was probably unique. Holes were drilled around the face of the drum and little alloy scoops mounted on the outside so, as the brake spun, the air was sucked out. This seemed to work well when the spokes got black which showed that the dust was coming out. VG95 linings gave no troubles.

Adjusting the drum brakes was difficult because you had to rotate the drum round to get the screwdriver through, not easy when the drum was hot and the screwdriver kept falling off the adjuster. I made up a special screwdriver which had a sleeve on it so that once on the screw it would not fall off.

New throttle springs were fitted, there were tougher oil cooler pipes, a new design of throttle return spring, hardtops coming airborne at high speed was cured by improved anchorages. There were better seats but the passenger seat only reclined about 10 degrees, as far as you could go!

On the 1956 Liège I did about 40 per cent of the driving. John was generous and he knew his limitations. He knew when he got tired. We would plan beforehand who would drive which sections and we would stick to it until the third night on the road when, depending upon the driving conditions and other factors, we might agree to change the schedule. If either of us got tired he would hand over whatever the section or the conditions – the safety of the crew and being sure of a finish always came first – there was no false pride and no arguments. Sometimes when things got really bad we would drive for no more than 15 minutes at a time.

Some of the other crews were less well disciplined and I recall on one Liège we came

across the crew of a TR wandering all over the road and we realised that the crew were on their last legs and were about to have an accident. We managed to get in front of them and when the car came to a halt the driver slumped over the wheel and was out cold – as was the co-driver. We left them safely by the side of the road!

Tiredness and the pressure of the event caused some remarkable scenes between crews. I recall seeing two chaps arrive at the finish covered in blood; apparently they had had a fight with spanners and tyre levers just before the finish because they could not agree which one was going to have the honour of driving into the finish!

Some of the Continental crews were less than sporting and their determination to finish the Liège was amazing. The wild Willy Miresse who drove Ferraris and Porsches was reputed to have told his co-drivers when they left the start that either they would win or crash!

One well-known crew of an open works Porsche used to carry a large box of old sparking plugs in the back and if you did not immediately pull over and let them pass the co-driver would stand up in his seat and pelt the car in front with them!

We got very little sleep, there were certain stages which I would memorise before the event so that John could get his head down and I can remember some of them to this day. My problem was that I really did not know how I would perform when I got really tired. John had done extensive military service and this, added to his police training and experience, meant that he knew exactly how to cope physically and mentally. I had never done anything like that and it was not until after we had done a few long distance events together that I set out with rather more confidence. Preparations before the event were pretty elementary. I used to do a lot of walking, and gave up smoking and drinking.

We used to take Benzedrine tablets to keep awake which worked quite well although they tended to give you hallucinations although not everyone owned up to it! I remember one incident when I found myself driving very slowly along the road viewing a lovely imaginary estate which I was going to buy!

Eating on the Liège was not so much a problem of finding the food but having time in hand to eat it. In every town and at controls the locals would offer you bottles of wine, chicken legs and sandwiches, all of which you had to accept. This all got stuffed under the seat hoping that you might have time to snatch a snack at some later point. A wine bottle once rolled from under John's seat and got jammed under the pedals which caused a certain amount of alarm and anger! My fault of course!

We really had very little trouble with the MGA. In particular this was one of the only BMC cars in which I ever rallied when the exhaust system did not fall off. The only problem we had in 1956 was that the drive came off the back of the speedo in Yugoslavia and I had to invert myself under the dashboard to screw it back on. We did the whole event on one set of tyres and really experienced very few punctures. We carried quite a bit of oil, used to change the plugs at times and we were careful to remove the carburettor air filters if they got blocked and possibly adjust the mixture on the SUs when we were using bad petrol.

The fuel in Yugoslavia was awful and we would all carry cans of benzole but usually by the time you needed it the cans had been smashed in the boot and had been thrown out. Coming out of Yugoslavia at the Italian border I recall seeing a fuel station at the bottom of the hill so I drained all the bad fuel out of the tank and we free-wheeled into Italy to take advantage of a full tank of better stuff. The fuel tank floats always broke up on a rough event such as the Liège and we carried little dip sticks.

Servicing was pretty bleak – we were usually able to get only one major service a day. Such was the straight-line route that most of the time the mechanics did not have many opportunities to leap-frog the competitors. Budgets were tight in those days and most teams could not afford to send too many crews. More important than mechanical attention to the car, I remember, was the wonderful thick green soup that Marcus and his wife Pat used to provide!

Most of the time you had very little information about placings at controls or service points. Most of the information came from the crews exchanging section times but you could go for many hours without seeing another car. It was therefore very difficult to know how to pace yourself and this is where John's notes and forward planning paid off.

On the 1956 Liège we had one major incident

in the Italian Alps when we went round a corner and came face to face with a big bus. John had the choice of the rock face or the bus and chose the rock face as it was not going as fast as the bus! This pushed the bumper and the wing onto the front tyre. The bus driver stopped and leapt towards us brandishing the biggest starting handle you have ever seen. I thought that we were going to be clubbed to death but he dived under the car and levered the offending bodywork clear and we were able to continue. After that incident the works cars ran without bumpers (where the regulations permitted) on the basis that if you are going to have a front-end accident it is better to have to straighten out the wing rather than the stronger bumper!

On the 1956 Liège there was a horrifying section in Yugoslavia which had not been used before. The only maps available were Italian, the mileages were hopelessly optimistic and most of the place names were Italianised versions of the Yugoslav names. We set off on this section where I remember the control was run by the village priest with his robes blowing in the wind, and then we had the co-driver's nightmare of being totally lost. The roads did not tie up with the map, two cars followed us and then their lights disappeared which is always a worrying factor. The road got narrower, and rougher, we charged through the woods, farmsteads and I was convinced we were going to end up in a dead end on the top of a mountain. John kept on going and eventually we came to a better bit of road which eventually turned out to be the right route. The joy of reaching the control on time (and later that the two crews following had not turned back but had both stopped with punctures) inspired us to carry on!

A unique feature of the Liège was the starting system for sections whereby you were sent off three abreast. This led to some pretty hectic racing starts as everyone tried to get to the serious stuff before the others, often to get a clear run out of the dust. The problem was it was a bit of a Le Mans start for the co-driver because he had to get the time card stamped and run to the car and jump in. We were handicapped because the control table was always on the wrong side for us being right-hand drive. I used to simply dive into the car head first, slam the door and sort myself out once the initial racing start was over. I recall the start of the section over the Stelvio which started in a village and 200 yards down the road was a right-angle hairpin bend over

a bridge. John was determined to get there first and he did so by being the last of the late brakers! That was the most frightening 200 yards of the Liège!'

Lessons learnt on the Alpine paid off on the 1956 Liège, with three out of the four MGAs finishing, the Abingdon cars coming second to Volvo in the Team Prize which MG would have won had one of the BMC service crews not repaired one of the Volvo team car's throttle cables. (Good sportsmanship in those days!) Gerry Burgess was the only casualty, hitting a big rock when he was pressing on a bit too fast for the conditions – a situation which angered John Gott. Nancy Mitchell narrowly missed out on the Ladies' Award through navigational errors.

1957 Marathon

The Suez crisis and the shortage of fuel did much to curtail rallying activities at the start of 1957 and it was not until the Liège that four MGAs appeared again for John Gott, John Milne, Nancy Mitchell and a guest car for Belgian Georges Harris who had impressed by winning his class in a Volvo the previous year. Little development had taken place since then although the MGs were now running with the standard 4.3 differential (4.5 in 1956) which made them a lot easier to drive in the mountains.

Harris, obviously keen to impress, set a very fast time over one of the opening sections just after the Cortina start on a very tough stage at Giau. This was rutted and very rough, and they set a class-winning time but then went off the road, damaging the suspension which later collapsed, forcing them to retire.

Co-driver John Milne was asleep when John Williamson went round a right-hand corner and his door flew open. Williamson, trying to grab him, went off the road and wrote the car off against a telegraph pole. The amusing sequel to this story was that when they walked to the local village to phone for help they were told by the operator that they could not get through because some 'clown' had knocked the telegraph pole down!

Nancy Mitchell finished a superb 16th overall and won the Ladies' Award which, with her consistent Magnette performances, clinched the European Ladies' Rally Championship.

Chris Tooley recalls his second Liège with John Gott.

'I was naturally highly delighted to be asked by John to go on a second excursion together into the now better-known unknowns of the Liège. That we

Marathon de la Route

Supporting the Chris Tooley/John Gott entry on the 1957 Liège-Rome-Liège, Nancy Mitchell and Joan Johns collected another Coupe des Dames.

were going in an MGA again was also satisfying as now owning one myself – the previous year's Liège car, MJB 191 – I felt better qualified to drive it well, or as well, as I could.

I was determined this year to keep the office work and the housekeeping side of the rally more under control. Last year there were too many cards around and, as a result, I redesigned John's excellent route cards to give us just as much information in less space. Also, having a specially made map board with the right amount of space for map, watch and route card on it helped a lot. To prevent the floor getting littered with odds and ends, I made extra shelves behind the seats including a compartment for the road book. Holdalls were banished to the boot and the general result was that throughout the rally the car was much tidier and, except for two occasions when the map disappeared for a time, life was much easier.

Our research into the Everest Expedition's food packs paid off in that we were less tired and did not have to resort to pills at all. As a result, I had no recurrence of my hallucinations. I did however have a recurrence of my last night "blues" when I overdid things on the climb up to the Chatelard. I hit a wall on this easy climb when I was very tired. John later reversed into a post and smashed all the rear lights so we were 'one all'.

Funny business, fatigue. One form slows you up when driving and yet gives you quick reactions to pull yourself out of trouble when you realise you are dozing at the wheel; the other makes you think you are driving like Stirling Moss and in fact lets you drive fast, but yet leaves you with poor reactions when you overcook it. Mine was the latter!

On the run through the Dolomites to the Yugoslav border I noticed that the speedometer and the Halda had stopped working. This was serious enough at the best of times but particularly irritating here because it prevented me from giving John an accurate warning of when the right hand turn at the foot of the pass was coming up.

To find out that we were running late on the run to Ljubljana was certainly a shock but the car responded beautifully to my demand for a cruising gait of just over the 90mph mark. Although there are many level crossings on this section, I noted that there were no gates. This shook me as well as giving me encouragement against them being shut.

The Giau stage was indeed appalling and I was amazed that any car could stay together on it. The general din of rocks clanking the wings (from underneath I hasten to add) and stones bouncing along the propeller shaft was pretty alarming.

The series of loose-surfaced Cols that lead eventually to Castello Tesino was taken in typical Gott fashion. I had enjoyed being slung round these sections the previous year, and I did so again this time. It seemed to me that the higher axle ratio made this sort of running much easier for the car and for John. We seemed to stay in the right rev range all the time.

Starting off up the Stelvio without lights was my fault but this should not have accounted for the loss of all those seconds. Without any competition on the "starting grid" this time, I am sure John was not so smartly away as in 1956 when we had our regular grand prix.

I did not enjoy my trip down the Autostrada. It was narrow, the edges were badly defined, there were many lorries which did not believe in dipping their headlamps and every so often we had to stop to show our ticket at a check point. At Pray we drank coffee in a little cafe with Pat and Ann although the girls asked for tea and by the time the confused proprietor had brought it, they were on their way to Bollengo.

The error on this stage was in my department as I had not got the map marked up sufficiently accurately among the maze of roads in that area. If you are going to mark up a map, do it properly and don't just put a line across the general direction to be taken. We were very lucky to pick up the right road again – worst moments of the Rally for me!

And so to the French Alp sections. I reckon we made a strategic blunder when we stopped to adjust the brakes just before a level crossing. The ensuing dice to wind up the jack and adjust the brakes before signing on at Forcalquier was something out of a Keystone Cops film although at the time it was not funny. I have never adjusted brakes so fast in my life.

Our run to the finish was uneventful and we made it up with the big Healeys which took the Manufacturers' Team Prize.'

Moss on Midnight Sun

Having driven a Morris Minor through the 1957 season (including an heroic finish on the Liège), Pat Moss was back with an MGA on the 1958 Midnight Sun Rally partnered as usual by Ann Wisdom.

'Our car was OBL 311, a red one, it was a foolish car to use because the only class for it was the one for Grand Touring cars of up to 3,500cc which meant that we were up against really fast stuff with engines twice our size.

Soon after we started I could see we were going to get nowhere because we were much slower than anything else in our class which included a lot of Porsches. They all gave us a terrible beating straight away on the first stage. I think we were much slower than everyone else in the class and I was a bit worried so I asked a Swedish chap: "What can I do?"

"It's simple," he told me. "You're slowing down on the brows of each hill and you shouldn't. You should take them all flat out." I was a bit younger and madder then, so I thought that if these mad Swedes do it, I will. So I did and, of course, the inevitable happened. On the second special stage we came over a brow as fast as the MG would travel which, with the hill to cope with, was not the 100mph it would do on the flat, but must have been well over 80mph. We jumped nicely, well off the ground; while we were in the air I looked down and saw that the road turned left, and there was nothing I could do about it. In front of us was rough ground with really big rocks scattered about and we went through them, bouncing from one to the other, bang, bang, bang, and still in the air. The noise was terrific and although it must have lasted less than a second it seemed to go on for minutes. Then we landed and stopped. The front and sides were damaged and the wheels were splayed out in an odd way, but the engine was still running.

There was nobody around when we went off, but suddenly about 50 Swedes appeared from the bushes and behind the rocks and "Wiz" jumped out and shouted: "Come on, lift it back on to the road." Once we reached the road again we *found that the MG was still a runner. They were as tough as nails those cars and we motored on all right in spite of the damage and the wheels being splayed out.'*

It was while waiting for the start of one of the tests that Pat was to meet up with one Erik Carlsson (who was to be her future husband) when the big Swede came over and offered the girls a slice of his orange!

'We carried on with the rally and came last of the five cars in our class. I do not remember where we came in the Ladies' but we won no points towards the Championship, so our only prize was Erik's orange!'

Twin Cam power

With the introduction of the Twin Cam in mid-1958, the MGA became a more competitive proposition. First seen three years previously in prototype form in the Tourist Trophy Race, the Twin Cam in standard tune gave a useful 108bhp at 6,700rpm. Unfortunately,

the engine's sensitivity to fuel mixture and ignition timing was very critical and this, coupled with early excessive oil consumption problems, did not endear it to enthusiasts.

The first rally outing for the Twin Cam was on the 1958 Liège when John Gott took a virtually standard car, the team's main effort being with the four-car entry of big Healeys which had received their baptism on the Alpine. Despite being delayed by a loose distributor clamp bolt, John was delighted with the Twin Cam. He finished ninth overall and for the first time felt that the car had the capability of challenging the eternal class-winning Porsches and even keeping up with the big Healeys. John was to drive the Twin Cam again on the 1959 Monte but slid off the road on the final mountain circuit.

Abingdon's works mechanics had to be jacks of all trades for they built complete race or rally cars from scratch including chassis, bodywork, engine, transmission and suspension work. They usually ran the cars in themselves and serviced 'their' car on events. Here, Johnny Organ works on the Morley twins' MGA for the 1962 Monte Carlo Rally.

A pair of Twin Cams was entered for the 1959 Tulip Rally for John Gott and John Sprinzel, a colourful character equally at home racing or rallying and who enjoyed great success with little cars like his Austin A35 and Austin-Healey Sprite.

John Gott was again partnered by Chris Tooley who recalls that they did not have a very happy event.

'As John reckoned that the results would be decided on the road sections rather than the timed stages, we used a close ratio gearbox with a 4.8 axle ratio which would make the car more suited to the road sections. Unfortunately, this made first-gear take-offs on the tests pathetic, we had to resort to slipping the clutch and the Twin Cam power band was not so flexible.

We had a major drama on the Col de Pin in France. It was a rough night, raining heavily and because of the bad weather the controller had lost us a minute and we ended up starting on the same minute as John Sprinzel partnered by the canny Stuart Turner in the other works Twin Cam. John was away first but it was not long before Sprinzel

was on our tail and pushing John hard which annoyed him intensely. John was sure that the event would be won or lost on the road sections (which turned out to be true) and was not too worried about special test times. We ended up racing through a village side by side, John was getting more and more annoyed because this, in his mind, was not the sort of thing that should be going on between two team members.

For the first time on a rally the tension and in particular John's fury, started to make me feel ill and I missed a crucial turn in the village near Lamastre as we roared into the open country. The more experienced Stuart Turner noticed that the colour on the top of the kilometre stones by the side of the road was wrong, Sprinzel turned round and it was some distance later that I realised our mistake. John was seething mad and

Above: Johnny Organ assembles the disc brakes on the 1962 Monte Carlo Rally Twin Cam. Right: John Sprinzel at the start of the 1959 Acropolis Rally with the MGA Twin Cam.

from then on lost all interest in the event. John's written report afterwards was unprintable when Sprinzel, who was lying fourth, decided to have a real go on the final Zandvoort race test and put the MG off the road!'

The Tulip Rally that year was won by the Morley twins in their privately owned Jaguar, a result which was to earn them a place with the BMC team. Don and Erle, famed for rallying in immaculate tweed suits, were one of the most courteous crews whose charm disguised a shrewd cunning and determination demonstrated by their legendary sports car achievements.

The rest of the works Twin Cam's rally sorties were generally not distinguished. On the 1959 Acropolis Rally John Sprinzel fell victim to the notoriously slippery polished bitumen roads, slid into a field and his only consolation was that he was promptly joined by a growing number of equally over-enthusiastic Greek competitors who did the same.

John Milne with Stuart Turner crashed out of the Alpine Rally, an incident which deputy foreman Den Green remembers with some amusement:

'When I arrived on the scene, the two of them were sitting on the ground about 100 yards apart. Obviously there was a certain lack of good feeling at this point. I was sent off to a local garage to try to find some suspension parts to get the car

going again and found a garage with two or three "dead" Twin Cams in the workshop – all customers' cars suffering from the dreaded engine problems. I asked the garage owner if I could "borrow" some of the suspension parts from one of these cars and replace them with new parts which I would arrange to be sent out from England – but when he discovered that I worked for MG he gave me hell about the unreliability of Twin Cam engines and threw me out of the place!'

A new era

Stuart Turner was soon to take over from Marcus Chambers as Competitions Manager. A former ace club navigator and later a works co-driver for most of the top teams, Stuart's inside knowledge of the sport, coupled with the timely arrival of the Mini-Cooper was to herald a new era for the team.

To try to squeeze the ultimate performance from the Twin Cam, Stuart played the homologation game and had a De Luxe 1,600 Mark II Coupé prepared. This had four-wheel disc brakes, centre-lock disc wheels and the

Don Morley, seen here in recent years with his wife, former navigator Val Domleo, was the supreme sports car driver, scoring successes with the MGA, MGB and in particular the big Healey on the Alpine Rally.

The talking point of the 1962 Tulip Rally was the performance of the young Finn Rauno Aaltonen who, partnered by Gunnar Palm, set remarkable times in the MGA Twin Cam against the works big Healeys and Mercedes.

optional single Weber carburettor homologated. The bodywork was lightened with the bumpers removed, a new front valance fitted, glassfibre wings and perspex door windows. Twin spare wheels were accommodated in the boot along with a 15-gallon fuel tank by modifying the rear bulkhead and putting a small bulge in the boot lid. With a free-flow exhaust manifold and a hot camshaft the car gave 115bhp. The MGA ran with the new Dunlop Duraband studded tyre.

Don and Erle Morley took this car on the 1962 Monte Carlo Rally and won their class, finishing runners-up in the GT category. The event was run on a handicap formula but on scratch times the MGA was impressive, challenging the works big Healeys on mainly dry roads and over one stage the Morleys beat the winning Saab of Erik Carlsson.

On the 1962 Tulip Rally Rauno Aaltonen, having survived his debut drive with the team on the Monte

when his Mini-Cooper rolled and caught fire, was given another chance – a drive with the Twin Cam Coupé. The little-known Finn's performance was the talking point of the event. Rauno won his class but more significantly on scratch times finished sixth overall behind two big Healeys, a Jaguar E-type and two works Mercedes, actually setting fastest time on one of the Turini tests and beating the big Healeys by some 13 seconds. The crew only had one incident when co-driver Gunnar Palm discovered too late that borrowed notes for one of the timed climbs were actually made for running in the opposite direction – a hairpin bend was called 'flat' which caused the talented Rauno to use all of his skills! As an aside, the Competitions Department were so busy preparing the works Minis and big Healeys for this event, the Twin Cam was only given the 'once over' before the start by Abingdon's Service Department after the Morleys' Monte run.

Despite this promising showing by the Twin Cam, by now the big Healey was spearheading Abingdon's attack on the European Rally front while the Mini-Cooper had just appeared on the scene.

The rallying days for the works MGAs were numbered.

CHAPTER 13

MGA IN RACING 1956–62

SEBRING 1956–62;
LE MANS 1959–61

Testing the 1962 Sebring Twin Cams at Silverstone.

The decree from Longbridge that there should be no more official works race entries following the 1955 Le Mans and Tourist Trophy accidents, was a sad blow to those at MG who had been involved in Abingdon's racing heritage for so long and, in particular, those who had put so much good work into the successful prototype racing MGAs.

Then as now, racing and rallying had their separate followers and at the time when the Competitions shop was a section within the MG Development Department, most of the staff had been brought up through racing and record breaking, so there was not unanimous enthusiasm for the prospect of having to drop the MGA race programme and switch to the European rallying scene. Needless to say the racing men soon found a way of channelling their enthusiasm back on to the race track.

The team had already been working on one or two special project cars for racing, including an MGA fitted with de Dion rear suspension (EX186), while one of the spare light-alloy MGA bodies had been built upon a tubular frame chassis (EX183). These cars were to have had Twin Cam engines but, with the abandonment of the racing programme, both had to be shelved; EX186 was sold to North America, while EX183 was dismantled.

With America being the prime market for the MGA, the annual 12 Hours Sports Car Race at Sebring in Florida was seen as an ideal showcase for the new model. As a round of the World Sports Car Championship, Sebring was contested by all of the major teams of the day and the event also attracted a strong entry of amateur drivers mainly at the wheel of British sports cars.

The circuit was a former airbase and the track used

The racing programme with the works MGA Twin Cams did something to calm anxiety amongst owners about engine unreliability and often an excessive thirst for oil. Johnny Organ checks the oil level on one of the 1960 Sebring race cars being tested at Silverstone.

Americans Jack Flaherty (left) and Jim Parkinson were regular and successful works MG drivers at Sebring.

a combination of runways and perimeter tracks; the surface was pretty rough and poorly defined with strawbales and cones marking the way. This led to considerable opportunities for corner cutting and nudging the cones out of the way, particularly at night when the marshals tended to be less vigilant. Generally the circuit facilities were pretty basic and one member of the BMC team accurately described the place as 'Snetterton in the Sahara'. However, Sebring was always a prime trip for MG mechanics (usually their first visit to the States) and after the rigours of the British winter and the Monte Carlo Rally, the sunshine and the warm welcome by the Americans was a great tonic.

It was Donald Healey who first visualised the value of Sebring to US sales when, in 1954, he entered an Austin-Healey 100S and after a good showing returned

to Sebring on a regular basis with big Healeys and later Sprites with consistent success. With the cars prepared at Warwick and entered under the name of the US importer, the Healey activity was not considered to have infringed the BMC 'no racing' ban. This was to lead to a combined policy from Hambro Automotive Products in New York, the USA BMC importers and BMC Canada, to officially support MG entries at Sebring – a development which one suspects was craftily supported by John Thornley in an endeavour to see MGs show their paces on the track in front of the all-important American market.

Sebring successes

Thus the 1956 race saw the entry of three almost completely standard MGAs driven by local drivers but entered and prepared by dealers in New York, Washington and Pennsylvania. Running in virtual showroom trim except for safety modifications, the

MGAs finished fourth, fifth and sixth in class behind the Porsche Spyders, the leading car averaging 65.43mph. The exercise was repeated the following year when the MGAs finished 1-2 in their class and collected the Team Prize.

In 1959 a full team of Twin Cams running with hardtops was prepared at Abingdon and shipped to the States to be driven by top regional drivers from the USA and Canada. The mechanics were drawn from the workshops of BMC Hambro in New York and BMC Canada. The race was run in wet weather and Gus Ehrman/Ray Saidel finished runners-up in the class to Porsche, while Jim Parkinson/John Dalton lost over an hour with starter motor troubles but were nevertheless placed third in the class. The third car of Jack Flaherty/Ray Pickering/Sherman Decker stopped with engine troubles but was pushed over the line to qualify as a finisher.

The three-car Twin Cam team for 1960 ran with aluminium hardtops, no bumpers, 17-gallon fuel tanks, cold air intake for the carburettors, extra twin driving lamps, wing vents to cure under-bonnet temperatures and oil coolers. As a reward for their MGA Le Mans efforts (reported later in this chapter) Ted Lund/Colin Escott drove one of the cars but were out after only two laps with a broken valve spring. Canadians Fred Hayes/Ed

Leavens averaged 69.11mph to finish third in class just ahead of the Jim Parkinson/Jack Flaherty car. The MGs ran well other than suffering from cracked brake pipes.

For 1961 a pair of 1600 Coupés was entered in Stage 6 tune fitted with the optional disc brakes and knock-off steel wheels. Main opposition that year was to beat the works Sunbeam Alpines (one of which was driven in spirited style by one Paddy Hopkirk) which was achieved in no uncertain fashion with the class-winning car of Jim Parkinson/Jack Flaherty. This American partnership was to achieve an impressive record of consistent Sebring successes with MG over the next six years.

Runners-up in the class were Peter Riley and John Whitmore. Peter was a larger than life former Cambridge University student who started rallying with a Healey Silverstone and went on to drive Minis and big Healeys with the BMC team. John Whitmore was to

Opposite page: Consistently good results in the 12-Hours World Championship Sports Car races at Sebring, Florida, did much to promote MG in the USA – these are the three 1962 MGA team cars.

Drivers for Sebring 1962 (from left): Jack Sears, Bob Olthoff and John Whitmore.

become a leading light in Mini-Cooper racing circles. Bob Olthoff attended as reserve driver, the popular South African working in Abingdon's show shop at the time preparing motor show exhibits and road test cars and who raced his own Twin Cam with great success.

The production move from the 1,588cc Mark I to the 1,622cc Mark II MGA in 1962 did not really suit the international racing class limit of 1,600cc. It was therefore decided that the two cars entered for the 1962 Sebring race should be Mark Is and these ran with old style Mark I grilles with alternate bars removed to aid cooling, Twin-Cam chassis with four-wheel disc brakes and centre-lock disc wheels. The two MGs finished

Andrew Hedges was the most successful of the post-war MG drivers with the MGA, Midgets and MGB.

second and third in class driven by Jack Sears/Andrew Hedges and Jack Flaherty/Jim Parkinson. This was the first works MG drive for Andrew Hedges, London car salesman and British bobsleigh team member, who was to become the most successful post-war works MG driver and a regular race partner to Paddy Hopkirk.

At Sebring in 1962, the MGA of Jack Sears and Andrew Hedges on the way to 16th place overall and fourth in class.

Le Mans Twin Cam

While the MGA racing programme at Sebring took place under the banner of BMC America and Canada, it was the enthusiasm and persuasion of British MG driver Ted Lund which was to see an MGA appear in three consecutive Le Mans races from 1959. The fact that the project was officially run under the auspices of Ted Lund's local North-Western Centre of the MG Car Club as a 'private' entry was probably a cleverly engineered plan by John Thornley as a convenient cover-up for Abingdon's considerable involvement, albeit behind closed doors! This was one of those MG

Under-bonnet view of the Lund/Escott Le Mans MGA Twin Cam as it is today.

projects which deserves inclusion in this story of the works cars although at the time, for obvious reasons, there were strenuous denials that Abingdon was officially involved.

For the 1959 race, Abingdon built a special Twin Cam

Seen in 1960, the Abingdon-built special-bodied MGA Twin Cam that ran at Le Mans in 1959, 1960 and 1961, driven by Ted Lund and Colin Escott under the banner of the MG Car Club.

open tourer (SRX 210) with light-alloy body and low racing screen, possibly using one of the original 1955 Le Mans body shells. Driven by Ted Lund and Colin Escott, the car ran for 19 hours then hit a dog on the Mulsanne Straight damaging the bodywork and the car finally retired with gearbox failure when the gearbox drain plug came undone.

The following year, a change in the Le Mans regulations saw the car converted to a full coupé top designed by Don Hayter from Abingdon's design office with a deeper windscreen as required by the new rules. Ted Lund was now the official 'owner' of the car and, although clearly Abingdon was still supporting the project, the party line was that funding came from a syndicate of North-Western Centre MG Car Club members.

The engine was now bored out to 1,762cc, ran with twin 2in SU carburettors and a 4.1 axle which gave 130mph top speed. The car finished 13th overall, averaged 91.12 mph, achieved a fastest lap of 99.46mph and won the 2-litre class.

While there were rumours of a special MG for Le Mans in 1961, this was shelved and the Lund car was re-modelled with a modified nose, the headlamps being moved back a few inches. Power output was now 128bhp and the car topped 140mph with a best lap at 101.66mph before being sidelined with a blown engine.

The three consecutive Le Mans entries with SRX 210 were a brave effort from a basically private entry (albeit with Abingdon's technical support) while the MGAs' performances at Sebring had laid the foundations for a revival of a post-war MG racing programme.

The special Twin Cam Coupé makes a good start in the 1960 Le Mans race.

CHAPTER 14

MIDGETS AND 1100S 1961–65

MIDGETS ON 1961 RAC AND 1962 MONTE CARLO RALLIES;

THE DICK JACOBS COUPÉS, 1965 SEBRING AND TARGA FLORIO;

1100S AT 1962 BRANDS HATCH SIX-HOURS, 1963 MONTE CARLO AND LIÈGE

Class-winning performance on the driving tests by Derek Astle in the works Midget on the 1961 RAC Rally.

With the arrival of Stuart Turner as the new Competitions Manager, taking over from Marcus Chambers, not only did the team step up a gear in terms of professionalism and competitiveness, significantly with the importation of fresh driving talent from Scandinavia, but there was also a more purposeful, publicity-seeking programme.

Thus, to support the regular rally entries of Mini-Coopers and big Healeys, a team of MG Midgets was prepared with the prospect of picking up class wins in the small GT category. Two cars were prepared for the 1961 RAC Rally in November and one for the Monte Carlo Rally of the following year. To make up a three-car team for the RAC Rally, the works prepared Tommy Gold's own Midget.

The RAC Rally Midgets brought exactly the right results with a 1-2 in the class from Derek Astle and Mike Sutcliffe, who recalls the event.

'The cars really went very well and we were delighted for Derek that he won his class. Our only problem was with a broken rear spring in the dead of night with the rain lashing down somewhere in Wales. I remember this mechanic lying under the car with it propped up on a kerbstone and the water running down his neck and out of his trouser legs! Great lads!'

Another Midget class win came on the Monte Carlo Rally with Peter Riley putting up a stirring performance in the little car supporting the Morleys' class win in the MGB. A repeat Monte class win for the Midget was achieved in the following year by the Rev Rupert Jones, a BMC team stalwart equally at home driving or navigating and who combined a long and versatile motorsporting career with his clerical ministry.

Jacobs Midgets

Talk of post-war racing MGs and the name of Dick Jacobs comes to mind. Ever since he bought his first Midget in 1937, Dick became an MG enthusiast, racing was always a part of his life and he raced TC, TD, YB, ZA and MGAs plus many MG specials. Dick's racing career came to an end with the 1955 Le Mans crash in the works MGA and he then concentrated on his flourishing MG dealership in North London and later turned to team management.

He began preparing a privately owned MGA in 1957 and in the following year ran a couple of Magnettes, one of which won its class in the BRSCC Saloon Car Championship. Next came the well-known pair of pale green MGA Twin Cams which established the Jacobs tradition for immaculate presentation and reliability. In two years of busy competition only twice did the quick Twin Cams fail to cross the finishing line – once with a puncture and once with dirty fuel.

Jacobs entered a Twin Cam for the Tourist Trophy at Goodwood in September 1958 driven by Alan Foster and Tommy Bridger finishing 14th overall, third in the 2-litre class behind two works Porsches averaging 76.20mph for the four-hour race. Later, the Twin Cams were to race mainly in the keenly contested *Autosport* championship races.

The announcement of the MG Midget in 1961 prompted Dick to trace the lines of the Aston Martin DB4 coupé on to the outline of the Midget on a sales brochure. He took his doodlings to Abingdon and

Despite finding the Midget's cockpit somewhat cramped (left), Peter Riley with Mike Hughes won the class on the 1962 Monte Carlo Rally.

persuaded John Thornley and Syd Enever to build him a pair of special coupés initially for club racing. The now-familiar and extremely attractive lines of the Jacobs Midgets and their track performance was to arouse great interest and some embarrassment to the Abingdon management who were pestered with requests for the coupé to go into production.

The new shape was wind-tunnel tested and with its lightweight construction contributed much to the cars' performance. Some 13bhp less was required to propel the little cars at 100mph. The pretty coupé body was built upon the standard Midget chassis platform using hand-beaten aluminium panels made to the standard wing, door and side panel shapes, extended to blend into the fixed hardtop and streamlined bonnet section. To produce a rigid join between the steel sub-frame and the aluminium panels, new construction methods were applied with the use of Araldite epoxy resin adhesive. Ready for the starting grid, the Midgets turned the scales at 1,242lb, 324lb lighter than the standard car.

Production Midget suspension was modified for racing with a heavier duty anti-roll bar at the front and stiffer Armstrong damper settings. At the rear,

adjustable Armstrong dampers were fitted and there were softer-rate rear springs re-cambered to suit the lighter load. The standard bump rubbers were replaced with Aeon progressive-type, standard equipment on early MGBs. Lockheed disc brakes were used at the front with drums at the rear. Dunlop wire wheels were used with 5.25-13 Dunlop racing tyres at the rear, 4.50-13 at the front.

The engine was modified as far as Group 3 regulations allowed and the early Midgets ran with the 948cc unit bored out to the maximum permitted 0.040in oversize bringing the capacity to 972cc which produced a power output of around 75bhp. A single 45DCOE Weber carburettor was used and there was a special camshaft, inlet and exhaust manifolds and modified cylinder head giving raised compression.

Later in the Midgets' racing career a little more power was coaxed from the A-series engine by boring out still further to 995cc. Then, when the 1,098cc engine was

Just to confuse the archivists, YRX 737 (previously one of the three works Midgets) became an Austin-Healey Sprite for the 1962 Alpine Rally when it was driven by John Williamson and David Hiam.

The rallying vicars, Rupert Jones and Philip Morgan, on their way to a works Midget class win on the 1963 Monte Carlo Rally.

introduced, this was used in 1,139cc form. Finally, when the 1,275cc power unit was homologated, this was raced in the Midgets in 1,293cc form using Mini-Cooper 'S' cylinder blocks when running in the prototype category.

During their final racing season the cars were converted to dry-sump lubrication which gave a slight increase in power due to less oil drag and, although the oil consumption remained the same, it meant that the engine could run longer without topping up – important in long-distance races.

Transmission was via a competition Borg & Beck diaphragm clutch to a close-ratio gearbox. A variety of rear axle ratios were used to suit different circuits; with the normal 4.55 ratio the Midgets ran at 15.4mph per 1,000rpm. With the original 972cc engine the Midgets' terminal speed was timed at 119.5mph at 7,750rpm.

The interior of the Midgets was spartan but everything was beautifully tailored with a raked bucket seat, smart black-crackle dashboard, small wood-rimmed steering wheel, big-size rev counter. A typical Jacobs touch was the cleverly designed door catch which extended up through the top of the door and which needed only a quick downwards stroke through the open sidescreen to open the door. Just the job for Le Mans starts!

Class winners

Dick took over the two cars in the summer of 1962, a third car being sold to John Milne who campaigned the car for many years in his native Scottish sports and GT championships. Competing in the national GT races, the Jacobs Midgets in their first season were placed in the first four on 13 occasions. In their most important races, the Brands Hatch August International and the Snetterton Three Hours, the little green cars came home first and second in their class. Not once during the year did the MGs fail to finish.

The story was much the same in 1963. The two Midgets contested 14 GT races, all of national or

Dick Jacobs persuaded Abingdon to build him a pair of lightweight racing Midget coupés in 1962 and over two seasons they scored a succession of impressive results in national and international events, running with a series of engines from 948cc to the final 1,300cc Mini-Cooper-based dry-sump unit.

Andrew Hedges (in helmet) discusses plans for the 1965 Nürburgring 500km race with Keith Greene in the ex-Jacobs Midget.

Keith Greene loses no time with the Le Mans start in the Nürburgring 500km.

international status where there was some reasonable opposition. In some events the Midgets were obliged to run in the 1,300cc or even the 2-litre class and this year the two cars finished in the first four places on 20 occasions. Significant class victories were claimed at the International Snetterton Sports Car Race, the International BARC Easter Goodwood meeting, the British Grand Prix meeting at Silverstone and the August International at Brands Hatch. The season closed with a class win in the *Autosport* Championship.

In their final season, Jacobs moved up to contest more prestigious events in 1964, scoring places in the first three in 15 races. The team's greatest run was in the International 1,000km Race at the Nürburgring when the cars finished 1-2 in the class and the highest placed British finishers.

Alan Foster was the main driving force behind the Jacobs Midgets having previously raced MGs with Dick for some 12 years. Andrew Hedges later became a Jacobs regular and for the final season of long-distance two-driver races, Keith Greene and Chris Martyn joined the team.

The Jacobs Midgets were later entered by the works and taken to Sebring in 1965 where Andrew Hedges and Roger Mac (No. 68) won the class.

Return to Abingdon

The Jacobs Midgets were returned to Abingdon at the end of 1964 and were then prepared and entered by the works for various events during 1965. Both cars were taken to Sebring in 1965 with the works MGB team where Andrew Hedges and Roger Mac won their class handsomely beating the works Triumph Spitfires. Ironically after displaying total reliability when raced by the Jacobs team, the second car, driven by John Wagstaff and Chuck Tannlund, retired with a blown engine.

Better fortune came when Paddy Hopkirk and Andrew Hedges took one of the cars to the 1965 Targa Florio where it was ideally suited to the conditions. This was the first of many works MG drives for Paddy who joined the BMC team from Triumph, ostensibly to drive the big Healey, but very soon found himself behind the wheel of the Mini-Coopers joining the Scandinavian stars Rauno Aaltonen and Timo Mäkinen and bringing the team their first Monte Carlo Rally victory in 1964.

The Targa Florio, which in 1965 was to be the first of what was to become a regular trip to Sicily, had been run over a variety of courses on the beautiful north coast of the island, with that year's race – the 50th on

the series – being held over ten laps of the 45-mile Little Madonie course. Apart from the main four-mile coast road straight, which at anything over 100mph was neither wide nor smooth, the rest of the course was just bend after bend after bend. This is the mountain road inland to Cerda, up and over the heights to Caltavulturo, down through the valley to Collesano and back along the coast road to Campofelice. The scenery is breathtaking but you would be crazy to take your eyes off the road. The variety of corners, uphill and downhill, with their steep cambers and rough cobbled gutters, make the course incredibly tricky. The road is just about two cars wide but passing is only really possible on the straights.

Racing through the villages presented its own hazards. Crowd control was virtually non-existent and at least one car in the 1965 race crashed to avoid a spectator who decided that he might get a better view from the other side of the road! The race was made more hazardous because of the weather, which changed dramatically when a freak storm blew its way across the island. Thus one section of the course which was dry on one lap could well be running with slippery, muddy water the next time around.

Apart from the local drivers and those who make an annual pilgrimage to the event, very few can hope to know their way around the whole of the course. For visiting drivers the days before the race mean endless practice. This can be more dangerous than the race itself, for the roads are open to normal traffic and the 'swervability' of a donkey cart is not all that good!

Many drivers make their own unique form of pace notes by painting coded markings on the road, tree trunks, walls or other bits of the Sicilian scenery. These take the form of a variety of multi-coloured letters, words, numbers and other hieroglyphics. Usually, just before the race, rival teams go out and paint over other people's signs, or change the letters, which always adds to the excitement on the opening laps!

Unofficial practice is made even more fun when the locals, who have had a whole year to prepare the circuit, decide that this is the time when they should try to make some attempt to re-surface the worst bits of road. As race day approaches the roads are crowded with old men with shovels leading rickety donkey carts and decrepit wagons loaded with asphalt and

Ready for the 1965 Targa Florio, the ex-Jacobs Midget was driven by Paddy Hopkirk and Andrew Hedges, finishing a spirited 11th overall.

Stuart Turner (checked shirt) talks Targa tactics with (from left) Clive Baker, Paddy Hopkirk, Rauno Aaltonen and (behind) Andrew Hedges.

chippings. Their road-mending efforts are well-meaning but quite useless as the combination of continuous high-speed practice motoring plus the roasting Sicilian sunshine breaks up the new surface just as fast as it has been laid, which makes things twice as dangerous as it had been in the first place.

The number of practice accidents is quite alarming but no-one seems to worry, except perhaps for the local rent-a-car man for whom it must be a nightmare as every team uses hire cars for practising. It was rumoured that for the week of the Targa he used to take delivery of just about every worn-out hire car in Italy, most of which never found their way back to the mainland.

The Midget's race in 1965 ran completely to form with Paddy Hopkirk and Andrew Hedges finishing 11th overall, just conceding the class by 65 seconds to a very quick, locally-driven Abarth Simca.

Two final entries complete the record of the works Midgets when a pair of cars were entered for the Bridgehampton 500 Race in 1965, one of the major US

East Coast sports car races. These were not the Jacobs cars but a pair of Donald Healey-prepared re-badged Sprites, MG presumably being the favoured marque for US marketing at the time. The flying Finns, Rauno Aaltonen and Timo Mäkinen, drove the cars, Rauno winning his class with Timo delayed with a broken exhaust pipe which required welding.

MG 1100

Just as the Midgets had provided useful competition sorties for the Abingdon team, so did the MG 1100 announced two years after the arrival of the Austin and Morris 1100s with the more sporty 1,098cc twin carburettor engine. The model was launched at the London Motor Show in October 1962 and as a publicity

To celebrate the launch of the MG 1100 in October 1962, a Dick Jacobs-entered car won its class in the Brands Hatch Six-Hour Race driven by Andrew Hedges and Alan Foster. Works support is verified by the two casual spectators in the next-door pit, Stuart Turner and tuning wizard Don Moore, who built the engine!

The BBC's Raymond Baxter (left) with Ernie McMillen battled their way through tough conditions to finish the 1963 Monte Carlo Rally with an MG 1100.

Hydrolastic suspension did not save the day for Pauline Mayman and Val Domleo in their MG 1100 on the fast, rough 1963 Spa-Sofia-Liège when suspension troubles put them out.

exercise Abingdon immediately supported the Dick Jacobs 1100 entry in the Brands Hatch Motor Six-Hour Saloon Car Race run on the Grand Prix circuit. Driven by Andrew Hedges and Alan Foster the car won its class, averaged a respectable 69.25mph and beat the fancied Alan Mann-entered Ford Anglias.

An Abingdon-prepared 1100 was entered for the RAC Rally in November to be driven by David Seigle-Morris but this retired with a broken piston in Scotland. Two works 1100s ran in the 1963 Monte Carlo Rally for John Cuff and the BBC's Raymond Baxter, a regular with the team who was later to serve as BMC's popular Publicity Director. Cuff's car was written off when another competitor ran into the back of him, Raymond Baxter with Ernie McMillen finishing thanks to a bottle of brandy recalls Raymond.

'This was a very cold year and a hard event. Our 1100, running in Group 1, went very well and was really quite a pleasure to drive and it coped okay with the bad weather. Ernest and I benefited from some good pace notes which we had spent some five days making in the pleasant company of old friends like Peter Harper and Henry Taylor.

Our only problem was with the electrics, the heater was not really strong enough to de-ice the windscreen and the wiper blades were not capable of dealing with the ice and snow, the motor was starting to burn out and the lights were dimming. I remember Ernest solving our iced-up windscreen by telling me to stand by because he had the ultimate solution in the glove pocket. He had a half bottle of brandy for emergencies (as we always did) and declared that this was an emergency! To my horror he poured the whole bottle over the windscreen – but it worked a treat and at least we could then see where we were going! But for these problems and the frightful weather we might have won the class. Another of those "if only" rallying results!'

Following the showing of a pair of works Morris 1100s on the 1962 Liege driven by Pat Moss and Peter Riley, when the hydrolastic suspension was well up to the rough roads but the cars suffered frustrating engine problems, a lone MG 1100 was entered for the 1963 Liège for Pauline Mayman and Val Domleo. Again the car was well suited to the conditions but a broken suspension ball joint finally caused retirement.

The Midget and the 1100 had maintained the MG marque's presence in competition at a time when the MGA in rallying was being eclipsed by the growing competitiveness of the works big Healeys. Now in 1962 came the car which was to bring a new era of MG competition activity for Abingdon – the MGB.

CHAPTER 15

MGB IN RACING 1963–66

DEBUT AT 1963 SEBRING,
LE MANS 1963–65,
SEBRING 1964–69;

WINNING THE 1964
NÜRBURGRING MARATHON
AND 1965 BRANDS HATCH
GUARDS TROPHY;

1966 TARGA FLORIO

The MGB of Timo Mäkinen and John Rhodes presses on through a Sicilian village to finish ninth overall and first in the GT category on the 1966 Targa Florio. GRX 307D was one of most-used works MGBs: its events in 1966 comprised the Monte Carlo Rally, the Targa Florio, Mugello, the 84 Hours at the Nürburgring, Spa, Montlhéry – and the car is finally raced at Sebring in 1967.

The arrival of the MGB at the end of 1962 was to witness the start of a record-breaking production run for Abingdon with instant appeal for the new body style, specification, basically sound engineering and very competitive price. In terms of performance it may not have offered much more than the MGA but it was soon to gain a reputation for reliability with a good reserve of power for those who wanted to use it for competitions.

As the racing MGAs at Sebring had set such a good track record it was ironic that its successor – the MGB – which was to prove such a reliable competition car in subsequent years – should have made such a disastrous racing debut there in 1963.

The problems of preparing race cars in the depth of winter for events to be run in the tropical heat of Sebring and 1963 has been mentioned earlier, and this was a classic example. Britain was suffering near arctic winter conditions at the time and none of the usual race circuits was usable for a pre-event shakedown or serious testing. The cars had to be run-in by the

mechanics at night around the icy Abingdon lanes and, just before they had to be shipped to the States, they were taken for a quick test run at Finmere, a rough-surfaced airfield which had been used by the BMC Advanced Driving School. Under conditions more like a test run for the Monte Carlo Rally, no problems showed up and the cars were crated up for the docks.

The two cars thus raced at Sebring 'straight out of the box', driven by Sebring stalwarts Jim Parkinson/Jack Flaherty and a ladies' team of British Mini racer Christabel Carlisle and US lady journalist Denise McCluggage.

It was not long into the race when both cars suffered serious overheating problems and then engine failure due to oil surge – a problem which should have shown up had it been possible to give the cars a good high-speed run in the UK beforehand. Back home after the disaster the newly formed Special Tuning Department was quick to offer modified sump baffles which solved the problem.

As a test run for the new modifications, one of the Sebring cars was loaned to privateer Alan Hutcheson who won his class at the *Daily Express* Silverstone International GT Race – a more encouraging result. Hutcheson then took the car to the 500km Race at Spa but this time overheating caused retirement.

Fearless Mini racer Christabel Carlisle joined the team for the MGB's debut race at Sebring in 1963 when both cars suffered oil surge problems and retired.

Defying the 'no-racing' ban imposed by Longbridge following the 1955 Le Mans disaster, MG returned to the Le Mans 24 Hours in 1963 with this 'private' entry in the name of Alan Hutcheson partnered by Paddy Hopkirk. Despite Hutcheson putting the car into the sand at Mulsanne for some 90 minutes, the MGB finished 12th overall and won its GT class.

Le Mans 1962

These sorties were in preparation for Le Mans in June when Hutcheson, joined by the redoubtable Paddy Hopkirk, were to drive what everyone knew by now was an official works MGB, albeit the entry was in Hutcheson's name in deference to the BMC 'no official racing' ruling which was still in force as far as Europe was concerned.

A small contingent of Competitions mechanics and other Abingdon personnel were sent in support, including myself. I had gone to Abingdon in 1960 as the first General Secretary of the Austin-Healey Club, later joining the staff of the BMC sports car magazine *Safety Fast* and moving on to act as Competitions Press Officer. This had brought me into regular contact with the Competitions Department activities and, having

been an official RAC timekeeper, Stuart Turner had asked me to join the team on a number of races to do the timekeeping and lap charting. This had led to various opportunities of running the MG pit and, with Stuart pre-occupied with the rally programme, I was very happy to become MG's unofficial racing team manager.

Le Mans 1963

The 1963 Le Mans race was the first of three consecutive MGB entries for the 24 Hours which were to achieve highly creditable results. It was qualifying in practice, however, which was the greatest test. One of the most significant Le Mans regulations at the time, certainly as far as MG was concerned, was the minimum practice qualifying time for the race which, in the 2-litre class, was almost exactly 100mph (representing a five-minute lap). If you did not achieve this in practice you did not start. Thus the specification of the MGB was set very carefully to achieve this by the minimum margin, at the same time adopting a state of tune that would, hopefully, last the 24 hours. Nevertheless it was always touch and go whether the car would qualify and our one fear was always wet weather, some engine problem which could not be quickly solved or a minor incident which could mean missing a vital qualifying session.

Mechanical modifications were restricted to the basic works Group 3 Stage 5 tune: overbore from 1,798cc to 1,801cc, high-lift camshaft, single Weber 45DCOE carburettor, 10.4:1 pistons, large capacity sump, modified oil pump, oil cooler, flowed and polished cylinder head, competition exhaust manifold feeding a big bore tail pipe, balanced crankshaft and flywheel. The car ran with a competition clutch, close ratio gearbox and a 3.3:1 final drive ratio which was calculated to achieve a top speed of around 130mph at 6,000rpm. The suspension was standard apart from competition dampers front and rear. Tyres were 5.50 x 14 R6 Dunlops. An extra 6bhp and perhaps some 10mph in top speed was produced from the only non-standard part of the body, the droop-snout bonnet that was designed by Syd Enever.

Contrary to policy at the time, in particular for MG, the cockpit was completely stripped of trim and carpets – this was probably only allowed because it was a 'private' entry. With the maximum capacity of 20 gallons of fuel on board, the MGB turned the scales at 995kg, only 20kg lighter than the standard car.

Practice proved that our sums were just about right. With a rev limit of 6,500rpm, the car clocked 132mph through the Mulsanne speed trap and just qualified with a best lap of 4 minutes 50 seconds.

The race started with a major drama when Hutcheson ran off the road at Mulsanne after only 12 laps having got carried away with the customary 'grand prix' during the opening laps. He took 90 minutes to dig the MG out of the notorious sand trap using every conceivable thing he could lay his hands on including his crash helmet and the passenger's seat!

Apart from this incident, the car ran like clockwork, the MG making a pit stop every 2 hours 20 minutes for an average of about 2½ minutes for fuel and a driver change. Apart from attention to a loose exhaust pipe (probably due to the earlier off-road incident at Mulsanne), no other work was done on the car apart from changing the rear tyres at half distance and the front brake pads (which in fact proved to be unnecessary).

By Sunday morning, the MGB was placed second in the 2-litre class ahead of all the fancied Porsches but behind the works Sunbeam Alpine but, when that retired with bearing troubles, Hutcheson and Hopkirk cruised home to win the GT class and finish 12th overall amongst the 13 survivors. The MGB averaged 92mph for the race (99mph during the 22½ hours when running) with a fastest lap of 104.2mph.

Paddy Hopkirk and Andrew Hedges with the 1964 Le Mans MGB retaining the 1963 'droop-snout' nose (designed by Syd Enever), which gave the car a top speed of 139mph and a 104mph lap speed.

The 20-gallon fuel tank of the 1964 Le Mans MGB was fed via a re-positioned fuel filler through the boot lid; not many cars at Le Mans today carry a spare wheel!

Le Mans 1964

As MG now seemed to have successfully crept back into official racing in Europe without any adverse comments from Longbridge, and encouraged by the success of the previous year, the team returned to Le Mans in 1964 with a new car. This was identical to the 1963 MGB with another droop-snout nose, but as this was now an official works entry, it was fully carpeted and trimmed.

This year the drivers were Paddy Hopkirk and Andrew Hedges with Frenchman Patrick Vanson as reserve. The car was allocated the number 37, which pleased Paddy as this was his winning Monte Carlo Rally number. The fun-loving Irishman celebrated after an uneventful practice

by falling off his Moulton bicycle in the paddock and ending up with very sore gravel wounds.

Fortunately, that was just about the only drama for the MG team for the car went well against the class opposition of five Porsche 904s and a trio of Alfa Romeos. Again pit stops were scheduled for every 29 laps (242 miles) or about 2 hours 20 minutes which made just ten driving stints in the 24 hours. The MG climbed to 35th place out of the 55 starters through the first hour and was 27th by midnight, averaging just over 100mph. In ideal conditions in the cool of the evening, the car clocked its best lap of 104.9mph, Hopkirk setting 139mph through the speed trap.

Apart from the replacement of a tyre with a slow puncture, the only unscheduled work on the car followed the action of a clumsy French 'plombeur' who, with the best intentions of helping the team to make a fast refuelling stop, snapped off the quick-release filler cap at the hinge. Eight minutes were lost while the mechanics fitted a new one which had been kindly donated by

The author (left), pit manager of the Le Mans MGB entries, talks to Paddy Hopkirk, Dunlop's Oliver Speight and Andrew Hedges.

Opposite: The 1964 Le Mans MGB driven by Paddy Hopkirk and Andrew Hedges on its way to finishing the highest-placed British car and runner-up in its class.

Andrew Hedges and Paddy Hopkirk receive the Motor *Trophy for the highest-placed British car at Le Mans in 1964.*

MG's old team boss, Marcus Chambers, who was then running the rival Sunbeam Tiger team in a neighbouring pit. Brake pads were changed at 14 hours along with new rear tyres, this stop being a little longer than anticipated because brake wear had been excessive and the pads had temporarily welded themselves to the discs.

At the end of the race the MG was placed 19th overall and the highest-placed British finisher taking home the *Motor* Trophy. But the most publicised aspect of the performance was the MG's average speed of 99.9mph which drew more attention than if we had been able to achieve the magic 100mph!

Le Mans hat-trick

With two consecutive finishes, the team was obviously keen to go for the hat-trick with the lone entry so in 1965 it was back to Le Mans with another new car now running as a prototype and in Stage 6 tune with another droop-snout nose, lightweight alloy bonnet, boot lid and doors. Hopkirk and Hedges were again the team drivers and again the MGB ran like a train and the only unscheduled pit stop was for a broken tail light bulb. Final placing was 11th overall, and runner-up in the 2-litre class to a Porsche 904 that actually went into the pits on its very last lap with a wrecked engine. The MGB also just failed to win the *Motor* Trophy again being beaten by the whispering Rover-BRM gas turbine car which finished just one place ahead of the MG, the average speed of which was 98.26mph.

Paddy Hopkirk, later reunited with one of his former Le Mans cars at Silverstone, commented:

'I do think the MGs were very well driven, although it is obviously difficult for me to say this. It is very hard work in a race like Le Mans to do well in a virtually standard car. Today the rules make this impossible and at the time we had to struggle to qualify. Each year we only just scraped into the race, on the ragged edge of the time limit, for Abingdon wanted to enter in the original spirit of the Le Mans of old, to drive a very standard production sports car. That is why the Le Mans MGBs were so near to a production car. They would never have gone in for wild engines and fancy suspensions.

Up against full racing sports cars, the MG could only hope to do well on reliability, and Le Mans has always been an endurance test where reliability comes foremost. To win anything at all we had to finish, and it was the reliability factor which helped to move us up the leader board. I suppose after the start we must have been virtually last, but after the first few hours we moved our way up the field as others blew up.

It takes a special kind of driving at Le Mans. Firstly, we gained quite a lot of speed from towing. We were always on the lookout for a tow up the straight and once right up behind someone else there was quite a considerable tug. That was more difficult at night. When you start to get a bit tired and you catch someone's blazing headlights in your mirror, you begin to wonder whether it is really another car about to come up your exhaust pipe, or just a slower car you had overtaken. Not

that we did much overtaking!

Rally drivers make good long-distance racing drivers, of that I am certain. Rally drivers have to push themselves to the limit for very long periods, more than the comparatively brief spell of the average race, for instance, so perhaps a rally driver with race experience is more mentally prepared for Le Mans. A rally driver has had to drive fast in mist and fog and knows all about sudden changes of surface and, of course, he is much better experienced both mentally and physically when it comes to night-time driving.'

The MGBs were probably the last true production sports cars to run at Le Mans and in the history of the event I doubt whether any 'lone' entry ever achieved the hat-trick of finishes. I also reckon that unscheduled pit stops for a slow puncture, a loose exhaust pipe and a broken tail lamp bulb must be something of a record over some 7,000 miles!

Sebring sorties

Following the unfortunate debut of the MGB at Sebring in 1963, the team was to return annually to Florida through to 1969 in company with the works-entered Austin-Healeys prepared by the Donald Healey Motor Company at Warwick. The objective was to demonstrate reliability and go for class awards if possible, beating any other British opposition in the process.

Of the three-car MGB entry in 1964, Ed Leslie/John Dalton finished third in class, three Canadian drivers, Frank Morrell/Jim Adams/Merle Brennan, qualified as finishers, while Jim Parkinson/Jack Flaherty retired with a failed oil seal.

Two MGBs ran at Sebring in 1965 and in order to try to gain a class win in the always competitive 2-litre class one of the cars ran as a prototype, with an over-bored engine at 2,004cc. This car was driven by Merle Brennan/Frank Morrell; the second MG ran in the usual GT class and was driven by Brad Pickard/Al Pease.

This was the year of the amazing floods which was to enliven things for the 55,000-strong crowd who were getting somewhat bored with the processional race, despite the prospect of a dominating all-American victory by the Chaparral-Chevrolet of Jim Hall and Hap Sharp over the Ford GT of Bruce McLaren and Ken Miles.

With some five hours of racing to go the skies suddenly became overcast, and within seconds a miniature hurricane whipped along the dusty pit road and with a peal of thunder the skies opened and the rain came bucketing down in torrents. The volume

The 1964 Le Mans car was rebodied to compete at Sebring in 1965. No. 49 ran in the prototype category with a 2,004cc engine (to get out of the highly competitive 2-litre class) while No. 48 was entered in the GT category. With American and Canadian drivers, the prototype car finished runner-up in the class while the GT car finished but was delayed by pit stops following an off-course excursion.

of rain which fell within the next few minutes was incredible. Even the locals admitted that they had not seen anything like it in their lives.

Within minutes the scene in front of the pits was chaotic. The low dividing wall between the track and pit road trapped the water where it completely blanketed the circuit to a depth of at least six inches. In the pit road drainage was non-existent, and conditions were even worse as the mechanics sloshed around in up to nine inches of water.

It was an unbelievable sight, the cars creeping around at 20mph, submerged headlights looming through the water, windscreen wipers flaying hopelessly. The drivers of open cars were trying to stand up in their open 'baths' to see over the low screens; those in closed cars either stuck their heads out of the side window or drove along hanging out of open doors trying to see the way ahead. The noises coming from some of the

unenclosed sports car engines were amazing.

At first everyone thought that the race would be stopped but there was no word from the announcer so the cars were kept running, mechanics wading out on to the circuit guiding their cars through the shallowest parts of the track where conditions were at their worst opposite the pits.

In these conditions the BMC sports cars found themselves in a class of their own with reasonably snug fitting hardtops, windscreens that did not mist up too badly and wipers that dealt with the rain a lot better than most. The MGs and Austin-Healeys pressed on, considerably faster than most of the bigger-engined machines.

Timo Mäkinen, driving one of the works Sprites, actually passed the leading Chaparral right in front of the pits, much to the amusement of all concerned except the poor Chaparral driver who was totally swamped as the Sprite cruised by! Timo, who actually made up two complete laps on the race leader during the storm, commented in his characteristic 'Finglish':

'The Sprite is about four inches deep with water inside. I am fabulous dripping. When I accelerate the water it rushes up to the back of the car around my shoulders. When I brake it all runs down to my toes. In the corners it slops from side

Top brass at Sebring 1966 (from left): Paddy Hopkirk, Graham Whitehead (boss of the MG importers in the USA), Andrew Hedges and Stuart Turner.

The Paddy Hopkirk/Andrew Hedges prototype for Sebring 1966 was one of the most powerful and fastest MGBs built at Abingdon. Despite a second lap pit stop to replace a broken rocker arm (changed in 17 minutes) the car stormed back through the field to lead the class only to put a rod through the side in the closing stages of the race.

This MGB GT ran at Sebring in 1967, 1968 and 1969 (its highest place was 11th overall in 1967) and also participated in the Targa Florio in 1968 (12th overall).

to side. To empty the car I go fast round a corner and open the door at the right moment. It all fantastic fun!'

More humour came when one of the MGBs came in for a tyre change. A mechanic losing his balance while trying to lift the car on to the quick-lift jack, fell backwards into the water with the jack on top of him and ended up completely submerged! Another mechanic took a wheel off, dropped it on to the track, turned around to pick it up again only to find that it had floated off down the pit road!

Just as we were all wondering how long the rain was really going to continue, the skies brightened and gradually the rain eased. Around the circuit cars came to life, spluttered their way slowly around to the pits to dry out and continue the race.

Al Pease had lost time with an off-course excursion which damaged the battery cable that had to be replaced and the GT car finished with a lowly class placing. Brennan/Morrell in the prototype car finished runners-up in their class.

As in the previous year, the pair of MGBs entered

for the 1966 race ran in different classes. One car was run as a prototype fitted with a special cylinder block bored out to 2,009cc to accommodate offset big Healey valves, a nitrided five-bearing crankshaft and Twin Cam rods. Producing some 138bhp this was one of the fastest MGB race cars yet built by Abingdon.

Unfortunately this car, driven by Paddy Hopkirk/Andrew Hedges, did not have a good event. Hopkirk brought the car in on only the second lap with a broken rocker arm leaving mechanic Nobby Hall to fit a replacement in only 17 minutes. Within two hours they had carved their way back through the field, overhauled all the class opposition and passed the leading TR4 prototype all set for a comfortable ride to the flag. With 1½ hours to go the car suddenly dropped off the lap charts and was out with a rod through the side.

The second car, running to Group 3 specification, a roadster with a hardtop but not a GT, was driven by Australian Mini racer Peter Manton, British sports car

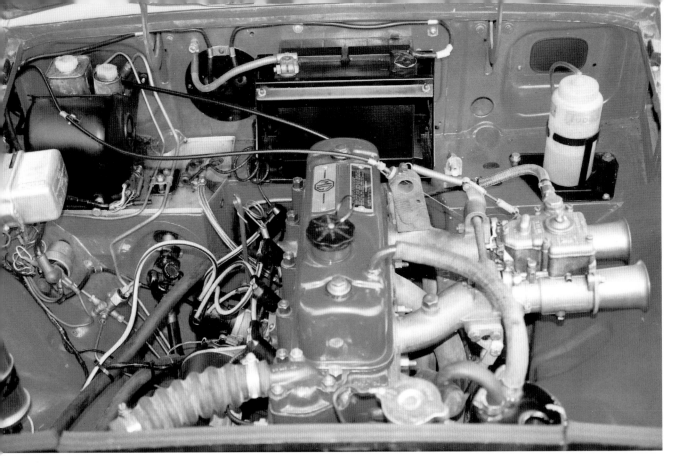

LBL 591E

exponent Roger Mac and American Emmett Brown. The GT car had a totally uneventful run and won the class when all the opposition retired. Towards the end of the race the drivers did battle with the fastest of the TR4s for the honour of being the first British car to finish. Thanks to some stirring night driving by Roger Mac, the MGB took the flag six laps up on the Triumph averaging 77mph and finishing third in the whole GT category behind a couple of 7-litre Chevrolet Stingrays.

Sebring 1967 saw the first entry for an MGB GT but this had to be entered in the prototype category because the GT was not yet homologated. The engine was increased to 2,004cc to get into the over 2-litre class and ran with a Weber carburettor, race camshaft and side exhaust. Driven by Paddy Hopkirk/Andrew Hedges, the GT lost time after being pushed off the circuit by a spinning Chaparral but nevertheless won its class and finished 11th overall, third in the category behind the 7-litre Ford GT 40s of Mario Andretti/Bruce McLaren and A. J. Foyt/Lloyd Ruby.

The second car ran in the GT category with a bored out 1,824cc power unit. Driven by Timo Mäkinen/John Rhodes it came in 12th behind Hopkirk/Hedges and third in class behind a Porsche 911.

John Rhodes, star works Mini-Cooper racer having his first drive with the MG team and his first trip to the States, recalls the experience.

'I have two vivid memories of Sebring driving with Timo Mäkinen. Firstly, driving back from the circuit in some enormous yank mobile, Timo was stopped by the police not only for speeding but clearly just about every other traffic violation in the book because all the cops had their guns out of their holsters and looked decidedly serious. Timo, of course, used the old trick of speaking only Finnish and it was left to me to explain that he was the greatest rally driver of all time – and that this was how he always drove. Timo got away with it.

Relaxing afterwards by the motel pool, Timo lifted up my sun bed and slid me into the pool which was fine except that I could not swim and everyone thought that my impersonation of a drowning whale was quite hilarious!'

The MGB GT appeared at Sebring again in 1968 this time with a three-man crew consisting of Gary Rodrigues and Richard McDaniel from the States and Canadian Bill Brack, the team finishing fifth in class. The same car ran in the 1969 race driven by Jerry Truitt/Les Blackburn, entered by the newly formed US British Leyland organisation but did not finish well-placed.

In summary the MGBs at Sebring performed pretty well. Every year from 1964 to 1968, at least one MG outclassed and outpaced the Triumph, Sunbeam, Lotus and Jaguar opposition and the only time that MG was not the highest placed British finisher was in 1965 when this honour went to one of the works lightweight Sprites.

Guards Trophy win

In my introduction I mentioned that there were a number of works MG entries which, for various reasons, were made in the name of private owners or teams. This was the case for the 1,000-mile Guards Trophy Race held at Brands Hatch in 1965. The event, although international, was really meant for amateur drivers and the works teams probably should not have been involved. A lone works car was prepared and entered by Don Moore, the redoubtable Cambridge-based tuner who was such a wizard with Group 1 engines. The event was split into two 500-mile legs, the first on Saturday and the second on Sunday, competitors being allowed to remove their cars from the circuit overnight and carry out repairs.

Driven by Mini racers John Rhodes and Warwick Banks, the Group 3 MGB won the first 500-mile race followed by Trevor and Anita Taylor in a J.C. Bamford-entered MGB. On the second day the MG held fourth place but on aggregate won the event by some eight laps over the Mike Garton/Mike Hughes ex-works Sprite, Jackie Oliver/Chris Craft (E Type Jaguar) and Paddy Hopkirk/Roger Mac (Austin-Healey 3000).

John Rhodes recalls the race:

'The car went magnificently – we ran a three-bearing engine because this was more free-revving giving more power in race tune and providing you did not over-rev it was utterly reliable.

We had two major problems, an oil leak from the filter in the first part of the race, I came into the pits and the mechanics saw what the problem was, sent me out again for another couple of laps and then they changed it in 2 minutes 17 seconds which has got to be some sort of a record! The other problem was that the clutch went towards the end of the first leg and we had to change it overnight.

There was a certain amount of aggravation with the neighbouring Morgan pit who had quite a few competitive entries and did not like being beaten by the MG. They put in a protest that we were using more than the regulation two mechanics but it was thrown out.

Warwick Banks had a bit of a battle with one of the other prominent MG drivers who seemed determined to have him off every time he was lapped. Warwick solved that one by making sure that he only lapped the other car right in front of the pits so that everyone could see if there was any naughty business!

I must say I was very proud to have co-driven the MG to win one of its two post-war outright international wins.'

Through the 1966 season Roger Enever and Alec Poole campaigned a works car prepared mainly by the Development Department in many major European events with creditable results. They finished third overall in the prestigious Brands Hatch BOAC 500.

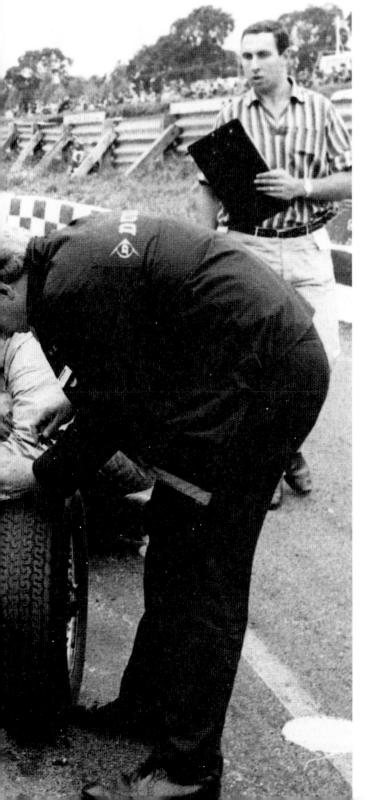

World Sports Car Championship

Through the 1966 and 1967 seasons works MGBs were made available for various European rounds of the World Sports Car Championship to a group of the team's drivers.

Roger Enever, Alec Poole, Andrew Hedges, Julien Vernaeve, Clive Baker and Robin Widdows raced in selected events, competing in the GT category. Their achievements, listed in Appendix D, were creditable: they regularly scored class wins and respectable overall placings, usually against more powerful opposition. The races concerned were the Brands Hatch 500, Monza 3 Hours, Mugello, the Nürburgring 1,000km, Spa 1,000km, Montlhéry 1,000km and Reims 12 Hours.

These were all low-budget sorties with the drivers loaned works-prepared cars and towing them to the circuits themselves on trailers, usually without any works mechanics present. The most regularly campaigned car was BRX 855B, which had been used by the Development Department as a test-bed for the five-bearing engine and was on permanent loan to Roger Enever.

Targa return

The MG team returned to the Targa Florio in 1966, two MGBs being entered for Timo Mäkinen/John Rhodes and John Handley/Andrew Hedges. The cars ran in the GT Category and in Stage 6 tune, power output being 107bhp on 1¾ SUs carburettors with standard inlet and exhaust manifolds, standard connecting rods, 40-thou oversize pistons, 10.8:1 compression ratio and a full-race camshaft.

The MGBs had no trouble other than one of the cars, for some reason, had arrived without bumpers and was in trouble with the scrutineers. This was solved when a spectator's MGB was spotted in one of the car parks and he was delighted to offer his bumpers for duty in return for a VIP tour of the MG factory and a set of new bumpers when he returned to England!

John Rhodes was paired with the redoubtable Timo Mäkinen and again recalled that the most frightening experience of the trip was not on the track!

'The most memorable thing for me about the Targa was not the actual race but being driven by Timo in a hire car from the circuit to our hotel. He would drive flat out on the wrong side of the road, lights on, horn blaring, lighting a cigarette as he drove and reassuring me that the locals would always move over in the end. Surprisingly

they always did, many of them ended up in the ditch, all of them certainly exhibited a wide-eyed open-mouthed expression of sheer horror before they took avoiding action!'

John Handley, more regularly seen racing the works Mini-Coopers, drove the second of the MGBs with Andrew Hedges, and recalls a practice drive with Timo Mäkinen.

'I was paired to practise with Timo in a Fiat 125 hire car and when you are paired to practise with Timo, he practises and you sit beside him. You don't get much driving so you have to pay rapt attention to what's happening and it is not so easy from the passenger seat to remember how the road goes; co-drivers can do it but drivers don't!

Timo's driving was the most amazing experience for me. We came to one of the little villages on the circuit right up in the mountains and there was a formal gate on the outskirts of the town where the circuit passed through. It was about a truck width wide. We were coming up to this town gate at a speed representing everything that this Fiat would do and a bit more. The poor car had not got many tyres or brakes left and as we approached the gate an enormous truck appeared in the middle of the gateway. Timo said "He go back". I muttered something like "Of course, Timo." There is no way you argue with Timo. Privately I thought to myself that he probably would not go back. I could not see where we were going other than through the wall or under the radiator of the truck.

We screeched up to the front of this truck and eventually he had to brake and as we were just about to lock horns with this giant machine, the driver juddered into reverse – the look of total disbelief and sheer terror on the driver's face being unforgettable!'

The Abingdon team were renowned for their off-duty escapades and on the Targa I recall a trip into Palermo one evening after practice to visit a funfair. Here the drivers found a race track with electric 'dodgem' cars and, of course, it was not long before the entire team was on board terrifying the locals with some bravado driving. It was probably Timo who thought that it would be a lot more exciting if the electric power could be turned up a bit to increase the speed and after an hilarious session with the operator, who eventually succumbed to most of the contents of a bottle of whisky, the mechanics located the master control lever and moved it to 'maximum' volts. The results were spectacular, the locals abandoned and watched in horror, the sparks flew, the air was thick with the smell of overheating electric motors and it all came to an inevitable halt when someone totally inverted a car and another went straight off the track through the barriers!

Back to the race, the event ran completely to form. Mäkinen and Hedges drove the first stints when the two MGs pulled out a one-minute lead over the best-placed Ferrari to lead the 2-litre GT class. Mäkinen was flying and was only 30 seconds down on the Lancia which led the whole GT category. The next two laps found the MG pair increase their class advantage to a comfortable five minutes.

With three laps completed Rhodes and Handley took over, both cars needing only refuelling and a top-up with oil. By this time the Sicilian sunshine had given way to the daddy of all storms, the roads running with water as the mountain streams washed stones and mud onto the circuit.

John Handley remembers the rain.

'In the race we did three laps each, Andy started, then I took over. Second lap out it started to rain on one side of the circuit, you came down to a very tight left over a bridge, almost a hairpin, and then square right away again. The surface was very slippery in the dry, in the wet it was diabolical. I banked into this left-hander, locked up and went straight off the road, there was no parapet other than on the bridge itself so I went off down a bank about 15 metres and ended up in the bed of this river. I engaged reverse, the car did not move and I thought that this was hopeless. This was my first drive for Stuart Turner and look what I have done. I was still sitting there in reverse trying to make the car shift when, all of a sudden, we start to move and I was aware that almost 100 people had appeared on the scene and they literally picked the car up and carried it back on to the road.

Off I went to complete my stint, Den Green checked the car in the pits, the exhaust pipe needed some attention and Andrew took over. After the race Stuart came up to me and said that I had done a very slow second lap and asked what had happened. I said that it had started to rain so I took it really carefully. Den Green and I kept our secret about how the exhaust pipe was flattened!'

John Rhodes recalls how he must be the only driver in a World Championship sports car race who has stopped in a village to top up with oil!

Described by some as the 'world's longest motor race', the 84-Hour Marathon at the Nürburgring in 1966 brought MG a memorable victory. With 'lap 0' showing on the pit board, the winning car comes in after a first-lap excursion to have smashed lights and a holed fuel tank repaired. Den Green (BMC overalls) leads the mechanics into action.

'The car went very well but started to use a lot of oil and during one of my sessions it got so bad that the oil warning light was blinking on all the corners – and the whole Targa Florio course is made up of corners. It got so bad that finally I felt that I had to try and find some oil before the 45-mile lap was up so I went slowly through all the villages shouting 'olio' to the peasants and the spectators. At first I could not remember what the Italian was for oil but luckily saw a big Fina advertising hoarding which reminded me! I finally got some from a little garage and staggered back to the pits. There the mechanics over-filled the sump and Timo took over and we made it to the finish.'

Laps seven and eight found the MGBs still way out ahead of all the class opposition, Rhodes and Handley having handed back to Mäkinen and Hedges. The leading GT Lancia then dropped back with a holed fuel tank so the Abingdon cars were now running 1-2 in the category.

I was acting as timekeeper for the team and I worked out that unless you kept a time chart going for every car in the race you would never know where your cars were placed. This was particularly significant because of the staggered 20-second rally-style starting procedure for the whole field which meant that positions on the road did not always represent race positions. I was pleased that I managed to keep my times and charts going for all 71 cars through the long hot race and we had our results out long before the organisers.

However, right at the finish the Targa rules produced a strange timekeeping and lap charting anomaly which deprived Hedges of his second place. It was not easy for me to explain to the excited Sicilian officials what had happened! The winning Mairesse/Muller Porsche took the chequered flag between the ailing Lancia and the Hedges MGB thus allowing the Lancia to have the advantage of being able to complete the full race distance of ten laps while Hedges was flagged off at nine laps. This situation, of course, happens regularly in conventional circuit races and when you have a proper scratch start a car which has completed ten laps will always beat a car that has only done nine. With the Targa, however, with its handicap-type start, this can make a complete nonsense of the result and I don't think the organisers had ever realised this before. Poor Hedges, therefore, failed to be credited with his second place in the GT category and we finished up with the ludicrous situation of the Lancia (placed 11th overall) averaging a slower race speed than the MGB (placed 16th overall). Not that we were all that fussed because we were very happy that the two MGs had finished 1-2 in the 2-litre class.

After the race I looked through the record books to see that the MGB's race average (and remember that part of the race was run in appalling weather conditions) was fast enough to have won the Targa outright five years previously, out-performing cars such as Ferrari, Mercedes and Maserati of the Moss-Collins-Hawthorne-Fangio era.

Marathon victory

When the last of the Spa-Sofia-Liège Marathons was run in 1964, the Belgian organisers created an entirely novel marathon, a 72-hour non-stop 'race' around the Nürburgring in Western Germany. Unfortunately the event suffered from hasty preparation and insurance restrictions which meant fairly sedate schedules (particularly at night) and far too much time was allowed for servicing. This meant that there were many more finishers than was in line with previous marathons.

In true Liège style, the organisers were quick to improve their event and when the regulations arrived for the 1966 marathon I got my slide rule out at Abingdon, and after some calculations, commented to Stuart Turner that I thought that this would be a good event for the MGB. Stuart, being totally committed at the time to the Mini-Cooper rally programme, somewhat reluctantly agreed to the preparation of two cars, gave me a modest budget and, with typical cynical good wishes, sent us on our way.

This was a bit of a mathematical marathon. Every car was set a bogey lap time according to its group capacity. For the GT cars this was 16 minutes in the day (19 minutes at night) which represented a speed of 66mph during the day (56mph at night). That may sound rather tame but a 16-minute lap around the 'Ring is only just about on in a standard MGB under ideal driving conditions (and conditions are seldom ideal at the 'Ring). The race was run over the full 17.5-mile track, incorporating both north and south circuits.

To allow time for refuelling an extra five minutes was allowed every ten laps. An extra 20 minutes was allowed every 50 laps for running repairs and service. Penalties for exceeding the bogey lap time were really severe and this is where I reckoned the event would be won or lost and why the reliable MGB could do well. For every one second late on a lap you were docked the equivalent of 200 metres from the total distance run. The severity of these penalties was apparent when you appreciated that you only have to be 2 minutes

20 seconds late on any one lap to loose the equivalent of one complete lap on your rival. And being one lap down at the 'Ring is some deficit!

A further illustration of how severe the penalties were can be seen from the final result of the event when one competitor who could not quite keep up to schedule, covered some 5,800km on the road but received some 7,000km in penalties and therefore ended up with a negative score of 1,200km. How demoralising to go racing for 3½ days only to find at the finish that in theory you have still got over 1,000km to go before you 'start'! The final straw was that the maximum lateness for any one lap was 30 minutes, so one major incident and you would be excluded.

It was, on the whole, a pretty fair marking system offering no real advantage to any particular type or size of car. Wet weather and early morning mist (traditional hazards at the 'Ring) also served as a good leveller between slower and faster cars. The only criticism was that the schedule for all the GT cars was the same, thus an MGB had to compete on equal terms with a Ferrari – but that was to make our victory even more rewarding.

The MGB was the obvious choice for the event on the basis of reliability, ease of servicing (and repairs if anything major went wrong) and driveability in all conditions. When Abingdon's Mini-Coopers and Austin-Healeys were having more than their fair share of rallying success at the time, there was enthusiastic anticipation for this MG sortie.

The two MGBs were the ex-Targa Florio car, which had actually been prepared by the Special Tuning Department, and a car from Development which had already done 10,000 miles in ten days at an average speed of 100mph at the MIRA test track for a publicity stunt with Shell.

For the drivers we selected racers rather than rally men – Andrew Hedges being paired with Julien Vernaeve, a Belgian BMC dealer who made a name for himself racing and rallying Group 1 Minis. In the second car were Roger Enever and Alec Poole. Roger was the shy young son of MG designer Syd Enever, a quick and steady driver who regularly raced a Development-prepared MGB. Alec Poole came from the family BMC dealership in Ireland, was an MG apprentice who raced Midgets and went on to capture the British Saloon Car Championship in a 1-litre Mini-Cooper.

In an endeavour to retain something of the old Liège traditions, the marathon started and finished in the city of Liège, there being a non-competitive but compulsory road section to and from the 'Ring. Scrutineering was held in the beautiful grounds of the Palais des Princes-Eveques, a fairly informal affair although one or two competitors were sent away to fit bumpers to their cars to comply with the 'rally' regulations.

Midnight start

The start on the circuit at midnight after the run-in from Liège was an anxious time for the drivers, for no practising was allowed, the cars were despatched rally-style at one-minute intervals, and there was no allowance as far as penalties were concerned for the standing start, so the drivers had to get down to their bogey times immediately. Many of them had never driven over the full circuit before, the Nürburg's south curve being seldom used for events – and of course it was pitch black!

For the MG team those opening laps were disastrous and it was very nearly a mighty short marathon for the Abingdon team. Roger Enever took the first spell in MGB No. 46 because he knew the circuit pretty well having done a bit of private practice during the previous weekend. Unknown to Roger, however, road menders had since been at work and had resurfaced one of the corners leaving a treacherous coating of loose chippings on the circuit. Poor Roger arrived on the scene on his very first lap, got the MG into a wild slide, went flying off the road, down a ditch, up the bank on the other side, back down into the ditch again and just managed to make enough headway to crawl back over the rise back on to the circuit. Shaken and pausing only to kick the fog lights back into shape, Roger pressed on to the pits, the MG having the honour of making the first pit stop. More serious, Roger was 3½ minutes over the bogey time which put us some half a lap behind the opposition before the race had even started!

As if that was not a bad enough start, no sooner had the mechanics straightened out Roger's car than Andrew Hedges went missing on lap two. He had found exactly the same patch of loose chippings, but he had made a far better job of his accident. The MG completely cleared the ditch, ploughed its way through a hedge and ended up in a field. With smashed lights, Andy had trouble finding his way back on to the track and several precious minutes were lost before he could find the hole in the hedge and take a running jump out of the field back on to the circuit. Losing 4½ minutes, the second MG hobbled back to the pits, fog lights akimbo, all the front jacking points smashed, bodywork crumpled, one headlight missing and fuel pouring like Niagara Falls out of a split in the fuel tank. While onlookers thought that our race was run, and that this activity in the MG pit so early on

The 84-Hour Marathon could have seen a 1–2 overall for MG but the second MGB of Alec Poole (left) and Roger Enever dropped out with a broken half-shaft in the closing hours.

in the race was quite a joke, the gallant mechanics – Den Green, Eddie Burnell and Cliff Bray – set to work repairing the lights and stemming the fuel tank with the magic Isopon. Within a couple of minutes Andy was back in the race, heavily penalised for his delay but at least the MG was running.

Back in the pits there were sighs of relief as the two MGs settled down to some steady lappery well within their bogey times. The marathon was under way albeit after a highly dramatic start.

Our plan for the race was to run the cars to a carefully controlled schedule, fast enough to keep them well-placed amongst the leaders without undue strain on the car or the crew. While we certainly hoped to do well in the class, and perhaps the GT category, I don't think any of us really expected to win the event outright. Our race plan was to stop every ten laps (175 miles – 2½ hours) for fuel and an oil check. The drivers were to change every third stop, giving them about 7½ hours' driving followed by an equally long rest halt. While this seemed a pretty long driving spell, it proved to be the right decision for it allowed the drivers to really get some rest so that they could get a proper meal and some six hours' sleep. Several of our rivals choose shorter driving stints only to find that their drivers were not really fully rested between turns.

The misfortunes of the opening laps had put us right at the bottom of the field in the early stages and everyone in the team was on their toes during that first night as the MGs sped on to make up for lost time. The mechanics were kept busy during those early hours for the cars were still in bad shape after their shunts and, unlike a normal race where one long pit stop could have got them roadworthy, with the constant pressures of the bogey lap times, it was a case of making rally-style repairs – a little bit here and a little bit there – at each pit stop.

Fortunately that first night was fine and there was only a little early morning mist in the mountains, so we were able to make up some time. By breakfast the Enever/Poole car had moved up to a more respectable 16th place while the Hedges/Vernaeve car trailed in 34th place, more time being lost during the night with repairs to the fuel tank. Taking an early lead was the Equipe National Belge Ferrari which was setting a pace which nobody could match.

As the sun came up and we changed from night to day schedules, morale was fairly high in the MG camp. As one wit remarked, 'Oh well, only three days to go!' Through the first morning the cars continued their climb up the field and after 12 hours of racing the Enever/

Poole car had reached eighth place while the second MG had jumped up to 19th place. There were a number of retirements, one of the most notable being the very quick Alan Mann Cortina of Bohringer/Kaiser which had gone out with a mild fire under the dashboard.

First day

The first day continued without drama, the two MGs running like clockwork, our only concern now being broken wheels. The first indication of trouble came when Alec Poole lost time when he had to change a collapsed wire wheel out on the circuit, a subsequent inspection revealing that the wheels on both cars were starting to shed spokes. Although we had a fair stock of wheels at the circuit, an SOS was sent to Abingdon for fresh supplies, just in case.

Even by slowing down a little to save the wheels and suspension, both cars were still making up ground. Hedges/Vernaeve were now lying tenth while the Enever/Poole car had climbed to fourth place behind one of the works Porsche 911s, a remarkably fast Swedish-entered Volvo and the leading Ferrari.

Into the second night – one Le Mans gone – and two to go! Early morning brought 100 laps completed (1,750 miles) and time for the second 20-minute stop for servicing. The near-side rear hubs on both cars showed signs of wear at this stage so it was decided to change the bearings as there was time. The pit crews on each car made a race of it, the first taking eleven minutes for the job, the second crew bettering this by two minutes. Apart from this the drivers reported the cars to be in fine fettle, so there was no other work to be done and the two MGs were soon back in the race having only used up half of their allotted service time. Oil consumption was working out at no more than a pint every ten laps (175 miles) with fuel consumption running at a constant 16mpg.

There were dramas amongst the leaders on the second night. The second driver in the leading Ferrari had twice been off the road and the yellow GTB was starting to look very battered. The Porsche 911 remained second but the third-placed Volvo was dropping back with overheating and water pump troubles. Enever/Poole clung to fourth place while Hedges/Vernaeve were now up to sixth.

The second day brought glorious sunshine with little of the dreaded early morning mist. Things in the MG pit were looking good for now the second-place Porsche had been disqualified for reversing out on the circuit and the fifth-placed Alfa Romeo had disappeared off the lap charts. Now the MGs sat in third and fourth places.

Half-time

As half-distance approached there were strange scenes in the pits as the mechanics carried out servicing more in line with a record attempt than a motor race. By now the MGs had clocked up some 2,500 miles so it was time to check things like battery levels, grease the steering and suspension and check the gearbox and axle oil levels. All was in order and there were some muffled cheers when the second-placed Volvo dropped right back and the MGs moved up to second and third behind the Ferrari. Just behind the MGs however danger lurked for the remaining Alan Mann Cortinas had been playing a waiting game with the strong entries of Ickx/Staepelaere and Elford/Neerpasch.

The early hours of the next morning saw the Ford challenge make its mark when the Elford/Neerpasch car came through to split the two MGs and take third place. With both our cars running well and comfortably within their limits, we decided to let Enever/Poole off the leash a little to see whether we could bait the Cortinas into speeding up. Some spirited early morning driving by Alec Poole set the Cortina a fair pace, the Ford crew taking up the challenge and, just as we had hoped, Elford's car started to overheat and finally blew up.

The second Cortina gave up the chase and Ickx decided to drop back and play for a safe finish in the touring category. So with 24 hours to run, the status quo was resumed with the two MGs in second and third spots.

Obviously, we had no chance of catching the Ferrari on the road but nevertheless there was now hope of an MG victory, for clearly there was concern in the Ferrari camp for their less-experienced and now very tired second driver. Poor Bianchi, their number one, had been forced to do more than his fair share at the wheel, driving one spell of over 18 hours!

Then came the big drama of the marathon! In typical Nürburg style, the daddy of all thunderstorms suddenly hit the circuit. Within seconds the track, which was now thickly coated with rubber dust, was turned into a skating rink. The very first casualty was the poor number two Ferrari driver who put the GTB off the road in no uncertain manner.

So now the MGs were first and second overall but, before we could signal the good news to the drivers, the smiles were wiped off our faces. Coming down the straight towards the pits Roger Enever had the terrifying experience of the car aquaplaning right out of control as it hit a river of water running across the track. The MG skimmed across the road and landed in a ditch on its side. It took 18 minutes to get the car

back on the track and into the pits, Roger dropping to fourth place.

At the same time Andrew Hedges came in to change to wet tyres, this stop costing him valuable time and now the situation on the leader board showed the Ickx/Staepelaere Cortina in the lead with Hedges/Vernaeve second, the Volvo having recovered to take third place and Enever/Poole fourth.

With 12 hours to run the battle against the Cortinas was well and truly on, as Julien Vernaeve took over for the final early morning spell. Making the best use of wet weather tyres, Julien slowly whittled away the Cortina's advantage and put the MG back in front. Alec Poole had also put up a splendid show to bring the other car back into second place, so once again it was an MG 1-2.

But our luck did not hold. As the Enever/Poole car pulled away from the refuelling pits (these were in special bays situated before the main pits) a half-shaft snapped and, as the car would have been disqualified if it were pushed to the pits or if a spare had been brought to the car, there was nothing to do but accept retirement. A tremendous disappointment for the young crew who had really driven their hearts out to overcome earlier problems.

Now, with only one car running, those final hours became sheer torture, everyone checking off the 15-minute laps as MG No. 47 sped on its way to victory. Andrew Hedges drove the final stint and slowly pulled out an amazing three-lap lead over Ickx in the Cortina. Seven laps down was the third-placed 2-litre BMW.

I fear there were some somewhat wild antics going on in the MG pit when Andrew finally came flying over the brow to take the chequered flag, swerving to avoid a carefully aimed champagne cork and some unmentionable pit signals! The final distance covered was 5,620 miles in 84 hours, only 14 cars were still running at the end and the MG was the only survivor in the GT category. It had been a marathon well worth winning – one of MG's only two post-war international outright victories.

When I phoned Stuart Turner to tell him the good news and said that we had won, he commented something to the effect that he expected us to win the class. When I repeated the message he still presumed that I meant the GT category. He took some convincing that an MGB had actually won outright!

The Marathon winner, Belgium's Julien Vernaeve, enjoys his Moulton bicycle; the drivers used these novel British-designed bicycles to get from the circuit to their hotel during the event.

CHAPTER 16

MGB IN RALLYING 1963–66

THE 1963–64 TOUR DE FRANCE WITH JOHN SPRINZEL;

1964 MONTE CARLO RALLY WITH THE MORLEYS;

1964 LIÈGE AND RAC RALLY, 1966 MONTE CARLO

The Morley twins' magnificent GT category win with the MGB on the 1964 Monte Carlo Rally was somewhat overshadowed by the much-publicised outright victory by Paddy Hopkirk's Mini-Cooper.

By 1963 Abingdon's rallying programme was concentrating on the Mini-Cooper with the big Healey still favoured for events such as the long, fast power-climbs of the Alpine Rally and the rough, tough Liège-Rome-Liège Marathons. The MGB was only to appear on selected events where there was a chance of a 2-litre class win in the GT category.

Such an event was the Tour de France which attracted almost as much hysteria and publicity amongst the French and Italian motoring press as did the tour on bicycles. For the 1963 event, run in September, the Le Mans car was prepared for Andrew Hedges and John Sprinzel who takes up the story.

'The Tour attracted a different city to sponsor the start each year and sometimes visited circuits in Germany in the same way as the bike event. The finish was generally in Nice, the home of the organising club, and the event lasted ten days with about half the nights spent in hotels. Although the main challenge was in the one-hour and two-

hour races at tracks around France, there were also special stages and hill-climbs. Also, the road sections were rarely longer than half an hour or so, to prevent a large build-up of time for repairs. The event had Shell as the overall sponsor and there were big money prizes for winners of each individual stage, hill-climb or race. So you did not even have to finish to get some of Shell's cash, which was an unusual touch.

There were tents full of food and drink at many controls and really huge five-course "knees-unders" at the circuits. On the road stages food would be served on the basis of one course per control – you might get your oysters and Chablis starter at one control, the roast beef a few miles along the road and peaches

Andrew Hedges and John Sprinzel took the ex-Le Mans 'droop-snout' MGB on the Tour de France in 1963. They retired when Hedges fell asleep. 'This was unfortunate because he was driving at the time!' recalls Sprinzel.

and brandy at a third control. Remember, this is France we are talking about, and at a time when drinking and driving was still socially acceptable – although obviously we did not take more than a token sip or two.

As you passed through each region the cars would be showered with gifts of the local speciality. At the circuit in the Cognac region, for instance, Monsieur Martel himself would hand out half-bottles of best five-star. We were just glad that we had service crews to carry all this loot.

The entry list always read like a Who's Who? of motorsport with grand prix drivers in their Ferraris and Porsches, most of the top rallymen in whatever exotica they could lay their hands on, and the factory teams anxious not to miss out on the tremendous publicity to be gained.

Policing was exceptional and virtually every car had a motorcycle escort through the towns – often it was quite hard and a bit nerve-wracking to keep up with the gendarme motoring at 80mph through dense rush hour traffic, his whistle glued to his lips, blasting at any poor Simca driver who dared to exercise his right of way. To see the procession of these raw and powerful race cars – for this is essentially what they were – attracted millions of spectators who would gather at every junction whatever the hour.

At each circuit knowledgeable commentators would keep the vast audience on its toes and the cheering and clapping far exceeded anything I have seen at a normal race meeting.

Donald Morley could not get away at the last moment so Stuart offered me the seat with Andrew Hedges in the droop-snout Le Mans MGB. Andrew took to our Le Mans class-winning MGB like a duck to water and we slowly worked our way up through the ranks until we arrived at the Pyrenees. On two foggy hill-climb tests I read from Pauline Mayman's pace notes – the first time I had ever read notes in action. Andrew, whose eyesight is about the same as Mr Magoo's and who had never listened to pace notes, stormed up through the mist to take half a minute off the leading Ferraris on each of these climbs.

Suddenly we were in fourth place overall behind two GTO Ferraris and a Porsche 904 – in a blooming MGB! Next morning the banner headlines in L'Equipe, the French Sporting Life, screamed "Sprinzel-Hedges MG batters the Ferraris" as if they could not quite believe it themselves.

Mind you, our glory did not last too long, as the following night Andrew had a little nap. Unfortunately, he was driving at the time, so we spent the rest of the night in the local clinic having our wounds dressed.'

Morley's Monte GT win

Moving into the 1964 season and the Monte Carlo Rally, which was totally overshadowed by Paddy Hopkirk's Mini victory – probably the most publicised rally win of all time – Don and Erle Morley's MGB won the GT category outright, their only problem being a leaking radiator which had to be replaced.

In an interview with Andrew Roberts in *MG Enthusiast* magazine, Don and Erle talk about their Monte drive.

'The MGB was not really seen as a rally car in the same way as the big Healey. The main thrust of Stuart Turner's programme was that the Mini should be the main contender in the rally effort supported by the big Healey. The MGB was the choice for long distance racing at which it performed very well. As for the 1964 Monte, Erle and I had thought about taking a big Healey – Timo Mäkinen and Christabel Carlisle had managed a class win the previous year – but we decided we weren't ready to die yet!

The MGB was totally different to the big Healey. With the big Healey you had to tame it. You really had to take it by the scruff of the neck because if you had not got the measure of the car it could be impossible to drive. The MGB, on the other hand, was a complete contrast – lovely to drive, comfortable, spacious and very forgiving. And what a difference to the MGA which was very cramped in comparison.'

Some have ascribed the Morleys' success to the fact that they were twins and naturally there was a very close bond between them. Erle considers that their attention to pace notes was a vital ingredient to their success – particularly on the Monte.

'Donald and I took the question of pace notes very seriously, and I admit to having been very fussy about getting distances absolutely spot-on. At one stage we talked to some RAF scientists at Cambridge about preparing our notes relative to the speed that the car was travelling over a special stage. Of course, the accuracy of the notes was crucial and it did relate to the results you achieved.'

Cockpit of the works MGB for the 1964 Monte Carlo Rally with (from left) windscreen washer control for co-driver's use (driver's control next to the heater controls), Halda speedpilot beneath illuminated magnifying screen, space for the Heuer rally clocks, auxiliary light switches in the radio panel, fuses (brought inside the car for instant access and clearer identification), mileage trip recorder control (brought forward on a special bracket for ease of use), electric windscreen demister bar, massive metal accelerator and brake pedal pads, three-spoke wood-rimmed steering wheel and overdrive switch on the gearlever knob.

To appreciate the significance of the Morleys' Monte performance the equivalence formula of that year has to be taken into account. This tended to favour smaller-engined cars, and certainly not the GT cars, thus the MGB suffered an overall 5 per cent handicap.

Starting from Oslo the Morleys were amongst the 73 crews unpenalised on the road when they reached Monte. Thus the 82 miles of special stages, the final mountain circuit and the somewhat inappropriate

round-the-houses 'race' on the GP circuit, was to determine the results.

The MGB was running against the mighty Ford Falcons of Bo Ljungfeldt, Anne Hall, Peter Harper, Peter Jopp, Jo Schlesser and Graham Hill, the Mini-Coopers of Paddy Hopkirk, Rauno Aaltonen and Timo Mäkinen, the Saabs of Erik Carlsson and Pat Moss, the Mercedes of Eugene Bohringer, the Volvo of Tom Trana – all possible outright winners.

The MGB was consistently placed amongst the top six and on the 14-mile Col Saint Martin stage they were only 12 seconds behind Ljungfeldt's leading Falcon. At the finish, overshadowed by the Hopkirk Mini victory, the Morleys won the GT category outright and, although classified 17th overall through the equivalence formula, would actually have finished fifth overall on a scratch basis. A superb drive.

Final sorties

Don and Erle took the same car on the Scottish Rally in June but crashed and the car was written off.

The only team of works MGBs entered on an

international rally appeared on the 1964 Spa-Sofia-Liège in August when three cars were prepared for Pauline Mayman, Julien Vernaeve and David Hiam. It was not a successful sortie with Mayman and Vernaeve retiring with clutch troubles caused by overheating due to the close-fitting sump guard, while David Hiam was forced out with a smashed rear spring shackle.

Andrew Hedges and John Sprinzel were again paired for the 1964 Tour de France – comment again by John Sprinzel.

Mechanics Bob Whittington (left) and Gerald Wiffen put the finishing touches to the MGB of Pauline Mayman and Val Domleo for the 1964 RAC Rally.

'Stuart forgave us for our retirement the previous year and we were given another droop-snout MGB. Once again my man Hedges worked his magic all around France, gradually creeping up the leader board as the Ferraris and Porsches hit things and fell by the wayside. By coincidence we were within 5km of the spot where we had crashed the year before when we stopped again, this time with a blown head gasket.'

Racers John Fitzpatrick and John Handley were paired in an MGB for the 1964 RAC Rally, an event which ended ignominiously in the depth of a forest recalls John Handley.

'Somewhere in the depths of Wales, we left the road on a long fast left-hander and entered a silver birch plantation at considerable speed. There were whippy little trees of about an inch girth all over the place and we mowed them all down and then they all spring up behind us. When we came to a standstill there was no way out at all, we could not get up enough speed to knock them all over again. We finally had to pull up a path of trees by the roots to get back on the road. I am sure the Forestry Commission were not impressed. Not long afterwards we were out with clutch failure.'

John Fitzpatrick recalls . . .

'I went testing the car on some rough roads before the event and was surprised to see that there were chains fitted to the inside of the doors. When I asked the mechanics what they were for they said I would soon find out when I went over a big

Pauline Mayman and Val Domleo (pictured) were forced out of the 1964 RAC Rally with clutch trouble, while the second team car of John Fitzpatrick and John Handley crashed.

bump. Sure enough the first time I took off over a crest the doors tried to fly open with the flexing of the chassis!'

The remaining works MGB rally entries were not particularly notable. Andrew Hedges/Jack Scott joined Paddy Hopkirk (Mini-Cooper) on the 1965 Nordhein-Westfalen Rally. There were nine special tests including the 'Ring and Zolder race tracks but this was really a glorified 'hunt the marshal' club event, Hedges and Hopkirk exchanging fastest stage times, with results being decided on handicap which did not suit the sports car class.

The last appearance of a works rallying MGB was on the 1966 Monte Carlo Rally – the event notable for the disqualification of the winning team of Mini-Coopers.

Tony Fall/Ron Crellin were entered for a GT category win but they were unlucky, recalls Tony Fall.

> *'Stuart Turner lent me a works Austin-Healey 3000 over Christmas and I thrashed this around to polish up my rear-wheel drive technique – and succeeded in removing quite a bit of polish from the big Healey in the process. On the Monte we were going quite well with a reasonable time on the opening stages when an oil cooler pipe chafed through on the steering column and put us out of the event. A pity because I was starting to get the hang of it!'*

In 1967 I took over from Stuart Turner as Competitions Manager at a time when the European rally opposition was starting to seriously challenge the supremacy of the Mini-Cooper. The regulations of the day made competition in the GT category even tougher for cars like the MGB while the big Healey was no longer in production. Under the coming regime of British Leyland the competition programme was soon to concentrate on the new generation of marathons, London to Sydney and then London to Mexico.

At this time there was a desperate search amongst the Leyland model range to find a new competition winner. The MGC-GTS project was to be the most promising.

Unsung heroes. The works co-drivers plotting their maps for the 1963 RAC Rally (from left): Ross Finlay, Val Domleo, Henry Liddon, Mike Wood, Tony Ambrose, Erle Morley and Ron Crellin.

CHAPTER 17

MGC-GTS
1967–68

BRITISH LEYLAND RULE;

1967 TARGA FLORIO,
1968 SEBRING AND
NÜRBURGRING MARATHON;

THE CLOSURE OF
COMPETITIONS

*The last official works MG entry from Abingdon was
the two-car MGC-GTS team for the 1968 Marathon at
the Nürburgring. This is the car driven by Andrew
Hedges, Julien Vernaeve and Tony Fall, which gave
the works Porsches a run for their money for 67
hours of racing before brake problems forced it to
drop to sixth overall at the finish.*

With the British Leyland takeover came the new brief for the Competitions Department to evaluate the motorsport potential of all the cars in the group. Thus I found myself in a unique situation of being one of the few people in the company who had access to the Design and New Model departments of Austin/Morris, Triumph, Rover and indeed Jaguar – although I was told that I would be wasting my time going to Coventry!

Looking back, I probably was not the right man in the hot seat at the time, my background within the Competitions world being administration and team logistics rather than engineering know-how and I have to say that I found it hard work trying to talk with any technical authority to the respective Chief Engineers. These people at the time were under considerable pressure to make their mark with the new Leyland management in terms of new model development, very few of them were personally interested in competitions, and they probably resented someone from MG turning up and wasting their time asking distracting and penetrating questions about their secret projects. Despite the fact that all the Chief Engineers at the time sat on a corporate Engineering and Design Committee, there was still inherent inter-marque rivalry and certainly reluctance to divulge plans to those from other factories.

Rallying at the end of the 1960s had developed to the point where most major European manufacturers had appreciated that in order to be competitive you had to engineer competition options into the car at the earliest design stage. From this you could then build the required number of special competition versions of the model – or offer for sale the required number of homologated competition parts. You can probably make any soundly engineered production car into a competition model if you start with that intention on the drawing board. It is really no good taking the finished production model then seeing how you can modify it for competition because inevitably you will come across inherent engineering design barriers which cannot be overcome.

None of the current models in the British Leyland range which I saw showed any motorsporting potential off the shelf to beat Renault Alpine, Lancia and Porsche, who were the main European opposition at the time. Trying to talk design chiefs into building in homologated options for future models was hopeless when the overall directive and commitment from the top management was not there.

Triumph had some enthusiastic competition-minded people around who I felt would have liked to have been co-operative if they had been given the green light (as proved by the later competition activities with the Triumph 2.5 PI, the Dolomite and the TR7). Austin/Morris was hopeless when you considered models such as the 1100, 1800, Allegro and Marina. There was a glimmer of hope from Rover when permission was obtained to evaluate the 3500 V8 and possibly produce a special edition competition version. We commissioned a racing Rover project from Bill Shaw and Roy Pierpoint which made its sensational debut in the 84-Hour Marathon de la Route at the Nürburgring in 1970, but this exciting project got no further, appearing on the eve of the closure of the Competitions Department itself.

MGC project

The only project which came close to fruition was what was to become known as the MGC-GTS, a lightweight special-bodied competition version of the MGC. This unquestionably got further than the other projects because it was an MG which was developed in-house at Abingdon at a time when the factory itself was facing the threat of closure and there was clearly a desire to try to do anything to boost morale and impress the pro-Triumph and anti-MG British Leyland management.

The objective of the GTS was to produce a rally car to take over from the Mini-Cooper, probably a bit ambitious but at least try to hold our own against the rising strength of the European opposition. The MGB chassis was basically well-proven in competitions and was rigid enough to stand up to rallying or at least good enough as a starting point for a big Healey-type chassis development programme. In lightweight form it was possible to shed quite a bit of weight while the GT was a sensible size for a rally car, certainly more attractive than a four-seater saloon.

Initially the car would have to be developed with MGB mechanicals prior to the MGC launch when the six-cylinder engine could be used. We were aware that in the pipeline was the prospect of a lightweight alloy competition engine which would do wonders for the MGC's inherent nose-heavy handling problems. Cavernous under-bonnet space allowed plenty of room for development.

The stages of the project were to first build a handful of prototypes, test in races, then evaluate them for rallies. The final and most difficult stage would then be to produce the required number of production versions for homologation – hopefully easier to achieve by MG at Abingdon than if we were dealing with any other British Leyland marque. There was confidence that such was the enthusiasm for MG that a limited

The MGC-GTS project was aimed to produce a more competitive MG racer and later possibly a challenge to the new generation of European rally opposition. The cars continue to attract interest at MG Car Club gatherings.

edition competition model, albeit highly priced, could be sold through dealers, particularly in the States, where possibly the whole production run could be sold at whatever price.

As a race car it probably was not going to be a Porsche-beater but we felt that certainly in long-distance races it could probably fight its way into the top ten on reliability. For rallying, we were to rely on Abingdon's know-how to make it competitive.

Styled by the Development Department, six sets of special GT panels were built by Pressed Steel Fisher at Swindon, a tricky process using light-alloy instead of sheet steel on the standard press tools, an operation which unquestionably only happened through 'old pals' contacts between Abingdon and Pressed Steel Fisher. The main differences from the standard design were the large flares on the front and rear wing panels to accommodate wide racing tyres.

Three of the new lightweight bodies were then assembled by Bodies Branch at Castle Bromwich, and the first car was built up at Abingdon by Tommy Wellman and Gerald Wiffen upon a standard steel MGC floorpan and bulkhead in March 1967.

The new production MGC torsion-bar front suspension was used but fitted with adjustable dampers. The ride height could be adjusted from a control under the driver's seat. At the rear there were heavy duty police springs and the floorpan was modified with turrets to take adjustable Armstrong telescopic dampers instead of the lever-arm design. There were anti-roll bars front and rear, a ZF limited-slip differential was fitted and the axle was located with special radius arms.

Centre-lock 6.5in Minilite wheels were fitted with 5.50 x 15in Dunlop tyres. Girling disc brakes were used all round with cooling scoops at the front and twin vacuum servos. There was a non-overdrive straight cut gearbox. The standard MGB steering rack was used with a shortened column. A full roll-cage was fitted and there was a 21.9-gallon fuel tank with 4in diameter filler with the cap just behind the off-side rear quarter light. Perspex windows were used. There were quick-lift jacking points and Sebring headlight cowls.

Targa trial

As the production MGC was not to be announced until the London Motor Show in October 1967 it was not possible initially to use the C-type six-cylinder engine. With plans to enter the car for the Targa Florio in May, the ex-Sebring MGB unit was used with 84.8mm bores increasing the capacity to 2,004cc giving 150bhp. The idea of entering it in the over 2-litre class and in the prototype category was to try for an easier class win away from the production Porsches. Tested at Castle Combe by Andrew Hedges and Geoff Mabbs, the GTS first ran with Weber carburetters and then with SUs, the latter showing an improvement and the Targa car ran in this form.

Driven by Paddy Hopkirk and Timo Mäkinen on the Targa, the car had some brake problems and lost 12 minutes in the pits but finished third in class behind two glassfibre-bodied Porsche 910-8s, one of which won the race outright. Because the MG was in the same class as the race winner and covered less than 90 per cent of the race distance, it was not officially classified but nevertheless finished ninth overall on the road.

With the MGC now in production, the Hopkirk/Hedges GTS entry for Sebring in 1968 was in the GT category. The car was tested at Silverstone in November where severe understeer and axle patter under heavy braking proved a problem which was overcome by lowering the suspension and increasing negative camber. Changes were also made to the cooling ducts to the front brakes. The new MGC engine had a gas-flowed alloy head upon the standard cast-iron seven main bearing block bored out to 2,968cc, producing some 200bhp at 6,000rpm on triple Weber carburettors.

The first of the MGC-GTS cars is tested by Paddy Hopkirk at Thruxton prior to the 1967 Targa Florio.

The final stage in the MGC-GTS development programme was the fitting of an all-aluminium engine block, which did wonders for the weight distribution and overall handling.

Timo Mäkinen signs on for the 1967 Targa Florio where he drove the MGC-GTS with Paddy Hopkirk to finish ninth overall.

The MGC-GTS had to be entered as an MGB GT for the 1967 Targa Florio as the MGC had not yet been announced. The car ran with a 2,004cc MGB engine giving 150bhp and, driven in spirited style by Paddy Hopkirk and Timo Mäkinen, finished a stirring ninth overall on the road.

MG works swansong

In the Sebring race the only unscheduled stop was to remove some paper from the radiator grille, the MGC running faultlessly and finishing tenth overall, and third in the prototype class behind the winning Porsches.

For the 1968 Marathon de la Route at the Nürburgring a second GTS car was built up to be entered with the original prototype car. This was the first of the cars to be fitted with the new all-alloy engine block developed by Engines Branch at Coventry which gave an impressive improvement in weight distribution and handling. For this event the cars ran with road-going exhaust systems. During testing there were problems with the centre-lock Minilite wheels and a hasty switch was made to wire wheels for the race.

Driven by Clive Baker/Roger Enever/Alec Poole, the alloy-engined car retired with engine overheating and a blown head gasket. The second car, driven by Tony Fall/Andrew Hedges/Julien Vernaeve was running in a fine third place overall after 67 hours, and catching the leading Porsche 911, when severe brake pad wear caused the front pads to wear right through and the back plates to become welded to the discs.

After a panic pit stop, Tony Fall was forced to do two completely brake-less laps having to move out of the pits to avoid disqualification according to the marathon regulations. The GTS finally finished sixth overall, covering some 6,000 racing miles and running only ten miles short of the leading Porsches at the finish.

The two GTS cars were to have one more outing at Sebring in March 1969 when they were entered by British Leyland North America and driven by Paddy Hopkirk/Andrew Hedges (15th overall) and local drivers Craig Hill/Bill Brack (34th overall).

Sadly, the cars were not to return to England for, after the Marathon, British Leyland announced the closure of the Competitions Department. Thus the promising GTS project never came to fruition and MG's post-war works racing and rallying activities came to an end.

Almost exactly 15 years since the Competitions Department was set up, the team was disbanded. More seriously, seven years later the MG factory itself was to be closed. As one wise MG archivist said later: 'It was amazing that at the time the only people who did not appear to appreciate the worldwide heritage and value of the MG name were the very people who owned it.'

Certainly the pre- and post-war competition activities of the works MGs, those who designed them, built them, raced and rallied them, contributed in no small way to that heritage.

The two original MGC-GTS cars – the last competition works MGs to be built at Abingdon.

APPENDICES

A–C BY MICHAEL ALLISON

D–F BY PETER BROWNING

APPENDIX A
PERSONALITIES

The following is a summary of the main characters of the MG pre-war competition story. Apart from Cecil Kimber and Frank Tayler, I met them all and worked with most of them during my time at Abingdon. These notes are supplementary to the many stories which appear in the main text, and is by no means exhaustive and I apologise for the omission of anyone not mentioned – I hold them all in the highest possible esteem. After each name I have appended their contemporary sobriquet, by which they were generally known by their fellows.

Cecil Kimber – 'CK'

Kimber was the founder of the MG Car Company, and its inspiration throughout the pre-war period. His ability to get people motivated was of paramount importance in getting the fledgling company into a state of financial viability, while fighting off others close to William Morris who envied him his success and foresight.

Cecil Kimber was born in Dulwich, London during 1888, son of a wealthy businessman who owned and ran a printing ink manufacturing business. He showed little interest in the family business and, although he started his career as a salesman in the firm, he disagreed with his father as to a likely way of earning a living.

He was a keen motorcyclist and his interest in things mechanical ultimately led him to the motor industry. However it was a motorcycle accident that presented him with the opportunity to do this, for with the insurance compensation, he not only bought a car, but also left the family firm to make his own mark.

Kimber was not by training an engineer, but had secured a job in the then respected firm of Sheffield Simplex, it is believed in the drawing office. After a spell with AC Cars, under S. F. Edge, he had moved to E. G. Wrigley Ltd, the transmission specialists, and it was there that he impressed William Morris enough to be offered the job with Morris Garages. Kimber's real strength was that he was an expert sales and promotion man, and had even written a paper on organisation and management. Privately he was an enthusiastic motorist, and by all accounts a fast and safe road driver. When it became obvious that there was a ready clientele for tuning motorcycles and cars amongst the richer students and residents around Oxford, it was natural for Kimber to encourage continuation of this service to these people at the Longwall Street Service Depot of Morris Garages Ltd.

After the service department of Morris Garages burgeoned into the MG Car Company, Kimber's leisure time interests became the growing MG Car Club, and yachting. The latter enabled him to get away from motors and motoring and to relax completely.

Although a short man in stature, he had, by all accounts, quite a presence. Popular stories have him named as 'Kim', but this appears to have been a name by which he was only known outside the Factory. Very few at the Factory dared to refer to him in such a familiar way, and where he was always known as Mr Kimber, or amongst senior colleagues as 'CK'.

Kimber was eventually effectively sacked from the company he had built up, by Miles Thomas, reputedly over war-time contracts with the War Department. It almost certainly rankled Thomas that Kimber was able to win contracts by using personal contacts, by-passing the red tape which was to bedevil the UK for the next 20 years of so. Kimber was not able to accept that this was the way of the future, and took a job with the Specialloid Piston Company. He died in 1945 in a railway accident.

Hubert Noel Charles – 'HN'

Hubert Charles was the real technical genius of the pre-war MG cars and their triumphs. If this has never been stated before it was because by the time histories came to be written he had left the orbit of Morris Motors, possibly not happily.

He trained at Cranwell College in Bedfordshire, where he achieved a BSc in engineering, and worked on fighter aircraft production during the First World War attaining the rank of captain in the RFC. After the war he started to work for the Zenith Carburettor Company but moved quickly to the company which eventually became Automotive Products. He took a job as designer with William Morris at Cowley in 1924, but had helped Kimber with design work on the early MG models, probably without Morris being aware of what was going on.

His real forte was in thinking things from first principles, which is mentioned more than once in the foregoing chapters. During the early days he worked closely with the practical Reg Jackson and Cecil Cousins, leading them to develop their own abilities. He was able to see the latent talent in Sydney Enever, and brought him on within the MG company from 1934.

After he left MG Charles spent the rest of his life in industry, initially with Morris Motors at Cowley, where it seems that he did not fit into the new Nuffield order, but he was responsible for the designs of the SA, VA and TA cars. He completed his time in the petro-chemical industry, before retiring in around 1970. He died a few years later.

It was while he was working at Associated Octel Company that I was to meet him, and talk to him about his time at MG but he was reluctant to do this, and it seems that he was badly hurt emotionally by the wheeling and dealing that went on, rather than concentrating on the future designs and engineering of the products.

John Thornley – 'JWT'

For many years 'Mr MG' to the many members of the MG Car Club, and indeed the President of that Club until his death in 1994.

John was originally training to be an accountant, but was elected as Secretary of the newly formed MG Car Club in 1930. He was recruited on to the staff at the Works by Kimber, and worked in the Service Department initially as a receptionist, and later as Service Manager. In that position he became team manager of the Trials teams, the Cream Crackers and The Three Musketeers.

During the war he was away on active service, and came back to MG to find the rule from Cowley being very strictly run. In due course he was appointed General Manager and was responsible for the introduction of the TD, and the later cars. He always fought the senior management of the larger corporation for the right of MG to produce sporting cars designed and built at Abingdon, although using the readily available components from the BMC parts bins. In this aim he followed the policy originally laid down by Kimber.

He was able to encourage private owners to compete in much the same way as CK had done before the war, by providing Factory support, and this policy he continued right up to his retirement.

When BMC was formed, in 1953, he found that company politics was the name of the game, and was very disappointed that the MGA was not put into production, but was able to get this done two years later.

He retired due to ill health in 1968, but continued to take an interest in all things MG including presidency of the MG Car Club, which he had helped to found.

Cecil Cousins – 'Cuz'

Cousins was able, even proud, to boast that he worked at MG before Kimber! He was Workshop Foreman at Morris Garages, Longwall depot when Kimber joined the company as Assistant Sales Manager. Cousins it was who got many of the earliest MG cars built including Old Number One. He went on to become the Team Manager of the racing teams, and selected those who could be trusted to work for customers.

He had a keen sense of humour and an entertaining turn of phrase, speaking with a broad Oxford dialect . . . he once told me that he spoke one foreign language: '. . . the King's English, but not very well'.

The Works Superintendent since pre-war days, he became Works Manager under John Thornley, retiring from that position in 1967. He spent time visiting various home and foreign MG Car Club meetings, often entertaining members with his stories of the early days. He died in 1974, unfortunately before he could write his memoirs, in spite of being encouraged to do so, but he did give me many graphic pictures of the early days at MG which are recorded in these pages.

Reginald Jackson – 'Jacko'

A time-served motor technician, brought up when the motor trade was still a sideline to blacksmith work. He went to work at GWK in Maidenhead around 1921 as a fitter, but was not too impressed with the way they worked, although he stuck at his job and gained experience. He bought a motorcycle, and was able to tune this to be more efficient, and faster, although he did not, so far as I know, ever compete in an organised competition.

Discontented with his lot at GWK, he went off job-hunting in Cowley, but was turned down by Morris Motors, and was directed to MG at Edmund Road which had just opened, so this must have been in 1927.

Initially he worked under Cousins, but quickly became recognised as a self-starter and motivator of men, as well as being able to work out job solutions on his own. His enthusiastic knowledge of tuning motorcycle engines led him to tuning the engine of M-types and then on to even greater things.

Jackson was probably responsible for most of the greatest of MG achievements before the war, but was always extremely modest of these when discussing them to the extent that he often allowed others to take the credit.

Just before the war, Jackson was charged with the job of setting up an inspection department to Air Ministry specifications, which he did, and continued as Chief Inspector right through the war. At the conclusion of hostilities, he continued as the Chief Inspector at MG, which title he held until he retired in 1968, preferring it to the more pretentious 'Inspection Manager'. He was involved with most of the MG record-breaking attempts and with the initial forays into racing in 1952, and again in 1955.

I had the pleasure of working for him from 1965 until he retired. He could not understand my

enthusiasm for the 'yesterday's cars' as he somewhat disparagingly called them. A keen gardener and DIY man, he showed little interest in cars after his retirement, although he was always interested in the activities of the MG Car Company. He died a few years after his retirement in 1974.

Fred Kindell

Chief tester for the Mercedes plant in London, Kindell was a Londoner by birth. A fine mechanic who loved working with engines and getting the best from them, he had a specialist knowledge in superchargers which few could rival, and with Jackson was responsible for much of the success enjoyed by MG in the racing days.

He was also a fine driver, who according to Jackson was able to make a car go through gaps barely an inch wider at speeds which ordinary mortals would think crazy!

Kindell left MG at the end of the racing period to work for various private vehicle owners and other employers, and died around 1964.

Gordon Phillips – 'Gordie'

Gordon Phillips was a fine mechanic, who was one of the original MG people from Pewsey Lane days. A painstaking worker, who could always complete what was wanted. He became Service Manager after the war, from which position he retired in 1967. He died a few years later in Abingdon.

Sydney Enever – 'Squeak'

An Oxfordshire man, Syd Enever started work as a tea-boy in the Cowley works, and was brought to MG by Reg Jackson in 1929, just as MG was moving to Abingdon. Reg and Syd were friends from the earliest days, and it was natural that Syd should follow along the road opened by the older man, although they were barely 18 months apart in age.

Syd was involved with the racing when he earned his sobriquet because he was apparently inclined to chirp into conversations with a short 'But . . .' The name stuck, and even the drivers knew him as that. In due course he was commandeered into H. N. Charles's drawing office where he learned about design. His thinking out of problems from first principles was developed by Charles and stood him in good stead for his best work on the MGA and MGB models.

Syd and Jacko became a two-man travelling advice group for the late pre-war and early post-war record-breaking attempts of Goldie Gardner, and although working for the company they worked on the record-breaker as an 'out of hours' activity!

Immediately before the war, he became the link man between the official Design Office at Cowley, and the MG outpost at Abingdon. After the war he worked for Gerry Palmer before becoming Chief Designer at Abingdon, from which post he retired in 1973.

Always a 'hands on' man, Syd was not one to suffer fools gladly, and was often thought to be autocratic and uncommunicative, but in fact he was a good man to work for with a very sharp mind who could always see a fault if it existed in a proposal.

Alec Hounslow – 'The boy'

Alec Hounslow was 'the boy' from 1929, when he joined MG as a tea-boy, until he first left MG in 1936, after racing stopped. He was a first class mechanic, initially spotted by Jackson and brought into the Experimental Department during 1931. He stayed there, riding with Nuvolari in the TT and being responsible for many of the successful cars in that period.

During the war he was seconded back to Abingdon for war work, and stayed on after to work in Syd Enever's Experimental Department until he retired as foreman in 1974. He was able to travel with Cecil Cousins on some of his foreign trips to entertain enthusiasts with his memories. He died a couple of years later. In the early post-war years he worked as unpaid mechanic for Curly Dryden, who was the owner of the ex-Harvey-Noble Q-type . . . as well as licensee of a well-known public house!

He was involved in the post-war exploits of racing and record-breaking until the formation of the official Competitions Department of BMC.

Henry Stone

Henry Stone worked at MG all his life. He started as a tea-boy, soon translating to be a production line worker, and quickly becoming recognised as a good mechanic by Jackson, and seconded to Experimental in 1933. He was an invaluable member of the team.

Perhaps an illuminating story, I once asked Jackson who the best mechanic of the 'insomnia gang' was, and he replied Henry. When I asked Henry the same question, he replied 'Jacko': so there was more than a small amount of mutual admiration there!

He was to work during the war on various military projects at Abingdon, and after the war was first of all a rate fixer, where his ability to perform complicated tasks quickly ensured that the unions could not press

for long times for the production operations, and so kept MG production costs down! He later became number two to Alec Hounslow, travelling all over on various racing and record-breaking activities. Henry retired as Deputy Foreman of Experimental in 1978, but during his retirement he enjoyed remaining part of the MG Car Club family of members for several years. He died in 1990.

Bert Wirdnam – 'Ginger'

Bert Wirdnam was a highly respected senior foreman when I joined MG, and, never being one to call a spade a digging implement, he was highly suspicious of college-educated 'smart-arses', as he put it. He quickly found that I was interested in 'real MGs' and we had several interesting talks about the old times.

When I knew him he had hardly any hair, and what was there was white, so I was interested that he was known as 'Ginger' . . . in the 1930s he had a mass of ginger locks, and was apparently often accused of being Irish, which for a Berkshire man, is not kind! Many of the tales of the racing days were contributed to by Bert Wirdnam.

Bob Scott

One of the original 'insomnia gang', Jackson's group who were often known to work an 80-hour week, to the chagrin of the pay office. He died in 1996 at Abingdon, having lived there all his life.

Frank Tayler – 'Frankie'

Frankie Tayler was one of the legendary figures of MG. A first class mechanic, who started working with Cousins before there was an MG Car Company, he was part of the crew who made MG a famous name. His life was cut short in a needless accident involving a racing car off the circuit, which resulted in a jail sentence for the driver.

Ron Gibson

Ron Gibson was something of an enigmatic character. He worked at MG as a mechanic in Experimental, but appeared to have some money, and was even an early customer for one of the C-types. He died during the late 1950s and all his old trophies were given to the MG Works Auto Club.

APPENDIX B
RESULTS AND ACHIEVEMENTS

To list every result achieved by an MG car would probably fill this book, for many of the cars are still winning events and taking records to this day. I have therefore selected significant results achieved during the period in which MG cars were supported by the Factory. As explained in the text, MG never officially entered Works cars, but supported private owners with a more or less even hand, the 'evenness' of this support being determined mainly by the results achieved, but also by the persistence of individual entrants. George Eyston ran teams of cars throughout 1932/35 which were as near a Works entry as any ever became, but in fact Eyston had to put money down before the cars were made available, and it was he who usually arranged for their sale when their racing days were over.

The results here listed are, in the main, prompted by claims by the Factory to various victories up to the outbreak of the Second World War. It is not comprehensive, but where possible, I have attempted to accredit the main prize winners and identify their cars. Results are listed in purely alphabetical order of the title of the event. Where speeds are given, these are in mph.

1924

Edinburgh Trial

Gold	C. R. B. Chiesman	14/28 Super Sports

Lands End Trial

Gold	C. Kimber	11hp Raworth
	C. R. B. Chiesman	11hp Raworth

1925

Edinburgh Trial

Gold	W. Cooper	14/28 Super Sports
	C. R. B. Chiesman	14/28 Super Sports

Lands End Trial

Gold	C. Kimber	MG Old No. 1
	R. V. Saltmarsh	14/28 Super Sports
	C. R. B. Chiesman	14/28 Super Sports

MCC Brooklands High Speed Trial

1st Class award	C. Kimber	14/28 Super Sports
	W. Cooper	14/28 Super Sports

1926

MCC Brooklands High Speed Trial

1st Class award	W. Cooper	14/28 Super Sports

1927

San Martin 90km circuit race, Buenos Aires, Argentina

1st place	A. S. Cires	14/40

1928

C. F. Dobson secured the first MCC Triple Award for MG. This was also known as the Marian, and was made to competitors having clean sheets in the Exeter, the Lands End and the Edinburgh trials in one season.

1929

JCC High Speed Trial, Brooklands

1st Class award	L. Callingham	M-type
	H. D. Parker	M-type
	Earl March	M-type
	M. H. Scott	M-type
	C. G. H. Dunham	M-type

MCC High Speed Trial, Brooklands

1st Class awards (five)	M-type

Monte Carlo Rally: Mont des Mules Hill-climb

3rd fastest time	F. Samuelson	18/80 Mark I Saloon

1930

BARC Double Twelve Race, Brooklands

Team Prize	C. Randall Team	C. C. Randall/
		F. M. Montgomery
		R. R. Jackson/
		Townend
		G. Roberts/
		A. A. Pollard

London to Lands End Trial

18 1st Class awards secured by MG cars

Monte Carlo Rally Mont des Mules Hill-climb

1st 1,100cc Class	F. M. Montgomery	M-type

Spa-Francorchamps 24-Hour Race

5th in 1,100cc Class, but first car under 1,000cc to finish a 24-hour race: Samuelson/Murton-Neale, M-type Le Mans.

1931

BARC Double Twelve Race, Brooklands

1st overall	Lord March/C. S. Staniland	C-type 65.62
2nd	R. Gibson/L. Fell	C-type
3rd	H. C. Hamilton	C-type

The first three home won the Team Prize. These cars also, naturally, won the 750cc Class. MG cars also 4th and 5th.

BRDC 500-Mile Race, Brooklands

3rd overall, 1st 750cc	E. R. Hall	C-type

The MG Team of Hall, Horton and Gardner won the Team Award.

Irish Grand Prix, Phoenix Park, Dublin

1st	N. Black	C-type 64.76
3rd	R. T. Horton	C-type

RAC Tourist Trophy Race, Ards Circuit, Belfast

1st	N. Black	C-type 67.90
3rd	S. Crabtree	C-type

These cars were 1st and 2nd in 750cc class.

Saorstat Cup Race, Phoenix Park, Dublin

1st	N. Black	C-type 64.76
2nd	R. T. Horton	C-type
3rd	A. T. G. Gardner	C-type

These three also won the Team Prize.

1932

Brooklands JCC 1,000-mile Race

1st 750cc Class, 3rd overall	N. Black/R. Gibson	C-type

Craigantlet Hill-climb, near Belfast

1st in class	E. R. Hall	C-type

Monte Carlo Rally Mont des Mules Hill-climb

1st 800cc class	H. C. Hamilton	C-type 59.08

RAC Tourist Trophy Race, Ards Circuit, Belfast

3rd overall,	E. R. Hall	C-type
1st in class		

Shelsley Walsh Hill-climb, near Worcester

1st in class	E. R. Hall	C-type

1933

Alpine Trial

Glacier Cup/	W. E. C. Watkinson/	L2
1st Light Car Class		
	H. A. F. Ward-Jackson	
Manufacturer's	Watkinson/Ward-Jackson,	
	L. A. Welch/D. F. Welch,	
Team Prize	Mr & Mrs T. H. Wisdom	L2s

Australian Grand Prix, Philip Island

3rd	Jennings	F-type

Avusrennen, Berlin, Germany, Voiturette Race

1st 800cc Class	R. T. Horton	C-type
		90.90

BRDC India Trophy Race, Brooklands

1st	M. B. Watson	J4
		101.23
2nd	K. D. Evans	C-type
3rd	R. T. Horton	C-type

BRDC British Empire Trophy Race, Brooklands

3rd,	G. Manby-Colegrave	K3
1st 1,100cc Class		

BRDC 500-Mile Race, Brooklands

1st,	E. R. Hall	K3
1st 1,100cc Class		106.53
2nd,	C. E. C. Martin	L2
2nd 1,100cc Class		

Coppa Acerbo Junior Race, Pescara, Italy

1st	W. Straight	K3
		75.48

Craigantlet Hill-climb, near Belfast

FTD,	E. R. Hall	K3
1st 1,100cc Class		86.6 sec

Eifelrennen, Nürburgring, Germany, Voiturette Race

1st 800cc Class	H. C. Hamilton	J4
		59.31

JCC International Trophy Race, Brooklands

2nd,	E. R. Hall	K3
1st 1,100cc Class		
3rd, 2nd in Class	Mrs E. M. Wisdom	K3

LCC Relay Race, Brooklands

1st	MGCC Team	L2
	A. C. Hess, C. E. C. Martin,	88.62
	G. W. J. H. Wright	

24-Hour Race, Le Mans, France

1st in	J. L. Ford/M. H. Baumer	C
750cc Class		61.7

Mannin Beg Race, Douglas, Isle of Man

2nd	D. K. Mansell	J4
3rd	J. G. Ford/M. H. Baumer	C

Mille Miglia Road Race, Italy

1st 1,100cc Class	G. E. T. Eyston/G. Lurani	K3
		59.7
2nd	Earl Howe/H. C. Hamilton	K3
Team Award	MG Magnette Team	

Monte Carlo Rally, Mont des Mules Hill-climb

FTD and	F. M. Montgomery	K3
		prototype
1st 1,100cc Class		
1st 750cc Class	W. C. Platt	J3

Phoenix Park Junior Race, Dublin

1st	A. H. Potterton	F1
		73.70

Phoenix Park Senior Race, Dublin

2nd	H. McFerran	
3rd	G. Beaty	

RAC Tourist Trophy Race, Ards Circuit, Belfast

1st,	T. Nuvolari	K3
1st 1,100cc Class		78.65
2nd,	H. C. Hamilton	J4
1st 750cc Class		
4th,	E. R. Hall	K3
2nd 1,100cc Class		

Southport 100-Mile Race, near Blackpool
1st in Class wins at the following hill-climb events:
Freiburg, and Riesengeberg, Germany
1st Class awards in MCC Trials.

1934

Alpine Trial

Glacier Cup	H. Symons	NA

ARCA American Grand Prix

1st	M. Collier	P-type

Australian Grand Prix, Philip Island

2nd	L. Thompson	K3
3rd	Clement	

Avusrennen, Berlin, Germany

3rd 1,100cc Class	R. Kohlrausch	K3

Bol d'Or 24-Hour Race, St Germain

1st, tied with	P. Maillard-Brune	P-type
		46.97
		Chevalier

BRDC British Empire Trophy Race, Brooklands

1st	G. E. T. Eyston	EX135
		80.01

Team Prize to MG Team of Eyston, Dodson and Handley.

BRDC 500-Mile Race, Brooklands

1st	J. D. Benjafield/	
1,100cc Class,	A. T. G. Gardner	K3
3rd overall		

Brooklands 120mph Badge

	R. T. Horton	K3

Circuit of Modena, 1,100cc Race, Italy

1st	R. Cecchini	K3
		59.4

Coppa Acerbo Junior Race, Pescara, Italy

1st	H. C. Hamilton	K3
		73.42
2nd	R. Cecchini	K3
3rd	R. J. B. Seaman	K3

Eifelrennen, Nürburgring, Germany

1st 800cc Class	A. Brudes	J4
		60.00

LCC Relay Race, Brooklands

3rd	MG Team	NE

Entered by Miss Irene Schwendler: Miss I. Schwendler,
Miss M. Allen, Miss D. B. Evans

Le Mans 24-Hour Race, France

1st	C. E. C. Martin/R. Eccles	K3
1,100cc Class,		68.99
4th overall		

Mannin Beg Race, Douglas, Isle of Man

1st	N. Black	K3
		70.99
2nd	C. J. P. Dodson	K3
3rd	G. E. T. Eyston	EX135

MG cars also 4th and 5th.

Nuffield Trophy Race, Donington

2nd	R. J. B. Seaman	K3
3rd	K. D. Evans	Q-type

Phoenix Park Handicap Race, Dublin

2nd	A. Corry	F-type

Prix be Berne, Bremgarten, Switzerland

1st	R. J. B. Seaman	K3
		74.91

RAC Tourist Trophy Race, Ards Circuit, Belfast

1st	C. J. P. Dodson	NE
		74.65

1,100cc Championship of Italy

1st	R. Cecchini	K3

FTD, and four Class wins, Craigantlet Hill-climb,
near Belfast.

1st in Class at the following hill-climb events:
Shelsley Walsh, Felsberg, Riesengeberg, Gabelbach,
Kesselberg, Klausen, Lueckendorfer, Freiburg, Stelvio,
Mont Ventoux, Vermiccino

London to Lands End Trial: 35 1st Class awards.

London to Edinburgh Trial: 39 1st Class awards.

1935

Australian Grand Prix, Philip Island

1st	L. Murphy	PA
		66.96
2nd	W. Thompson	K3
3rd	P. Jennings	L

BRDC 500-Mile Race, Brooklands

1st in	Marquis Belleroche	K3
1,100cc Class		106.60
5th		

British Empire Trophy Race, Brooklands

1st in	A. R. Samuel	Q
750cc Class, l		69.72
4th overall		

Brooklands 120mph Badge

	A. T. G. Gardner	K3

Bol d'Or 24-Hour Race, St Germain

1st	P. Maillard-Brune	R-type
		50.86

County Down Trophy Race, Bangor,

1st	M. H. Fleming	PA
		61.83

Coupe de l'Argent, Montlhéry

2nd	P. Maillard-Brune	R-type

Craigantlet Hill-climb, Belfast

FTD	E. R. Hall	N-type

(car known as the *Zoller Special*)

Eifelrennen, Nürburgring, Germany

1st 800cc Class	R. Kohlrausch	EX127
		61.64
2nd	J. C. Wren	J4
3rd	A. Brudes	J4

JCC International Trophy Race, Brooklands

1st in Class,	E. R. Hall	K3
3rd overall		

Team Prize to MG Team

Le Mans 24-Hour Race, France

1st 1,100cc Class	P. Maillard-Brune/P. Druck	PA

Rudge-Whitworth Cup 1934/5:

2nd	P. Maillard-Brune/P. Druck	PA

Leinster Trophy Race, Tallaght Circuit

2nd	A. P. Huet	P-type

Nuffield Trophy Race, Donington Park

3rd	D. L. Briault	R-type

Phoenix Park 200-Mile Race, Dublin

1st	H. W. Furey	N-type
		69.94
3rd	L. R. Briggs	K3

Welsh Rally

Premier Award	C. W. Nash	NE
Team Prize	MGCC Team: The Three Musketeers	

Class wins at the following hill-climbs: Shelsley Walsh, La Turbie, Stelvio, Grossglockner, Feldberg.

1936

Bol d'Or 24-Hour Race, Montlhéry

2nd,	P. Maillard-Brune	R-type
1st 750cc Class		

BRDC 500-Mile Race, Brooklands

1st 1,100cc Class	W. E. Cotton	K3
1st 750cc Class	W. E. Humphreys	Q

Brooklands 120mph Badge

	R. Parnell	K3

County Down Trophy Race, Bangor

2nd	L. R. Briggs	K3

Grand Prix des Frontières, Belgium

1st	E. Hertzberger	Q-type
		74.72

Limerick Road Race, Town Circuit Limerick

1st	A. Hutchinson	PA
		57.1

MCC Trials Championship 1936

Winners	MGCC Team:	Magnette
	The Three Musketeers	Specials

200-Mile Race, Phoenix Park, Dublin

1st	H. W. Furey	N-type
		77.16
3rd	T. W. McComb	P-type

Class wins at La Turbie, Feldberg, Ratisbona, Bussaco, Santarem, Mount Washington, and Craigantlet hill-climbs.

1937

Australian Grand Prix, Victor Harbour, SA

1st	L. Murphy	P-type
		68.50

Brooklands Outer Circuit Record, 750cc Class

Held in	G. P. Harvey-Noble	Q-type
perpetuity		122.42

Brooklands Outer Circuit Record, 1,100cc Class

Held in	A. T. G. Gardner	K3
perpetuity		124.40

Brooklands 120mph Badge

	W. E. Cotton	K3

Cork Grand Prix, Carrigrohane Circuit

1st	H. B. Prestwich	K3
		76.33

12-Hour Sports Car Race, Donington Park

Team Prize	Cream Crackers	TA

JCC International Trophy Race, Brooklands

1st 1,100cc Class	W. E. Cotton/	K3
3rd overall	W. E. C. Wilkinson	

24-Hour Race, Le Mans Rudge Whitworth Biennial Cup

2nd	Miss D. M. Stanley-Turner/	PB
	Miss E. Riddell	

Leinster Trophy Race, Tallaght Circuit

2nd	R. D. Cox	F-type

MCC Trials Championship 1937

1st	Cream Crackers	TA

Rand 170-Mile Race, Johannesburg

3rd	J. D. McNichol	PA

Rand 120-Mile Race, Johannesburg

2nd	R. O. Hesketh	R-type

100-Mile Race, Phoenix Park, Dublin

3rd	I. H. Nickols	J4

100-Mile Race, Kimberley, South Africa

1st	R. O. Hesketh	R-type

Ulster Trophy Race, Ballyclare Circuit

2nd	J. R. Weir	K3
3rd	H. B. Prestwich	K3

1938

Australian Grand Prix, Bathhurst

3rd	Crago	PA

Bol d'Or 24-Hour Race, Montlhéry, France

1st 1,100cc Class	de Burnay	K3
2nd overall		

Brooklands lap record, Campbell Circuit, 1,100cc Class:

Held in	J. H. T. Smith	K3
perpetuity		70.60

Circuit of Ireland Rally

1st	R. G. Chambers	PB

Coronation Trophy, Donington Park

4th	I. H. Nickols	J4

JCC International Trophy Race, Brooklands

4th overall	J. H. T. Smith	K3

JCC 200-Mile Race, Brooklands

1st	A. Cuddon-Fletcher	K3
		65.92
3rd	J. H. T. Smith	K3

Limerick Road Race, Town Road Circuit

1st	J. D. McClure	TA

Phoenix Park Handicap Race, Dublin

2nd	I. H. Nickols	J4

Rallye Paris-St Raphael Feminin

1st	Miss B. M. Haig	PB

Brooklands 120mph Badge

	W. E. Humphries	MG Midget
		Q-type

1939

Australian Grand Prix

1st	Tomlinson	NE

Grand Prix des Frontières, Belgium

3rd	H. Herkuleyns	K3

Imperial Trophy Race, Crystal Palace Circuit, London

3rd overall	H. Stuart-Wilton	K3

Leinster Trophy Race, Tallaght Circuit

2nd	A. J. Welch	P

Phoenix Park Handicap Race

2nd	A. P. McArthur	K3
3rd	M. Cahill	N-type

Achievements in record-breaking, 1930-50

The records listed here are those achieved by the three Factory-sponsored cars as recorded in the text. Exact dates are given where these are known, otherwise the month and year.

The international class divisions, as recognised, were:

E	1,501 to 2,000cc
F	1,101 to 1,500cc
G	751 to 1,100cc
H	501 to 750cc
I	351 to 500cc
J	251 to 350cc

EX120

30.12.30	Montlhéry	G. E. T. Eyston	Class H	50km	86.38
				50-mile	87.11
				100km	87.30
2.31	Montlhéry	G. E. T. Eyston	Class H	5km	97.07
	Montlhéry	G. E. T. Eyston	Class H	5km	103.13
				5-mile	102.76
				10km	102.43
				10-mile	101.87
3.31	Montlhéry	G. E. T. Eyston	Class H	1km	97.09
				1-mile	96.93
9.31	Montlhéry	G. E. T. Eyston	Class H	1 hour	101.10

EX127

9.31	Montlhéry	G. E. T. Eyston	Class H	5km	110.28
2.32	Pendine	G. E. T. Eyston	Class H	1-mile	118.39
16.5.32	Brooklands	G. E. T. Eyston	Class H	Outer Circuit Lap	112.9
12.32	Montlhéry	G. E. T. Eyston	Class H	1km	120.56
				1-mile	120.56
				12-hour	86.67

With A. E. Denly and T. H. Wisdom

9.33	Brooklands	G. E. T. Eyston	Class H	50km	105.76
				50-mile	106.67
				100km	106.72
10.33	Montlhéry	G. E. T. Eyston	Class H	1km	128.63
				1-mile	128.62
				5km	127.8
				5-mile	127.8
				10km	127.23
				10-mile	125.43
11.33	Montlhéry	A. E. Denly	Class H	50km	115.00
				50-mile	114.47
				100-mile	111.17
				1-hour	110.87

19.5.35	Gyon, Hungary	R. Kohlrausch	Class H	1km	130.891
				1-mile	130.481
				1 km	81.798 standing
				1 mile	93.405 standing
10.10.36	Frankfurt	R. Kohlrausch	Class H	1km	140.51
				1-mile	140.60

EX135

1934	Montlhéry	G. E. T. Eyston	Class G	1-mile	128.7
				200km	129.4
				50-mile	120.72
				100-mile	121.13
				1-hour	120.88
	Frankfurt	A. T. G. Gardner	Class G	1km	186.6
				1-mile	186.5
	Dessau	A. T. G. Gardner	Class G	1km	203.5
				1-mile	203.2
				5km	197.5
	Dessau	A. T. G. Gardner	Class F	1km	204.3
				1-mile	203.9
				5km	200.6
	Jabbeke	A. T. G. Gardner	Class H	1km	159.1
				1-mile	159.2
				5km	150.5
	Jabbeke	A. T. G. Gardner	Class I	1km	118.04
				1-mile	117.49
				5km	114.10
				5-mile	110.53
	Jabbeke	A. T. G. Gardner (Jaguar engine)	Class E	1km	176.76
				1-mile	173.66
				5km	170.52
	Jabbeke	A. T. G. Gardner	Class I	1km	154.8
				1-mile	154.2
				5km	150.5
	Jabbeke	A. T. G. Gardner	Class J	1km	120.394
				1-mile	121.048
				5km	117.510
8.51	Bonneville	A. T. G. Gardner (XPAG engine)	Class F	50km	127.8
				50-mile	130.6
				100km	132.0
				100-mile	135.1
				200km	136.6
				1-hour	137.4
8.52	Bonneville	A. T. G. Gardner (Wolseley engine)	Class E	50km	143.23
				50-mile	147.4
				100km	148.72
8.52	Bonneville	A. T. G. Gardner (XPAG engine)	Class F	5-mile	189.5
				10km	182.84

Except where stated, the engine used was the six-cylinder block ohc MG engine, with variations applied to reach the capacity desired.

APPENDIX C
THE PRE-WAR RACING CARS: TECHNICAL SPECIFICATIONS

Below are summarised the major specifications of the models specifically sold for competition purposes. In general, although each model was developed to be an improvement on its predecessor, most of the actual parts used in the racing models were standard production items, and could be found on the standard touring and sports models sold to 'ordinary' customers.

Differences from the normal production parts could be summarised as follows: Engine valves were different, having tulip heads and made of KE965 material. The triple valve springs were in fact the standard 'doubles' fitted with an extra inner spring. From 1933 most of the gears in the engines and rear axles had straight-cut teeth, which, contrary to popular belief, did not materially increase general gear noise, because they were properly set up. Bearing metal was special, but the crankshafts and connecting rods were standard items, although crack-tested and polished before metalling. An interesting story was told to me by Reg Jackson.

I had asked him about crack checking, and whether this was carried out. In fact it was, the method was the spraying of the unit to be inspected with paraffin, and then drying off with a cloth. A light dusting of French chalk followed, after which cracks would show up as the paraffin was absorbed into the cracks leaching into the chalk dusting. This was carried out on all used units which were returned for repair to the Competitions Department, and the failed parts would be replaced with new if cracks were detected. By 1932, the procedure was carried out on all stressed parts, even new items, and Jacko said that there several new crankshafts drawn for use in K3s which were found suspect in this respect. I asked what happened to the rejected items, and he said that they were returned to stores so that another could be drawn . . . I wonder if those rejected parts then went into production cars?

Some of the parts developed for racing use were certainly brought into production, which no doubt reduced costs of the 'special' parts. At the end of 1931 12in brakes were developed for use in racing the C-types, were made available during 1932, and were brought into production in the F-type Magna that year. The four-cylinder crossflow head originally developed for the C-type racers was quickly used in the J-type sports cars as they were introduced, and no doubt led to the success of that model. There is little doubt that the quick absorption of racing practice into sports cars was one of the reasons why MG was successful commercially at a period when it was difficult to sell a sports car.

MG as a company may have struggled financially in the mid-1930s, and a measure of this may have been due to the expense of the rapid development of the small sports car, but the company survived at a time when many others failed. Wolseley, part of the Morris Group, struggled at producing cars which were not out-and-out sporting cars in the sense that their cousins were, but gradually fell back into the production of saloon cars that were more expensive than those produced at Cowley.

Amongst other domestic manufacturers, Morgan produced sports cars and three-wheelers of undoubted sporting character, but only in very small numbers. Singer stopped producing true sports cars in 1937, Frazer Nash also did so a year or so earlier, becoming instead a retailer of an advanced German car, the BMW. Rapier cars were shed off by their parent Lagonda Company, and went under in 1937. Riley never produced sports cars in large numbers, but they fell under the Nuffield umbrella after struggling through the 1930s with failing balance sheets. Most of the other sports car manufacturers only produced in very small numbers or at very high prices, or both, neither of which permutations could survive for long.

The fact was that during the 1930s MG car sales rose and fell with the economic barometer, and there is no doubt that the MG Car Company Ltd survived because it fell under the overall blanket of the Morris empire.

There is little doubt that the cessation of production of racing cars was influenced because of a deep dislike of the breed by the new management team at the helm of the Nuffield organisation, and influenced by their personal disregard, if not downright jealousy, for the success of Cecil Kimber.

At what is now termed the 'Nuffield Takeover', in 1936, when Sir William Morris sold all his companies to the Nuffield Group, MG and Wolseley cars were to be based on a common Morris set of parts, at least in theory. Racing these cars was out of the question, partly because they were not capable of being developed to a racing standard, but chiefly because motor racing had evolved into a highly specialised activity, where production cars had no common base. This was to change for a period immediately following the Second World War, but gradually racing and sports cars moved away from each other to the detriment of grass roots motorsport.

If MG competition cars had a better than expected performance than their competitors, then the only reason is that those cars prepared by the Works were carefully assembled and fine-tuned by people who had made it their business to prove that their cars were superior to the opposition. In short, it amounted to sheer hard and meticulous work.

The MG Six Mark III, or 18/100, or Tigress

The MG Six Mark III was a logical development of the 18/80 cars, evolving from the Mark II Model. The name Tigress was not appended in the original announcement, but has since become common usage. The type nomenclature 18/100 came about because Kimber had wanted the car to be sold with a certificate that each one had reached 100mph at Brooklands, but this was never achieved. The car used many parts from the 18/80 Mark II, but was special in respect of the cylinder head layout, engine oiling system, gear ratios, and bodywork.

Production period 1930

Chassis

Steel channel section side members and cross members, riveted construction

Wheelbase	9ft 6in
Track	4ft 4in
Suspension	Semi-elliptic laminated leaf springs, Andre-Hartford dampers
Steering	Marles worm and peg box
Turning Circle	44ft
Toe-in	0.1875

Brake gear	Four-wheel mechanical system, cable-operated, self-compensating
Drum diameter	14in
Drum material	Cast iron

Wheels	
hubs	Rudge pattern centre lock, 50mm
Diameter	19in
Width	3in
Tyre size	19 x 5.00
Tyre pressure	40psi

Engine

Six-cylinder in-line, iron block, detachable head. Overhead camshaft

Bore	69mm
Stroke	110mm
Cubic capacity	2468cc
Power output	80bhp @ 4,800rpm according to Morris Engines Branch, 1963
Maximum crankshaft speed	5,000rpm

Compression ratio	6.8 : 1
Firing order	1 5 3 6 2 4
Valve timing	IO: 14 BTDC IC: 56 ABDC EO: 55
	BBDC EC: 15 ATDC
Cam lift	Not recorded
Valve lift	Not recorded
Valve clearance	Inlet: 0.012in Exhaust: 0.020in
Valve seat angle	30 degrees
Valve head diameter	Not recorded
Valve spring type	Double coil spring
Valve spring rate	Not recorded
Valve spring seat pressure	
	Not recorded
Installed length	Not recorded
Free length	Not recorded
Connecting rods	H-section steel, machined from
	solid, white metal lined
Length	8.5in
Small end type	pinch bolt
Big end bearing material	
	S6 racing metal
Piston	Solid skirt type, aluminium alloy
Rings	Three, two compression,
	one oil control
Compression height	Not recorded
Engine oil	Castor oil
Oil pressure, hot	60/80psi at 3,000rpm
Sump capacity	5 gallons, dry sump, located at front
	of car, ahead of radiator

Ignition system

Lucas coil and distributor

Ignition timing	Points about to break at TDC,
	hand lever retarded
Distributor points gap	
	0.015in

Carburettors

Twin SU, down draft 1.5in choke

| Jet size | 0.090in |
| Needle | 24 |

Clutch

Two-plate cork insert, running in engine oil

Gearbox

Four-speed ENV made unit

First gear	3.42
Second gear	1.84
Third gear	1.206
Fourth gear	1.000
Grade of oil	Castor
Capacity	3 pints

Propeller shaft

Fully enclosed, torque tube drive,
single universal joint at front end

Rear axle

Fully floating, fitted with four star differential.
Straight cut gears

Ratio	4.25 : 1
MPH/1,000rpm	21
Grade of oil	Castor
Capacity	3 pints

Cooling system

Thermosyphon, pump assisted. No engine fan

| Capacity | approximately 5 gallons |

Fuel tank capacity

25 gallons

| Location | Rear of car |

Fuel pump type

Two Autopulse pumps located at rear of car

Body style

Four-seat AIACR body type fitted with wings and lights

| **Price** | £895 |

| **Number built** | 5 |

12/12 Midget, M-type

The 12/12 M-type model was directly evolved from the standard M-type car, and used more or less standard chassis parts throughout. A special camshaft was introduced for this model, but this became the standard for the M-type from mid-1930. A special carburettor, inlet manifold and exhaust system were used, and the bodywork was slightly modified.

In addition to the 'standard' 12/12 model, two special cars were created for the 1930 Le Mans race, with bodies further modified to comply with the regulations for that race, but these were otherwise standard.

Production period 1930

Chassis

Steel channel section side and cross members, riveted construction

Wheelbase	6ft 6in
Track	3ft 6in
Steering	Adamant worm and wheel type
Turning Circle	34ft

Castor angle	3 degrees
Camber angle	2.5 degrees
King pin Angle	6.5 degrees
Toe-in	0.125in
Brake gear	Four-wheel drum system, mechanically operated by cables, self-compensating
Drum diameter	8in
Drum material	Cast iron, with cast on alloy ribs

Wheels

Wire spoked bolt-on type, supplied by Dunlop.
40-spoke pattern

Diameter	19in
Width	2.5in
Tyre size	19 x 4.00
Tyre pressure	Approximately 40psi

Engine

Four-cylinder in-line detachable head. Overhead camshaft

Bore	57mm
Stroke	83mm
Cubic capacity	847cc
Power output	27bhp @ 4,500rpm, this was 1930 standard engine
Maximum crankshaft speed	5,500rpm
Compression ratio	6.2 : 1 for 12/12 race
Firing order	1 3 4 2
Valve timing	IO: TDC IC: 50 ABDC EO: 32 BBDC EC: 7 ATDC
Cam lift	0.200in
Valve lift	0.282in
Valve clearance	Inlet: 0.008in Exhaust: 0.010in
Valve seat angle	30 degrees
Valve head diameter	Inlet & Exhaust: 1.125in
Valve spring type	Double helical coil spring
Valve spring rate	55lb/in
Valve spring seat pressure	35lb
Installed length	1.406in
Free length	1.75in
Connecting rods	H-section steel, machined from forgings
Length	6.5in
Small end type	Pinch-bolt. Pin diameter, 0.5625in
Big end bearing material	S6 racing metal, directly applied to rod
Piston	Aluminium alloy solid skirt type
Rings	3: 2 compression rings, one oil control
Compression height	1.406in

Engine oil	Castor
Oil pressure, hot	60/80psi @ 50mph
Sump capacity	One gallon, wet sump

Ignition system

Lucas coil and distributor

Ignition timing	Points just about to break at TDC, lever set fully retarded
Distributor points gap	0.015in
Carburettors	Single SU Downdraft instrument, 1.25in choke size
Jet size	0.090in
Needle	C

Clutch

Single dry plate, Wroper & Wreaks made unit, 6.5in diameter

Gearbox

Three-speed and reverse Wolseley built-in unit with engine

First gear	3.5
Second gear	1.83
Third gear	1.000
Grade of oil	Castor
Capacity	1.5 pints

Propeller shaft

Fabric joint Hardy-Spicer type, not balanced

Rear axle

Bevel gear crown wheel and pinion, two-star differential

Ratio	4.89 : 1
MPH/1,000rpm	16.4
Grade of oil	Castor
Capacity	1.5 pints

Cooling system

Thermosyphon type, no fan or pump

| Capacity | Approximately 2 gallons |

Fuel tank capacity

7 gallons

| Location | Under scuttle, over driver's legs |

Fuel pump type

SU, mounted on nearside chassis frame, just behind radiator

Body style

Two-seat Brooklands type. Supplied with wings and lights and gauze windscreen

Price	£245
Number built	6 racing cars, plus 19 'Replica' models sold late 1930 – 25 in all

Montlhéry Midget, C-type

The C-type was derived directly from the successful EX120 record attempt car. It shared little with previous production cars, but laid the foundations for most of the successive models up to 1955.

Production period: 1931/2

Chassis
Channel side members, tubular cross members. Bolted together

Wheelbase	6ft 9in
Track	3ft 6in
Suspension	Semi-elliptic laminated leaf springs with Andre-Hartford dampers
Steering	Adamant worm and wheel type
Turning Circle	32ft
Castor angle	6 degrees on axle beam
Camber angle	9 degrees
King pin Angle	6.5 degrees
Toe-in	0.1875in
Brake gear	Four-wheel drum brake system, mechanically operated by cables
Drum diameter	8in
Drum material	Cast iron, with cast on alloy ribs

Wheels

	Centre-lock Rudge pattern splined hubs, 48-spoke
Diameter	19in
Width	2.5in
Tyre size	19 x 4.00
Tyre pressure	Approximately 40psi

Engine
Four-cylinder in-line overhead camshaft

Bore	57mm
Stroke	73mm
Cubic capacity	746cc
Power output	1931, unsupercharged AA head, petrol fuel: 37.4bhp @ 6,000rpm
	1931, supercharged, AA head, Benzole fuel: 44.9bhp @ 6,200rpm
	1932, unsupercharged AB head, petrol fuel: 44.1bhp @ 6,400rpm
	1932, supercharged, AB head, Benzole fuel: 52.5bhp @ 6,500rpm

Maximum engine speed	6,500rpm
Compression ratio	Unsupercharged: 8.5 : 1 Supercharged: 5.8 : 1
Firing order	1 3 4 2
Valve timing	IO: 15 BTDC IC: 55 ABDC EO: 50 BBDC EC: 20 ATDC
Cam lift	AA Head: 0.200in AB Head: 0.220in
Valve lift	0.282in 0.308in
Valve clearance	Inlet: 0.008in Exhaust: 0.010in (AA head) 0.014in (AB head)
Valve seat angle	30 degrees
Valve head diameter	Inlet: 1.250in Exhaust: 1.125in
Valve spring type	Triple helical coil spring
Valve spring rate	Unsupercharged: 60lb/in Supercharged: 90lb/in
Valve spring seat pressure	40lb 50lb
Installed length	AA head: 1.406in AB head: 1.36in
Free length	1.75in
Connecting rods	H-section steel, machined from forgings
	Length 7.281in
Small end type	Bronze bush, gudgeon pin retained by dural plugs
Big end bearing material	S6 racing metal
Piston	Solid skirt aluminium alloy type
Rings	3: two compression, one oil control
Compression height	1.406in
Engine oil	Castor
Oil pressure, hot	80/100psi hot, at 3,000rpm
Sump capacity	8 pints

Ignition system	Rotax coil and distributor
Ignition timing	Varied according to state of tune
Distributor points gap	0.015in

Supercharger: 1931/32

Powerplus No. 7 running at 78% crankshaft speed blowing at 10/12psi boost

Carburettors

AA head, unsupercharged:
Single SU D/draft 1.25in diameter

AB head unsupercharged:
twin SU HV2, 1.125in diameter

Supercharged, either head:
Single SU HV5, 1.625in diameter

Jet size	0.090in, unsupercharged.
	0.100in supercharged
Needle	Unsupercharged: C
	Supercharged: RLB

Clutch   Two dry plate, Wroper & Wreaks, 6.5in diameter

Gearbox

Four-speed and reverse, ENV built in unit with the engine

First gear	3.58 or 2.69
Second gear	1.96 or 1.86
Third gear	1.36 or 1.29
Fourth gear	1.000
Grade of oil	Castor
Capacity	2 pints

Propeller shaft

Hardy-Spicer, metal bushed universal joints at each end

Rear axle

Bevel gear crown wheel and pinion, two-star differential

Ratio	5.375 : 1 or
	5.625 : 1 or
	5.875 : 1
MPH/1,000rpm	15.2
	14.5
	13.9
Grade of oil	Castor
Capacity	1.5 pints

Cooling system

Thermosyphon system, pump assisted on supercharged engines.

| Capacity | Approximately 2 gallons |

Fuel tank capacity

Approximately 15 gallons

| Location | Rear of car, mounted inside tail |

Fuel pump type

Twin Autopulse pumps

Body style

Two-seat Brooklands racing style, supplied with wings and lights fitted, and gauze windscreen

Price

1931, on release, £245 unsupercharged. Mark 2 £495, supercharged. 1932, Mark 3, unsupercharged: £495. Supercharged: £575

Number built   44

Midget, J4 type

The Montlhéry Midget had, to all intents and purposes, reached the end of its development in 1931, but the new racing model was not ready for release until the end of 1932. With longer wheelbase and more power it was destined to be a very fast car, but the deficiencies of the model soon came to the surface, and it gained a reputation for being a difficult car to drive.

Production period 1933

Chassis

Channel side members, tubular cross members. Riveted construction

Wheelbase	7ft 2in
Track	3ft 6in
Suspension	Semi-elliptic laminated leaf springs with Andre-Hartford dampers.
Steering	Bishop Cam steering box, worm and peg type
Turning Circle	34ft
Castor angle	6 degrees on axle beam, plus 2 degrees with taper plate under beam
Camber angle	9 degrees
King pin Angle	6.5 degrees
Toe-in	0.1875in
Brake gear	Four-wheel drum brake system, mechanically operated by cables
Drum diameter	12in
Drum material	Cast iron, with shrunk-on steel ribs.

Wheels

Centre-lock Rudge pattern splined hubs, 48-spoke

Diameter	19in
Width	2.5in
Tyre size	19 x 4.00
Tyre pressure	Approximately 40psi

Engine

Four-cylinder in-line overhead camshaft

Bore	57mm
Stroke	73mm
Cubic capacity	746cc
Power output	72bhp @ 6,500rpm, using 60/40 methanol benzole mixture
Compression ratio	5.4 : 1
Firing order	1 3 4 2
Valve timing	IO: 15 BTDC IC: 55 ABDC
	EO: 50 BBDC EC: 20 ATDC
Cam lift	0.220in
Valve lift	0.275in
Valve clearance	Inlet: 0.008in Exhaust: 0.014in
Valve seat angle	30 degrees

Valve head diameter   Inlet: 1.250in   Exhaust: 1.125in
Valve spring type   Triple helical coil spring,
                         retained by circlips
Valve spring rate   90lb/in
Valve spring seat pressure
                         50lb
Installed length   1.36in
Free length   1.75in
Connecting rods   H-section steel,
                         machined from forgings
Length   7.281in
Small end type   Bronze bush, gudgeon pin
                         retained by dural plugs
Big end bearing material
                         S6 racing metal
Piston   Solid skirt aluminium alloy type
Rings   3: two compression, one oil control
Compression height   1.406in
Engine oil   Castor
Oil pressure, hot   80/100psi hot, at 3,000rpm
Sump capacity   8 pints

Ignition system
Lucas coil and distributor
Ignition timing   Varied according to state of
                         tune and fuel used
Distributor points gap
                         0.015in

Supercharger
Powerplus No. 7, blowing at 12psi or No. 8, blowing at
14psi both types geared to run at 69% engine speed.

Carburettor
Single SU HV5, 1.625in diameter
Jet size   0.125in
Needle   O1

Clutch
Two dry plate, Wroper & Wreaks, 6.5in diameter

Gearbox
Four-speed and reverse, ENV built in unit with the engine
First gear   2.69
Second gear   1.86
Third gear   1.29
Fourth gear   1.000
Grade of oil   Castor
Capacity   2 pints

Propeller shaft
Hardy-Spicer, metal bushed universal joints at each end

Rear axle
Bevel gear crown wheel and pinion, four star differential
Ratio   5.375 : 1
MPH/1,000rpm   15.2
Grade of oil   Castor
Capacity   1.5 pints

Cooling system
Thermosyphon system, pump-assisted
Capacity   Approximately 2 gallons

Fuel tank capacity
Approximately 15 gallons
Location   Rear of car, mounted outside body,
                         Ulster style

Fuel pump type
Twin Autopulse pumps
Body style
Two seat Ulster racing style, without doors, supplied with
wings and lights fitted, and gauze or glass windscreen

Price   £495 in 1933

Number built   9

Midget, QA type

With the relative failure of the J4, its replacement was required
to be even faster. It ended up being much more powerful, as
well as being longer in wheelbase and wider in track which in
turn meant it was heavier. However, even these changes only
showed that the days of the cart-sprung car were over, and
like its predecessor, only a small number were sold.

Production period 1934

Chassis
Channel side members, tubular cross members.
Riveted construction
Wheelbase   7ft 10.1875in
Track   3ft 9in
Suspension   Semi-elliptic laminated leaf springs
                         with Andre-Hartford dampers at the
                         front, Luvax hydraulic at the rear.
                         Cable torque reaction stays fitted to
                         front suspension
Steering   Bishop Cam steering box,
                         worm and peg type
Turning Circle   35ft
Castor angle   6 degrees on axle beam, plus 2
                         degrees with taper plate under beam
Camber angle   10.5 degrees
King pin Angle   7.5 degrees
Toe-in   0.1875in

Brake gear	Four-wheel drum brake system, mechanically operated by cables
Drum diameter	12in
Drum material	Cast iron, special design

Wheels

Centre-lock Rudge pattern splined hubs, 48-spoke

Diameter	18in
Width	2.5in
Tyre size	18 x 4.75
Tyre pressure	Approximately 40psi

Engine

Four-cylinder in-line overhead camshaft

Bore	57mm
Stroke	73mm
Cubic capacity	746cc
Power output	113 bhp @ 7,200rpm using MG1 fuel
Compression ratio	6.25 : 1
Firing order	1 3 4 2
Valve timing	IO: 15 BTDC IC: 55 ABDC EO: 50 BBDC EC: 20 ATDC
Cam lift	0.220in
Valve lift	0.309in
Valve clearance	Inlet: 0.008in Exhaust: 0.014in
Valve seat angle	30 degrees
Valve head diameter	Inlet: 1.250in Exhaust: 1.125in
Valve spring type	Triple helical coil spring, retained by circlips
Valve spring rate	92lb/in
Valve spring seat pressure	50lb
Installed length	1.36in
Free length	1.75in
Connecting rods	H-section steel, machined from forgings
Length	6.70in
Small end type	Bronze bush, gudgeon pin retained by dural plugs
Big end bearing material	S6 racing metal
Piston	Solid skirt aluminium alloy type
Rings	3: two compression, one oil control
Compression height	1.406in
Engine oil	Castor
Oil pressure, hot	80/100psi hot, at 3,000rpm, 60psi at idle speed.
Sump capacity	8 pints

Ignition system

Lucas coil and distributor

| Ignition timing | Varied according to state of tune and fuel used |
| Distributor points gap | 0.015in |

Supercharger

Zoller type Q4, running at 69% crankshaft speed, 28psi boost

Carburettor

Single SU HV8, 1.875in diameter

| Jet size | 0.1875in |
| Needle | RM0, RM1, RM2, or RM3, according to fuel used |

Clutch

Two dry plate, Wroper & Wreaks, 6.5in diameter, but no operating mechanism

Gearbox

Four-speed and reverse, ENV built Wilson-type preselector in unit with the engine

First gear	QA type:	3.40
	QH-type:	3.10
Second gear		2.00
		1.84
Third gear		1.34
		1.31
Fourth gear		1.00
		1.00
Grade of oil	Castor	
Capacity	3 pints	
	5.25 pints	

Propeller shaft

Hardy-Spicer, metal bushed universal joints at each end

Rear axle

Bevel gear crown wheel and pinion, straight cut and four-star differential

Ratio	4.89 : 1, with optional 4.5 : 1 or 4.125 : 1 also available
MPH/1,000rpm	17.2
Grade of oil	Castor
Capacity	1.5 pints

Cooling system

Thermosyphon system, pump assisted.

| Capacity | Approximately 2.5 gallons |

Fuel tank capacity

Approximately 19 gallons

| Location | Rear of car, mounted inside tail |

Fuel pump type

Twin Autopulse pumps

Body style

Two-seat Brooklands racing style, without doors, no wings, lights or windscreen. An aeroscreen was supplied for driver only

Price	£595
Number built	8

Midget, RA type

The most revolutionary MG built. Even now, more than 75 years later, it is difficult not to marvel at its construction and specification. If to modern eyes it is heavy and tall, these are possibly lessons which could have been learned if the models had been properly developed.

Production period 1935

Chassis
Steel box-section frame, Y-shaped,
electrically welded construction

Wheelbase	7ft 6.5in
Track	3ft 10.375in, front. 3ft 9.5in, rear
Suspension	Independent on all four wheels using equal length wishbones
Spring medium	Torsion bars, adjustable for trim on car
Dampers	Luvax vane type all round.
Steering	Bishop Cam steering box, worm and peg type, with two drop arms
Turning Circle	28ft
Castor angle	5 degrees
Camber angle	10.5 degrees
King pin Angle	7.5 degrees
Toe-in	0.1875in
Brake gear	Four-wheel drum brake system, mechanically operated by cables: Girling system, with shoes expanded by wedges
Drum diameter	12in
Drum material	Cast iron, special design

Wheels
Centre-lock Rudge pattern splined hubs, 60-spoke

Diameter	18in
Width	3.0in
Tyre size	18 x 4.75
Tyre pressure	Approximately 40psi

Engine
Four-cylinder in-line overhead camshaft

Bore	57mm
Stroke	73mm
Cubic capacity	746cc
Power output	113 bhp @ 7,200rpm using MG1 fuel
Compression ratio	6.25 : 1
Firing order	1 3 4 2

Valve timing	IO: 15 BTDC IC: 55 ABDC EO: 50 BBDC EC: 20 ATDC
Cam lift	0.220in
Valve lift	0.309in
Valve clearance	Inlet: 0.008in Exhaust: 0.014in
Valve seat angle	30 degrees
Valve head diameter	Inlet: 1.250in Exhaust: 1.125in
Valve spring type	Triple helical coil spring, retained by circlips
Valve spring rate	92lb/in
Valve spring seat pressure	50lb
Installed length	1.36in
Free length	1.75in
Connecting rods	H-section nickel-chromium alloy steel, machined from forgings
Length	6.70in
Small end type	Bronze bush, gudgeon pin retained by dural plugs
Big end bearing material	S6 racing metal
Piston	Solid skirt aluminium alloy type
Rings	3: two compression, one oil control
Compression height	1.406in
Engine oil	Castor
Oil pressure, hot	120psi hot, at 3,000rpm, 80psi at idle speed
Sump capacity	8 pints

Ignition system
Lucas vertical magneto

Ignition timing	Varied according to state of tune and fuel used
Distributor points gap	0.015in
Supercharger	Zoller type R4, running at 69% crankshaft speed, 28psi boost

Carburettor
Single SU HV8, 1.875in diameter

Jet size	0.1875in
Needle	RM2, or RM3, according to fuel used

Clutch
Two dry plate, Wroper & Wreaks, 6.5in diameter, but no operating mechanism

Gearbox
Four speed and reverse, ENV built Wilson-type preselector in unit with the engine RH-type

First gear	3.10
Second gear	1.84
Third gear	1.31
Fourth gear	1.00

Grade of oil   Castor
Capacity   5.25 pints

Propeller shaft
Hardy-Spicer, metal bushed universal joints at each end

Rear axle
Bevel gear crown wheel and pinion, straight cut and four star differential. This was mounted rigidly on the chassis frame, with universal joint half shafts transmitting the drive to rear wheels

Ratio   4.5 : 1
MPH/1,000rpm   18.5
Grade of oil   Castor
Capacity   1.5 pints

Cooling system
Thermosyphon system, pump assisted
Capacity   Approximately 2.5 gallons

Fuel tank capacity
Approximately 21 gallons
Location   Rear of car, forming the tail

Fuel pump type
Air pressure

Body style
Monoposto racing style, with aeroscreen.
No equipment supplied

Price   £695

Number built   10

Magnette, K3 type

The undisputed best of the MG racing car production in terms of competition results. An immensely strong and safe car, it often got to the finish when others failed demonstrating the contention of the greatest post-war World Champion: to finish first, first you must finish!

Production period 1933 and 1934

Chassis
Channel side members, tubular cross members.
Riveted construction
Wheelbase   7ft 10.1875in
Track   4ft
Suspension   Semi-elliptic laminated leaf springs with Andre-Hartford dampers, twin sets for the rear suspension. Cable torque reaction stays fitted at front

Steering   Bishop Cam steering box, worm and peg type
Turning Circle   36ft
Castor angle   6 degrees on axle beam, plus 2 degrees with taper plate under beam
Camber angle   10.5 degrees
King pin Angle   7.5 degrees
Toe-in   0.1875in
Brake gear   Four-wheel drum brake system, mechanically operated by cables
Drum diameter   13in
Drum material   Cast magnesium alloy, with cast iron liners interference fitted, and screw retained

Wheels
Centre-lock Rudge pattern splined hubs, 60-spoke
Diameter   19in
Width   2.75in
Tyre size   19 x 4.75
Tyre pressure   Approximately 40psi

Engine
Six-cylinder in-line overhead camshaft
Bore   57mm
Stroke   71mm
Cubic capacity   1,087cc
Power output   120bhp @ 6,000rpm using MG1 fuel
Compression ratio   6.4 : 1
Firing order   1 4 2 6 3 5
Valve timing   IO: 15 BTDC IC: 55 ABDC EO: 50 BBDC EC: 20 ATDC
Cam lift   0.220in
Valve lift   0.309in
Valve clearance   Inlet: 0.008in   Exhaust: 0.014in
Valve seat angle   30 degrees
Valve head diameter   Inlet: 1.250in   Exhaust: 1.125in
Valve spring type   Triple helical coil spring, retained by circlips
Valve spring rate   92lb/in
Valve spring seat pressure
                      50lb
Installed length   1.36in
Free length   1.75in
Connecting rods   H-section Nickel-Chromium alloy steel, machined from forgings
                      Length   6.50in
Small end type   Bronze bush, gudgeon pin retained by dural plugs
Big end bearing material
                      S6 racing metal
Piston   Solid skirt aluminium alloy type
Rings   3: two compression, one oil control
Compression height   1.406in

Engine oil   Castor
Oil pressure, hot   80/90psi hot, at 3,000rpm,
                         60psi at idle speed
Sump capacity   1933 sump: 12 pints.
                         1934 sump: 16 pints

Ignition system

BTH horizontal magneto.
Ignition timing   Varied according to state of
                         tune and fuel used
Distributor points gap
                         0.015in

Supercharger

1933: Powerplus No. 9, blowing at 12/14psi
1934: Marshall No. 85, blowing at 10/12psi

Carburettor

Single SU HV8, 1.875in diameter
Jet size   0.1875in
Needle   RM0, RM6, RM7, or RM8
                         according to fuel used

Clutch

Nil

Gearbox

Four-speed and reverse, ENV built Wilson-type
preselector in unit with the engine
First gear   3.40
Second gear   2.00
Third gear   1.34
Fourth gear   1.00
Grade of oil   Castor
Capacity   3 pints

Propeller shaft

Hardy-Spicer, metal bushed universal joints at each end

Rear axle

Bevel gear crown wheel and pinion, straight cut
and four-star differential
Ratio   4.89 : 1, with optional 5.78
                         and 4.33 also available
MPH/1,000rpm   17.85
Grade of oil   Castor
Capacity   1.75 pints

Cooling system

Thermosyphon system, pump assisted
Capacity   Approximately 3 gallons

Fuel tank capacity

Approximately 23.5 gallons (1933 model)
or 27.5 gallons (1934 model)

Fuel pump type

1933: Twin Autopulse pumps.
1934: Pressurised tank system.

Body style

1933: Two seat Ulster racing style, with wings, lights and
full windscreen. Optional long streamlined tail offered.
Slab-type fuel tank at rear
1934: Two-seat Brooklands racing style body, with no
lamps or mudguards, aeroscreen provided for driver's
position only. Tank formed part of tail

Price   £795

Number built   33

Magnette, NE Type

Conceived and built in an amazingly short time to meet
regulations for the RAC Tourist Trophy Race this was the
first unsupercharged racing MG since the original C-type.
Much closer to its prototype production model than some
of the more exciting cars, this model did its job well, and
proved to be not much slower than the supercharged
models. Unlike the earlier cars, it was never intended to
sell this model, which was not listed, and was probably
the only MG ever produced in this way. Its production
counterpart was the ND model which was likewise not
listed, but was sold to the public at a price of £345.

Production period 1934

Chassis

Channel side members, tubular cross members.
Riveted construction
Wheelbase   8ft
Track   3ft 9in
Suspension   Semi-elliptic laminated leaf springs
                         with Andre-Hartford dampers at
                         the front, supplementary Luvax
                         dampers also fitted.
                         Rear, Luvax units only
Steering   Bishop Cam steering box,
                         worm and peg type
Turning Circle   30ft
Castor angle   8 degrees on axle beam, plus 2
                         degrees with taper plate under beam
Camber angle   10.5 degrees
King pin Angle   7.5 degrees
Toe-in   0.1875in
Brake gear   Four-wheel drum brake system,
                         mechanically operated by cables
Drum diameter   12in
Drum material   Cast iron, with shrunk on steel ribs

Wheels

Centre-lock Rudge pattern splined hubs, 48-spoke

Diameter	18in
Width	2.5in
Tyre size	18 x 4.75
Tyre pressure	Approximately 40psi

Engine

Six-cylinder in-line overhead camshaft

Bore	57mm
Stroke	83mm
Cubic capacity	1,271cc
Power output	75 bhp @ 6,000rpm using petrol/benzole mixture
Compression ratio	9.8 : 1
Firing order	1 4 2 6 3 5
Valve timing	IO: 25 BTDC IC: 60 ABDC EO: 60 BBDC EC: 25 ATDC
Cam lift	0.230in
Valve lift	0.32in
Valve clearance	Inlet: 0.012in Exhaust: 0.016in
Valve seat angle	30 degrees
Valve head diameter	Inlet: 1.250in Exhaust: 1.125in
Valve spring type	Triple helical coil spring, retained by circlips
Valve spring rate	92lb/in
Valve spring seat pressure	50lb
Installed length	1.36in
Free length	1.75in
Connecting rods	H-section Nickel-Chromium alloy steel, machined from forgings
Length	6.50in
Small end type	Bronze bush, gudgeon pin retained by dural plugs
Big end bearing material	Finlays L1 racing metal
Piston	Solid skirt aluminium alloy type with raised crown
Rings	3: two compression, one oil control
Compression height	Not quoted
Engine oil	Castor
Oil pressure, hot	100psi hot, at 3,000rpm, 60psi at idle speed
Sump capacity	12 pints

Ignition system

Lucas coil and distributor, auto advance, twin contact breaker

Ignition timing	Varied according to state of tune and fuel used
Distributor points gap	0.015in

Supercharger

Nil

Carburettor

Twin SU HV3, 1.375in choke

Jet size	0.100in
Needle	C1

Clutch

Wroper and Wreaks twin plate

Gearbox

Four-speed and reverse, Wolseley built, in unit with the engine

First gear	3.58
Second gear	2.14
Third gear	1.36
Fourth gear	1.00
Grade of oil	Castor
Capacity	2 pints

Propeller shaft

Hardy-Spicer, with needle-roller bearing joints

Rear axle

Bevel gear crown wheel and pinion, straight cut and four-star differential

Ratio	4.89 : 1, with optional 5.375, 5.125 and 4.5 also available
MPH/1,000rpm	17.85
Grade of oil	Castor
Capacity	2.0 pints

Cooling system

Thermosyphon system, pump assisted

Capacity	Approximately 3 gallons

Fuel tank capacity

Approximately 27 gallons

Location	Rear of car, mounted inside tail

Fuel pump type

Twin SU pump, with common pumping chamber

Body style

1934: Two-seat Brooklands racing style body, with lamps and mudguards, aeroscreen provided for driver's position only. Tank enclosed within tail

Price	£595
Number built	7

APPENDIX D

INTERNATIONAL MG RACE
AND RALLY ENTRIES 1955–1969

Entries made by the BMC Competitions Department at Abingdon from the formation of the department in 1955 to the final Works entry in 1969.

1955

Month	Event	Crew	Car	Reg	No.	Result
January	Monte Carlo Rally	G. Holt/S. Asbury/J. Brooks	Magnette	KJB 910	49	178th overall
		L. Shaw/B. Brown/F. Finnemore	Magnette	KJB 909	36	202nd overall
		R. Holt/A. Collinson/W. Cave	Magnette	KJB 908	58	237th overall
March	RAC Rally	P. Moss/P. Faichney	TF	KRX 90	193	3rd in Ladies
		G. Holt/J. Brooks	Magnette	KJB 910	198	1st in class
		R. Holt/B. Brown	Magnette	KJB 908	200	Retired
		L. Shaw/A. Collinson	Magnette	KJB 909	199	Retired
April	Circuit of Ireland	I. Appleyard/Mrs I. Appleyard	TF	KMO 836	192	4th overall, 1st in class
		J. Flynn/Mrs Flynn	TF	KMO 837	193	Finisher
		C. Vard/L. Young	TF	–	–	–
May	Tulip Rally	P. Moss/S. Cooper	Magnette	KJB 908	139	Retired
		L. Shaw/D. Lawton	Magnette	KJB 909	137	Retired
		G. Holt/J. Brooks	Magnette	KJB 910	148	Retired
May	Daily Express Silverstone	R. Jacobs	Magnette	JRX 251	32	1st in class
June	Scottish Rally	N. Paterson/A. Craig	TF	KMO 835	63	1st in class
		E. Herrald/P. Chisholm	TF	KMO 836	62	2nd in class
		R. Kay/D. Mickel	TF	KMO 837	61	3rd in class (Manufacturers' Team Prize)
June	Le Mans	K. Miles/J. Lockett	MGA	LBL 301	41	12th overall, 5th in class
		E. Lund/H. Waeffler	MGA	LBL 303	64	17th overall, 6th in class
		R. Jacobs/J. Flynn	MGA	LBL 302	42	Crashed
September	Tourist Trophy, Ulster	J. Fairman/P. Wilson	MGA 1500	LBL 303	35	20th overall, 4th in class
		E. Lund/R. Stoop	MGA 1500	LBL 304	36	Retired

		R. Flockhart/J. Lockett	MGA Twin-Cam	LBL 301	34	Retired
September	Montlhéry Records	K. Wharton	MGA 1500	–	–	100 miles in hour

1956

January	Monte Carlo Rally	N. Mitchell/D. Reece/ S. Hindermarsh	Magnette	KJB 910	327	59th overall, 3rd in Ladies
		G. Grant/N. Davis/C. Davis	Magnette	JRX 251	34	Retired
March	RAC Rally	P. Moss/A. Wisdom	MGA 1500	MJB 167	79	5th in class, 3rd in Ladies
		N. Mitchell/D. Reece	Magnette	–	–	–
March	Lyons Charbonnières Rally	N. Mitchell/D. Reece	Magnette	JRX 251	132	47th overall, 1st in Ladies
April	Mille Miglia	P. Scott-Russell/T. Haig	MGA 1500	MJB 167	229	70th overall, 4th in class
		N. Mitchell/P. Faichney	MGA 1500	MBL 867	227	72nd overall, 5th in class
May	Tulip Rally	N. Mitchell/D. Reece	Magnette	KJB 910	147	Disqualified
May	Daily Express Silverstone	A. Foster	Magnette	JRX 251	–	2nd in class
May	Dieppe Rally	P. Moss/A. Wisdom	Magnette	MBL 417	–	2nd in Ladies
May	Geneva Rally	N. Mitchell/P. Burt	Magnette	–	–	2nd in Ladies, 7th in class
June	Midnight Sun Rally	N. Mitchell/D. Reece	Magnette	–	–	4th in Ladies, 17th in class
July	Alpine Rally	N. Mitchell/P. Faichney	MGA 1500	MBL 867	326	15th overall, 3rd in class, 1st in Ladies
		J. Milne/D. Johns	MGA 1500	MJB 314	314	4th in class
		W. Shepherd/J. Williamson	MGA 1500	MJB 167	308	5th in class
		J. Gott/R. Brookes	MGA 1500	MJB 191	324	Crashed
		J. Sears/K. Best	MGA 1500	MRX 42	330	Crashed
August	Liège-Rome-Liège	J. Gott/C. Tooley	MGA 1500	MJB 191	75	13th overall, 6th in class
		J. Milne/R. Benstead-Smith	MGA 1500	MRX 43	15	14th overall, 7th in class
		N. Mitchell/A. Hall	MGA 1500	MBL 867	38	26th overall, 2nd in Ladies
		G. Burgess/S. Croft-Pearson	MGA 1500	MRX 42	24	Retired
September	Viking Rally	N. Mitchell/D. Reece	Magnette	KJB 909	45	64th overall

1957

Month	Event	Crew	Car	Reg	No.	Result
February	Sestrière Rally	N. Mitchell/A. Hall	Magnette	NJB 365	–	60th overall, 2nd in Ladies
March	Lyons-Charbonnières	N. Mitchell/D. Reece	MGA 1500	MBL 867	98	32nd overall, 1st in Ladies
May	Tulip Rally	N. Mitchell/P. Burt	Magnette	–	–	76th overall, 9th in class, 3rd in Ladies
August	Liège-Rome-Liège	J. Gott/C. Tooley	MGA 1500	MJB 167	48	14th overall, 8th in class
		N. Mitchell/J. Johns	MGA 1500	OBL 311	5	16th overall, 9th in class, 1st in Ladies
		J. Milne/W. Shepherd	MGA 1500	MRX 43	24	Crashed
		G. Harris/G. Hacquin	MGA 1500	MRX 42	87	Retired

1958

Month	Event	Crew	Car	Reg	No.	Result
January	Monte Carlo Rally	N. Mitchell/J. Johns	Magnette	–	341	Retired
April	Tulip Rally	N. Mitchell/G. Wilton Clarke	MGA 1500	–	49	34th overall, 4th in class, 3rd in Ladies
		D. Seigle-Morris/J. Sprinzel	Magnette	D20	–	Retired
June	Midnight Sun Rally	P. Moss/A. Wisdom	MGA 1500	OBL 311	25	5th class, 9th in Ladies
August	Liège-Rome-Liège	J. Gott/R. Brookes	MGA Twin-Cam	PRX 707	78	9th overall, 4th in class

1959

Month	Event	Crew	Car	Reg	No.	Result
January	Monte Carlo Rally	J. Gott/R. Brookes	MGA Twin-Cam	RMO 101	106	Crashed
April	Sebring 12 Hours	G. Ehrman/R. Saidel	MGA Twin-Cam	–	28	2nd in class, 27th overall
		J. Parkinson/J. Dalton	MGA Twin-Cam	–	29	3rd in class, 34th overall
		J. Flaherty/R. Pickering/ S. Decker	MGA Twin-Cam	–	30	45th overall
April	Tulip Rally	J. Gott/C. Tooley	MGA Twin-Cam	SBL 707	28	Finisher
		J. Sprinzel/S. Turner	MGA Twin-Cam	RMO 101	29	Crashed
May	Acropolis Rally	J. Sprinzel/R. Benstead-Smith	MGA Twin-Cam	RMO 101	12	Crashed

Month	Event	Drivers	Car	Reg.	No.	Result
June	Alpine Rally	J. Milne/S. Turner	MGA Twin-Cam	SBL 707	–	Crashed
June	Le Mans	E. Lund/C. Escott	MGA Twin-Cam	SRX 210	33	Retired

1960

Month	Event	Drivers	Car	Reg.	No.	Result
March	Sebring 12 Hours	F. Hayes/E. Leavens	MGA Twin-Cam	UMO 96	39	24th overall, 3rd in class
		J. Parkinson/J. Flaherty	MGA Twin-Cam	UMO 94	40	4th in class
		E. Lund/C. Escott	MGA Twin-Cam	UMO 95	38	Retired
June	Le Mans	E. Lund/C. Escott	MGA Twin-Cam	SRX 210	32	13th overall, 1st in class
September	German Rally	P. Riley/A. Ambrose	MGA 1600	777 EMK	8	2nd in class

1961

Month	Event	Drivers	Car	Reg.	No.	Result
March	Sebring 12 Hours	J. Parkinson/J. Flaherty	MGA 1600 C	–	44	14th overall, 1st in class
		P. Riley/J. Whitmore	MGA 1600 C	–	43	16th overall, 2nd in class
June	Le Mans	E. Lund/R. Olthoff	MGA Twin-Cam	SRX 210	58	Retired
November	RAC Rally	D. Astle/P. Roberts	Midget	YRX 727	31	8th overall, 1st in class
		M. Sutcliffe/R. Fidler	Midget	YRX 723	21	2nd in class
		T. Gold/M. Hughes	Midget	473 TEH	15	60th overall

1962

Month	Event	Drivers	Car	Reg.	No.	Result
January	Monte Carlo Rally	D. Morley/E. Morley	MGA 1600	151 ABL	314	28th overall, 1st in class, 2nd in GT category
		P. Riley/M. Hughes	Midget	YRX 747	44	33rd overall, 1st in class
March	Sebring 12 Hours	J. Sears/A. Hedges	MGA 1600	–	51	16th overall, 4th in class
		J. Flaherty/J. Parkinson	MGA 1600	–	53	17th overall, 5th in class
		J. Whitmore/R. Olthoff	MGA 1600	–	52	20th overall, 6th in class

Month	Event	Drivers	Car	Reg	No.	Result
May	Tulip Rally	R. Aaltonen/G. Palm	MGA 1600	151 ABL	11	15th overall, 1st in class
		T. Gold/M. Hughes	Midget	YRX 737	59	38th overall, 3rd in class
June	Alpine Rally	J. Williamson/D. Hiam	'Spridget'	YRX 737	23	–
September	Liège-Sofia-Liège	J. Gott/W. Shepherd	MGA 1600	151 ABL	49	Retired
November	RAC Rally	D. Seigle-Morris/R. Jones	MG 1100	977 CBL	11	Retired

1963

Month	Event	Drivers	Car	Reg	No.	Result
January	Monte Carlo Rally	R. Jones/P. Morgan	Midget	YRX 747	158	1st in class
		R. Baxter/E. McMillen	MG 1100	399 CJB	268	4th in class
		J. Cuff/Anderson	MG 1100	–	162	Crashed
March	Sebring 12 Hours	J. Parkinson/J. Flaherty	MGB	7 DBL	47	Retired
		C. Carlisle/D. McCluggage	MGB	6 DBL	48	Retired
April	Spa 500km Race	A. Hutcheson	MGB	8 DBL	–	Retired
May	Daily Express Silverstone	A. Hutcheson	MGB	7DBL	–	1st in class
June	Le Mans 24 Hours	P. Hopkirk/A. Hutcheson	MGB	7 DBL	31	12th overall, 1st in class
June	Acropolis Rally	B. Consten/J. Herbert	MG 1100	399 CJB	–	Retired
August	Spa-Sofia-Liège	P. Mayman/V. Domleo	MG 1100	399 CJB	57	Retired
		D. Hiam/R. Jones	MGB	8 DBL	38	Retired
September	Tour de France	A. Hedges/J. Sprinzel	MGB	7 DBL	155	Crashed

1964

Month	Event	Drivers	Car	Reg	No.	Result
January	Monte Carlo Rally	D. Morley/E. Morley	MGB	7 DBL	83	17th overall, 1st in GT category
		T. Wisdom/J. Miles	MG 1100	399 CJB	243	Retired
March	Sebring 12 Hours	E. Leslie/J. Dalton	MGB	–	–	17th overall, 3rd in class
		F. Morrell/J. Adams/M. Brennan	MGB	–	–	22nd overall
		J. Flaherty/J. Parkinson	MGB	–	–	Retired
June	Scottish Rally	D. Morley/E. Morley	MGB	7 DBL	–	Crashed
June	Le Mans	P. Hopkirk/A. Hedges	MGB	BMO 541B	37	19th overall, 2nd in class, Motor Trophy

August	Spa-Sofia-Liège	P. Mayman/V. Domleo	MGB	BRX 853B	78	Retired
		J. Vernaeve/D. Hiam	MGB	BRX 854B	–	Retired
September	Tour de France	A. Hedges/J. Sprinzel	MGB	BMO 541B	153	Retired
November	RAC Rally	J. Fitzpatrick/J. Handley	MGB	BRX 854B	177	Crashed
		P. Mayman/V. Domleo	MGB	BRX 853B	39	Retired

1965

March	Sebring 12 Hours	M. Brennan/F. Morrell	MGB Prototype	BMO 541B	49	25th overall, 2nd in class
		B. Picard/A. Pease	MGB	DRX 256C	48	32nd overall, 6th in GT class
		R. Mac/A. Hedges	Midget	771 BJB	68	12th in GT category, 1st in class
		C. Tannlund/J. Wagstaff	Midget	770 BJB	82	Retired
April	Tulip Rally	K. Tubman/Stefanoff	MGB	BRX 854B	12	Retired
May	Welsh Rally	T. Fall/R. Crellin	MGB	8 DBL	7	34th overall
May	Targa Florio	P. Hopkirk/A. Hedges	Midget	771 BJB	44	11th overall, 2nd in class
May	Guards 1000, Brands Hatch	J. Rhodes/W. Banks	MGB	8 DBL	28	1st overall, 1st in class
May	Nürburgring 1,000km	A. Hedges/K. Greene	Midget	770 BJB	98	6th overall, 1st in class
June	Le Mans	P. Hopkirk/A. Hedges	MGB	DRX 255C	39	11th overall, 2nd in class
July	Nordrhein-Westfalen Rally	A. Hedges/J. Scott	MGB	BRX 853B	116	11th overall, 3rd in GT category
July	Bridgehampton 500	P. Hopkirk	MGB	–	48	4th overall, 2nd in GT category
		R. Aaltonen	Midget	–	50	6th overall, 1st in class
		T. Mäkinen	Midget	–	49	11th overall, 3rd in class

1966

January	Monte Carlo Rally	A. Fall/R. Crellin	MGB	GRX 307D	183	Retired

March	Sebring 12 Hours	P. Manton/R. Mac/E. Brown	MGB	HBL 129D	59	3rd in GT category, 1st in class, 17th overall
		P. Hopkirk/A. Hedges	MGB	8 DBL	44	Retired
April	Targa Florio	T. Mäkinen/J. Rhodes	MGB	GRX 307D	64	9th overall, 1st in class
		J. Handley/A. Hedges	MGB	JBL 491D	66	16th overall, 2nd in class
May	Brands Hatch 500	R. Enever/A. Poole	MGB	BRX 855B	74	3rd overall, 1st in class
May	Spa 1,000km	A. Hedges/J. Vernaeve	MGB	GRX 307D	59	12th overall, 1st in GT category, 1st in class
June	Monza 3 Hours	R. Enever/C. Baker	MGB	BRX 855B	–	1st in class
June	Nürburgring 1,000km	A. Hedges/J. Vernaeve	MGB	JBL 491D	107	Retired
July	Mugello	A. Hedges/R. Widdows	MGB	GRX 307D	92	3rd in GT category
August	Marathon de la Route	J. Vernaeve/A. Hedges	MGB	GRX 307D	47	1st overall, 1st in class
		R. Enever/A. Poole	MGB	BRX 855B	46	Retired
October	Montlhéry 1,000km	R. Enever/A. Poole	MGB	BRX 855B	33	12th overall, 2nd in class
		A. Hedges/J. Vernaeve	MGB	GRX 307D	31	13th overall, 3rd in class

1967

March	Sebring 12 Hours	P. Hopkirk/A. Hedges	MGB GT	LBL 591E	30	11th overall, 3rd in GT category, 1st in class
		T. Mäkinen/J. Rhodes	MGB	GRX 307D	48	12th overall, 3rd in class
April	Monza 1,000km	R. Enever/A. Poole	MGB	BRX 855B	59	16th overall, 1st in class
May	Spa 1,000km	R. Enever/A. Poole	MGB	BRX 855B	71	10th overall, 1st in class
May	Targa Florio	P. Hopkirk/T. Mäkinen	MGB GTS	MBL 546E	230	Unclassified
		A. Hedges/A. Poole	MGB	MBL 547E	48	Crashed

| May | Nürburgring 1,000km | R. Enever/A. Poole | MGB | BRX 855B | 102 | 16th overall, 4th in class |
| June | Reims 12 Hours | R. Enever/A. Poole | MGB | BRX 855B | 49 | 16th overall, 2nd in class |

1968

March	Sebring 12 Hours	P. Hopkirk/A. Hedges	MGC GTS	MBL 546E	44	10th overall, 1st in class, 3rd in category
		G. Rodrigues/R. McDaniel/ B. Brack	MGB GT	LBL 591E	66	18th overall, 5th in class
		J. Truitt/R. Canfield	Midget	LNX 628E	74	15th overall, 1st in class
May	Targa Florio	P. Hopkirk/A. Hedges	MGB GT	LBL 591E	130	12th overall, 2nd in GT category
June	Marathon de la Route	A. Fall/A. Hedges/J. Vernaeve	MGC GTS	MBL 546E	4	6th overall
		C. Baker/R. Enever/A. Poole	MGC GTS	RMO 699F		Retired

1969

March	Sebring 12 Hours	P. Hopkirk/A. Hedges	MGC GTS	RMO 699F	35	15th overall, 9th in Prototype category
		J. Truitt/L. Blackburn	MGB GT	LBL 591E	62	28th overall, 8th in GT category
		C. Hill/W. Brack	MGC GTS	MBL 546E	36	34th overall, 15th in Prototype category

APPENDIX E
THE POST-WAR
WORKS MG DRIVERS

The post-war works MG drivers

The following short driver biographies feature those who drove the works MGs along with their individual achievements from the formation of the BMC Competitions Department in 1955.

Rauno Aaltonen
Former Finnish motorcycle and speedway rider, first works drive with Mercedes, joined BMC in 1962 to become leading works Mini driver, European Rally Champion in 1965.
Works MG drives
1962 Tulip Rally, MGA, 15th overall, 1st class
1965 Bridgehampton, Midget, 6th overall, 1st class

Jim Adams
Started racing MGs and Sunbeam Tigers in SCCA events, progressed to a McLaren sports car in Can-Am events.
Works MG drives
1964 Sebring, MGB, 22nd overall

Ian Appleyard
Leading British rally driver in post-war era mainly with Jaguar, winning Gold Cup for three Alpine Rally victories
Works MG drives
1955 Circuit of Ireland, TF, 4th overall, 1st class

Derek Astle
Successful northern privateer who finished third on 1959 RAC Rally in Riley 1.5 and went on to drive the first works 850 and later the works big Healeys.
Works MG drives
1961 RAC Rally, Midget, 8th overall, 1st class

Clive Baker
Best known for driving the works Sprites and big Healeys for Donald Healey at Le Mans, Sebring and the Nürburgring.
Works MG drives
1966 Monza, MGB, 1st class
1968 Nürburgring 84 Hours, MGC, retired

Warwick Banks
Drove F3 for Tyrrell, contested European Touring Car Championship and British Saloon Car Championship with Mini.
Works MG drives
1965 Brands Hatch, MGB, 1st overall

Raymond Baxter
Well-known BBC commentator who regularly drove BMC cars on the Monte Carlo Rally.
Works MG drives
1963 Monte Carlo Rally, MG 1100, 4th class

Les Blackburn
Experienced British driver of big-engined cars in British Touring Car Championship, Thundersports and World Endurance Championship.
Works MG drives
1969 Sebring, MGB, 28th overall, 8th class

Bill Brack
Started ice racing Minis in Canada and progressed to drive Lotus and BRM in F1 and later Formula Atlantic Champion.
Works MG drives
1968 Sebring, MGB, 18th overall, 5th class
1969 Sebring, MGC, 24th overall, 15th class

Merle Brennan
Notable Jaguar driver in SCCA racing, from Nevada.
Works MG drives
1964 Sebring, MGB, 22nd overall
1965 Sebring, MGB, 25th overall, 2nd class

Gerry Burgess
First drove in the BMC team in 1955 with Austin Westminsters and later big Healeys.
Works MG drives
1956 Liège-Rome-Liège Rally, MGA, retired

Christabel Carlisle
Young music teacher who came to fame driving a Don Moore-prepared Mini in British saloon car races and later a Sprite.
Works MG drives
1963 Sebring, MGB, retired

Bernard Consten
French rally champion and multiple winner of the Tour de France.
Works MG drives
1963 Acropolis Rally, MG 1100, retired

John Dalton
Long career driving production sports cars in British events.
Works MG drives
1959 Sebring, MGA, 34th overall, 3rd class
1964 Sebring, MGB, 17th overall, 3rd class

Roger Enever
Son of MG designer Syd Enever who had a successful racing career with works-supported Midgets and MGB.
Works MG drives
1966 Brands Hatch, MGB, 3rd overall, 1st class
1966 Monza, MGB, 1st class
1966 Nürburgring 84 Hours, MGB, retired
1966 Montlhéry, MGB, 12th overall, 2nd class
1967 Monza, MGB, 16th overall, 1st class
1967 Spa, MGB, 10th overall, 1st class
1967 Nürburgring, MGB, 16th overall
1967 Reims, MGB, retired
1968 Nürburgring 84 Hours, MGC, retired

Gus Ehrman
Worked for USA BMC importers, long career driving MGs and Austin-Healeys.
Works MG drives
1959 Sebring, MGA, 27th overall, 2nd class

Colin Escott
Successful northern competitor with the MG Car Club and regular co-driver to Ted Lund.
Works MG drives
1959 Le Mans, MGA, retired
1960 Sebring, MGA, retired
1960 Le Mans, MGA, 13th overall, 1st class
1961 Le Mans, MGA, retired

Jack Fairman
Drove Bristol, Jaguar and Aston Martin before Grand Prix career including Connaught and BRM.
Works MG drives
1955 Tourist Trophy, MGA, 20th overall, 4th class

Tony Fall
Car salesman for Appleyards of Leeds, started rallying Minis in 1964 and had first works BMC drive in 1965, becoming a regular member of the team.
Works MG drives
1965 Welsh Rally, MGB, 34th overall
1966 Monte Carlo Rally, MGB, retired
1968 Nürburgring 84 Hours, MGC, 6th overall

John Fitzpatrick
Drove Mini in British Saloon Car Championship, went on to win Championship in Ford Anglia, later successful career with Porsche in European GT events.
Works MG drives
1964 RAC Rally, MGB, crashed

Ron Flockhart
F1 driver with BRM and Le Mans winner with Jaguar
Works MG drives
1955 Tourist Trophy, MGA, retired

Alan Foster
Regular driver for the Dick Jacobs Team especially with the famous Jacobs Midgets.
Works MG drives
1956 Silverstone, Magnette, 2nd class

Jack Flaherty
Californian sports car driver who regularly partnered Jim Parkinson at Sebring.
Works MG drives
1959 Sebring, MGA, 45th overall
1960 Sebring, MGA, 4th class
1961 Sebring, MGA, 14th overall, 1st class
1962 Sebring, MGA, 17th overall, 5th class
1963 Sebring, MGB, retired
1964 Sebring, MGB, retired

Joe Flynn
Successful Irish MG privateer.
Works MG drives
1955 Le Mans, MGA, crashed

Tom Gold
Well-known privateer rallying an Austin-Healey Sprite.
Works MG drives
1961 RAC Rally, Midget, 60th overall
1962 Tulip Rally, Midget, 38th overall, 3rd class

John Gott
After rallying HRG and Frazer Nash, joined the BMC team in 1958 mainly driving the big Healey as BMC Team Captain. Served as Northampton's Chief Constable.
Works MG drives
1956 Alpine Rally, MGA, crashed
1956 Liège-Rome-Liège Rally, MGA, 13th overall, 6th class
1957 Liège-Rome-Liège Rally, MGA, 14th overall, 8th class
1958 Liège-Rome-Liège Rally, MGA, 9th overall, 4th class
1959 Monte Carlo Rally, MGA, crashed
1959 Tulip Rally, MGA, finisher
1962 Liège-Sofia-Liège Rally, MGA, retired

Gregor Grant
Founding editor of *Autosport* magazine who took part in many major classic events with cars from various manufacturers
Works MG drives
1956 Monte Carlo Rally, Magnette, retired

Keith Greene
Drove F1 Gilby Grand Prix car and later became F1 and sports car team manager.
Works MG drives
1965 Nürburgring, Midget, 6th overall, 1st class

Tom Haig
Chief test driver for the MG Car Company at Abingdon.
Works MG drives
1956 Mille Miglia, MGA, 70th overall, 2nd class

John Handley
One of the first to rally the Mini, drove for Cooper, Broadspeed and British Vita, European Saloon Car Champion, partner to John Rhodes in the 1969 BL Mini team.
Works MG drives
1964 RAC Rally, MGB, crashed
1966 Targa Florio, MGB, 16th overall, 2nd class

Fred Hayes
Successful SCCA sports car driver.
Works MG drives
1960 Sebring, MGA, 24th overall, 3rd class

Andrew Hedges
Regular driver with Paddy Hopkirk, also drove the Jacobs Midgets, British bobsleigh competitor.
Works MG drives
1962 Sebring, MGA, 16th overall, 4th class
1963 Tour de France, MGB, crashed
1964 Le Mans, MGB, 19th overall, 2nd class
1964 Tour de France, MGB, retired
1965 Sebring, Midget, 1st class
1965 Le Mans, MGB, 11th overall, 2nd class
1965 Targa Florio, Midget, 11th overall, 2nd class
1965 Nürburgring, Midget, 6th overall, 1st class
1965 German Rally, MGB, 11th overall, 3rd class
1966 Sebring, MGB, retired
1966 Targa Florio, MGB, 16th overall, 2nd class
1966 Mugello, MGB, 3rd class
1966 Nürburgring 84 Hours, MGB, 1st overall
1966 Nürburgring 1000k, MGB, retired
1966 Spa, MGB, 1st class
1967 Sebring, MGB, 11th overall, 1st class
1967 Targa Florio, MGB, crashed
1968 Sebring, MGC, 10th overall, 1st class
1968 Targa Florio, MGB, 12th overall, 2nd class
1968 Nürburgring 84 Hours, MGC, 6th overall
1969 Sebring, MGC, 15th overall, 9th class

David Hiam
Privateer driver who went on to become Dunlop's Rally Manager.
Works MG drives
1963 Spa-Sofia-Liège Rally, MGB, retired

Craig Hill
Canadian sports car driver and successful Porsche competitor at Mosport.
Works MG drives
1969 Sebring, MGC, 24th overall, 15th class

Geoff Holt
Works MG drives
1955 Monte Carlo Rally, Magnette, 179th overall
1955 RAC Rally, Magnette, 1st class
1955 Tulip Rally, Magnette, retired

Reg Holt
Works MG drives
1955 Monte Carlo Rally, Magnette, 237th overall
1955 RAC Rally, Magnette, retired

Paddy Hopkirk
Joined the BMC team after a long career with Triumph and Rootes to drive the big Healey but soon became linked with the Mini after his Monte Carlo Rally win in 1964.
Works MG drives
1963 Le Mans, MGB, 12th overall, 1st class
1964 Le Mans, MGB, 19th overall, 2nd class
1965 Le Mans, MGB, 11th overall, 2nd class
1965 Targa Florio, Midget, 11th overall, 2nd class
1965 Bridgehampton, MGB, 4th overall, 2nd class
1966 Sebring, MGB, retired
1967 Sebring, MGB, 11th overall, 1st class
1967 Targa Florio, MGC, 9th overall, 3rd class
1968 Targa Florio, MGB, 12th overall, 2nd class
1968 Sebring, MGC, 10th overall, 1st class
1969 Sebring, MGC, 15th overall, 9th class

Alan Hutcheson
Privateer who raced Riley 1.5 and was the first to race the MGB in international events.
Works MG drives
1963 Spa, MGB, retired
1963 Silverstone, MGB, 1st class
1963 Le Mans, MGB, 12th overall, 1st class

Dick Jacobs
Well-known post-war driver of T Types and Magnettes, went on to race works MGA but retired after Le Mans crash to run successful MGA and Midget teams.
Works MG drives
1955 Silverstone, Magnette, 1st class
1955 Le Mans, MGA, crashed

Rupert Jones
The rallying vicar equally at home driving or navigating, pioneer driving the 850 Minis and later his favourite big Healeys.
Works MG drives
1963 Monte Carlo Rally, Midget, 1st class

Ed Leavens
Regular US BMC sports car driver.
Works MG drives
1960 Sebring, MGA, 24th overall, 3rd class

Ed Leslie
Leading US Formula Junior driver who went on to race Shelby Cobras.
Works MG drives
1964 Sebring, MGB, 17th overall, 3rd class

Johnny Lockett
Professional Grand Prix motorcyclist with Norton in 1940s and 1950s.
Works MG drives
1955 Le Mans, MGA, 12th overall, 5th class
1955 Tourist Trophy, MGA, retired

Ted Lund
Successful northern driver with local MGCC Centre, regular partner with Colin Escott.
Works MG drives
1955 Le Mans, MGA, 17th overall, 6th class
1955 Tourist Trophy, MGA, retired
1959 Le Mans, MGA, retired
1960 Sebring, MGA, retired
1960 Le Mans, MGA, 13th overall, 1st class
1961 Le Mans, MGA, retired

Roger Mac
Young and successful production sports car driver, mainly with Jaguar, who joined the BMC team to drive at Sebring.
Works MG drives
1965 Sebring, Midget, 1st class
1966 Sebring, MGB, 17th overall, 1st class

Timo Mäkinen
Started ice racing and rallying in Finland in 1960 with Volvo and Saab, joined the BMC works team in 1962 driving Minis and went on to memorable results with big Healeys.
Works MG drives
1965 Bridgehampton, Midget, 11th overall, 3rd class
1966 Targa Florio, MGB, 9th overall, 1st class
1967 Sebring, MGB, 12th overall, 2nd class
1967 Targa Florio, MGC, 9th overall, 3rd class

Peter Manton
Top Mini competitor in the Australian Touring Car Championship.
Works MG drives
1966 Sebring, MGB, 17th overall, 1st class

Pauline Mayman
Started with BMC team as co-driver to Pat Moss and later became the team's leading lady driver with Minis and then big Healeys.
Works MG drives
1963 Spa-Sofia-Liège Rally, MG 1100, retired
1964 Spa-Sofia-Liège Rally, MGB, retired
1964 RAC Rally, MGB, retired

Denise McCluggage
American lady journalist who partnered Christabel Carlisle in the works MGB at Sebring.
Works MG drives
1963 Sebring, MGB, retired

Richard McDaniel
National SCCA Champion and owner of leading motor dealership.
Works MG drives
1968 Sebring, MGB, 18th overall, 5th class

Ken Miles
Early racing career in UK with Bugatti, Alfa Romeo and Alvis, then moved to USA where he became a regular SCCA Champion with MGs.
Works MG drives
1955 Le Mans, MGA, 12th overall, 5th class

John Milne
Scottish whisky distiller, compatriot and regular co-driver with John Williamson.
Works MG drives
1956 Alpine Rally, MGA, 4th class
1956 Liège-Rome-Liège Rally, MGA, 14th overall, 7th class
1957 Liège-Rome-Liège Rally, MGA, crashed
1959 Alpine Rally, MGA, crashed

Nancy Mitchell
Drove for most of the British teams in the years before joining the BMC team and twice winning the European Ladies Rally Championship.
Works MG drives
1956 Monte Carlo Rally, Magnette, 59th overall, 3rd Ladies
1956 Lyons-Charbonnières Rally, Magnette, 47th overall, 1st Ladies
1956 Tulip Rally, Magnette, disqualified
1956 Geneva Rally, Magnette, 7th class, 2nd Ladies
1956 Midnight Sun Rally, Magnette, 17th class, 4th Ladies
1956 Viking Rally, Magnette, 64th overall
1956 Mille Miglia, MGA, 72nd overall, 3rd class
1956 Alpine Rally, MGA, 15th overall, 1st Ladies
1956 Liège-Rome-Liège Rally, MGA, 26th overall, 2nd Ladies
1957 Lyons-Charbonnières Rally, MGA, 32nd overall, 1st Ladies
1957 Sestrière Rally, Magnette, 60th overall, 2nd Ladies
1957 Tulip Rally, Magnette, 76th overall, 3rd Ladies
1957 Liège-Rome-Liège Rally, MGA, 16th overall, 1st Ladies
1958 Monte Carlo Rally, Magnette, retired
1958 Tulip Rally, MGA, 34th overall, 3rd Ladies

Don Morley
With twin brother Erle, started rallying in 1952; they made their names with the BMC team, in particular driving works big Healeys on the Alpine Rallies.
Works MG drives
1962 Monte Carlo Rally, MGA, 28th overall, 1st class
1964 Monte Carlo Rally, MGB, 17th overall, 1st class
1964 Scottish Rally, MGB, crashed

Fred Morrell
Works MG drives
1964 Sebring, MGB, 22nd overall
1965 Sebring, MGB, 25th overall, 2nd class

Pat Moss
Started rallying a Morris Minor and Triumph TR2 in the early 1950s, went on to works BMC drives in MGs, big Healeys, Riley 1.5 and Austin A40; twice European Rally Champion.
Works MG drives
1955 RAC Rally, TF, 3rd Ladies
1955 Tulip Rally, Magnette, retired
1956 Dieppe Rally, Magnette, 2nd Ladies
1956 RAC Rally, MGA, 5th class, 3rd Ladies
1958 Midnight Sun Rally, MGA, 5th class, 9th Ladies

Bob Olthoff
Most successful South African driver who worked at MG Abingdon, raced an MGA in UK and went on to race Cobras and Formula 5000 in South Africa.
Works MG drives
1961 Le Mans, MGA, retired
1962 Sebring, MGA, 20th overall, 6th class

Jim Parkinson
Ran leading MG dealership in California, regular West Coast sports car driver and regular partner to Jack Flaherty at Sebring.
Works MG drives
1959 Sebring, MGA, 34th overall, 3rd class
1960 Sebring, MGA, 4th class
1961 Sebring, MGA, 14th overall, 1st class
1962 Sebring, MGA, 17th overall, 5th class
1963 Sebring, MGB, retired
1964 Sebring, MGB, retired

Al Pease
Canadian F1 driver and national Championship winner.
Works MG drives
1965 Sebring, MGB, 32nd overall, 6th class

Brad Picard
Canadian production sports car driver.
Works MG drives
1965 Sebring, MGB, 32nd overall, 6th class

Ray Pickering
Successful SCCA driver from Kansas.
Works MG drives
1959 Sebring, MGA, 45th overall

Alec Poole
Former MG apprentice who enjoyed a long career driving Minis and MGs as a private entrant; won the 1969 British Saloon Car Championship in a 1-litre Mini.
Works MG drives
1966 Brands Hatch, MGB, 3rd overall, 1st class
1966 Nürburgring 84 Hours, MGB, retired
1966 Montlhéry, MGB, 12th overall, 2nd class
1967 Monza, MGB, 16th overall, 1st class
1967 Spa, MGB, 10th overall, 1st class
1967 Nürburgring, MGB, 16th overall
1967 Targa Florio, MGB, crashed
1967 Reims, MGB, retired
1968 Nürburgring 84 Hours, MGC, retired

John Rhodes
Early career driving F3 Cooper but best remembered for his spectacular Mini racing career, first with Coopers and then with the BL works team.
Works MG drives
1965 Brands Hatch, MGB, 1st overall
1966 Targa Florio, MGB, 9th overall, 1st class
1967 Sebring, MGB, 12th overall, 2nd class

Peter Riley
Started racing and rallying while at Cambridge University, first BMC works drive in big Healey and Minis in 1959, married Ann Wisdom.
Works MG drives
1960 German Rally, MGA, 2nd class
1961 Sebring, MGA, 16th overall, 2nd class
1962 Monte Carlo Rally, Midget, 33rd overall, 1st class

Gary Rodrigues
Former driver for BMC importer, moved on to run Star Mazda series for up-and-coming young drivers.
Works MG drives
1968 Sebring, MGB, 18th overall, 5th class

Ray Saidel
Prominent SCCA driver and special builder.
Works MG drives
1959 Sebring, MGA, 27th overall, 2nd class

Jack Sears
Started racing in the 1950s driving various MG-engined specials, won the National Saloon Car Championship in Austin A105 and drove sports cars for the BMC team.
Works MG drives
1956 Alpine Rally, MGA, crashed
1962 Sebring, MGA, 16th overall, 4th class

Peter Scott-Russell
MG privateer who was the regular race commentator at Silverstone.
Works MG drives
1956 Mille Miglia, MGA, 70th overall, 2nd class

David Seigle-Morris
Started club rallying with Vic Elford, joined works Mini
team in 1960 and went on to drive the works big Healeys
and MGs.
Works MG drives
1962 RAC Rally, MG 1100, retired

Len Shaw
Pioneer privateer who was among the first to drive the
works-prepared Y Types and Magnettes.
Works MG drives
1955 Monte Carlo Rally, Magnette, 202nd overall
1955 RAC Rally, Magnette, retired
1955 Tulip Rally, Magnette, retired

Bill Shepherd
Along with John Williamson, was recruited to the BMC
team from the HRG team to drive the big Healeys.
Works MG drives
1956 Alpine Rally, MGA, 5th class

John Sprinzel
Successful and versatile racing and rally privateer with
Austin A30, Triumphs, Riley 1.5 and his favourite Sprite.
Works MG drives
1959 Tulip Rally, MGA, crashed
1959 Acropolis Rally, MGA, crashed
1963 Tour de France, MGB, crashed
1964 Tour de France, MGB, retired

Dickie Stoop
Former Squadron Leader who enjoyed a long career
driving production sports cars.
Works MG drives
1955 Tourist Trophy, MGA, retired

Mike Sutcliffe
Campaigned a works Riley 1.5 before gaining a works Mini
drive; also regular co-driver to Derek Astle.
Works MG drives
1961 RAC Rally, Midget, 2nd class

Chuck Tannlund
SCCA driver with Lotus, Jaguar XK, Porsche and Aston
Martin.
Works MG drives
1965 Sebring, Midget, retired

Jerry Truitt
1967 SCCA Production National Champion.
Works MG drives
1969 Sebring, MGB, 28th overall, 8th class

Ken Tubman
Round Australia Rally winner and driver of BMC 1800 on
World Cup Rally.
Works MG drives
1965 Tulip Rally, MGB, retired

Julien Vernaeve
Belgium Group 1 Mini exponent in racing and rallying,
regularly supported the works team to win team prizes
and class awards as a privateer.
Works MG drives
1963 Spa-Sofia-Liège Rally, MGB, retired
1966 Nürburgring 84 Hours, MGB, 1st overall
1966 Nürburgring 1,000km, MGB, retired
1966 Spa, MGB, 1st class
1968 Nürburgring 84 Hours, MGC, 6th overall

John Wagstaff
Regular British sports car driver and former works Lotus
Elite driver.
Works MG drives
1965 Sebring, Midget, retired

Hans Waefller
Swiss driver whose only other international drive was with
a BMW 328.
Works MG drives
1955 Le Mans, MGA, 17th overall, 6th class

Robin Widdows
F1 Cooper driver, drove F2 and F3 and Le Mans, Olympic
bobsleigh competitor.
Works MG drives
1966 Mugello, MGB, 3rd class

Peter Wilson
Former naval officer who started racing in 1954 with
Bristol and Frazer Nash.
Works MG drives
1955 Tourist Trophy, MGA, 20th overall, 4th class

Tommy Wisdom
Doyen motoring correspondent who drove works cars for
various manufacturers in many pre-war and post-war races
and rallies; father of Ann Wisdom.
Works MG drives
1964 Monte Carlo Rally, MG 1100, retired

John Whitmore
Prominent Mini racer who won British Saloon Car
Championship, contested the European Touring Car
Championship and drove works Ford GT40 at Le Mans.
Works MG drives
1961 Sebring, MGA, 16th overall, 2nd class
1962 Sebring, MGA, 20th overall, 6th class

John Williamson
Former member of the HRG team recruited to drive the
big Healeys.
Works MG drives
1965 Alpine Rally, MGA, 5th class

APPENDIX F

WORKS MGB
BUILD SHEET

The following is an example of a Competitions Department build sheet for a works racing MGB. This detailed information would have been prepared by the Shop Supervisor or Foreman based on a previous sheet for a similar specification which would have been modified and updated where appropriate. The sheets were given to the mechanic who was responsible for preparing the car and he would check off and sign each item and each page. The sheets ran to some ten foolscap pages and would have included about half as much information again for the more detailed modifications on a rally car.

This build sheet was for MBL 547E which was prepared by mechanic Nobby Hall for the 1967 Targa Florio, driven by Andrew Hedges and Alec Poole, and written off in a crash.

With the closure of the Competitions Department by British Leyland a policy instruction was given that all of these build sheets, which were kept in bound volumes and covered most of the post-war race and rally MGs, Austin-Healeys and Minis, should be destroyed. A similar instruction was given to destroy all of the photographic library held within the Competitions Department. How fortunate that certain people at Abingdon at the time took it upon themselves to ignore that instruction and rescue this material, most of which has now rightfully found its way into the hands of the proud owners of original ex-Works cars.

Cylinder block
Bore size: .020 1,822cc. Modified: pistons .015in down bore. Fume Pipes: one with long hose. Camshaft: AEA 770. Crankshaft: balanced double drilled and blanked off as drawing 707/823 standard. Flywheel: standard lightened. Clutch: diaphragm balanced. Release bearing: note this is carbon on MGB. Cam bearings: standard. Crank bearings: special Vandervell. Con rods: standard line-up and balance, Twin Cam machined with oil groove cut in. Pistons: .020 for three main bearing engine. Oil pump: standard modified with spacer. Oil pump drive: standard mechanical. Camshaft gear: steel lightened. Crankshaft gear: standard steel. Timing chain: standard. Core plugs: Isopon around edges, ping round. Dip stick and washer: blue dipstick and check length. Oil filter element: re-new.

Distributor: latest condensor and rotor arm, grease pivot point. Ignition setting: test on rolling road and report (8 degrees BTDC). Engine rubbers: standard. Check engine number plate: yes. Oil pressure: check and report. Sump and protection: deep type. Sump plug: standard wire lock. Oil cooler: large latest type C-ARO 9875 with special flex pipes, check for fouling.

Cylinder head
Type: MGB latest. Modified: Downton. Compression ratio: 11:1. Amount removed: .060 ins. Combustion space: 40.2. Exhaust valves: standard Nimonic 80. Inlet valves: standard modified Nimonic 80. Top caps: Marked W AEH 760. Bottom caps: AEA 403 AEH 801. Valve spring inner: AEA 652 AHH 7265. Valve spring outer: AEA 524 AHH 7264. Thermostat: fit blanking insert. Exhaust manifold: standard. Inlet manifold: standard line up with cylinder head. Plugs: N60Y racing. Rocker assembly: standard.

Transmission
Gear ratios: close ratio. Gear material: special crack tested. Type: standard spur cut gears. Sump plug: standard wire locked. Selector bars and forks: check and tighten, wire lock. Dip stick: Healey modified. Check oil leaks: yes. Gear lever: standard. Propshaft: latest type Hardy Spicer needle rollers. Diff ratio: 4.3 ZF. Sump protection: nil. Rear axle casing: standard modified. Half shafts: special for ZF. Breathers: fit special to gearbox and rear axle.

Carburettors
Type: Twin 1¾ in SU HS6. Modified: nil. Needles: SY. Dash pot springs: blue. Dampers: AUC 8114. Air cleaners: ram pipes. Choke cables: standard. Heat shields: standard. Induction: standard. Linkage: fork and peg. Accelerator cable: special nylon insert Smiths, check alignment. Float level: standard. Vibration: check.

Chassis
Anti-roll bars: GT type special ⅞ in OD split pin at bottom. Anti-roll bar links: standard. Rear shackles: standard. Wishbones: standard. Bump rubbers: standard. U bolts: special. Front shockers: special competition. Rear shockers: special competition. Chassis strengthening: nil.

Engine mounting brackets: standard. Shocker mounting brackets: standard. Bumpers: standard. Jacking points: quick lift brackets front and rear. Height of car: low as possible. Front hubs: standard check and packed with FCB grease. Rear hubs: standard Timken from T&T with FCB grease. Stub axles: standard. Radius arms: standard.

Cooling system
Type of fan: three-bladed for race. Radiator: DEV 3023. Water pump: standard. Hoses: bottom hose Morris Minor. Fanbelt: MGB 13H 923. Radiator cap: 7lb. Header tank: standard. Temperature gauge: special Smiths. Radiator drain plug: wire lock. Radiator drain tap: wire lock. Flush system: test.

Electrics
Alternator: fit. Starter: special small type. Coil: HA 12. Regulator box: 28 amp. Battery and fixing: standard. Wiper motor: two speed. Wiper motor switch: two speed. Wiper blades and arms: special for racing. Headlamps: standard. Fog lamps: FST 576. Tail lamps: standard. Stop lamps: standard. Flasher lamp: standard. Flasher switch: standard. Horns: small. Panel lights: standard. Panel light rev counter: standard. Focus lamps: yes. Ammeter: nil. Headlamp flick switch: standard. Battery: standard. Battery cable: fit large type terminal covers to insulate and run inside car. Screen washer: Lucas electric, fit switch to driver's panel. Headlamp washers: nil.

Steering
Column: standard check bottom clamp bolt. Steering wheel: leather covered. Steering wheel nut: tighten. Rack and pinion: standard checked. Steering arms: standard. Track arms: standard split pin nuts. Camber and castor: check. Lubricate: well. Lock nuts: fit castellated nuts and split pin both ends of the rods. Adjustment: check $\frac{1}{16}$ to $\frac{3}{32}$ toe in. Line up steering wheel: yes. Track wheels: yes.

Exhaust
System: special competition. Silencer: special competition. Hanging brackets: special. Support front bracket: special.

Fuel system
Tank: competition in boot. Tank fixing: standard. Fuel gauge: standard with bi-metal strip. Pumps: back to back pump in boot. Pipes: run inside car. Tank filler: Le Mans type 4in. Leaks: check. Petrol filters: clean. Tank breather: in cap.

Body
Drivers seat: special MGC GT. Drivers harness: special Irvin lap and diagonal, Sebring type. Windscreen: laminated. Windscreen washers: Lucas electric. Perspex windows: nil. Heater: nil. Front wings: standard. Rear wings: standard. Doors: standard. Panels: standard. Fairings: standard. Bonnet: standard. Bonnet fixings: standard with straps. Doors: check for shut. Safety catches: check. Hard top: wire lock. Hard top fixings: wire lock. Crash bar: yes with cover. Window fixings: standard check. Carpets: removed. Trim: standard. Parcel shelf: standard. Door draughts: check. Water test: check. Paddings: as driver requests. Switch positions: standard. Registration number: stick on fablon. GB plate: yes. Competition numbers: matt black, bonnet and doors, 14in high, 2in strokes. Fire extinguisher: yes large type. Driving mirror: MGC GT. Kit stowage: small kit. Safety Fast sticker: yes. Union Jacks: yes. Crew names: yes.

Controls
Accelerator pedal: modify for heel and toe. Accelerator pedal brackets: modify for heel and toe. Accelerator cable: nylon insert Smiths and line up for ease. Accelerator linkage: standard fork and peg. Brake pedal: standard made larger area. Pedal box: standard. Clutch pedal: standard. Handbrake lever: modify for fly-off. Handbrake cable: grease well.

Instruments
Speedo: MPH with trip. Rev counter: Smiths electric special check. Safety gauge: special check. Ignition key: yes and spare. Boot key: yes and spare.

Tyres and wheels
Tyres: Dunlop R7. Tubes: yes. Spare wheels: one. Valve caps: yes. Balance: yes. Wheels: 5½ in 70-spoke special offset.

Brakes
Master cylinder: standard. Master cylinder mountings: standard. Rear wheel cylinders: special checked. Front callipers: standard. Pads: DS 11. Shoes: VG95/1. Bed brakes and fade: as many sets as possible. Pipes: inside car. Bleed: standard. Fluid: Lockheed disc. Air cooling: yes.

Kit
Jack: standard stowed. Plug carrier: yes. Spare coil: yes. Wheel hammer: large stowed.

INDEX

Mugello 227
Muller, Hans 230
Mussolini, Benito 65

Nash, R.G.J. 44, 77
Nash, Sam 10, 115
National Motor Museum 11
Neale, Murton 31, 39, 42
Neerpasch, Jochen 234
Nordheim-Westfalen Rally 242
Nuffield Group 24, 100, 106, 108, 125, 128
Nurburgring 43, 54, 64, 73, 139, 144, 169, 205, 227, 229, 230-4, 246, 251
Nuvolari, Tazio 65, 70, 73, 77-83, 93, 95

Oliver, Jackie 225
Olthoff, Bob 192, 194, 290
Organ, Johnny 142, 162, 183, 190
Osca 169

Palm, Gunnar 187
Palmer, Gerald 169
Palmes, Jimmy 34-5, 49
Parker, Harold 21, 23, 28, 39, 44, 45, 73
Parkinson, Jim 191-4, 214, 221, 290
Parnell, Reg 119
Paul, Cyril 56, 58
Pease, Al 220, 223, 290
Pendine Sands 51-2
Penn Hughes, C. 66, 90
Phillips, George 138, 152, 166-7
Phillips, Gordon 35-8, 48, 59, 132, 256
Phoenix Park 41, 75
Pickard, Brad 220, 290
Pickering, Ray 192, 290
Pierpoint, Roy 246
Pohl, Zdenek 97
Pomeroy, Laurence 118, 119, 122
Poole, Alec 227, 231-4, 251, 290
Porsche 145, 147, 169, 171, 176, 179, 182-3, 192, 201, 216-17, 225, 230, 233, 239, 241, 246, 248, 251
Porsche, Dr 43
Porlock Hill 30
Prescott Hill Climb 174
Pressed Steel Co 100, 247
Price, Bill 138, 153
Propert, George 40, 49

RAC Grand Prix 152

RAC Rally 21, 143, 146, 152-3, 157-61, 174-5, 200, 211, 241-3
Railton, Reid 40, 121
Randall, Cecil 31, 39
Raworth of Oxford 15
Renault 246
Rhodes, John 138, 225-30, 290
Richmond, Joan 53
Riddell, Enid 65, 75
Riley 34, 39, 41, 44, 53, 55, 58, 66, 78, 80, 83, 93, 105, 171, 174, 266
Riley, Peter 143, 192, 200, 201, 211, 290
Rippon, Allen 167
Robinson, Harry 48, 68, 102
Roberts, Andrew 239
Robson, Graham 138
Rodrigues, Gary 225, 290
Rolls-Royce 121
Rose-Richards, Tim 78, 81
Rothschild, Lord 23
Rover company 16, 220, 246
Rubin, Bernard 64, 65, 70, 75
Ruby, Lloyd 225

Saab 187, 240
Saidel, Ray 192, 290
Saltmarsh, R.V. 16
Samuels, A.R. 88
Samuelson, Francis 20, 31, 39, 42-3, 53, 73
Schlesser, Jo 240
Schwendler, Irene 93
Scott, Bob 95, 257
Scott, Jack 242
Scottish Rally 159-60
Scott-Russell, Peter 138, 175, 290
Seaman, Richard 93, 97, 109
Sears, Jack 162, 176, 192, 194, 290
Sebring 146, 148, 152, 162, 190-6, 206, 214, 220-5, 248, 251
Seigle-Morris, David 211, 291
Selby 39
Sharp, Hap 220
Shaw, Bill 246
Shaw, Len 138, 152, 154, 160-1, 291
Shelby, Carroll 152
Shell company 21, 23
Shepherd, Bill 162, 169, 176, 291
Shorrock, Chris 122, 128-30
Silverstone 142, 148, 152, 169, 174, 190, 206, 214, 248
Simister, Tommy 78
Simons, Jean 128
Singer 25, 26, 28, 30, 93, 105, 115

Smith, John 97
Snetterton 203, 206
Spa 31, 214, 227, 241
Special Tuning Department 214, 231
Sprinzel, John 138, 184-6, 238-9, 241, 291
Squire, Adrian 70, 71
Staepelaere, Gilbert 234
Stanley Turner, Dorothy 116
Stevens, Frank 10, 16, 35, 100
Stisted, H.H. 31, 39, 42
Stone, Henry 10, 70, 87, 95, 102, 170, 257
Stoop, Dickie 171, 291
Straight, Whitney 77, 78, 83, 92, 93
Sunbeam 145, 192, 216, 219, 225
Sutcliffe, Mike 138, 200, 291
Symons, Humfrey 113

Talbot 20, 21, 45, 53, 58, 78
Tannland, Chuck 206, 291
Targa Florio 206-7, 223, 227-31, 248-51
Taruffi 90
Tayler, Frank 28, 40-2, 48, 52, 57, 91, 257
Taylor, Anita 225
Taylor, Henry 211
Taylor, Trevor 225
Temple, John 31, 72, 113
1,000 Mile Race 53
Thomas, George 54, 64, 66, 82, 90
Thomas, Miles 125
Thomas, Parry 52
Thompson & Taylor 54, 56, 72
Thornley, John 30-1, 72, 114, 119, 138, 152, 157, 166-8, 175, 191, 195, 201, 255
Three Musketeers 114-16, 119
Thyslethwaite, 'Scrap' 38
Tongue, Reggie 104
Tooley, Chris 138, 177-86
Torquay Rally 115
Toulmin, J.M. 112, 114, 117
Tour de France 238-9, 241
Tourist Trophy 42, 43-5, 78-81, 109, 152, 169-71, 201
Trana, Tom 240
Triple M Register 11
Triumph 25, 26, 28, 153, 157, 169, 206, 225, 246
Truitt, Jerry 225, 291
Tufanelli 68
Tulip Rally 160-1, 184-7
Turner, Stuart 153, 184, 186, 200,

208, 209, 215, 222, 228, 230, 234, 239, 243

University Motors 44, 54, 57
Urban-Emmerich, Hugo 43, 45, 54-5

Van Damm, Sheila 159
Vanson, Patrick 217
Vautibault, Comtess de 169
Vernaeve, Julien 139, 227, 231-5, 241, 251, 291
Volvo 180, 233, 234, 240

Waeffler, Hans 169, 291
Wagstaff, John 206, 291
Waite, Captain 39
Ward-Johnson 74
Watkinson, W.E.C. 74-5
Watson, Michael 74, 83
Watts, Doug 142, 153, 162, 168-9, 171, 176
Welch, Lewis 83, 114-16
Wellman, Tommy 138, 153, 166, 168-71, 247
Weslake Engineering 168
Wharton, Ken 169, 171, 291
Whitcroft, Cyril 55
Whitehead, Graham 222
Whitmore, John 192, 291
Whittington, Bob 241
Widdows, Robin 227, 291
Wiffen, Gerald 142, 169, 241, 247
Wiggins, Harold 168
Williamson, John 162, 169, 176, 202
Wilson, Peter 171
Winterbottom, Eric 167
Wirdnam, Bert 10, 70, 76, 257
Wisdom, Ann 159-61, 183
Wisdom, Elsie 53, 70, 72, 74
Wisdom, Tommy 59, 74, 291
Wolseley 11, 19, 20, 23-6, 28, 34-5, 48, 62-4, 100, 116-17, 132, 171
Woodhouse, Jack 118-20
Woolard, Frank 19, 62
Worsley, Victoria 31
Wright, G.W.J.H. 58, 74, 90
Wrigley, E.G. 19

Yallop, Ronnie 70-1, 75, 76, 78, 83

Zandvoort Circuit 186
Zolder Circuit 242